The World of Samuel Beckett, 1906–1946

The

World

of

Samuel

Beckett

1906–1946

Lois Gordon

Yale University Press

New Haven and London

Published with assistance from the
foundation established in memory of
Philip Hamilton McMillan of the Class of
1894, Yale College.

Designed by James J. Johnson and set
in Monotype Joanna types by
Tseng Information Systems, Inc.,
Durham, North Carolina.
Printed in the United States of America
by Edwards Brothers, Inc., Ann Arbor,
Michigan.

A catalogue record for this book
is available from the British Library.

The paper in this book meets the
guidelines for permanence and durability
of the Committee on Production
Guidelines for Book Longevity of the
Council on Library Resources.

10 9 8 7 6 5 4 3 2 1

Library of Congress
Cataloging-in-Publication Data

Gordon, Lois G.
The world of Samuel
Beckett, 1906–1946 /
Lois Gordon.
 p.   cm.
Includes bibliographical
references (p.   ) and index.
ISBN 0-300-06409-8 (alk. paper)
1. Beckett, Samuel, 1906–1989—
Biography.   2. World War, 1939–1945—
Literature and the war.   3. Authors,
Irish—20th century—Biography.   4.
Authors, French—20th century—
Biography.   I. Title.
PR6003.E282Z6666   1996
848'.91409—dc20
[B]   95-22851

To Alan and Robert

Contents

Acknowledgments

I wish to thank a few friends and colleagues for their abiding support throughout this project: Peter and Dominique Benson, Robert Coven, Barbara Deblat, Ilene Engelmayer, Mary Farrell, Warren French, Cara Fuchs, Bill Huott, Charlotte London, Sybil Maimin, Marvin Rechter, Ruth Schwartz, Patricia Tobin, and Aukse Trojanas. I owe a special debt of gratitute to Laurence Wylie, who shared invaluable information with me. Of the many librarians who offered generous assistance, I should like specifically to mention Beth Diefendorf, Eileen McIlvaine, Georgia Higley, Travis Westly, Eilis Ní Dhuibhne, Philip Dunn, Ian Carter, Norma Pomerantz, Toby Hopkins, and Stewart Gillies. I am especially appreciative of the good-natured and tireless efforts of Judy Katz and Laila Rogers.

It has been my good fortune to work with two exceptional people at Yale University Press. I am deeply grateful to Noreen O'Connor, my peerless manuscript editor, for her many intelligent and insightful suggestions and for the meticulous care she gave the preparation of this book. Above all, I can never express the full extent of my respect for Jonathan Brent. He possesses a wonderful combination of intellectual brilliance and personal kindness. His consistent support and empathic advice were instrumental in the completion of this project. I owe him my enduring gratitude.

Finally, I must acknowledge my family. My son, Robert, has throughout been a reliable source of cheerful encouragement. My husband, Alan, has given me the inestimable comfort and benefit that an ever-willing and thoughtful reader can provide. I consider myself blessed to have a bountiful in-house supply of intelligence, attention, and nurturance.

Beckett as Hero

The Kafkaen hero has a coherence of purpose. He's lost but
he's not spiritually precarious, he's not falling to bits. My
people seem to be falling to bits. . . . I think anyone nowadays,
anybody who pays the slightest attention to his own
experience, finds it the experience of a non-knower.
—SAMUEL BECKETT

All poetry . . . is prayer. —SAMUEL BECKETT

[Beckett] gave me 10,000 francs, and a double brandy and a
lecture on the evil of drinking. —BRENDAN BEHAN

Samuel Beckett was a kind, modest man. Through-
out his life, he avoided interviews, audiences, and, when it finally arrived,
celebrity. He declined to surround himself with a coterie of admirers, or to
propose political or moral solutions before a public perpetually in search of
celebrity wisdom. Yet, over the decades, he met informally and readily — if
briefly — with many who expressed an interest in his work. He elicited, as
the common element in the efforts to portray him, the words *goodness* and
compassion. His "common decency" is "almost unnatural," wrote one acquaintance, explaining: "He never disparages anyone, for he seems unaware of the
hygienic function of spite — [and] its salutory possibilities."[1] A close friend
similarly remarked: "His only real social lack is that commonest of social
accomplishments — hypocrisy. Beckett is unable to tell the smallest white lie
or engage in the smallest dishonesty."[2]

Beckett's thoughtfulness and generosity were apparent in any number
of situations — from his unsolicited financial aid to friends and artists to the
handwritten notes he returned to inquiring students, scholars, and even, on
one occasion, the warden of a German penitentiary.[3] It would apparently
never have occurred to him, regardless of the public attention or inconve-
nience involved, to withhold help from someone in need. Alec Reid, the
nearly blind Trinity lecturer and critic, recalls a "gentle and tender" Beckett
attending to him at their earliest Paris meeting, at a time when Beckett himself was having difficulties with his eyes: "We were virtually the blind leading the blind out the hotel, down the stairs [and] into a cab."[4] Harold Pinter
also tells of how, at their first meeting, Pinter developed a "bad digestion,"

1

and Beckett scoured the apothecaries for the proper bromide.[5] Beckett's em-
pathetic nature was characteristic of both his personal and professional deal-
ings—from his discretion and obvious pain over Lucia Joyce's unrequited
love for him (and his loyal friendship to her until her death) to his sensitivity to the many actors and directors with whom he worked.[6]

2

And yet, until 1989, when he authorized James Knowlson to write his
biography, he remained silent about his life—perhaps the predictable response of a modest, private person. Indeed, given his advancing age, one
may wonder if his authorization occurred more from a sense of duty than
an impulse of vanity. He had, after all, told Deirdre Bair, regarding her six-
year project nearly twenty years before, that he would neither help nor hin-
der her.[7] And despite Bair's abundant correspondence and interviews with
others, when her highly controversial book of more than seven hundred
pages appeared, Beckett again remained silent.[8] Now, although Knowlson—a
longtime friend of Beckett's and a founder of the Beckett Archive at the University of Reading in England—continues to have access to Beckett's papers,
he was able to interview him "formally" only during the last year of his life.
Much about Beckett's life may thus remain a mystery. An enormous amount
of biographical detail, however, is embedded within the massive accumula-
tion of critical studies published to date, some of it troubling in its contradictions and qualifications.

Descriptions of Beckett's modesty and kindness, for example, have often
been followed by conflicting reports about his mental health. On the one
hand, Beckett has been described as "surprisingly the most balanced and
serene of men"—"initially shy and reserved," soon "thoroughly charming, witty, and at times, even sentimental."[9] Kenneth Rexroth characterized
his "mind [as one] of singular toughness and stability—a mind like an
eighteenth-century Englishman, as sly as Gibbon, as compassionate as Johnson, as bold as Wilkes, as Olympian as Fielding."[10] On the other hand, Beckett
has been portrayed as fragile or anguished. Early photos were accompanied
by such captions as "Beckett: An Air of Horror."[11] Essays referred to him
as "a fiery apostle," a "gaunt, imposing figure," a ghostly specter of a man,
who seemed to have "come within a hairsbreadth of death and survived."[12]
Frequently Beckett was described as gloomy and depressed—an eccentric
profoundly controlled by an inner torment. In perhaps the most graphic of
terms, we were told that he spent long periods of time curled upon the bed
in a fetal position, searching for the happiness, perfection, and immobility
he remembered from the womb; again, in a further contradiction, we were
told that his fetal recollections were dark and agonizing.[13]

Certainly the most ambitious biography to date, Bair's book—which
continues to influence Beckett researchers—has focused on Beckett's eccen-

tricities. Bair's overview is typified by: "When something went wrong, he never showed his temper; instead he broke out in boils. . . . He had taken Geulincx [the seventeenth-century Cartesian philosopher] to heart: he would control his own fate without pandering to the outside world, no matter how dearly it cost him."[14] Speaking of Beckett's wartime experiences in southern France, Bair goes so far as to write: "[Beckett] was scathing in his denunciation of life [there] and hated the circumstances that placed him there. He followed a bizarre schedule of strange ritualistic tramps throughout the countryside despite the ridicule of his fellow exiles and the taunts of the villagers. . . . He felt guilty that he wasn't with his mother every time a letter came from her. . . . Self-hatred and his instinctive reach toward self-preservation were at war within him, and they caused a split; a 'center' failed to hold, so that fragments of himself seemed to fly off in so many directions that he was on the verge of total disintegration."[15]

The present book, collating details from a wide assemblage of Beckett scholarship and focusing on the historical events through which he lived, creates an entirely different profile.[16] My basic assumption is that *despite* Beckett's artistic images of debilitation and impotence—too often taken as projections of Beckett's own mental state—the public record describes a man of courage and resilience. This volume proposes that Beckett was a gentle but heroic man with a reservoir of toughness and strength that enabled him to pursue both an altruistic bent and the need for personal and artistic fulfillment. I would venture to say that Beckett's life—even in brief summary—was inspiring.

Beckett graduated from Trinity College, Dublin, a prize-winning athlete and honor student, well regarded by both his peers and professors, a young man of varied gifts and great promise. To his family and friends this was not unexpected; since childhood he had been singled out for his many talents, remarkable memory and wit, and considerable athletic abilities.[17] In response to Bair, who suggests that Beckett had a disturbed childhood and ongoing, guilt-ridden relationship with a domineering and highly neurotic mother that resulted in paralyzing, schizoid behavior, a few comments are in order. First, from his earliest school days Beckett exhibited—and cultivated—his intellectual and physical gifts, a meticulous code of honor and duty, and a unique, and perhaps ameliorative, sense of humor. Second, Beckett was always the devoted son of loving if unempathetic parents. They were deeply caring and devoted, but, typical of their time, more concerned with inculcating their own values and ambitions than fostering their child's unique inclinations. Specifically, Beckett's parents wished him to remain in their upper-middle-class Irish society—literally, in the family business—although they eventually realized that this was not his calling. Beckett preferred to travel and pursue the unconventional life of the artist. All the same, his parents helped finance his bohemian life, and he always treated them, along with his extended family, with respect and affection. Their relationship typified how love, goals, and understanding between family members are sometimes tunes of entirely different drummers.

That Beckett was neither reclusive nor solipsistic—he was merely shy— is also implicit in other important details. Throughout his early travels to and from Ireland, England, and the continent—and at the same time that he retained strong family allegiances—he also began what were to be abiding friendships with numerous people, including Alfred Péron, Thomas McGreevy, Jack B. Yeats, Kay Boyle, Maria Jolas, and, perhaps most significant, James Joyce. In later years, he became a caring mentor to several younger writers, including Harold Pinter (who sent him every new play), and he championed many musicians and artists—from Jack B. Yeats and Bram van Velde to Abigdor Arikha. He had a fifty-year relationship with his wife, Suzanne, whom he met shortly before World War II broke out and who also died in 1989, barely six months before Beckett.

Further noteworthy details characterize a man of personal and worldly interests, rather than solipsistic reclusiveness. During most of World War II, Beckett served in the Resistance, although as an Irish citizen he could have remained a neutral; for his fearless dedication and courage, he was awarded high distinctions, including the Croix de Guerre. After the war, he performed the most boring and menial of tasks when he helped the Irish Red Cross build a hospital in Saint-Lô, Normandy. Even after he returned to Paris in 1946, he continued to support the Red Cross in its restoration of the war-torn city. Throughout Beckett's productive life, he also endured a number of physical ailments—cysts and boils since his youth, and recurrent bronchitis, pleurisy, and lung infections following a near-fatal chest stabbing in 1938.

Perhaps most impressive about Beckett's steady self-determination was his passionate commitment to his craft. After a long and difficult process of rejecting his family's dreams, their society's expectations, his fellow artists' established conventions—and after studying the wisdom of both the ancients and his contemporaries—he was left with what he could only call "the mess." Accepting this—the external and internal absence of coherence and "meaning"— he determined to find his own way. Lacking fame and funds until nearly his fiftieth year, and with little encouragement from the publishing establishment, he persevered in molding an instrument with which to express "the mess," the inexpressible. He worked steadily and self-sufficiently—until he forged a new language and vision of human identity amid the eschatological fragments of a disordered universe and, in many ways, an incomprehensible and alien self.

Beckett's life was different, but it was neither damaged nor pathological. Although he admitted to considerable inner suffering, he was obviously able to endure his pain and not be broken by it, either clinically or artistically. It is perhaps time to focus on the strength that grew out of Beckett's distress, just as it is fruitful to consider the historical period in which he developed as a man and writer — Dublin and its environs during the Irish civil war and World War I, Paris in the two decades after the Great War, England in the terrible depression of the thirties, and France during World War II. This book, essentially a portrait of Beckett's world until he was forty, asserts that the external reality in which Beckett functioned from day to day shaped the man who would advance to that extraordinary "siege in the room" — his great creative outpouring that began in 1946. While respectful of Beckett's extraordinary erudition and its influence upon his work, this study challenges the majority of scholars who, like Andrew Kennedy in his 1989 *Samuel Beckett*, maintain: "Nor were the child and the young man subjected to the turmoil of war and rebellion," and "It is the orderliness and the sheltered old style gentility of a pre–First World War childhood, at the relatively quiet edge of the Western world, that strikes one."[18] I suggest that the world of Foxrock and Beckett's youth may not have been orderly, quiet, and genteel and that Beckett was very much aware of Dublin's — indeed much of this century's — sociopolitical and religious crises — and that these would mold the man and gain poetic formation in his work. Beckett's art might well be viewed as a product of and testament to his times.

Daniel Bell has proposed that it is the children of the bourgeoisie, not of the workers, who are likely to embody the rebellion against bourgeois values and the status quo.[19] Although the 1960s in America provides a later example, late nineteenth- and early twentieth-century middle-class Europe (as well as America) also produced children who rejected their origins to pursue great creative vision — Wittgenstein, Kafka, Cocteau, Stein, Pound, Breton, Proust, and Gide, not to mention the Irish Oscar Wilde and John Millington Synge. Beckett, in this regard, may be typical of certain gifted children of the middle class who turned to the life of the mind in revolt against the often limited vision of middle-class privilege and propriety. But Beckett was also unique.

Coming to maturity somewhat later than Synge and the others, and at a time of far greater social, political, and religious upheaval, Beckett was uniquely situated, historically, to become the poet of the most dramatic stage in the disintegration of Western bourgeois culture. His life spanned the demise of unqualified optimism with regard to the exalted triumvirate of science, materialism, and industry. It also spanned the triumphal maturation of many postwar "isms," from Surrealism and Freudianism to existentialism and deconstructionism — many of which promised to fill the void left by shattered nineteenth-century and prewar ideals. More important, Beckett witnessed, literally, extremes in human destruction hitherto inconceivable to the civilized mind. He lived through two terrible depressions (in Belfast and London); two world wars; and virtually two civil wars (in wartime France, as well as in Ireland). He witnessed the power of totalitarianism as it swept through the modern world—from Hitler's assumption of power and Japan's takeover of China to the grotesqueries of World War II. Throughout, one must speculate, he could not help but observe the degrees of caring and indifference, of pettiness and megalomania that accompanied each event— the panoply of human behavior, from self-sacrifice to utter barbarism, that were the personal and national responses to each of these occurrences. In thus reminding ourselves of the world in which Beckett matured and prepared—or was prepared—for the "siege in the room," given the specifics now on record, we may see how the world from 1906 to 1946 formed the man who would create the definitive literary forms of our time.

ONE | Ireland

Foxrock

I had a very good childhood, and a very normal childhood as
childhoods go. . . . But I was more aware of unhappiness
around me. —SAMUEL BECKETT

Samuel Barclay Beckett was born at Cooldrinagh, the
family home in Foxrock, a wealthy Dublin suburb, on April (or May) 13, 1906.
Although his official birth certificate designates the latter, Beckett always insisted on the former, and the date had a special significance for him. It was
not only a Friday the thirteenth but also Good Friday. The thirteenth day of
a month was, oddly enough, the day Dante, Samuel Johnson, James Joyce,
and Beckett's only brother, Frank, died—all people of inestimable importance in his life; Saint Augustine was also born on the thirteenth.

Beckett's parents, William (Bill) and Mary (May), and their parents as
well, were part of the dominant turn-of-the-century Protestant upper-
middle class. Irish by birth, they were English by style and temperament,
and their primary goal was hard work in fulfilling the duties of the station
to which they had been called, which included passing on to their children
the proper manners and values that were "for their own good." People of
this rank typically believed that progress via the sacred trinity of science, industry, and materialism would better the lot of humankind, and that wealth
and status were signs of divine grace. To most children of these families
there was little to do but follow in their elders' footsteps, as Beckett's brother
and uncles did.

Beckett's father, Bill, was descended from the French Huguenot Becquets
who had immigrated to Ireland during the seventeenth century. Not inter-

ested in university education, he entered the family construction business at fifteen and later purchased a partnership in the Dublin firm of Beckett and Medcalf, where he was a quantity surveyor. Beckett's mother, May, also pursued a somewhat independent youth following her family's financial reverses and became a nurse; it was in this capacity that she met Bill.[1] Of Bill's three brothers, two became widely respected physicians, and the third, severely injured in World War I when he fought with the British in France, became a successful businessman. Their only sister, Frances (Cissie), the artist and bohemian of the family, married Bill (Boss) Sinclair, who was half-Jewish and always described as charming and bright. Boss, who was in the art and antiques business, enjoyed and cultivated the company of writers and artists.

The Becketts lived eight miles from Dublin in what was, at the time, an undeveloped country hamlet with unpaved roads, one general store (McEvoy's), one service garage, and a countryside of cows, sheep, hens, and dogs. Foxrock was within walking or biking distance of the Dublin mountains, the sea at Dun Laoghaire, and the coast of Killiney harbor. The Beckett house, built in 1903, was of sufficient architectural interest to be exhibited in the respected Irish Builder magazine. "Only a house of a certain value could be built there," explains one neighbor, and the Beckett three-story Tudor had tennis courts, stables, a croquet lawn, and large lawns and gardens. It was decorated in traditional Edwardian style, with a wood-paneled room with fireplace (for afternoon tea), and several other spacious and dark mahogany-paneled sitting rooms with heavy drapes. Large, comfortable, cushioned sofas and chairs were covered in loose fabrics of "peasant" embroidery in reds, blues, and greens.[2] One might well imagine the house filled with the smells of fresh jam cakes and lemon verbena, which Mrs. Beckett cultivated in her kitchen and gardens.

The William Beckett family, in their affluent Protestant community, enjoyed the prerogatives of the well-to-do, including at least two house maids, a gardener, and numerous pets—dogs, donkeys, and hens. Although May Beckett did not enjoy hosting stylish dinner parties, she was a visible, revered, and well-liked member of the community and a renowned doyen of children's parties that featured much-loved donkey-cart rides and games of every variety. As Vivian Mercier characterizes the Becketts' neighbors, the women were "ladies of leisure," and the men, when not playing golf, took themselves off on the hourly "puffer" (also called the "Slow and Easy") to Dublin for work, shopping, or meetings.[3] Deirdre Bair emphasizes May's reclusive and moody nature and her lifelong battle for control with Samuel. She insists that May suffered debilitating headaches, insomnia (which kept her walking the house at night), depression, and temper tantrums—the combination of which frequently sent her to bed and kept Bill away at business. She also suggests that May may have been more nurturing to her plants and animals than to her children.[4]

Most other commentators, however, describe May Beckett as caring, thoughtful, and shy—an intelligent, strong, and clever woman who was also capable of charm and engaging wit.[5] Her apparent life goal, typical of the times, was to be a good wife and mother. Dorothy Coote Dudgeon, one of Beckett's childhood friends, in protest to the depiction in Bair's book, has made a public defense of May Beckett in this regard.[6] Dudgeon recalls May's extraordinary maternal kindness, which extended to nursing neighbors through their most delicate physical ailments.

In many ways, Beckett's mother was a typical Victorian wife. In addition to her devoted attention to the children—inventing games and instructing them in proper manners and congenial hobbies, like piano, drawing, and singing—she was stern and religious. Beckett once said that he was raised "almost a Quaker," adding the caveat, "But I soon lost faith. I don't think I ever had it after leaving Trinity."[7] Nevertheless, the Tallow Parish church provided the community with important social events: the annual church garden party, for example, was a celebrated occasion, in anticipation of which the women speculated for weeks—was So-and-So wearing her feathered boa and was So-and-So presented at Court?[8] Like their neighbors, neither May nor Bill appears to have had very much interest in Irish culture or popular Irish life. Describing how their only contact with the Catholic world was with their servants, Mercier adds that if "one preferred to think of oneself as English here in Foxrock, there was really no reason not to." He adds that, for an Irish lad brought up like Beckett, subsequent "alienation and search for identity" were inevitable.[9]

Bill Beckett was very much interested in his children. "I can see him now," Dudgeon writes, "smiling down at Sam and myself playing on the floor. I remember looking up and thinking what a lovely, kind smile."[10] Rugged (a "man's man"), hardworking, and sometimes quiet, although frequently jovial and sentimental, Bill shared a keen interest in sports with his two sons; he himself was a prize-winning swimmer, an agile fisherman, and on more than one occasion a visitor to the Leopardstown races. He took his boys hiking across the Wicklow Hills regularly, shared his love of nature with them, and fished, bicycled, and played golf with them. He tried his best to understand his children, but he was strict and, in the style of the times, demanding of a kind of physical perfection and fearlessness. He would, for example, take the young boys to a granite promontory above the sea at Sandycove ("Forty Foot") and force them to jump into the water.[11] Alec Reid concludes of such activities: "Sam early acquired a physical toughness" and "a taste for open-air pastime" that would "stand him in good stead through-out his life."[12] Beckett, not just neighbors or observers, frequently described the enormous love both he and his brother, Frank, felt toward their father.[13]

Beckett spoke repeatedly of his happy childhood ("You might say I had a happy childhood"), although he added, "but I was often lonely."[14] He was keenly sensitive to the suffering around him, a quality that would remain with him throughout his life. "I had a very good childhood, and a very nor-mal childhood as childhoods go," he once said, also adding, "but I was more aware of unhappiness around me."[15] Whereas for most children of Beckett's Irish Protestant class there was little to do but follow in their elders' foot-steps, for the intellectually gifted or the more emotionally sensitive, the cloistered, well-fed, well-bred world of devout mother and doughty father might have seemed claustrophobic. Their goals might have extended beyond Father's office in town and Mother's late afternoon teas. For such children of attentive and determined (if single-minded) parents, disaffection might have been predictable, if slow and subtle.

Beginning a proper education at age five, Beckett followed his brother, four years his elder, to Miss Ida Elsner's Academy, a kindergarten run by two German sisters; they provided him with an early introduction to French and were themselves particularly interested in music. The next year, in 1912, he attended Earlsfort House, one of Dublin's private Protestant schools (run by a Frenchman, Alfred Le Peton), where, typical of the times (and reminis-cent of Stephen Dedalus's Clongowes), children were caned for misbehav-ior. There, Beckett indicated a precocious talent in French and the piano. In 1920, when he was fourteen, Beckett entered Portora Royal, a tradition-filled Anglo-Irish boarding school in Enniskillen, County Fermanagh (now North-ern Ireland), a prep school for Trinity. Although founded by King James I in 1618 for the sons of Protestant "gentlemen" (Oscar Wilde was among its illus-trious alumni), the school emphasized sports more than academics and was often described as "tough plus." Its motto was "Omnes Honorate" (Honor All Men), and its focus on self-reliance was apparent in its various publica-tions, which promoted student independence, character development, and ecumenical social service.[16] As Reid notes, Wilde notwithstanding, Portora was better known for producing generals and public servants than men of letters.[17]

Beckett's brother had already established an impressive reputation at Por-tora in cricket, rugby, and acting, but this did not daunt Beckett. He was popular with the boys, a good-looking child and a superior athlete in cricket, rugby, swimming, and boxing (an undefeated light-heavyweight).[18] Harvey writes that Beckett's sympathetic nature and talent for sports helped him make friends quickly.[19] His courses included French, English, Latin, and the classics, and he is recalled as "most discriminating and critical in thought and blessed with a wonderful memory."[20] He also played tennis, bridge, and the piano, and sang (he knew all of Gilbert and Sullivan by heart), and his stories and poems were published in the school newspaper. He was also popular with his masters, although some recall him as "withdrawn" and "moody" — a typical adolescent, perhaps. He is said to have been fond of doodling, a habit he long enjoyed, and his drawings were of battered, vagrant hoboes, those weary tramp figures who would later inhabit his fictional landscapes. There is some evidence that, when he was sixteen, he wrote a review in sonnet form and signed it "John Peel," for a school performance of Haydn's "Toy Symphony":

> One would think
> Such noises are the one surviving link
> Between this world and that where Dante found
> His wild exotic phantoms.[21]

The Easter Uprising and the Great War

Dudgeon indicates that Beckett's early years were generally happy ones. The children enjoyed trips to Dublin to visit the museums, libraries, and cathedrals, and they heard concerts and saw light shows. Mostly, they roamed the countryside in search of mysterious and beautiful new territories — all the "lovely places almost unknown. The beautiful scenery, and glorious banks of primroses . . . bluebells . . . herons . . . streams of kingcups . . . cuckoos and beautiful larks."[22] They watched aeronautical displays at the Leopardstown race course, and had a number of magical play areas and hideouts: the ancient ruins at Foley's Folly, the cromlech (monolith) at Glen Druid, the Tully church and cemetery with its Celtic and Latin crosses, and Barrington's Tower, where Beckett would often retreat with a book and bag of peach apples.[23]

Specific details from this early period, however, elucidate Beckett's remark about the "unhappiness around me." First, beggarwomen and tramps frequently roamed the Foxrock countryside or sat with outstretched hat or hand on the Dublin bridges.[24] In addition, the Foxrock children who played together were aware of but confused by the retarded and mentally ill neighbors' relatives who were "hidden" at home. Dudgeon writes, "I remember such a family near us, of two sisters and a brother who always had a 'keeper' — the man played the same tune on his piano all day long. This 'keeper' somewhat puzzled us children, as it was the word used for the men who looked after lions and tigers etc. in the zoo. There were quite a few such cases around."[25] Dublin also had two asylums for the insane, as well as

During the Irish rebellion, Beckett's father took his ten-year-old son to see Dublin in flames, a scene that long remained with Beckett. (*Daily Sketch*)

several hospitals, and tuberculosis was common.[26] Moreover, following the war many retired service people of the army, navy, and colonial service lived in the Foxrock area. There was a war pensioners' hospital close to the Beckett home, and, as Jack MacGowran reports, Beckett saw the patients "regularly every day" in "various stages" of physical and mental "disability."[27]

One of the most memorable events of this time—and Beckett's life— was the day his father took him to see Dublin in flames during the Easter Uprising of 1916.[28] As John St. Ervine described the burning of O'Connell Street: "The finest street in Europe was consumed in one night." A scene that long remained with Beckett,[29] this would surely not have been the only event of the Rising that Beckett witnessed. A family friend recalls how worried the Foxrock community was immediately after the Uprising, when it took the neighbors "four days to get back . . . on foot" from the Dublin races.[30] Beckett's parents could hardly have been indifferent to the monumental social and political events of the time. Beckett's uncle Howard was fighting with the British army in World War I. The continuing Irish civil war would anticipate years of dreams and disappointment regarding Ireland's autonomy, along with an increasingly brutal animosity between the English and Irish; the Great War would end any lingering English Victorian dreams of limitless power and expansion. Throughout Beckett's childhood, adolescence, and early manhood, he would have heard about and read newspaper and magazine reports on national and international issues. For example, Irish conscription into the military was proposed at the very time (1918) the British had tabled Home Rule legislation (presumably because of their own involvement in "more important" world events). The Dublin newspapers were filled with headlines regarding conscription, Home Rule, and the war. And, of course, depending on one's religious or political convictions, reportage was either for or against England. The same held true regarding Roger Casement and the Irish Republican Brotherhood plotting revenge on the English and the voluntary army corps organized in Ulster.

It is also likely that throughout this time Beckett would have heard about the internecine struggles within the already splintered Irish political groups. The press covered every quarter, and even now, Paul Johnson, Sheila Lawlor, and other historians struggle with the profusion of conflicting reports regarding such issues as the military dimensions of the Irish Republican Brotherhood by 1919, Eamon de Valera's true intentions, and such lesser matters as the political positions of the Gaelic Athletic Association, the Irish literary groups, and the Gaelic League.[31]

In Dublin, where Beckett had been attending school, not only were many sections of the city devastated by bombs and other artillery, but posters and flags were reminders of the terrible events of the time. Beckett would have seen many of these. Lawlor reports that between 1916 and 1918—Beckett's tenth to twelfth years—children ran about Dublin booing British soldiers and waving small Irish flags. Dreaming of a happy ending for their daily problems—an independent Irish parliament—they sang the following:

> When I am a Member of Parl-i-a-ment,
> The War will be over I ween,
> You'll never see me in Westminster,
> I'll be sitting in old College Green.[32]

Beckett's family and the bright young Samuel could not have been immune to the chaos of the times.

13

Political proclamations decorate Dublin's buildings. (Library of Congress)

The Germans had sent rifles to both the Ulster and Irish Volunteers in 1914, which precipitated a highly audible outcry against "German sympathizers." The latter shipment arrived the day before Austria declared war on Serbia and nine days before England entered the war. Now, in 1916, the Easter Uprising—as planned—was once more dependent upon a shipment of German arms. In supporting the Rebels, the Germans hoped to divert the British from the Great War. The British, however, discovered and destroyed the German ship *Aud* (and the arms on board), and the leader of the Volunteers, Eoin MacNeill, was forced to cancel the uprising. In the Saturday newspaper he announced: "All orders for tomorrow, Easter Sunday, are hereby rescinded,

North Earl Street, Dublin, after the Easter Uprising. (Library of Congress)

and no parades, marches or other movements of Irish Volunteers will take place." [33]

In spite of this, one thousand of the ten thousand Irish Volunteers and about two hundred from the Citizens Army forged ahead on Easter Monday—a bank holiday when most Dubliners were out of town. For those people of obstinate dedication (as William Butler Yeats put it, their hearts "enchanted to a stone"), their hoisting of the green flag with its golden harp above the O'Connell Street post office was symbolic of Ireland's righteousness, of what the Fenians called the "immutable natural law." As George Bernard Shaw shrewdly observed, at that very moment a world war was

16

COLLAPSE OF SINN FEIN RISING.

INSURGENTS SURRENDER IN LARGE BODIES.

SUDDEN ORDER TO CEASE FIRE.

GREAT DESTRUCTION OF PROPERTY.

MANY DEAD AND WOUNDED.

MARTIAL LAW THROUGHOUT IRELAND.

Shortly before 4 o'clock on Saturday we received the official announcement that the rebels in Dublin were surrendering unconditionally.

The following communication was issued by the Field-Marshal Commanding-in-Chief the Home Forces early on Saturday morning :—

The military operations for the suppression of the rebellion in Dublin are proceeding satisfactorily.

What may be described as the organised forces of the rebels are confined to a few localities, the principal one being the Sackville street district, in which the rebels' headquarters appear to be the General Post Office.

The cordon of troops round this district has been drawn closer, and the rebels in this locality appear now to be confined behind the line of their barricades.

Sniping from houses in which small parties of the rebels have established themselves in various parts of the city still continues.

The district where this is most prevalent is that to the north-west of the Four Courts which is still in possession of the rebels. The clearance of the snipers is a matter of time.

Considerable damage was caused by fires on Thursday, and a large fire is still burning in Sackville street.

In other parts of Ireland the principal centres of disturbance are County Galway and Enniscorthy.

Disturbances have also been reported at Killarney, Clonmel, and Gorey.

Other parts of Ireland appear to be normal.

The general trend of the reports received indicates that the disturbances are local in character.

Headlines following the Uprising. (*The Irish Times*)

being fought for the rights of little nations like Ireland.[34] And "little" aptly describes the fighting power of the Rebels: 450 were killed and 2,600 were wounded.

The issues were complicated. The Rebels, some thought, had allied themselves with the Germans by asking for arms at the same time that young Irishmen were being slaughtered in the trenches of World War I. Rumors circulated that the Rising was a prelude to a German invasion or the signal of a socialist revolt.[35] However, James Connolly's repeated statements, and the banner that covered Liberty Hall, proclaimed: "We will serve neither King nor Kaiser but Ireland."[36] To Connolly, "Irishmen are ready to die endeavoring to win for Ireland those natural rights which the British government has been asking them to die to win for Belgium. As long as that remains the case, the cause of Irish freedom is safe."[37]

To many Protestants, because the only accomplishment of this ill-planned and ill-executed Easter event was massive looting and gratuitous killing, the subsequent executions and martial law (which continued periodically through 1921) were not inappropriate. But if the Rebels lacked broad support earlier, the retaliatory measures of the British only gained them wider favor. Padraic Pearse, Connolly, Thomas MacDonough, and the others understood that bloody rebellion and the retaliatory executions that would follow were the necessary catalysts for change, that only through violence and sacrifice would sufficient solidarity mount to ensure the nation's resurrection.[38] Connolly stated repeatedly: "There are many things more horrible than bloodshed, and slavery is one of them."[39] The week of street fighting that ensued after the Uprising set the tone for those men and women who would initiate the 1919–1921 war of independence.[40]

Connolly was able to rouse support from people of every walk of life — "publicists, philanthropists, literary men, lovers of their kind . . . archibishops" (as he called them).[41] He always qualified the sacred nature of their mission: "Men still know how to die for the holiest of all causes," which he then defined as "the practical brotherhood of the human race."[42] This, along with his other pronouncements—like, "We recognize that of us, as of mankind before Calvary, it may truly be said: 'Without shedding of Blood there is no Redemption'"—is a statement Beckett would have heard about or read.[43] Indeed, the notion of suffering redeemed through camaraderie— and, if possible, altruistic action—would resound throughout his work and life. In *Waiting for Godot*, for example, each figure repeats in his own way, "To every man his little cross," aware that salvation arises only from hearing those "cries for help" addressed to "all mankind" when "all mankind is us." Beckett's extraordinary activities during World War II suggest a similar sense of responsibility.[44]

After the Rising, lists of the subsequent two thousand imprisonments and numerous executions, along with names of those deported, appeared immediately and regularly in the press.[45] They would have stirred the imagination of a child like Beckett (who had recently turned ten). One middle-aged eccentric, for example, Francis Sheehy-Skeffington, whose worst offense was an untidy beard and devotion to minority causes, was—in error— arrested and shot. (James Joyce, his friend, followed this event closely.)[46]

To the People of Ireland!

"Our Freedom must be had at all hazards."—Wolfe Tone.

The time has come to practice the advice of Fintan Lalor, namely: to train our hands and our sons' hands, for the day will come when we and they will have to use them.

The workers must be disciplined and alert if they are to enjoy the just proceeds of their labour. It has been well said:

"The Price of Liberty is Eternal Vigilance."

The methods of discipline and alertness and the means of power to train our hands, are provided by

THE IRISH CITIZEN ARMY.

This organisation embraces the full principles of Republican Democracy; its aim is to sink the difference of Birth, Privilege and Creed under the common name of the Irish People. It stands for a Union of Progressive Nationalism with the Democratic forces of Ireland, and its policy is to achieve that, for which

Theobald Wolfe Tone died, and John Mitchel suffered—

AN INDEPENDENT IRELAND.

Irishmen! Join the Citizen Army NOW and help us to build up an Irish Co-operative Commonwealth.

Large crowds gather to hear James Connolly preach sacrifice for the cause of Irish independence: "Men still know how to die for the holiest of all causes—the practical brotherhood of the human race." (photo: Hulton Deutsch collection; poster: Imperial War Museum, London)

British soldiers stand guard amid the rubble of the General Post Office, Dublin.
(Imperial War Museum, London)

The beautiful Countess Constance Markiewicz, who dramatically surrendered her "station" at Saint Stephen's Green only after kissing her revolver,
subsequently escaped execution; her sentence was commuted to a prison
term. Many others stood before a firing squad. A debilitated Joseph Plunkett,
who had left his hospital bed to fight (swathed in bandages from recent surgery to treat tuberculosis), was shot in the prison where he had married his
fiancée just two hours before.

A priest reported how the wounded James Connolly was carried to his
death on May 12, 1916: "They carried him from his bed in a stretcher to an
ambulance and drove him to Kilmainham Gaol. They carried the stretcher
from the ambulance to the gaol yard. They put him in a chair . . . and asked

him: 'Will you pray for the men who are about to shoot you?' And he answered: 'I will say a prayer for all brave men who do their duty.' . . . And then they shot him."[47]

Pearse's emancipation proclamation, although recited before a very small audience on April 24, had also been a stirring tribute to heroic commitment, and it was later repeated and posted throughout Dublin: "IRISHMEN AND IRISHWOMEN: In the name of God and of the dead generations from which she receives her old tradition of nationhood, Ireland, through us, summons her children to her flag and strikes for her freedom. . . . We pledge our lives and the lives of our comrades-in-arms to the cause of its freedom, of its welfare, and of its exaltation among the nations. . . . In this supreme hour the Irish nation must, by its valour and discipline and by the readiness of its children to sacrifice themselves for the common good, prove itself worthy of the august destiny to which it is called." Pearse's rhetoric was irresistible: "Life springs from death and from the graves of patriot men and women spring living nations," he began, at a memorial for one of the Fenian founders. But then he added: "They think they have foreseen everything. They think they have provided against everything. But the fools, the fools, they have left us our Fenian dead, and while Ireland holds these graves, Ireland unfree shall never be at peace." One of his remarks, on the day of the Rising, recalls W. B. Yeats's "madness" and "terrible beauty" of the times. Said Pearse: "It's madness, yet it's glorious madness and I want to be in it."[48]

The terrible "retaliations" of the Black and Tans (the British occupying soldiers) and Sinn Fein during Beckett's youth were also widely publicized. On Bloody Sunday in November 1920, the Black and Tans opened fire on a large crowd at a football match at Croke Park in Dublin because fourteen British soldiers had been killed that morning. A month later, a large area in Cork City was set on fire. Other frightening and much-discussed events included the hanging of a popular, promising, and possibly innocent university student, Kevin Barry, as well as the "sack" of Balbriggan after two policemen were shot. Beckett would bear witness to these kinds of activities twenty-five years later in occupied France. But through the end of 1920, "Hardly a day passed without an ambush, an assassination, a raid or a reprisal," as D. G. Boyce puts it.[49] Women were shot with children in their arms, people fired blindly into crowds, and many were deported or sent to internment camps after secret trials. Reports of such occasions are preserved in the journals of playwrights Lady Augusta Gregory and Lennox Robinson and in both Irish and British histories and many Home Rule and Unionist papers and magazines that covered the news at the time.[50]

Lady Beatrice Glenavy, a schoolgirl friend of Beckett's aunt, Cissie Sin-

clair, reports the terrible confusion of the period. Glenavy, whose father
was later Lord Chancellor of Ireland, sympathizes with both the righteousness of the Protestants and the courage of the Rebels. Even under the most
stressful circumstances—her house had been set on fire—she expresses little
hostility toward the Rebels: "It was difficult for a young susceptible person
not to be swept up in a flood of patriotism." Betraying her ambivalence,
she continues: "To be really involved in this movement it was necessary to
have a great hate of England and everything English. . . . I could never work
myself up to that." Again and again, and during the most trying situations,
Glenavy showed remarkable sympathy toward both the Irish and English. On
another occasion, when the Rebels raided her house, she could only view
her persecutors like the sacrificial lambs of the Great War: "There were German submarines in the Irish Sea. . . . In Ireland . . . houses of families whose
sons were known to be in the British Army were being raided." The Rebels
entered, "masked men with revolvers," but they were "gentle, only there to
collect" goods. "We always parted," she concludes, "the best of friends."[51]

In a similarly nonpartisan way, P. O. O'Hegerty reveals the ambivalence
of a surviving Irish Republican Brotherhood leader, for whom the major
outcome of all the bloody warfare was, ironically, the annihilation of moral
clarity: "We adopted political assassination as a principle; we decided the
moral law. Every devilish thing we did against the British went its full circle,
and then boomeranged and smote us tenfold; and the cumulatory effect of
the whole of it was a general moral weakening and a general degradation,
a general cynicism and disbelief in either virtue or decency, in goodness or
uprightness or honesty."[52]

The Great War, with its unprecedented fatalities and casualties, caused
unspeakable human grief. Boys were killed "barely out of school," who
"went into action with very little training and not even the slight protection of a steel helmet." But in Ireland, such losses persisted long after the
armistice, and reports of the dead young men continued to be published.
The Great War may have ended, but the civil war endured, "with shooting,
curfews, ambushes, murders in the street, and every kind of horror."[53]

A profound sense of indignity and injustice—as well as the fighting—
continued in Ireland beyond the agreements of 1923, when Britain recognized the independence of Ireland (except Northern Ireland), the year
Beckett enrolled at Trinity. The mayhem of the times must have entered
Beckett's reservoir of experience, molding his understanding of human
nature, affecting his feelings about Ireland, England, and Germany, further
dispelling any illusions of his youth—that world which children ordinarily
assume to be based on rational systems of rational adults, if not on ratio-

nal reflections of a divine and just order. In this context, Beckett's remark that he was raised "almost a Quaker," but "soon lost faith . . . after leaving Trinity," is significant.

T r i n i t y

Beckett entered college after the armistice and establishment of the Irish Free State, the offspring of a well-to-do Protestant family and the product of Protestant schools for the sons of Protestant gentlemen. Trinity, however, like Portora (which had a Roll of Honor for the heroes of both the civil war and the world war), was not removed from the global transformations that had shaken the roots of every social institution.

By 1923, hundreds of books had been published that reflected the impact of the Great War in the areas of philosophy, psychology, religion, and science. Many, questioning God and country, science and progress, morality and nationalism, were timely purchases of the Trinity College Library.[54] Greene's Library bookshop on Clare Street (across the road from Beckett and Medcalf, the Beckett family business) probably carried some of these books, for many had been reviewed or at least listed in local magazines, including the Irish Book Lover and Dublin Magazine. Bertrand Russell's Icarus, or the Future of Science, for example, with its provocative statement, "The sudden change produced by science has upset the balance between our instincts and our circumstances," was debated, along with Spengler's "decline of the West" theories, in Dublin Magazine.[55] Books like E. B. Poulton's Science and the Great War, C. B. Thomson's Old Europe's Suicide, I. M. Clayton's Shadow on the Universe, R. B. Perry's The Present Conflict of Ideals, J. N. Figgis's The Will to Freedom; or, The Gospel of Nietzsche and the Gospel of Christ, F. Grierson's Illusions and Realities of the War, and J. B. Hunt's War, Religion, and Science argued along similar lines — with the unambiguous intent of undermining the righteous self-glorification of prewar ideals and stressing the waste and despair of the present.

The eager willingness to sacrifice life and limb for God, king, and country — a Charge of the Light Brigade mentality — along with Crystal Palace dreams of world mastery through hard work, prayer, and good manners became grist for the mills of the hundreds of books published between 1914 and 1928. "The seed of Europe" has been slain "one by one," observed Wilfred Owen to the ignorant and callous middle classes that had permitted the war.[56] Indeed, the ideal of the British Empire, divinely ordained to disseminate Christian values, was forever impugned; the only truth that remained was the meaningless slaughter of war and emptiness of the old morality. Science had become a two-edged sword: once heralded as the instrument of humankind's grace and preferment, it had now both theoretically (through

Darwin) and practically (in the war) furnished testimony of human besti-
ality. The cohesive social-political-religious prewar ideals had been pulverized by the mechanical ingenuity of the very nations that epitomized Victorian and Edwardian glory. The creative forces of the previous hundred years
had been defeated; "progress" had led to war, and science had provided its
instrumentation; and democracy would soon die two deaths—in the totali-
tarianisms of the Right and Left.

Throughout the Western world, art bore witness to these truths, as artists bitterly demanded an examination of the pipedreams of the nineteenth
century—from the literature of Hemingway and Remarque to the paintings
and music of a similarly diverse generation, of Beckmann and Picabia, Antheil and Bartók. All were clearly postimpressionists, post-Futurists—post-
political idealists—in one form or another. As Paul Fussell observed, sur-
veying Britain's postwar literature, World War I was the "archetypal origin"
of the modern ironic vision of life as one of bondage, frustration, and absurdity. The difficulty, he bitterly concluded, was in admitting that the war
had been made by men.[57]

In his widely read *The Modern Temper* (1929), Joseph Wood Krutch observed, with unrelieved pessimism, that the dilemma of Beckett's generation
was a consequence of no longer being able to sustain unreasoning faith or
rational doubt. He explained the new disharmony of thought and feeling:
"Try as he may, the two halves of [his] soul [could] hardly be made to co-
alesce, and [he could] either feel as his intelligence tells him that he should
feel or think as his emotions would have him think, and thus he is reduced
to mocking his torn and divided soul."[58] Frederick Hoffman, generalizing
about the twenties, added a final bitter insight: "Man is capable of an apparently endless extension of his intelligence, but he is not happy in the
knowledge."[59] In retrospect, these observations could have been made about
the writer Samuel Beckett.

In 1923, Beckett enrolled in Trinity as a day rather than a resident student. Although we have little knowledge about the books and magazines
Beckett read during this time or the conversations he had with friends and
professors, it is likely that he discussed the issues raised by the war and
its aftermath. The Donellan lectures on religion, philosophy, and contemporary issues, a tradition at Trinity, addressed these questions. One of the
most active campus debates remained how to honor the 450 Trinity graduates who had died in the Great War.[60] In 1928, an £11,000 Hall of Honor was
dedicated at the Library. And although Deirdre Bair says of the civil war
that "the reality of its aftereffects seldom penetrated the gates," this is apparently untrue.[61] Newspapers reported the continuing sectarian violence, and
the college felt its severe economic repercussions.[62]

Beckett concentrated in the arts and humanities, whose degree requirements dated to the seventeenth century—logic, moral philosophy, physics,
metaphysics, rhetoric, ethics, Latin, Greek, Hebrew, and mathematics.[63] But
given Beckett's voracious intellectual interests, in addition to his course assignments over this period, he may well have read Malinowski's *Myth in
Primitive Psychology*, I. A. Richards's *Science and Poetry*, Tawney's *Religion and the Rise of
Capitalism*, and Wyndham Lewis's *Time and Western Man*. Other much-discussed
books were Cassirer's *Language and Myth*, Dewey's *Experience and Nature*, Whitehead's *Science and the Modern World*, and Bertrand Russell's *Mysticism and Logic*,
Causes of the Present Chaos, and *What I Believe*. Vivian Mercier writes that by 1927
Beckett was very much changed, for he "had begun not only to hold opinions but to express them and was ready to argue about whatever intellectuals
argued about in 1927."[64] Some years later, he was sufficiently interested in
the New Science to give his uncle Gerald a copy of Schrödinger's *What Is
Life: The Physical Aspects of the Living Cell*. As James Knowlson puts it, Beckett's
interest in science as an attempt to understand and explain life on earth is
little known.[65] An enormous amount of work in the new mathematics and
quantum physics was being published and publicized at the same time that
science was being reevaluated as an instrument of human destruction.[66]

Beckett's life at the university was, in many ways, a continuation of his
life in Foxrock. As a Trinity student, he found himself in one of the last bas-
tions of English Protestant culture in Dublin. Although his father lacked a
university education, there was a family tradition at Trinity, for his uncles
Gerald and James were Trinity graduates, and his brother, Frank, had studied
engineering there. There was also a long and tumultuous school history
which all the undergraduates were encouraged to respect. Founded by Pope
Clement V in 1311, the school had endured a turbulent decline in the late six-
teenth century; it was rechartered during Queen Elizabeth I's reign in 1592.
In Beckett's time (as now), the catalogue cover displayed a royal blue flag in
heraldic flight above the Irish green.

Trinity also boasted an impressive alumni roster, including Wilde, Synge,
Swift, Farquhar, Congreve, Berkeley, Goldsmith, Edmund Burke, and Nahum
Tate, as well as Increase Mather. The chancellors during Beckett's matricula-
tion were earls of Iveagh from the Guinness family. Among the best-known
arts faculty associated with the college were Wilbraham Fitzjohn Trench,
Louis Claude Purser, George W. Mooney, William A. Goligher, and Alfred
Perceval Graves.[67] Douglas Hyde, the poet-scholar and founder of the Gaelic
League, was an officer and regular contributor to the Irish Texts Society.

Once at Trinity, Beckett quickly gained a reputation for unconventional
brilliance, and during his third and fourth years he established himself as a
distinguished scholar. The much-coveted Foundation Scholarship, which he

won in his third year after an intensely competitive examination, granted him reduced tuition, free use of the Commons, and a room at half rate, in addition to a stipend of twenty pounds sterling.[68]

University officials were facing a crisis during this period: they were encouraging their best students "to seek fortune in the higher spheres of banking and big business" and opened a School of Commerce, yet they feared decreasing business opportunities and massive emigration. "What does the Free State offer to these young people, with their brains, their education and their fresh and liberal outlook upon national affairs—potential citizens of the best type? . . . Commerce is depressed and the professions are overcrowded."[69] Not interested in the more traditional majors, including law and chartered accountancy (which he had briefly considered), and setting aside what MacGowran implies was a lifetime desire to become a painter, Beckett pursued a general liberal arts curriculum and concentrated in modern languages, particularly French and Italian, with a secondary interest in German and Spanish.[70]

Beckett's tutor was the philosopher Arthur Aston Luce, an authority on Berkeley, Descartes, and Bergson; for his "Dante revelation," Beckett acknowledged Walter Starkie (who also introduced him to Pirandello) and his Italian teacher Bianca Esposito.[71] That Beckett became intensely interested in Dante and Descartes is an early indication of the tidy pairing of opposites which would fascinate him throughout his life. In Dante he found the last great synthesizer of medieval thought, the last major architect of a coherent system of ideals by which to live. In Descartes, he could identify with the first modern investigator into the mind's functioning, as well as the originator of radical skepticism. The systematizer and the doubter: these must have been intellectually irresistible.

The French professor Thomas B. Rudmose-Brown soon became Beckett's mentor. He had an extensive knowledge of linguistics and was an authority on Racine, Corneille, Marivaux, Ronsard, and Scève, as well as contemporary writers like Fargue, Larbaud, Le Cordonnel, and Jammes. Rudmose-Brown had also edited the plays of Racine and Corneille, as well as collections of short stories, and he had written a history of French literature and numerous scholarly essays published in local journals during Beckett's student days.[72] It would have been extremely flattering to Beckett that this esteemed scholar enjoyed discussing literature with him, including the array of better- and lesser-known French Symbolists. "Ruddy" clearly recognized Beckett's extraordinary mind and encouraged him to teach; he even invited him to be his assistant.

Beckett did not limit himself to academic pursuits at Trinity. He spent time at the National Gallery of Ireland studying the Dutch, Flemish, and Italian masters, and he cultivated his sporting interests, although he restricted these to cricket, golf, rugby, billiards, and snooker.[73] He won golf awards and was so successful a cricketer that he toured England with the school team and was celebrated in one of Trinity's annuals. At one point he was elected to the College Athletic Council. Beckett also developed a habit at Trinity, begun by many an undergraduate, of sleeping until noon.

Despite the impact of the war and Ireland's new dominion status, Dublin in many ways had not changed socially since the prewar period. As in previous years, those newly planted in the ivory tower, in particular would-be artists and scholars, aspired to the local literary salons, with their genteel conversation, poetry readings, and musical entertainments. The blasphemous James Joyce portrayed the contemporary intellectual scene as one of contagious torpor in Dubliners and A Portrait of the Artist As a Young Man. But to attend Sarah Purser's "at homes" was the aspiration of many a young student, for these gathered the likes of W. B. Yeats, Lady Gregory, G. K. Chesterton, Bernard Shaw, A.E., John McCormack, Hugh Lane, George Moore, and Oliver St. John Gogarty. Other renowned writers and artists were frequently invited to Dublin, although we do not know if Beckett attended the following well-publicized series (or how many of these marathon events materialized). The March 1924 issue of the Dublin Magazine, for example, advertised the visits of D'Annunzio, Anatole France, Georg Brandes, Maurice Maeterlinck, Selma Lagerlof, Henri Bergson ("who is, by the way, half an Irishman"), Gerhart Hauptman, H. G. Wells, and Maxim Gorki.

The Dublin cultural scene was diverse and vibrant at the time, although we can only speculate on the extent of Beckett's interest (and participation) in it. During his first term at Trinity, a Dublin music festival advertised the appearance of Lauritz Melchior, Fritz Kreisler, Eugène Ysaÿe, Wilhem Backhaus, and Alfred Cortot.[74] In any given week, a variety of relatively new films opened, such as The Sheik, Passion, and Secrets of Paris. Films of Charlie Chaplin, Laurel and Hardy, and Harold Lloyd were also popular fare among undergraduates. A number of literary magazines published new poems and stories, as well as plays by Synge, Yeats, Lady Gregory, and others—many of which were performed at the time and became classics of the modern stage. At the Abbey, Gate, Queens, Theatre Royal, or Olympia, actors including Barry Fitzgerald, Sara Allgood, Arthur Shields, Michael J. Dolan, F. J. McCormick, and Eileen Crowe performed in the plays of Sean O'Casey, Lennox Robinson, Lady Gregory, Denis Johnson, Yeats, Synge, and the more experimental Europeans like Pirandello. Knowlson reports that at the Abbey Beckett saw Robinson's Never the Time and Place and The White Blackbird, numerous Yeats plays, most of Synge's works, O'Casey's Shadow of a Gunman, Juno and the Paycock, and Plough and the Stars, Ibsen's Enemy of the People, and (perhaps at the Gaiety) Shaw's

Fanny's First Play.[75] Beckett's theatergoing would have no small effect on him, and it remains of interest that many of his greatest interpreters—Jack Mac-Gowran and Patrick McGee, to name two—have been Irish, as though his lines were written for the Irish tongue.

Beckett also joined in the musical evenings at his parents', as well as at the home of their friends the John Mannings, and at the home of the renowned Mrs. Starkie (the mother of his Italian professor), who gathered together people like W. B. Yeats, Oliver St. John Gogarty (a raconteur-poet-surgeon who was a friend of Beckett's uncle Boss Sinclair), and James Stephens. On Sundays, he traveled to Malahide for tea and conversation with the Rudmose-Browns.[76] Finally, like many an undergraduate pursuing the common custom of undergraduate life, Beckett was introduced to the charms of stout at the local pubs. Here he discussed poetry and whatever was on the minds of Dublin students and poets on a given day. Some of the poets on view at the popular pubs and restaurants were Liam O'Flaherty, F. R. Higgins, and Austin Clarke.

While the vitality of Dublin's cultural scene may have been appealing, Mercier and others indicate that Beckett was long troubled by Ireland's religious narrowness, by what he would later call the "sterilisation of the mind and apotheosis of the litter"—its censorship and prohibitions against birth control.[77] (W. B. Yeats had also attacked the parochialism of the Irish, in poems like "September 1913.") In comments that apply to the problems of a young Irish would-be writer at the time, Seamus Deane writes that following the civil war, it took a long time for Ireland to transform "into a country of [unique] imagination."[78] Regardless of one's passion for or against recent Irish history, the postwar Irish artist had few external resources to rely upon in order to establish an individual voice. Both Yeats and Joyce were cumbersome legends with which to compete, and they represented the extremes in attachment to and rejection of Irish identity. But competing with (or, as Harold Bloom might put it, "killing") the successful "father" was not the issue. At this time in history, Deane continues, writers needed an entirely new idiom, not the linguistic extravagances that perpetuated an Irish English with its own semiology—in effect, its own history and identity. To the astute modern reader, the literariness and ideological (if not personally theological) strains of the Irish-English idiom were obvious. For Beckett, whom George Steiner finds representative of the "silence" of literary modernism, what was needed was pure form (without literariness)—Barthes's *écriture* divorced not only from Irish speech patterns, landscape, and personal ideals but also from any values of the past, regardless of whether one were sympathetic or antipathetic to them.[79]

During his Trinity years, Beckett would have found the local press and literary magazines debating these issues, in such essays as "Is Literature in a Blind Alley?" along with the more frequent celebrations of the Celtic tradition.[80] The revivalist Lennox Robinson, a noticeable presence on and off the Trinity campus, must have been a constant source of irritation or pleasure, depending upon one's point of view. As Beckett wrote in "Recent Irish Poetry" (1934), most contemporary Irish poetry was unacceptable in its "flight from self-awareness," in its abandonment of "the centre" for the circumference, regardless of its peasant or cosmopolitan setting. Language, along with "self," was the key to authenticity.[81]

Pursuing this argument that nationalism, parochialism, and provincialism — whatever one's political bent — could only "cramp" the "purer" writer, Carlos Fuentes argues that Joyce also struggled for a voice free of geographical, biographical, historical, or political coloration, although a pyrrhic victory was the best one could hope for. "A revolution," Fuentes writes, "is a battle for 'faces against masks.' The masks of subservience, of foreign power, of colonialism are stripped off the Irish psyche slowly." Still, he continues,

> the political impetus of the initial period of the Irish revolution was given added force by the capacity of the Irish writers to create for each mask its appropriate mirror, to give to nationalist history a physiognomy which betrayed in its changes the evolution of the face of truth. Red Hanrahan, Christy Mahon, Leopold Bloom, Stephen Daedalus, Father Moran are all, even to blatancy, representative Irish figures. Each incarnates an achievement in self-consciousness, a triumph of identity, which [perhaps ironically], is closely meshed in with the democratic impulses which produced Sinn Fein — the meaning of which (Ourselves) is precise and significant. (It's easier to scoff at the name if it is mistranslated as Ourselves Alone.)[82]

Bair describes Beckett's college years between 1923 and 1927 as a time of frequent drinking ("pub crawling") and sticky encounters with the authorities. Once again, she portrays Beckett as mentally and physically ill in response to his estranged but controlling family.[83] If, however, Beckett were meeting a variety of Catholic artists (McGovern reports that during this time, Beckett "mixed with a lot of artists, writers, painters and so on, most of whom would probably have been Catholic") — and if Deane's and Fuentes's assumptions are pertinent — Beckett may have been experiencing a number of predictable reactions.[84] First, typical for his age (in particular in his third and fourth college years when he had moved away from home), he was experiencing "growing pains" — the difficult process of separating from his family, especially severe in children who had a secure home life. Second, in his relationship with his Catholic writing acquaintances, he may have felt a conflict of loyalties regarding the very subjects and language that would constitute the "new" Irish art; his new friends might well be challenging certain traditions in which he had been raised and continued to share. Beckett did, in any case, announce to his father that he intended to pursue a teaching career instead of joining the family business. However, an astute Rudmose-Brown —despite his encouragement of Beckett's academic career—may have suspected the path of Beckett's later independence, having characterized him as the "grand ennemi de l'impérialisme, du patriotisme, de toutes les églises."[85]

The summer before his December 1927 graduation, Beckett took his second trip abroad and traveled to Florence. (He had bicycled through the Loire Valley the previous summer.) At his commencement, he received a first in modern languages and earned the large gold medal in modern literature, as well as the special prize of fifty pounds for exceptional scholarship for his work on Descartes. He planned to write on Jouve and the Unanimistes for the prestigious Moderatorship award (a tradition was building that Moderatorship awardees would go on to become Trinity Fellows and even provost).[86] Beckett's honors also included the highly regarded exchange position of lecteur d'anglais at the Ecole Normale Supérieure in Paris. The Ecole, which accepted France's intellectually gifted students (Henri Bergson, Jean Giraudoux, Romain Rolland, Maurice Merleau-Ponty, Jules Romains, Simone Weil, and Jean-Paul Sartre, a friend of Beckett's friend Alfred Péron, attended), invited the brightest language graduate from Trinity and from Oxford to teach there. Beckett would teach for two years, from the autumn of 1928 to 1930, after which he would assume a three-year Trinity teaching appointment. Taking his degree in December, however, allowed him at least a term during which to launch his career as a teacher.

Belfast

Beckett began teaching French at Campbell College in Belfast in January 1928. It was, as Beckett put it, a "grim" nine-month experience—perhaps an early indication of an unfortunate career choice. In addition, as he specifically commented to John Pilling, it was "a terrible place . . . full of bigotry."[87]

If, as both Protestant and Catholic historians report, a fitful peace had arrived in Northern Ireland by the mid-1920s, this was due only to its citizens' temporary exhaustion.[88] The nation remained bitterly divided, and political and social enmity was to accelerate during the remainder of the decade (and century). Belfast had been under curfew since 1920, and major strikes in shipbuilding and engineering were joined by sympathizers from all walks of life. The severe economic depression of the decade also reached a low point in 1927. The rise in unemployment, which escalated from 18 percent in 1923 to 25 percent by the end of 1926, seemed irreversible.

The poor educational system was also a subject of controversy. Protestants began holding Bible classes because a newly formed United Education Committee had declared that nonsectarian education was an "attack on the Bible."[89] Catholics deeply resented this because the Protestant schools were state funded.

The Civil Authorities (Special Powers) Act had in 1922 given the (Protestant) authorities wide and often unjustifiable powers of arrest, search, detention, and internment. The act, which was renewed annually until 1928, when it was extended for five years and then made permanent in 1930, guaranteed the arrest of any "threatening" types during a celebrity's visit. (Considerable precautions were taken when Henry Ford traveled through Northern Ireland in 1928 during Beckett's residence there.)

Courts in Northern Ireland had traditionally been associated with the Unionists, and juries were overwhelmingly Protestant, because jury selection was based primarily on property ownership.[90] The general situation was evaluated as follows: "To be Protestant is to be privileged; to be privileged is to require that Catholics be visibly deprived; and to deprive Catholics is to build the social order on overt as well as covert domination. Thus, rather than a liberal society invoking universal 'rights' . . . Northern Ireland is a colonial one based on individual and abiding privileges. It is this, far more than religion, that constitutes the key to understanding Northern Ireland's politics."[91]

During the darkest days of the depression, for example, "Protestant workers decided that if work had to be lost, it was better that Catholics lose it."[92] A march of the unemployed against Parliament was banned, and restrictions on freedom of speech were increased. John Darby, reporting the growing polarity of the Nationalist and Unionist communities, analyzed the discrimination against Catholics in public employment in areas like Derry and Fermanagh and concluded that such practices served the most outrageous goals of controlling the growth of the Catholic population. Disallowing Catholics work opportunities, he said, encouraged emigration, which then countered "the higher Catholic birth rate." These years "were among the most violent in the history of Ulster."[93]

A brief glance at both the Belfast and Dublin press from almost any day during the first half of 1928 reveals the ongoing prominent coverage of the continuing North-South struggle and the local depression, as well as the usual daily news. On Beckett's twenty-second birthday — April 13, 1928 — for example, most of the lead stories were detailed variations on the bold headline "The Terrible Depression and Unemployment," including reports from the Committees on Relief and Unemployment from different districts and discussions of the housing and education problems. In a typical editorial, the *Belfast Star* observed: "It is difficult for the working classes to be cheerful while the wolf is growling at their doors [and] our wealthy brothers abroad really lack interest in our problems." Debates continued over the old-age pension and an imminent strike in Cork. One resolution called for the government of the Irish Free State and Northern Ireland to provide public education for teachers. Other resolutions concerned "the drink traffic" and the Ulster Women Committee's proposed temperance legislation. Trinity College sent a group of students to Belfast to "interact" with university students there as "the only thing apart from the Great Northern Railway, which linked North and South." The papers contained open attacks on American industry: "No one . . . without degeneration, can deify the machine and conspire to make material wealth the be-all and end-all of life."[94]

After Beckett left Belfast, he returned to Dublin briefly and then took a month's holiday in Kassel, Germany, where he visited his father's sister, Cissie Sinclair, and her family. His aunt, an aspiring artist who had trained in Dublin and Paris, and her husband, Boss, the art and antiques dealer and an author of essays on contemporary painting, were instrumental in encouraging what became Beckett's lifelong interest in painting. Their daughter, Peggy, always referred to as an unconventional and green-eyed beauty (who died of tuberculosis only a few years later, at the age of twenty-two), engaged Beckett's deepest affection. At the end of September, under the terms of his exchange scholarship, he took up his teaching post at the Ecole Normale in Paris.

TWO

Paris, 1928

Paris in the twenties . . . was a good place for a young man
to be. —SAMUEL BECKETT

Paris in the 1920s was a dazzling city of frenetic
energy and prodigious creativity. Yet for all its gaiety and sophistication,
an underlying cynicism and sadness enveloped the city. Maurice Nadeau attributes its mercurial moods—its postwar "madness"—to the spiritual and
emotional devastation of the Great War; the grandest of human talents
seemed to have been subverted to the meanest of human purposes: "In [the]
disproportion between means and ends . . . the madness . . . appeared. . . .
Science, whose noblest efforts . . . perfected only another extermination
weapon; . . . philosophies, . . . fabricating excuses to keep [man] in ignorance of the shameful [war] trade he was being made to ply; . . . literature, merely an appendage to the military communiqué—[these] universally
bankrupt the civilization turning against itself, devouring itself. . . . Had it
all come to this?"[1]

After the war, the French, like people everywhere, searched for solutions to fill the void left by shattered prewar ideals. Older but still lively
radical political communities (communism, socialism, and anarchism) appealed to many. Also compelling were the philosophical ideologies systematized by Nietzsche, Freud, and the phenomenologists. A number of relatively new aesthetic ideologies were also attractive—vertiginous mixtures of
the Left and Right—Futurism, Dadaism, Surrealism, and even the less political, residual Cubism and early forms of Abstract Expressionism. Voices from
abroad, of Vorticists and Suprematists, Die Brücke and Der Blaue Reiter,
also gained a following. A revolution in the arts, with entirely new uses of
color, harmony, and linearity, might counter the decadence, waste, and distortions of reality—the "lies," as Hemingway called them—of earlier works
and times.

By 1928, Paris offered its expatriates any variety of replacement artistic, social, and moral systems, and, on occasion, one system served several
needs. The Surrealists, for example, found a broad and encompassing salvation in psychoanalysis. To them, Freud explained civilization and its discontents at the same time that he provided a kind of metaphysics for the exile,

adrift amidst the recent loss of religious, social, or family values. Psycho-analysis promised an inner coherence to fill the personal or cosmic loneli-ness of the times. It also provided validity for the "automatic" formulas of the new spontaneous and "pure" art forms.

Baudelaire and Rimbaud had already provided artists like T. S. Eliot and Ezra Pound examples of the purity of the creative life—the superiority of questing after *le mot juste*, regardless of the traditional everyday obligations of bourgeois society—a new version of art for art's sake. Baudelaire's insistence that the life of action, and even "evil," was preferable to that of middle-class ennui also remained appealing to Paris's new citizens. The combination of these artistic, moral, and social freedoms, and the basic rebellion against prewar values of ambition, industry, and materialism, made for a unique kind of bohemianism. One thing was clear: the immorality of the war ex-cused any and all current renegade behavior. The most outrageous acts or artistic or political statements were tame in comparison to the hypocritical (and lethal) manners of the older generation. The "lost generation" was lost only to the extent that it separated itself from the values of the recent past.

The implications and manifestations of this new attitude touched every aspect of life—from dressing, dining, and drinking styles (with the liber-ated flapper ordering the cocktail Between the Sheets) to the new popular culture, including jazz, which celebrated blacks as primitive and pristine, re-minders of preindustrial and prewar innocence.[2] Entertainers like Josephine Baker and Sidney Bechet became virtual culture heroes.

Paris in the late 1920s was like a magnet to people from everywhere—America, Spain, Belgium, Rumania, Germany, Russia. It was the home of Joyce, Picasso, and Mondrian, and of members of the newly launched Art Deco movement, as well as the now slightly passé Fauvists, Cubists, and Dadaists, and their successors, the Surrealists. It was also the home of Berg-son (who had won the Nobel Prize in 1927), Cocteau, Mauriac, Valéry, Gide, Aragon, Hemingway, Fitzgerald, Gertrude Stein, Ford Madox Ford, Varèse, Milhaud, Antheil, Copland, Virgil Thomson, Chagall, Dali, and Giacometti. Magritte and Miró arrived at about the same time as Beckett; Arp had resided there since 1927; Bram van Velde had been exhibiting since 1926.

The visual and aural imagery of the new arts had a powerful effect on Beckett's work. His photographic memory allowed him years later to dupli-cate in his stage settings and in his own productions (meticulously recorded in notebooks) the design of paintings he had not seen for decades.[3] Tech-niques of nonlinearity in painting, accomplished through image fragmen-tation, dream imagery, and the intentional use of blank canvas—like atonal music achieved through the statistical arrangement of notes and incorpo-ration of silence—influenced Beckett's use of language, gesture, and stage setting. (Beckett often appeared at rehearsals with a metronome.) He was also influenced by the avant-garde playwrights and cinematic innovators. The findings of the New Science concerning relativity, like those of the new linguists regarding the ambiguity of language, complemented the artistic revolution occurring around him.

Throughout Paris, the extremes of the avant-garde imagination were visible, along with the now more traditional forms of Cézanne, van Gogh, and Gauguin. Along the streets bordering the Luxembourg Gardens, the postimpressionists (a new word coined by Roger Fry) were on display, along with their Cubist and Fauve successors.[4] Picasso's guitars were now constructed of painted metal, rather than paper. Galleries like Georges Bernheim and Galerie Surréaliste were showing the biomorphic and geometric abstractions of Arp, Miró, and Mondrian. ("Good investments" included Modigliani, Soutine, and Chagall.) Man Ray's "Rayographs" spread the face of the sensuous model Kiki, with her dark bobbed hair and bangs, large green eyes, and heavily rouged cheeks, throughout the city. One can imagine Beckett's initial reaction on seeing, even in their many reproductions, a Duchamp "readymade" (a bicycle tire or signed urinal), his goateed Mona Lisa with its brash title L.H.O.O.Q. (translation: "Elle a chaud au cul," "She has a hot behind"), or Brancusi's elegant *Bird in Space*, at the same time abstract and representational.

Roger Vitrac and Antonin Artaud, famed for holding the mirror up to the unconscious, founded Théâtre Alfred Jarry in 1927, where they used dreamlike techniques·in plays by Vitrac and in adaptations of Strindberg and Shelley. Eisenstein was pursuing his experimental cinematography, and the boulevards were showing his work, along with that of Dreyer, Renoir, Gance, and Tourneur, as well as Beckett favorites Charlie Chaplin (*The Gold Rush*) and Buster Keaton (*The General*). The avant-garde compositions of Alban Berg, Arnold Schoenberg, and George Antheil were also gaining attention. Samuel Beckett, recently arrived from "grim" Belfast, must have felt a sense of relief in the dynamic environs of his new home.

The major artistic statements of Paris in 1928 emanated from the Surrealists. Not only did their work influence Beckett's creative development, but their bitterness toward World War I also recalled many arguments he had heard in Dublin. Primarily devoted to unifying the inner and outer worlds, the Surrealists were also committed to exposing the false dreams and hollow values that had produced the terrible war. Although this is an attitude one ordinarily associates with Dada because many Dadaists turned to Surrealism after 1920, Virginia Williams may be correct in suggesting that Surrealism remained a "rebellion" against the Great War. Many of its proponents had served in the war—Masson, Ernst, Eluard, Péret, Breton, and Aragon, among others. To Williams, underlying their revolutionary forms was a "diatribe against patriotism, religion, rationality, and organization," and these were "explicit reactions against [the] war. . . . Nothing was more central to their lives and their conception of the function of art." Many Surrealists wrote commentaries on the spiritual and physical mutilations of the war. In short, the subject of the Great War remained an abiding topic of conversation in Paris during 1928.[5]

The artistic goals of the Surrealists, expressed by their spokesperson, André Breton, were becoming common parlance ("pure psychic automatism, . . . the real process of thought [with] . . . all exercise of reason and every esthetic or moral preoccupation being absent").[6] His newly published *Surrealism and Painting* and *Nadja* each concluded with a demand for "convulsive beauty" born out of the automatic image—a reiteration of Lautréamont's description of beauty as something "shivering" and "trembling," like the "chance encounter of a sewing machine and an umbrella on a dissecting table."

The Surrealists' work gained increasing attention in various art forms. Films in 1928 included Man Ray's *L'Etoile de Mer* and Duchamp's *Anaemic Cinema*; Luis Buñuel and Salvador Dali were preparing *Un Chien Andalou*. The most significant art show of the year, "Au Sacré du Printemps," included Arp, de Chirico, Ernst, Malkine, Masson, Miró, Picabia, Man Ray, and Tanguy. Important, also, were the one-man shows, including Max Ernst's, at such galleries as Georges Bernheim, as well as the drawings and essays of Ernst, Schwitters, Klee, Man Ray, de Chirico, and Masson reproduced in the many little magazines.[7]

Wassily Kandinsky was a major influence on many of the Paris artists. He had attracted a large following with his brooding intimation of world disaster in *Composition No. 6* (1913), but he gained even more attention now for his book *On the Spiritual in Art* (1910), which extolled the artist's need to utilize the inner world because of the failure of external systems. In his own bold, synaesthetic work, Kandinsky conveyed musical response in color and line—a painter's perception of Wagnerian opera; Kandinsky would be one of many international artists to interest Beckett.[8]

Two bookstores across the street from one another—Sylvia Beach's Shakespeare and Company and Adrienne Monnier's La Maison des Amis des Livres—promoted the local artists and were gathering places for French, English, Irish, and American creative dignitaries. Here one could discuss the host of radically new perceptions of reality and self in the areas of science, philosophy, psychology, linguistics, and art. Bertrand Russell and Alfred North Whitehead might have established, in a single system, all the valid principles of mathematical reasoning—a set of axioms upon which all rules would follow. But others, like Werner Heisenberg and Kurt Gödel, were pursuing their claim that the observer influences the observed and that any axiomatic system has undecidable propositions (for example, although we ought to be able to see ourselves in a mirror, we cannot see ourselves with closed eyes). These and other bookshops in Paris stocked the most talked-about authors, including Heidegger, Wittgenstein, Saussure, Cassirer, Eddington, Jung, Freud, and Yeats. Not only did Beckett visit these bookshops, but, as Pilling reports, "during this period [he] was obviously engaged in reading everything he could lay his hands on."[9]

Finally, Paris in 1928 was the home of many new publishers in search of new authors.[10] J. P. Morgan's nephew Harry Crosby was expanding Black Sun Press (and in 1929, a young assistant from transition magazine, Kay Boyle, began selling stocks for Crosby). Black Sun soon published The Fall of the House of Usher, Sterne's A Sentimental Journey, Crane's The Bridge, Proust's Letters, and Joyce's Tales of Shem and Shaun. Robert McAlmon's Contact Press, Bill Bird's Three Mountains Press (sold in 1928 to Nancy Cunard, who renamed it the Hours Press), Edward Titus's Black Maniken Press, and Gertrude Stein's Plain Editions were other new houses dedicated to quality rather than profit.

When Beckett arrived in Paris, he plunged into the magical world before him and began his lifelong commitment to the city. He took up his responsibilities at the Ecole; one report says that he held afternoon "seminars with his sole student" at the Dôme, where the two read Shakespeare together."[11] He pursued his study of Descartes, Geulincx, and Romains. But he also sought out artists, writers, teachers, and publishers, and many became mentors of sorts, offering him not just personal encouragement but also their hope for some possible aesthetic or spiritual sustenance in a world gone awry. Unlike Joyce, however, whom he soon met (or Stravinsky, Eliot, or Picasso, for that matter), he would not find the key to salvation in the past. When Beckett began to write, he did not salvage and expand the fragments of language or form in the service of renewed mythic patterns. Nor did he declaim against present social forms and privilege like Ford Madox Ford. Beckett also rejected the grandiosity of the local artist-heroes—carryovers of the Romantic artist as legislator or prophet. He would never assume the role of the godlike creator, either publicly or artistically. The declarations of the aesthetes, or the French Symbolists, whom he had studied so closely, also proved inadequate, for the magic of language and form which they revered reflected a continuing belief in the coherence between the personal and external worlds—Hermes Trismegistus's "as above/so below" correspondence. Instead, Beckett retained a modest position, as he opened himself to the entire world around him—to a continual study of the ancients and contemporaries (and there have been few more erudite artists), as well as an involvement in the scientific, psychological, and philosophical thinking of the time. And when these proved unsatisfying, he worked toward his own solutions.

Three important events occurred shortly after his arrival. First, he began or renewed important friendships. In each, Beckett was like a magnet, absorbing or incorporating from those he respected specific interests and commitments (and, on occasion, mannerisms) that would last a lifetime. In these special attachments, he identified with the other so completely that in some ways he became the other's mirror. Second, he became involved with Paris's little magazines, began his career as a writer, and worked with the "Revolution of the Word" proponents. Third, he met a number of Surrealists whose interests, if not aesthetic and personal goals, profoundly influenced his later work.

Beckett had met Alfred Péron in 1926, when Péron was Trinity's visiting lecturer from the Ecole. Péron invited Beckett to join the college's literary activities, including its Modern Language Society, and they now resumed their discussions of art, literature, and language. It must have been important to Beckett to have this link with his recent and successful past at Trinity; his term at Belfast had been unhappy and probably lonely. Péron would join Beckett the following year in translating Joyce's "Anna Livia Plurabelle" passage from *Finnegans Wake*; Péron subsequently spent time in Japan but returned to Paris in 1937, when he and Beckett renewed what became an even deeper friendship; in 1940, he involved Beckett in the Resistance; Péron was subsequently captured and tortured by the Nazis.

The poet and later art critic Thomas McGreevy (later spelled MacGreevy) was a new friend. Born in County Kerry, McGreevy had been wounded in World War I, after which he recuperated and studied in France. Now a lecturer at the Ecole, he and Beckett lived in the same quarters on the rue d'Ulm. McGreevy introduced Beckett to the close circle of Dublin expatriates in Paris, including Arthur Power and Francis Stuart (married to Iseult Gonne, Maud's adopted daughter). He also introduced Beckett to many celebrated intellectuals, including Richard Aldington, Sylvia Beach, and James Joyce, who was beginning to publish *Work in Progress*. Although ten years apart in age, Beckett and the older, sophisticated McGreevy became intimate, lifelong friends. McGreevy took to calling Beckett "the melancholy Irishman," after Joyce's reference to himself as the "Melancholy Jesus." Beckett came to call McGreevy "an existentialist in verse." Bair says that McGreevy was "the only person to whom Beckett [was] ever absolutely truthful." [12]

McGreevy's books on Jack B. Yeats, Aldington, Eliot, Leonardo, and Poussin are as revealing of the author as they are of his subjects. They indicate McGreevy's deeply humanitarian bent, as well as his fierce independence — traits that must have been obvious to those who knew him, including Beckett. McGreevy emerges from his books as unabashedly idealistic, an unembarrassed advocate of universal human rights.

In approaching Jack B. Yeats, McGreevy makes abundantly clear that art criticism, to him, is philosophy: "I do not feel called upon to apologize for introducing questions of either religion or patriotism in . . . writing about art anywhere." Although the book was written in London in 1938 and not published for seven years, in the 1945 preface McGreevy confidently dismisses the London art establishment—indeed, the entire moral ethos of that period—recalling that "London [in 1938] was the London of appeasement," whereas his convictions were "those of a premature anti-Fascist." McGreevy does not appeal to any standard that deviates from what he considers to be the absolute and unequivocal good. This gains sharp focus after his questions: Is Jack Yeats merely a regional artist, a purveyor of Irish subjects? "Does anything in Ireland matter?"—and to both he immediately replies: "The answer is that every place in which there are human beings matters." He further defines his moral system and his faith in human nature: "What matters in Ireland is what has mattered at all times in all places, and in art as in life, the classical trinity of the true, the good, and the beautiful. That trinity constitutes the part of the kingdom that even profane philosophies allow to be within us." His conclusion is enthusiastically positive: what is essential is "the impulse in humanity to delight in its own potential truth, goodness, and beauty." [13]

Through McGreevy, Beckett met Joyce—perhaps the single most important man in his life after his father (see chapter 3), and it was not long before his literary circles widened. He was introduced to Philippe Soupault, Léon-Paul Fargue, Valéry, Edouard Dujardin, Romains, Monnier, Paul Léon, Nino Frank, Stuart Gilbert, and Ivan Goll. Among the many others to whom McGreevy eventually introduced Beckett (or arranged for their meeting) were William Butler Yeats, Jack B. Yeats, T. S. Eliot, Walter Lowenfels, Desmond MacCarthy, George Reavey, and Samuel Putnam, several of whom were important editors.

It is likely that shortly after they met, Beckett and McGreevy, who eventually became director of the National Gallery in Dublin, visited the local museums and galleries like the Bernheim Jeune, Paul Rosenberg, and Galerie Pigalle. The Zborowsky Gallery had an important exhibition of Henri Hayden, who spent the last years of World War II with Beckett in Roussillon, where they became close friends. Beckett had been interested in art since childhood, and he (perhaps with McGreevy) may have attended some of the most widely discussed shows: the Corot and Bonnard retrospectives, the Fauve shows, and the many Derain, Picasso, Bonnard, Manet, and Renoir exhibitions. [14]

During the 1928–29 season, there were at least four exhibitions of works by Cézanne—an artist whose technique of *passage* (creating shifting surfaces) influenced Beckett's stage designs—and the Louvre acquired three new Cézannes. With the 1929 Pellerin bequest to the city of another hundred and sixty Cézannes, a major cultural issue arose: where to house the collection. Because Cézanne's work had been rejected during his lifetime, it was now imperative to "have the courage to express repentance in the name of the State."[15] (This may have reminded some Irish art lovers of the embittered Dublin situation in 1908, when Hugh Lane's collection of French Impressionist paintings failed to find a suitable gallery and was removed from Ireland.) Smaller galleries showed Magritte, Dali, Arp, and Tanguy.

Beckett also encountered a city of numerous little magazines with which writers and artists might become affiliated (and where Beckett was able to earn money doing translations). These included not only *The Exile* and *Little Review* and, later, *Tambour* and *This Quarter*, but also Maria and Eugene Jolas's prestigious *transition*. An "international quarterly for creative expression," *transition* was, during 1928, chiefly associated with James Joyce and Gertrude Stein. Its earliest issues, from April through August 1927, had already published an extraordinary group of artists, including Joyce, Stein, Valéry, Hemingway, Hart Crane, William Carlos Williams, Breton, Picasso, Arp, and Miró.[16] But *transition* remains most famous for its seventeen installments of what was later entitled *Finnegans Wake*—the stunning show piece of the Jolases' promulgation of the "Revolution of the Word." The issues devoted to the "Language of Night" and "Revolution of the Word," as well as those containing Jung's essay "Psychology and Poetry" and the "On Verticalism" manifesto, are most relevant to Beckett's career. Some of Beckett's earliest poetry and fiction also appeared in *transition*.

Whether or not all the magazines of the period were flights from social reality, as Samuel Putnam maintains, most of *transition*'s eclectic contributors shared similar attitudes toward society, art, history, science, and the Great War. Contemptuous of the positivism and rationalism of the prewar century, and equally contemptuous of the neorationality of Formalism and Structuralism, they declared in the February and June 1929 issues (Beckett contributed to the latter): "We are still living in an epoch of transition . . . in the face of a materialistic despotism which places 'concept' before the living imagination, and the force of will before that of life. . . . The new TRANSITION, having little faith in reason or Science as ultimate methods . . . in a spirit of integral pessimism, proposes to combat all rationalist dogmas that stand in the way of a metaphysical universe."[17]

Eugene Jolas, a former reporter for the *Chicago Tribune*, published the expatriates, and he announced, in no uncertain terms, the reasons for their expatriation—their common "Revolt against the Philistine," their battle against "plutocratic materialism"—in short, their rebellion against "the ideology of a rotting civilization." The extent to which he and the others supported active social revolution is unclear; they lacked the political fervor of the Futurists and Dadaists. What they unanimously demanded was cultural transformation through the "Revolution of the Word" and rebellion against "all rationalist dogmas that stand in the way of a metaphysical universe." [18]

Art, as Jolas proposed in each issue, could provide salvation to the aimless age: "We live in disquiet and disorientation. 'Isms' come and go; the crisis of the imagination continues. What characterizes most this age is its lack of revolutionary faith." His solution was an art—or, more specifically, a language—that would unite the personal, inner experience with the "social world" and "cosmos"—a "collective" and "unifying" "mythos." That the painter and writer were responsible to serve this high function was restated in every issue of transition. Even its advertisements reinforced this moral obligation—from the listings of revived and lost films of André Delons, Henri Sauvage, Desnos, René Clair, and Soupault to announcements of paintings at 16, rue Jacques-Callot, the Surrealist Gallery. Adrienne Monnier publicized her bookshop with the following declaration: "A moral order demands that the bookseller be not only cultivated but that he or she undertake the task of a veritable priesthood." [19]

The "Revolution of the Word" gained slow but precise definition. As Kay Boyle, Hart Crane, Caresse and Harry Crosby, Elliot Paul, and Jolas prescribed, among their twelve demands, there must be a rebellion against "THE HEGEMONY OF THE BANAL WORD, MONOTONOUS SYNTAX, STATIC PSYCHOLOGY, DESCRIPTIVE NATURALISM [and the desire to] CRYSTALLIZE A VIEWPOINT." Pure poetry, they declared, is "A LYRICAL ABSOLUTE THAT SEEKS AN A PRIORI REALITY WITHIN OURSELVES ALONE." As such, time "IS A TYRANNY TO BE ABOLISHED," and "THE WRITER EXPRESSES, HE DOES NOT COMMUNICATE." With this as their aim, "THE PLAIN READER [of necessity] BE DAMNED." [20]

The goal—for painter and writer alike—was the creation of a verbal and visual art that was operative at a "pre-logical" level. Jolas explained this in terminology already popularized by Freud and which Jung used later in a transition essay. After providing a history of Hegelian rationalism and Schopenhauerian irrationalism and Will, Jolas focused on the importance of the nocturnal world in both Herder and Hamann, as well as in Freud's dream researches (a subject he traced back to Heraclitus, Aristotle, and Aquinas). He then referred to Janet's work on primitive humanity and Jung's redefinition of the subconscious. In "Night-Mind and Day-Mind" he added: "Gnosis accepted the principle that the universe partakes of a dual nature. . . . Gnosis is still with us. In order to understand the very springs of the human psyche it is imperative to study the nocturnal manifestations of the spirit. . . . They are found in such states of somnambulism, hypnotic sleep, stigmatisation, telepathy, telekineses, . . . and the numerous occult accidents of consciousness discussed by Dr. Freud and his disciples."[21]

Jung, Jolas astutely observed, had rejected Freud's notion of the "unconscious" as an area of unfulfillment or neuroses (as well as Freud's exaltation of the ego). Instead, Jung extolled the "subconscious" as an infinitely rich storehouse of universal experience through which imaginative and spiritual fulfillment might occur—a merging or unity of "it" and "I," "cause and effect"—a unity of *all* life experience. In the June 1930 issue of *transition*, Jolas reiterated: "For three years, *transition* almost alone of all the movements today, set its face against the pragmatism of the age. . . . In the chaos of the postwar period, a confusion of values . . . set in." *Transition* sought, he continued, "an ideology that would combine the primitive, instinctive mythology with a modern consciousness."[22]

In Jolas's view, the Surrealists, thus far nurtured on Rimbaud, Freud, and Lautréamont, had "failed" in their use of language: "In my opinion," he explained, "because [they] refused to consider the problem of the word in the struggle for a new reality," they retain "traditional" language. It remains the obligation of the creator, he continued, "to find the bridge between the primal and the objective worlds and to consciously fuse his discoveries into an organic whole." As he later defined it, the Surrealists had failed to "locate the language of the nocturnal world," the language of "a-logical grammar."[23] Beckett's mastery of this language—of and through "the mess"—occurred as early as *Waiting for Godot*.

The June 1930 issue of *transition* included Jung's "Psychology and Poetry," Jolas's "The Dream," and Beckett's poem "For Future Reference." Jung emphasized the nondidactic but universal quality of art: "[The poet's] great work is like a dream which . . . does not interpret itself, and is . . . unequivocal. No dream says: 'Thou shalt' or 'This is the truth'; it presents a picture, the way nature lets a plant grow." The poet touches "that salubrious and redeeming psychic depth where as yet no individual has secluded himself in the solitude of his consciousness in order to start forth . . . to reach out to all humanity." Jolas's essay repeated that the writer taps universal nature as he "penetrates" the "labyrinth of his own inner world," and it was illustrated by works of Tzara, Artaud, Williams, Eisenstein, Rilke, and Beckett (his poem). A list of contributors identified twenty-four-year-old Beckett as "an Irish poet and essayist . . . instructor at the Ecole Normale in Paris."[24]

Jolas's intentions were even more specific two years later in the "Poetry is Vertical" issue, with its handsome cover design by Arp. The contents page announced "Anamyths, Psychographs and Other Prose-Texts" by Asturius,

Calderón, Kafka, Rosenberg, Stein, Beckett (his story "Sedendo and Quies-
ciendo"), along with a "Metanthropological Crisis" manifesto by Gottfried
Benn, Martin Buber, Whit Burnett, Stuart Gilbert, C. G. Jung, H. L. Mencken,
D. A. Siquieros, Stein, Vitrac, and others. The Verticalist manifesto called for
the "hegemony of the inner life over the outer life" in an interesting blend of
Jolas, Freud, and Jung: "The transcendental 'I' with its multiple stratifications
reaching back millions of years is related to the entire history of mankind,
past and present, and is brought to the surface with the hallucinatory irrup-
tion of images in the dream, the daydream, the mystic-gnostic trance, and
even the psychiatric condition."[25] Jolas's ideology was then focused within
a set of goals for a unifying mythos of dream and external reality: the evocation of the instinctive, personal, and collective universe. In short, Jolas
provided a definition of the universal self in relationship to primal consciousness and the transcendent unity that connected all things; art would
contain and be a product of all the interdependent processes therein. The
manifesto was signed by Arp, Carl Einstein, Jolas, McGreevy, Georges Pelorson, Theo Rutra, James J. Sweeney, Ronald Symons—and Beckett.

That their primary goal was the "hegemony of the inner life over the
outer life" relates to Beckett's later use of unconscious thought functioning
in his work. Beckett successfully expressed the universal and "transcendental 'I,' " as he moved toward its "final disintegration"—in the creative act of
the I's measuring itself. His heroes, each in search of an irreducible self or
voice, became the refinement of each previous fictional hero and moved to
silence in the impossible task of touching the core of inner and outer reality.
"Assumption," Beckett's earliest fiction, begins this pattern, and its subject
matter and struggle with common Surrealist contradictions typify the kind
of work *transition* had been publishing.

The Surrealists were also affiliated with the newly planned *Variétés*. Breton
and Aragon edited a special 1929 issue called "Surrealism," which, in June, included an essay by Sigmund Freud.[26] They were also associated with Breton's
La Révolution surréaliste (later called *Le Surréalisme au service de la révolution* when
many aligned themselves with the communist party). The revived *This Quarter*
magazine, now owned by Edward Titus (who was married to Helena Rubin-
stein), like *transition* welcomed international contributors, and the September
1932 issue, edited by Breton, carried essays, poetry, and designs by Tzara,
Dali, Buñuel, Breton, Duchamp, Crevel, Ernst, de Chirico, Man Ray, Tanguy,
and Eluard. Beckett and Richard Thoma were hired to translate many of the
poems and essays; Titus later made "special acknowledgement" of Beckett's
"substantial contribution to the issue."[27] Beckett translated an Eluard essay,
which was later reprinted in England, along with work by Péret, Breton,
and Tzara. Breton's article, "Surrealism Yesterday, To-Day, and To-Morrow,"

again specified as the Surrealists' goal "to calculate the quotient of the unconscious by the conscious." The issue contained such landmark writings as Duchamp's notes for The Bride Stripped Bare by Her Bachelors, the script of Un Chien Andalou, and Dali's essay "The Object as Revealed in Surrealist Experiment."

Breton, the major theoretician of the Surrealists, brought to the group both his war and his psychiatric experiences. He had a brilliant mind and overpowering personality and, according to his lifelong friend Duchamp, became "the great catalyst" not just for the Surrealists but for all the writers and artists of the time "who were looking for a new focus for the arts"—including Picasso, Aragon, Eluard, Ernst, Dali, Octavio Paz, Tanguy, Durrell, Lacan, Lévi-Strauss, and numerous others.[28]

As early as 1919, largely through his treatment of World War I patient Jacques Vaché, Breton recognized that the mind has a continuous thought process that exists below consciousness—which Freud called "primary process." Breton had studied Freud's major theories and worked at the Charcot Clinic, where Freud had once been in attendance. Focusing on Freud's dream theory, Breton made the subtle observation that through the continuous operation of subterranean thought, the mind was naturally, as Lionel Trilling later phrased it, "a poetry-making organ." With its techniques of condensation, symbolism, ambiguity, and with its redefinition of time and space, poetry was "indigenous" to the very constitution of the unconscious mind.[29] Breton thus set forth as the first tenet of Surrealism the artist's obligation to retain the purity of unconscious thought process, which could be accomplished through automatic writing—writing without conscious control or awareness. He also proposed a series of techniques by which the rational mind could be kept at bay. Although some of his most important statements, including "Les Vases communicants," were not published until 1932, his notions regarding the relationship between consciousness and the unconscious, and between Freudianism and Marxism, were articulated in the early 1920s. By the time Beckett began his association with transition, Breton's notions of how reality and dream re-create and re-energize one another had been much discussed.

Like Jung, Breton clarified his divergence from Freud. Strict psychoanalytic theory, for example, proposed that dreams revealed the past; to Breton (and Jung), dreams were prophetic, acting in a dialectical relationship to the past and future. Breton found Freud's imagery, rather than his "science," most compelling, although Freud's explanation of humor appealed to him as well. Freud saw "wit" as the liberating mechanism that allowed the inner world a victory over the rational one, again a product of the dialectical interaction of consciousness and the unconscious.

Jarry had said that laughter is born out of "the discovery of the contradictory," anticipating Artaud's "We believe in the absolute power of contradiction." Vaché, Breton's patient, considered "umor" as "a feeling," a "sense . . . of the theatrical uselessness (and no joy there) of everything *when* you know."[30] Breton's earliest manifestos emphasized a number of elements that must have been of enormous interest to Beckett: dreams, paradox, chance, and coincidence (which reduced the disjunctures between the individual and nature). These early writings also discussed humor as visible at life's most tragic moments and the precarious distinctions between the self (*soi*) and ego (*le moi*). In *Surrealism and Painting* (1928), Breton spoke of "canalizing" from the "depths of our minds . . . [the] strange forces capable of increasing those on the surface or of successfully contending with them," and then submitting "to the control of reason." The intermingling of conscious and unconscious thought functioning would become both subject and technique in the Beckett canon.[31]

So too, Breton's emphasis on "objective chance," on "the geometric locus of coincidences"—where unrelated events gain synchronicity through an obscure common denominator within normal thought function—would have been of considerable interest to Beckett. In Breton's words, objective chance was "the manifestation of external reality which opens a path for itself in the human unconscious."[32] "Objective chance," that cosmic state of randomness that deprives events of final "meaning," may well have been a precursor of Beckett's sardonic treatment of logic and the tension between necessity and freedom that underlies his tragicomic forms.

Paris was filled with immigrant painters equally attracted to Breton's Surrealism. As the poets had rejected logic, syntax, and the traditional meanings of words for an automatic landscape of unconscious dreams, Magritte, Miró, and many others created "texts" in paint. They shocked their audiences by shaping dream images in strictly representational forms (realistic, "logical" forms), articulated in slick, pure color. The words and phrases they added to their canvasses created some of their most dramatic effects. *The Hunter (Catalan Landscape)*, for example, with its verbal hieroglyphics, was one of Miró's most innovative *tableaux-poèmes*. Magritte was also successful in his translations of Apollinaire, Rimbaud, and Cendrars onto canvas. In 1929, Magritte wrote his famous treatise on language (fascinating in its affinities with Wittgenstein), in which he made the declaration, "La poésie est une pipe." This became a useful gloss not just on his painting *La Trahison des images* (*"Ceci n'est pas une pipe"*) but on many Surrealist paintings of the period. Magritte later exchanged letters with Foucault, whose *Les Mots et les Choses* he had already studied.[33]

Beckett's contact with the painters and writers who gathered around

Breton, Aragon, Eluard, Péret, and, for a time, Soupault, not only introduced him to a variety of fascinating new art forms but to an entirely new
body of ideas. Perhaps most striking was the Surrealists' desire to reconcile
traditional contrarieties and dualities and to integrate chance, mystery, and
mysticism, in their quest toward the linkage of opposites, like the inner and
outer world, the conscious and unconscious life. Theirs was an art of constant flux and metamorphosis, as in dreams, where image and "meaning"
continually connect and separate, where a sense of transcendence or whole-
ness mingles with a sense of the fragile and tentative. The young Beckett may
well have been fascinated by the Surrealists' idealism, their faith in the con-
nectedness of all experience, and their quest for "liberation" in some state of
mystical, if temporary, synthesis. It seems unlikely that he would have taken
to their Marxist interests. All the same, his hero in "Assumption" aspires to
their point sublime of inner and outer revelation, although this is unique in
the Beckett oeuvre.[34] Given his later works, however, Beckett would have
been interested in their conviction that the unconscious re-creates external
reality, just as the external world refuels the inner one.

Mary Ann Caws speaks of the similarities between film and Surrealist
poetry in their common "metamorphosis of the instant"—possibly what
Balakian calls the Surrealists' "elasticity of experience."[35] One could clarify
"metamorphosis" and "elasticity" by emphasizing that the Surrealists embraced new parameters of time—as it operates on both unconscious and
conscious levels. In any case, if Breton used techniques similar to Eisenstein's montage—and we know of Beckett's fascination with this director—
this in itself might have appealed to Beckett, who had an uncanny skill in
incorporating any number of art techniques (film, painting, music) into his
own forms.[36]

Would Beckett have discussed with his new Surrealist acquaintances the
differences in their work compared with, say, that of the French Symbolists,
whom he had studied with Rudmose-Brown? Would he have asked them—
because many had been former Dadaists—the reasons for their new attitude
toward "contradiction"? As Jacques Rivière had defined Dada for the Dada
Almanac, published in Nouvelle Revue Français: "Dada managed to take hold of the
being . . . in all its incoherence, or rather, in its primal coherence, before the
idea of contradiction appeared and forced it to contain itself, structure itself;
to replace its acquired logical unity with its original, absurd unity."[37] Would
Beckett have been attuned to what had become the generally accepted conclusion that the "smirking" futility of the Dadaists was best summarized "by
the word 'rien' "[38]—a word to which Beckett would subsequently give new
dimension? ("Rien à faire," "Nothing to be done," Godot begins.) Or would he

have considered the Surrealists naive in their efforts to replace logic with a mystical mixture of Hegelian, Freudian, and Marxist doctrine? Finally, what would he have thought of the vitriolic attacks on the Surrealists that spewed out of magazines like the London *Enemy*? What would he have thought of the self-proclaimed realist Wyndham Lewis in his dogged defense of reason?

Beckett had begun to publish poetry and fiction in the small magazines, and in 1930, his first separate published work appeared, the ninety-eight-line poem *Whoroscope*. The circumstances of its publication tell us about Beckett's life during this period.

Whoroscope was submitted to a contest on the subject of time, sponsored by Nancy Cunard's Hours Press; Beckett heard about the competition just twenty-four hours before the deadline. As he wrote in a letter to Cunard many years later: "[I] wrote the first half before dinner [on Hotel Bristol stationery], had a guzzle of salad and Chambertin at the Cochon de Lait, went back to the Ecole and finished it about three in the morning. . . . That's how it was and them were the days." [39] Cunard and Richard Aldington judged the contest, and Beckett won the thousand-franc prize and a publication commitment. [40]

Cunard had actually been associated with the Surrealists in 1924, mainly through her affair with Louis Aragon. A leader in the Africana fad, she was known for her beauty, high style, financial generosity, and sexual freedom. She was also a very hard worker: she bought her press in 1928 for £300 and shortly thereafter tripled her investment, publishing such unusual combinations of works as Pound's *Probable Music of Beowulf*, George Moore's *Peronnik the Fool* (a reprint), and Norman Douglas's *Report on the Pumice-Stone Industry of the Lipari Islands*. [41] During the same year she also brought her black lover, the jazz musician Henry Crowder, to London. He had been living in Venice, a victim of fascism and racial discrimination. He and Beckett later became friends.

With "Horo" a pun on *hour*, *Whoroscope* is about the life of the superstitious Descartes, who refused to reveal his birth date for fear that an astrologer could predict his death. The poem, which centers around details from Adrien Baillet's *Life of Descartes* (1691), is obscure and arcane. The reader, for example, must connect the title with the Swedish queen Christina, who, in demanding Descartes's early morning court appearance, might have (like time itself) precipitated his final illness. (Descartes, like his disciple Samuel Beckett, preferred to stay in bed until noon.) But the poem is interesting for its treatment of what became some of Beckett's major interests, such as the mind-body duality. It begins, for example, with Descartes's calling for his favorite kind of egg, one hatched in eight to ten days. A telescopic womb-

tomb image, the broken egg suggests not just the mind-body split (and
the modern consciousness of self and time), but also the fetus condemned
to death and the rot and stench into which all organisms decay: "What's
that?/An egg?/By the brothers Boot it stinks fresh,/Give it to Gillot."

Descartes's several voices in the poem also anticipate the multiple inner
voices of Beckett's later fiction, like *The Unnamable*'s "I can't go on. I'll go on."
Descartes rages against fate, wishes for more time ("a second starless inscrutable hour"), envisions a time without light (a paradoxical state, since a
horoscope is cast by the stars), for then he would, presumably and finally,
contemplate time. At the same time, he is restrained to his "cogito," the
"sky of my skull." Here, all games are played, and, as such, the meaning of
the external world is forever "inscrutable." He will, nevertheless, persevere,
although once again, punning, he says: "Fallor, ergo sum." (Saint Augustine:
"I am deceived, therefore I am.") The way up and the way down are perhaps
the same; through cogito and deception, one might arrive at unreason, the
dark light of the inner voices and a new understanding of time and the self.

Beckett spent the summer of 1930 reading Proust's sixteen volumes twice
before completing his seventy-two-page *Proust*, commissioned by Chatto and
Windus through the recommendation of Richard Aldington. (McGreevy was
writing a similar volume on T. S. Eliot.) Another arcane and highly erudite piece of writing, it is one of the first in-depth analyses of *A la Recherche*
(and was positively reviewed by Rebecca West in the *Daily Telegraph* when it
was published in 1931).[42] Although Beckett deals with Proust's work con-
cretely, many of his observations are of interest as they relate to his future
work. Form and content must be one, he writes (as in *Our Exagmination*, discussed below)—"the one is a concretion of the other, the revelation of a
world." Because language is an approximation, translation, or distortion of
experience, the artist lacks precise "vehicles of communication": the "world
is expressed metaphorically by the artisan because it is apprehended metaphorically by the artist." Even the notion of the "world," or "reality," as the
subject of art demands clarification. Experience remains unknowable due to
the constantly fluid nature of the mind or self and the world—and the complex metamorphizing that occurs in their interaction.

Furthermore, the traditional measuring vehicle, the ego, along with its
instruments—logic and language—define one another in and through time,
and they are subject to all the distortions imposed by memory. As a result, ordinary or "voluntary memory" is "of no value as an instrument of
[artistic] evocation." Like ordinary language, voluntary memory functions
like habit and is itself the distorted product of one's imprisonment in time.
In a much-quoted statement, Beckett defines time as "that double-headed

monster of damnation and salvation," from which "there is no escape," as it "deform[s] us, or [has] been deformed by us"—through the rationalizations or misunderstandings of the self through time.

Nevertheless, one accommodates oneself to the fundamental challenge of survival through habit, which Beckett defines as "a compromise effected between the individual and his environment, or between the individual and his own organic eccentricities." As such, "life is habit. Or rather life is a succession of habits." The world thus becomes a projection of one's habits of mind or habits of behavior—an accommodation to what Beckett elsewhere calls the "mess," or buzzing confusion of the inner and outer worlds.

True nakedness of self—the "suffering" of existence and the "fertile" insights which accompany this—surfaces only at the instant one steps out of one particular habit before escaping into another. These "periods of transition that separate consecutive adaptations . . . represent the perilous zones in the life of the individual, dangerous, precarious, painful, mysterious and fertile, when for a moment the boredom of living is replaced by the suffering of being."

The most authentic connection one can make with the self occurs during such moments of "latent consciousness," during those preconscious or unconscious moments of experience over which one lacks rational control. Unlike moments of "voluntary memory," controlled by will and logic, these are the intuitive, disjointed, emotional, creative moments of mental functioning. They are "explosive" and "unruly"—"immediate, total and [a] delicious deflagration." They "cannot be importuned." They bring one in contact with the purest and least diluted part of self, as at the same time one remains powerless over the source from which they emanate.

Great artists put latent consciousness to effective use in reaching toward the union of subject and object. In so doing, and in moments of "solitude," they act as "translator[s]" of that "excavated" area of the deepest self. Ultimately, then, art is "neither created nor chosen." It is the consequence of the artist's surrender—in motivation, execution, and subject matter—to the deepest core of being. Beckett writes: "The only fertile research is excavatory, immersive, a contraction of the spirit, a descent. The artist is active, but negatively, from shrinking from the nullity of extracircumferential phenomena, drawn in to the core of the eddy."

Beckett considers numerous other matters in Proust, of interest in terms of his later work. He speaks of the "tragic figure" who, in "expiation of original sin," realizes that his fall is due to the mere "sin of having been born." That is, thrust into a condition of ignorance and powerlessness, he, at the same time, desires knowledge. But not only is knowledge an illusion, so is action. The tragic figure would know and act, but conclusions and destinations are similarly illusory. (As Beckett repeats throughout *Wait-ing for Godot*: " 'Let's go.' [They do not move.]") In the end, the artist, like all humankind, remains enfeebled—estranged both from understanding and connection with the world into which he has been born: "Reality, whether approached imaginatively or empirically, remains a surface, hermetic."

Beckett visited Sylvia Beach's and Adrienne Monnier's bookshops, and to Monnier he was "the new Stephen Dedalus," following "the Joycean path of 'silence, exile and cunning.' " At Beach's, "being too poor, and at the same time too proud, to accept, as many others did, a free library card," he "came to browse and talk."[43] That he came to "browse and *talk*" (emphasis added) brings us to another inescapable dimension of life in Paris: gossip. Indeed, in the bookshops and cafés, or at many shops or galleries on the boule-vards, one might have heard many of the local scandals or legends—many of which concerned people Beckett had met. As Beckett himself said, Paris in the twenties was a "good place for a young man to be," and we can envision him, like any young person, enjoying the lighter, more seductive, "wicked" side of Paris.

The tales—both large and small—of the Surrealists, for example, were well spun: their performance at Anatole France's funeral, where they mounted a furious demonstration with the manifesto "A Corpse (Have You Ever Slapped a Dead Man)"; Cocteau's and Breton's famous rivalry and Breton's "excommunication" of Vitrac, Artaud, Soupault, and Masson; Magritte and Breton's breakup when Masson insisted that the painter's wife, Georgette, dispose of the gold chain and cross she was wearing; Aragon's predictable tirades against his bourgeois roots; Breton's boycott of Strind-berg's *Dream Play*; Desnos's, Eluard's, and Soupault's sabotage of Aron's lec-ture on "The Average Frenchman"; the banquet-debacle at Closerie des Lilas for Saint-Pol Roux; the open letter to Claudel, after he called their actions "pederastic"; their "love celebrations" and "Hands off Love" essay (1927), which defended Charlie Chaplin for his "inherent right" to ask his aggrieved and divorcing wife to perform "unnatural acts"; and the fiftieth anniver-sary celebration of the scientific discovery of "hysteria." Less exotic but also frequently discussed were the Surrealists' severe attacks on artists pursuing different styles, as in Matisse's "pandering to middle class taste by offering insipid modernist paintings."[44]

Conversations about death added an additional piquant and glamorous note. Not only had the suicide of Breton's patient Vaché become legendary, but after the young Surrealist Jacques Rigaut took his life in 1929, a public debate ensued over Nietzsche's statement "Die at the right time" and whether or not suicide was a decisive act of freedom. (Harry Crosby, Mayakovsky,

Crevel, and Radiguet were other suicides.) It was also common knowledge that in 1929 Hemingway's mother had acceded to her son's request and sent him the pistol his father had shot himself with the year before. If Beckett were discussing suicide at this time, as Bair speculates, it may have been due less to his supposed morbid fantasies than the social and intellectual temper of the time.[45] Freud's and Bergson's findings on the divided personality and Freud's "death instinct" also precipitated numerous debates—from the "Nothing is left us" sentiments of the Discontinuité group to the public declamations against Surrealism from local personalities like Emmanuel Berl and those involved in creationism.[46]

By 1928, controversies about the "life" and "death" instincts—indeed, many of Freud's theories—were commonplace. An entirely new language—of fetishes, fixations, and Freudian slips—had entered the lexicon. As Paul Johnson puts it, the translation of Freudian texts during the twenties had become an industry unto itself. Johnson goes on to speak about Freud as a gnostic, believing in the existence of a hidden structure of knowledge beneath the surface of things, which, to Johnson, accounted for his great appeal to artists and intellectuals of the time. If Marx had attributed human behavior to economic interests, Freud aligned it with sexual drives, although, like Marx, he shared the conviction that religious belief was fantasy or narcotic, another concept comfortable to the postwar generation. In fact, Freud's *Future of an Illusion* was very much discussed in the late twenties. Here Freud labeled religion as a human construct designed to ameliorate personal unhappiness and called it "a protection against suffering through a remolding of reality." This "remolding," he furthermore qualified, was "delusional." That Freud's interest in sexuality, the death wish, and guilt met the needs of the time was manifest, Johnson broadly concludes, in much of the work published at the time. As Gide had put it: "[Freud writes] what I have always thought!"[47]

America was a subject of considerable interest in Paris during 1928. Despite the United States' integral role in ending the First World War, anti-U.S. sentiment surfaced in 1927. The American government was adamant that France pay its war debt at the very time its economy was on the verge of collapse. Furthermore, although Americans had brought a great deal of tourist money to Paris, they appeared to many as profligate, if not vulgar, in their tastes and manners. As Briton Clive Bell put it: "Some Americans had French mistresses, but very few had French friends."[48]

The daring success of Charles Lindbergh's transatlantic flight in May 1927 temporarily reversed this sentiment. Lindbergh accomplished an aeronautical feat that could link America and Europe (in only thirty-three hours), and the handsome, clean-cut young man restored a wholesomeness to the otherwise debauched "ugly American" image. But France's celebration of America was short-lived. The conviction of Sacco and Vanzetti only three months later, with its shades of the Dreyfus affair, precipitated riots in Paris that were exceeded in violence only by those in the United States. Celebrities protested in the streets, and demonstrators insulted even the former doughboys. As an indication of anti-American sentiment, few French people attended Isadora Duncan's funeral after her shocking accidental death, although the dancer had been one of France's greatest advocates.[49]

Perhaps coincidentally, a great deal of local news centered on specific Americans, many of whom Beckett would have known through their work, if not personally.[50] Hart Crane had been taken up by the publisher Harry Crosby and his wife as an artist to be pampered into writing. He had been escorted to their home where, given his own tower room, stationery, and all he could eat (and drink), he agreed to work on The Bridge. Instead, he engaged in drunken sexual binges (with their employees) and was finally given, again by the Crosbys, a last bottle of Cutty Sark and passage back to New York. He did not return at the time; in 1932, he drowned himself on the way to New York from Mexico.

A great deal of Paris gossip centered on the transition people and their allies and adversaries. Who took tea at Stella Bowen's art studio was a matter of instant concern. The same held true for gatherings at Stein's residence at 27, rue de Fleurus, Beach's at 12, rue de l'Odéon, and Natalie Clifford Barney's on rue Jacob. Although the Jolases held regular parties for the transition group, Bill and Mary Widney also actively cultivated these people. Sorbonne faculty, including Bernard Fay, hosted other groups, and Elsa Maxwell and Jean Cocteau competed for the "smart set."[51] The petty rivalries at these parties were numerous. Gertrude Stein once called Joyce "a third rate Irish politician," adding, as one might expect, "The greatest living writer of the age is Gertrude Stein."[52] At another transition party given by the Jolases, Stein and Alice B. Toklas arrived in the presence of Sylvia Beach and the Joyces. Kay Boyle felt she couldn't talk to Stein, for it would "have seemed almost a disloyalty." Furthermore, "Stein had made clear her opinion of Joyce both to Sylvia . . . and to [Maria] Jolas. Jolas was [then] insulted by Stein for paying too much attention to the 'dirty Irish politician James Joyce.' "[53] Boyle, who became a good friend of Beckett's, had the misfortune of finding herself in the middle of several competitions, in particular one between Stein and Maria Jolas. Boyle had observed about Jolas: "She [has] the head of a Roman emperor and the wild gaze of a poet." But Stein, who had been similarly described, retorted: "Perhaps there [is] not room for two such imperial heads in one expatriate kingdom."[54]

Establishing one's place in this kingdom made for some clumsy falls, and this, too, became part of the flourishing grapevine. After transition accepted the free forms of Lincoln Gillespie, for example, with Gillespie presumably a practitioner of the "Revolution of the Word," his work was interpreted as a parody of both Stein and Joyce. Future contributions from Gillespie were discouraged, but the man had already celebrated his success by discarding his wife with the explanation that he was entitled to a woman of equal intellect. Such trivialities and the enormous attention they elicited might have demonstrated for some, including Beckett, the desirability of remaining a private person.

A few artists received constant attention: Hemingway tales were legion, especially those involving his 1928 marriage to Hadley Richardson, shortly after which the itinerant bridegroom began a liaison with the wealthy Pauline Pfeiffer, along with a visible indulgence in food and wine. The latter not only produced serious symptoms of gout, initiating his lifelong battles with food and drink, but increased the audiences that followed the trail of his various appetites.

His mother's condemnation of The Sun Also Rises ("one of the filthiest books" she had ever read) also became public information. She urged him (as she had since his childhood) to call on God to reform his ways, which included his excessive drinking. Hemingway's private unhappiness was "covered up by . . . rudeness" and the pretense that he was beyond pain: he bragged that "he'd beat up any guy he didn't like." [55] As a result, he was always in need of a "timekeeper" for the many brief boxing matches he "playfully" initiated with accommodating celebrities such as Miró and F. Scott Fitzgerald. But the friendship between Hemingway and Fitzgerald suffered after the latter absent-mindedly allowed one game to exceed two minutes, and Hemingway was knocked down, not out. Because of Hemingway's great notoriety, his "knockout" was immediately picked up by the international press, and it became another subject of popular conversation.

Picasso was another artist whose adventures reached legendary proportions. For instance, after he began illustrating Ovid's Metamorphosis—with his mythical nymphs, satyrs, and minotaurs—he is said to have literally signaled his publisher, Albert Skira, every time he created a new image: he blasted notes on a clown's antique trumpet to alert Skira, who had rented a flat next to his. [56]

And so the legends grew. Yet in mythic status and magnitude of achievement, no one in the Parisian artistic pantheon exceeded an earlier arrival from Beckett's native land, James Joyce. Joyce's friendship with the twenty-four-year-old Beckett profoundly altered the young man's growth as a person and artist.

THREE | James Joyce

I welcome this occasion to bow once again, before I go, deep
down, before his heroic work, heroic being.
—SAMUEL BECKETT, on the centenary of Joyce's birth

I saw his stoicism before fate. . . . This tenacity was part of his
honesty of conviction, his horror of cheap compromise, his
fanatic belief in his own intellectual power.—EUGENE JOLAS

The function of literature, as Joyce and his hero Stephen
Dedalus both define it with unaccustomed fervor, is the eternal
affirmation of the spirit of man, suffering and rollicking. We
can shed what he called "laughtears" as his writings confront us
with this spectacle.—RICHARD ELLMANN

Central to Beckett's life in Paris during the late 1920s
and early 1930s was his relationship with James Joyce. Beckett and Joyce
were in close contact from 1928 to 1930 and again between 1937 and 1939.
Joyce left Paris in December 1939 and died in Zurich on January 13, 1941. I
shall concentrate on the 1928–30 period, as most of the available information focuses on these years.

Richard Ellmann's definitive Joyce biography, first published in 1959,
provides many of the specifics; indeed, subsequent biographical material on
both Joyce and the Beckett-Joyce relationship builds upon Ellmann's findings.[1] However, several of Joyce's closest friends whom Ellmann relied upon
extensively—Frank Budgen, C. P. Curran, Maria and Eugene Jolas, Stuart
Gilbert, Louis Gillet, Sylvia Beach, and Mary and Padraic Colum, among
others—have also published books about Joyce, in most cases, after the publication of Ellmann's first edition. A close study of these detailed descriptions
of Joyce, especially during the early years, is indispensable, for they help us
understand the "heroic being" of the person who, next to William Beckett,
was probably most influential in Beckett's development.

Joyce's commentators report that, despite the most trying financial,
health, and family problems, Joyce had a great tenacity for survival and a virtually holy commitment to his craft, family, and friends. Of his family ties,
one friend writes: "Joyce possessed an almost mystical belief in blood lines."
Louis Gillet commented: "In the chaos of the universe, as in the Deluge, his
family was for him . . . the Sacred Ark." Birthdays and anniversaries were

celebrations; they were Joyce's happiest days. They were also "rituals" to be performed "to appease the cruel forces of destiny."[2] Even his large and scattered family in Ireland always elicited his faithful vigilance: he helped brothers and sisters gain jobs in the various cities in which he resided; he "religiously" maintained a correspondence with anyone who could inform him of "all family affairs."[3] So, too, when he committed himself to a friendship, he treated his friend like a family member and was soon involved with his or her every family, domestic, and social problem. For Joyce, friendship was a serious moral obligation.

Joyce's longtime friend Constantine Curran once said that Joyce was "an exile of the soul," but he was speaking in traditional religious terms. Curran and virtually everyone who knew Joyce spoke of his unshakable faith in his own sacred calling—as "priest" of the "eternal imagination" (Stephen Dedalus's terms in *Portrait of the Artist As a Young Man*). Joyce used the same terminology in his personal correspondence: "I am . . . perhaps creating at last a conscience in the soul."[4] The Catholic priesthood had been an impossible option—and for one reason alone: "Mind you, it was not a question of belief," he said. "It was a question of celibacy. I knew I could not live the life of a celibate." In fact, when asked when he left the church, he said: "That's for the Church to say."[5] As Joyce's brother Stanislaus explained, Joyce believed that poets were the true priests, that "poets in the measure of their gifts and personalities were the repositories of the *genuine* spiritual life of their race" (emphasis added).[6]

Indeed, Joyce believed in his "own soul's," as he put it, "well, sexual department," and was repulsed by the church's "lying drivel about pure men and pure women and spiritual love and love forever"—to him, "blatant lying in the face of truth." For Joyce, there could be no distinction between body and spirit.[7] With this as a given, he remained deeply spiritual, and through the rituals of daily life and the sanctification of family and personal relationships created his own sacred "religion." His art was his instrument—the scripture—in which he forged and through which he revealed the holiness of everyday life. Even Joyce acknowledged that the "silence, exile, and cunning"—as he had projected them in Stephen Dedalus—were "equated with" his own "theological virtues . . . hope, charity, and faith."[8]

Joyce's life and art were two sides of the holy coin. Once, before he cut a birthday cake with a replica of *Ulysses* on it, he said: "Hoc est enim corpus meum" (this is my body). One might well say of Joyce, as Buck Mulligan did of Stephen, that he had the "jesuit strain" in him, "only it [was] injected the wrong way."[9] Yet "the wrong way" involved Joyce's "will of steel," rather than conventional faith, to guide both his life and art. But "the wrong way" also involved his ability to transform ("transsubstantiate") the ordinary into the

extraordinary, to make a birthday party into a festival, to envision Leopold
Bloom as Ulysses, to interpret the human tragedy as a kind of divine comedy.

Stanislaus recognized his brother's calling and said that any success in
his life would arise not from his "genius" but from his "extraordinary moral
courage," which he associated with Joyce's earliest religious inclinations: "I
confess I have no better explanation to offer of his triumphant struggle to
preserve his rectitude as an artist in the midst of illness and disappointment, in abject poverty and disillusionment, than this, that he who has loved
God intensely in his youth will never love anything less. The definition may
change, the service abides." After Joyce's death, he repeated that his brother's
greatest "passions" in life had "stemmed" from his "*ancient* love of God." [10]

Joyce's spiritual outlook thus may have accounted for his stoicism in the
face of his many afflictions. "No man has so much hope for the future,"
wrote his brother once again. The three volumes of Joyce's *Letters* offer repeated evidence of his determination and equanimity. Statements like, "My
reading sight seems to have come to an end but I was informed that both
eyes should be again operated," are followed typically by such comments as,
"Is it possible to have the Welsh-English dictionary?" [11] Perhaps Beckett was
referring to this kind of faith when, long afterward, in the year of his Nobel
Prize, he said that Joyce had had a great "moral effect" on him. [12]

Once [Joyce] had given his friendship, nothing could swerve him from his giant
loyalty. —EUGENE JOLAS

When Joyce chose a friend, his commitment aspired to the noblest con-
ceptions of the ideal of friendship. Maria Jolas, one of Joyce's (and Beckett's)
closest friends—the tall, handsome Kentuckyan and trained opera singer
most frequently associated with *transition*—remarks that Joyce "had a talent
for friendship that was quite extraordinary. . . . This is one of the reasons why
he didn't give his friendship very easily; it was a responsibility to him." [13]

Frank Budgen, a painter and occasional model (the sailor on the pack of
Players cigarettes), whom Ellmann calls Joyce's lifetime confidante, explains
that Joyce was "a man in need of friends" and that he regarded friendship as
a relationship of "egalitarian laws and constitution." He was consistent and
loyal; he both gave and received; and he was always both a sharing talker
and caring listener. Mary Colum, musing upon Joyce's absolute "devotion"
and "reliability"—which she "was to remark again and again about Joyce"—
elaborates on his "solicitousness." Available for the most everyday problems
as well as more serious matters, he "would help one with any old thing—
with finding an apartment or a maid or a doctor, [just as] if one . . . were
ill, he would shower him with attentions." Joyce was "even at pains to study

his friends' tastes and to serve them. His anxiety to give them pleasure and his sense of hospitality were so embarrassing," writes Curran, "that at times I had to keep him in the dark as to my own . . . movements so as not to disarrange unduly his own plans." Joyce regularly attended performances by his friends' friends.[14]

Joyce's modesty and pride needs were also unconcealed. If a friend offered an opinion about his work or kept an offprint or a copy, he was deeply "grateful. . . . Their piety was sweet to him and consoled many a bitterness." Beckett reported to Ellmann one such occasion after he first read a section of "Anna Livia Plurabelle." "On the other side," writes Mary Colum, "Joyce expected a lot of attention from those he knew, and, on account of his eyes, a great deal of help."[15]

Although Marvin Magalaner and Richard M. Kain conclude that Herbert S. Gorman tried to "make a martyr" of the author of *Ulysses*, Gorman does write the following in his early biographical sketch (1924): "Joyce was that type of literary artist who is thoroughly selfish and inwardly gazing at all times. The world as such meant less to him than the world's reactions upon his mind and spirit. . . . We can hardly picture him dying for a lost cause unless the lost cause happened to be himself." The fact that Joyce, when invited to edit Gorman's manuscript, allowed this to remain but deleted all mention of his daughter's mental illness[16] may illustrate Ellmann's (and many others') insistence upon Joyce's modesty, foreshadowing Beckett's later forbearance in response to unkind public portraiture: "Joyce met [people] face to face, as unassuming in his behavior as he was uncompromising in his aims. People lionized him but he would not roar." He once said to an academic who wanted to exalt him: "Don't make a hero out of me. I'm only a simple middle-class man."[17]

A more exacting reply to Gorman's comment—also pertinent in describing Joyce—might be that everything in Joyce's world became the raw material for his work, since, in his own terms, "imagination was memory." As Harry Levin put it, Joyce regarded strangers as "contemporary posterity."[18] As a result, his most casual activity—having his trousers measured at Galeries Lafayette, or a response like "Come in," when someone knocked at his door—found its way into his work.[19] The man's life and work were inseparable, as the artist devoured details that would inevitably reappear in his vast mirroring of nature. That this was Joyce's approach to life, however, is not incompatible with his reported kindness and humanity. Sylvia Beach well defines what I have alluded to as Joyce's ministry: "As for Joyce, he treated people invariably as equals, whether they were writers, children, waiters, princesses, or charladies. What anybody had to say interested him; he told me that he had never met a bore."[20]

As Beckett himself was to be, Joyce was uncommonly supportive to both friends and aspiring young artists. It was as though a legacy of kindness were being passed from one generation to the next. When he was twenty, Joyce had met William Butler Yeats, then thirty-seven, and Yeats invited him to review books and write for the new Abbey Theatre, introduced him to Lady Gregory and Arthur Symons, and became one of the relatively few established writers who consistently praised his work. Yeats wrote Joyce shortly after their first meeting in 1902: "I will do anything for you I can but I am afraid that it will not be a great deal. The chief use I can be, though probably you will not believe this, will be by introducing you to some other writers who are starting like yourself. One always learns his business from one's fellow-writers, especially from those who are near enough one's age to understand one's difficulties."[21] Ezra Pound had been similarly supportive of Joyce, publishing *Portrait of the Artist As a Young Man* in regular installments in the *Egoist* from February 1914 through September 1915.

Joyce managed to combine his strong personal and creative commitments. Regardless of his personal and family sorrows, he retained an interest in his friends and persevered in his calling—all through sheer strength of will. Yet he was also a man of deep feeling and often unabashed emotionalism. For example, after learning that his daughter, Lucia, had to be institutionalized and that he had to undergo yet another eye surgery, he said to Maria Jolas: "And I'm supposed to be writing a funny book." On another occasion he revealed to Harriet Weaver: "Perhaps I shall survive and perhaps the raving madness I write will survive, and perhaps it is very funny. One thing is sure, however. *Je suis bien triste.*"[22]

When Beckett and Joyce first met, Joyce's personal circumstances were better than they were in the late thirties, even though the earlier years at Square Robiac were marked by enormous suffering for virtually everyone in the Joyce family. Beckett would have observed Joyce in the "gloom" which Ellmann describes as of near tragic dimensions. His eye problems had begun in Trieste during 1917, but in the fall of 1928 they grew significantly worse: he was suffering from episcleritis, conjunctivitis, blepharitis, and incipient glaucoma. (He also suffered the discomfort of a large boil on his right shoulder.) Unable to read print, he tried maneuvering several magnifying glasses; he often collapsed from eye pain and experienced sporadic blindness. He underwent injections of arsenic and phosphorous and was given cocaine for his dizzying pain.

At about the same time, Nora was hospitalized for suspected cancer; she was released after several radium treatments, but the following February she returned for a hysterectomy, which provided a cure. Joyce slept at her bedside throughout both hospitalizations. During the same period, Joyce's daughter began behaving erratically; her condition would later be diagnosed as hebephrenia, a form of schizophrenia. As Jack MacGowran reports, despite Joyce's persistent efforts to find the proper care for Lucia (she initially resisted all treatment) and his eventual consultations with Freud, Jung, and other psychiatrists, Joyce felt an abiding guilt over her illness, believing she might have been conceived "in drink." As others report, Joyce also believed that he had genetically transmitted her condition and that his nomadic life-style had exacerbated her condition.[23] If all of this were not sufficiently trying, Joyce's son, Giorgio, a talented and aspiring singer, had become involved with a married woman eleven years his senior. In 1929, Giorgio began to withdraw from his father toward "a life that was almost his own."[24]

Given Joyce's difficult circumstances, along with an understanding of his special regard for friendship, it is not surprising that Beckett soon acted "like a slave" to his revered idol.[25] The contemptuous Ezra Pound was unable to be sympathetic to the young man's adulation of his hero. When Pound first saw Beckett and Joyce together, at a dinner, he was so rude to Beckett that shortly thereafter Joyce curtailed his friendship with Pound.[26] Given the degree to which Joyce enveloped the lives of those closest to him, when he was overwhelmed with a number of serious problems, his friends freely responded with the attention he required.

Alec Reid explains that Beckett, like the others in regular contact with Joyce, enjoyed doing "little jobs for Jimmy" (adapting Nora's phrase)—reading to him, assisting him in his work, doing anything at all. In a lighter vein, Nora remarked that if she died after her husband, she would "surely have to wait at the Heavenly Gates, since the Recording Angel would inevitably be busy doing some little job for Jimmy."[27] It is thus understandable that when Beckett returned from the Ecole to hear that Mr. Joyce had called, he "immediately . . . reached for [the] phone and gave the operator the number: Ségur 95–20. Ségur quatre-vingt-quinze vingt." In reporting this, Noel Riley Fitch adds that Beckett "spoke the words with a poetic rhythm that he would remember vividly for more than five decades." So, too, when Joyce wanted a companion for his evening walk, Beckett would hurry to meet him, "honored by the demand, which it was a privilege to fulfill."[28]

Perhaps, in understanding Joyce's earliest interest in Beckett, one might conjecture that Joyce found in him a "whole" child—a young person he could truly help (he had fiercely tried to advance Lucia's and Giorgio's careers), just as Beckett found in Joyce a fatherly figure who was entirely approving. Joyce would have also found in Beckett a unique intelligence that understood and appreciated his work. While Joyce's friends were supportive, many admitted they did not comprehend his new literary forms, and no one in his family read his work. Nora openly admitted her indifference to all literature; his children asked where they might find examples of good Irish humor.[29]

Perhaps another reason for Beckett and Joyce's close relationship was that Joyce recognized in Beckett an idealized image of himself as a youth. There were physical resemblances, and they had had similar childhood interests and experiences.[30] But as parents sometimes relive in their children their unfulfilled youth, Joyce may have vicariously experienced in Beckett's filial devotion the feelings he had never overtly expressed to his father. At the same time, he may have tried to be for Beckett the ideal father he had hoped to be for his own children.

Long before and after his own father's death in 1931, Joyce expressed regret for not returning to Ireland to visit him, but he feared physical harm from his enemies.[31] After his father died, he asked Padraic Colum, planning a trip to Dublin, to return to John Joyce's home and collect remembrances for him. He confessed to a number of people, including T. S. Eliot, his inconsolable grief in losing his father. When he met Thomas McGreevy on the street, he broke down and wept. He told Eugene Jolas: "I hear my father talking to me. I wonder where he is." [32] He even wrote Harriet Weaver that his "prostration of mind" was so great that he was "thinking of abandoning work entirely." [33] The birth of a grandson provided some comfort and was the occasion for one of his finest poems, "Ecce Puer," which concludes:

> A child is sleeping:
> An old man gone.
> O, father forsaken,
> Forgive your son!

Joyce's father was a "heroicomic man" who could sing in the moonlight at the same time he navigated his frightened and destitute family from one set of decrepit lodgings to another. Yet Joyce always loved him. Many years after John Joyce's death, Joyce commissioned Patrick Tuohy, a Dublin artist, to paint his father's portrait, which always occupied a special place in the Joyce home. A photograph of that painting was also taken after it had been placed high on a wall, with the next three generations in view—James, Giorgio, and Giorgio's son, Stephen. This too was always prominently displayed in Joyce's various residences.

Despite their differences in age and reputation (Joyce was twenty-four years older than Beckett), there was a strong basis for their friendship. They had many common interests—language, philosophy, theater, music, and the love of family. They also shared a great empathy with one another and a deep compassion regarding human foibles. Humbled by the inseparability of human tragedy and comedy, they both appreciated the extraordinary as it manifested itself in the most ordinary of human endeavors. "Life is so tragic—birth, death, departure," said Joyce, but "we are permitted to distract ourselves—[and] forget a little."[34] Their relationship, like that of most good friends, also included a number of more mundane interests—smoking, drinking, the pleasure of long walks, and a fascination with esoterica and superstition.

Many scholars suggest that at the heart of their relationship was their shared ambivalence toward Ireland. As Ellmann details, Joyce returned to Dublin three times after his initial departure in 1904, and one can assume, from Ellmann and others, that he had every intention of continuing these visits. But in 1912, his Irish publisher, Maunsel, humiliated him and literally destroyed his work. Anticipating the uproar Dubliners would create, the company broke up the set type and burned the galleys and copies thus far printed.[35]

Joyce fled Ireland, violated by this episode, the first of several such brutal rejections, and yet "up to the end of his life" he "wait[ed] patiently" to be honored by the Irish. During the 1920s, however, he began to believe that if he returned home, he would suffer the same bodily harm as Parnell. Because of his similar violation of church and state law (Parnell had an affair with Kitty O'Shea; Joyce and Nora were not legally married), he feared that he too would have quicklime thrown into his already fragile eyes. (Nora and Joyce were married in 1931, to ensure her inheritance of his estate, just as Beckett and Suzanne married after more than twenty years for similar testamentary purposes.) Joyce's tenacious belief that marriage was a personal matter, not one for church or state, cost him dearly. Even after he died, the regular clergy in New York City refused to say a customary mass for him; only a chaplain at Columbia University finally permitted the "ordinary prayers."[36]

Nonetheless, wherever Joyce lived, he remained deeply interested in Irish politics and Irish daily life. He may have settled in a foreign city because it was a good workplace "where you could be and let be," but he never abandoned his watch over Irish affairs or severed his contacts with his homeland. He opened his door to strangers, in Paris, Rome, Pola, Trieste, and Zurich—if they were from Dublin. And as he welcomed them (usually with a white wine), he posed question after question about his city and the people he remembered. "Was So-and-So still alive?" "Did Mrs. So-and-So still walk her dog at such an hour at night?" The first time he met Beckett, he asked him about Dublin news and gossip. Given the specifics of his writing and his many Irish friends, one might well take him at his word when, asked why he didn't return to Ireland, he replied: "Have I ever left it?"[37]

Joyce's closest friends maintain that his love of Ireland was so absolute that he did not consider himself a permanent exile until 1938. When he first arrived in Paris, he had stayed at the Hotel Corneille specifically because of its Dublin connections; John Mitchel, John O'Leary, Synge, and Stephen MacKenna had stopped there. Much later, he proudly displayed in his home the "wonderful carpet that Mrs. Bécat [Adrienne Monnier's sister]," designed for him; it represented, in Joyce's words, "the Liffey flowing through Dublin into the Irish Sea with the arms of Norway, Dublin and my own woven into the scheme." Even the frequently cynical Stuart Gilbert was moved by Joyce's frank, undaunted pride in Dublin and his unabashed bragging about the city.[38]

The event that virtually paralyzed him with regard to returning home occurred in 1922. Nora and their children, on a trip to Galway, had been trapped on a train in the midst of the civil war. Gunfire and bombing forced Nora to shelter the children under the seats, and the violence of that week gained wide circulation; one report described a decapitated head found without tongue or teeth in Phoenix Park. After this, Joyce developed what Curran calls a "preposterous fear" about returning home, although to Mary Colum, "what might be called a persecution complex" in someone else was appropriate in Joyce, "for he actually was persecuted." But he still spoke of returning (on one occasion, to T. S. Eliot).[39] His ambivalence, it would appear, was largely associated with his dread of bodily harm. "If the country had not been turned into a slaughterhouse," he remarked in the early 1920s, "of course I should have gone there."[40] Joyce passed his love of Ireland on to his son, Giorgio, who would correct others if they called him anything but an Irishman. Stanislaus Joyce wrote of his brother after his death: "[There were] two dominant passions of my brother's life: . . . love of father and of fatherland." At Joyce's very simple burial, only a green plant and green wreath, with a lyre woven in it as an emblem of Ireland, decorated his grave.[41]

If Joyce's "ambivalence" toward Ireland touched a responsive chord in Beckett, Joyce's absolute commitment to his work did as well. Regardless of his mental or physical stresses, Joyce "never threw down the reigns of will," according to Curran; his "whole nature" was "perpetually—often preposterously"—given to his craft. In the face of what to others might have been overwhelming adversity, he worked on the whole as he labored exactily on its parts; he spent entire days creating a single sentence. Budgen once asked him if he were looking for le mot juste, to which he replied: "No . . . I have the words already. What I am seeking is the perfect development of the words in the sentence."[42] Overriding all his activities was the ethical mandate of creating art, and in this regard he had what Jolas has called that will of steel. In following his specific calling—in re-creating the word—he demonstrated a purity of purpose and totality of devotion.

Beckett's idealization of the "master" may thus have helped him consolidate his own professional identity. That is, not only did Joyce's support and empathy encourage him to pursue a career that was incomprehensible to his parents; Joyce's very example—as perhaps the greatest artist of his time and a person of absolute moral integrity—also gave Beckett a model he could both internalize and identify with. Joyce provided Beckett with an "ideal-other"—rarely encountered in actual rather than fantasied experience. This kind of relationship, furthermore, would not have diminished Beckett's unique and loving kinship with his father; it would have complemented it.[43]

Beckett and Joyce's relationship, in more concrete terms, can be reconstructed through the memoirs of Joyce's friends. (Scholars focus primarily on the two men's works.) Such memoirs enable us to visualize Joyce—the man and his mannerisms—as Beckett would have met him in 1928.

Joyce was tall, slim, and elegant. He favored a fin-de-siècle style of dress at home—smoking jackets of plum and wine; perfectly pressed, starched, and flat but pointed shirt collars; gray, plaid, or striped cravats; light-hued or embroidered waistcoats (his favorite was one of his father's); narrow gray pants; and velvet slippers. When he went out, he wore blazers and enjoyed wearing various light or dark felt hats (in the summer, straw hats), just as he liked a wide variety of shoes—spats and kid pumps, with or without buckles, and, of course, the white canvas shoes he had favored since his youth. He also wore heavily wrought gold and jeweled rings (only on his left hand; the one on the third finger was a talisman against illness). When he grew a beard, it was orangey-brown, lighter than his thick, wavy, dark brown hair (always well-brushed-back and trim), and he styled his beard in the Elizabethan fashion, to a point; at other times, he wore a small mustache. His complexion during these early years was healthy and ruddy. By the time Beckett met him he had retired his pince-nez, and his beautiful light blue eyes were often obscured by powerful, dark, small, round lenses. The right lens was always thicker than the left; sometimes he wore a black patch. He also carried a cane or ashplant, which disguised his infirmity but aided him in his dimmed vision. His hands were large but narrow and soft, with the adroitness and sensitivity of a person who has learned to depend a good deal on touch.

In describing Joyce's manner during serious conversation, his friends present unconflicting reports. He preferred the company of one to many. Although he was given to moments of silence and introspection, he was far from antisocial; he enjoyed and cultivated conversation with others. But he was reserved, although never aloof—self-possessed but never arrogant. As he was formal in physical appearance, he was similarly formal in his social demeanor: he "eschewed surnames" and called everyone "Mr." or "Miss."

One day he "stopped calling his young friend 'Mr. Beckett,' and called him simply 'Beckett,' a concession which, being almost without precedent . . . gratified its recipient immensely."[44] He also avoided esoteric conversation, although he enjoyed this sort of exchange: "If your deceased grandfather or mine reappeared before us, we would be shocked," which might be followed by, "not because they were ghosts but because their costumes would be dissettling." Speculations on the subject of appearance and alienation might follow.[45]

Joyce was engrossed by the drama of daily relationships. He took an inordinate interest in human behavior and was keenly concerned about the welfare of those he knew. Insatiable for details, he would pose question after question until he satisfied his vast curiosity. But, again, there was never a scrap of malicious talk in his inquiries, for he abhorred unkindness.[46] One of the few abusive comments he is recalled as making, which reveals more humor than rancor, concerned the author of Lady Chatterley's Lover: "That man really writes very badly," he said. "You might ask instead for something from his friend Aldous Huxley, who at least dresses differently."[47] Always sensitive to human fallibility, Joyce objected to the denigration of friends and enemies alike. This attitude filtered down into his most ordinary daily interactions: he had, for example, few impatiences over a late meal or a missed bus.

So too — and unlike his defensive undergraduate persona, whose bravura was affected to disguise his obvious poverty — he had abolished profanity from his spoken language. At Joyce's home, "there were never any dirty stories told; even risqué ones were taboo." One "never heard him make a remark that would embarrass a nun." He never swore in God's name, and his favorite exclamation was the harmless ma ché ("but what"). In speech, bearing, and life-style, despite Brenda Maddox's allegations to the contrary, he was "scrupulously moral and ethically above reproach."[48]

Joyce once told Eugene Jolas that "Nothing so reveals us as our laughter," and, according to Budgen, Joyce had "the kind of laugh one would expect to hear if the president of the republic took the wrong hat, but not if an old man's hat blew off into the gutter." His humor, also free of belittling or mimicry, was "of a tonic and refreshing kind that delighted in strange words, puns, incongruities, odd situations, exaggerations, and impish angles of vision. There was no sniggering defeatism in it. [It was] for his own and his friends' pleasure." This is not to say that he didn't enjoy a good burlesque; Joyce was always ready for a good leg-pull. But he never practiced slick verbal wit with his friends. His humor was altogether unforced and boyish.[49]

Budgen emphasizes that even in moments of silence, introspection, and pessimism, there was always a "festive pause," when Joyce would start dancing and singing — with a "gaiety and humor that could, on occasion, approach a kind of delirium." His dancing was one of whirling arms, high-kicking legs, grotesque capers, and coy grimaces. Descriptions of Joyce's dancing are consonant with our image of a man who celebrated anniversaries to appease the cruel forces of destiny: he was performing the ritual antics of comic religion.[50] They also correspond to the transformations he was effecting in his art, intermingling matter and spirit, conquering tragedy through humor. Nora reported her own curious dilemma when her husband was in the process of composition: "I can't sleep anymore," she would say: "I go to bed, and then that man sits in the next room and continues laughing about his own writing. And then I knock at the door, and I say, now Jim, stop writing or stop laughing." [51] But humor, dance, and writing were not Joyce's sole defenses against life's tribulations. On many occasions when he felt glum, he would go out and buy a necktie.

These traits persisted in the older Joyce, the man Beckett knew in the late 1930s. During these very trying years—when he was bent over from pain or overwork, when he resisted Lucia's institutionalization (he always believed she would recover), or when he worried about a second world war—even in these blackest moods, he maintained a concern for others and a wry humor that made the strain on others tolerable. Immersed as he was in his writing, Joyce well understood the cycles of joy and sadness that characterize the human experience. His response, as an ordinary person, as well as an artist, was that of the healing comedian.

Ellmann and others describe how Beckett imitated Joyce. He sat like him, with his legs crossed and the toe of his upper leg under the instep of his lower one. He held books close to his eyes and smoked with his cigarette dangling from his mouth. He even bought pointed-toe, patent leather shoes in the same size as Joyce, even though they caused bunions and corns.[52]

The plethora of information detailing Joyce's pastimes and social interactions allows us to visualize stunning images—not just of Beckett and Joyce but of Beckett and Joyce's friends and family. There were musical evenings—when Giorgio might sing Schubert and Beckett play the piano. There were occasions when Joyce sang before any combination of friends. He was a talented musician with a light tenor voice, "pure in pitch and clear . . . [in] articulation of language." He had earned money after his college days by giving recitals; he had even competed in the same contest once won by the Irish-American tenor John McCormack (and won second prize only because he couldn't sight-read). In his early Paris days, his voice had been likened to Jean de Reszke's (whose *Pagliacci* was particularly meaningful to him and whose voice reminded him of his father's).[53]

Once again, determined to find an outlet for his sorrow, Joyce sang for sadness as well as joy: according to Mary Colum, "When anything hit him hard, [he] found relief in singing." But whatever his mood, he favored English and Irish songs, like "Blarney Castle" and "Billy Me Luv the Lad," and he often sang his father's favorite ballad, " 'Tis Youth and Folly Makes Young Men Marry," along with Elizabethan and Jacobean songs. He also sang his own musical settings for James Mangan's and Yeats's poems. His favorite parody of humorous Irish ballads was "Mollie Bloomagain." Joyce also played the piano as he sang (he played by ear), and played the lute (from which he had earned money one summer in his youth), and even the hornpipe.[54]

At other times, Joyce read verse aloud, which he apparently did "with a deliberateness, precision and naturally beautiful voice."[55] His friends often joined in by reading foreign literatures. Paul Léon read Hölderlin in German, and Eugene Jolas possessed a "strange and eloquent trilingual poetic gift."[56] Joyce himself read Norwegian, which he had learned specifically in order to read Ibsen. As Budgen describes his voice on these occasions: "The lower pitch of his speaking voice [was] darkly metallic, and he [would] slow down the tempo of the verse to the last reasonable degree to extract from each syllable its full essence of sound." On a given evening, his friends might hear readings from Flaubert, Tolstoy, D'Annunzio, Defoe, and Chaucer. Joyce liked reciting Shelley's "When the Lamp Is Shattered," Mangan's "Dark Rosaleen," and Yeats's "When the Heart Grows Old," about which he often remarked: "No living poet could write better than that."[57]

Music was one of Joyce's (and Beckett's) greatest interests. To the question of what in all music he thought to be most beautiful, Joyce told Budgen: "the flute solo in Gluck's *Orpheus*" because "it tells of the sick longing for earth of one in Elysian fields. I know of nothing more beautiful than that."[58] He apparently disliked Wagner and showed little interest in Bach, Beethoven, and Schumann. To him, "music was an atmosphere," a condition of thought, an aura that extended beyond words, which nevertheless, he believed could be found in words.[59] Of all instruments, he preferred the male voice, which reminded him of his father. In fact, he rarely attended orchestral concerts; he preferred opera, especially Italian opera. Joyce also declined any knowledge of the plastic and pictorial arts—perhaps because of his eyesight— although his apartment was filled with paintings and photos, mostly of his great-grandparents and other family members.

Beckett and Joyce took quiet walks along the Seine to the Ile des Cygnes. As Joyce took this relaxation from work, he may have discussed neighborhood history.[60] He and Beckett may have spoken of their common love of mountains and rivers. "They are the phenomena that will remain when all the people and their governments will have vanished," Joyce once remarked.[61] To what extent did Joyce reveal his personal fears and superstitions? He not only followed popular practices but he created his own—for example, he was frightened of thunder and all explosive noises, and he particularly feared dogs. "Joyce's fear of a great many things was real . . . I think . . . cultivated as a counterbalance to his fearlessness where his art was concerned. He was afraid of 'catching it' from God Almighty," said Sylvia Beach.[62] He also loved the fact that he had been born on the same day (February 2) as Eamon de Valera, Wyndham Lewis, and Frank Budgen, and that his birthdate and birth year (1882) were the same as the Irish writer James Stephens'. That his birthdate was not just Candlemas and St. Bridget's Day but also Groundhog Day also elicited his whimsical appreciation. Joyce tried to have all his books and translations published on his birthday, but he commemorated other important dates, as well. Bloomsday—June 16, 1904—was the day he had fallen in love with Nora, and they were married on his father's birthday, July 4. How remarkable that Joyce, his father, and his mother died on the dreaded thirteenth of a month, and his brother died on Bloomsday.

Ellmann reports that with their common dislike of literary groups and their uncommon affection for alcohol and cigarettes, Beckett and Joyce spent most of their time at Joyce's apartment, discussing such subjects as the responsibility of art to lend insight into the universal mysteries of experience. Ellmann also describes how empathically attuned they were to each other, directing "silences across each other's torsos" and frequently communicating "without words."[63] If, as his friends report, Joyce ordinarily avoided abstract and esoteric conversation, he made an exception with Beckett. In the midst of their silences Joyce might suddenly ask: "How could the idealist Hume write a history?" And after a period of meditation, Beckett might reply, "A history of representations."[64] Beckett and Joyce also discussed Aquinas. They may have recalled for each other their first excitement in reading Dante— Joyce's favorite author (whose work Beckett kept with him until he died)— or the French Symbolists (Verlaine was Joyce's favorite). Joyce had closely studied Schopenhauer's *World as Will and Idea* during his college days and had admitted the influence of Wyndham Lewis's *Time and Western Man* on his recent work, subjects of great interest to Beckett. Joyce's "prodigious memory" embraced many areas that he enjoyed talking about, not just music and poetry, but anthropology, education, philology, the new physics, geometry, and mathematics.[65]

Their conversations may have extended to the belief in God. Joyce once recalled to Beckett an experience in Zurich, when he told a priest who was attempting the cosmological proof of God's existence: "What a pity that the whole thing depends upon reciprocal destruction." At another time, Beckett reported to Ellmann that Joyce's response to the statement, "What do you think of the next life?" was, "I don't think much of this one."[66]

Although Ellmann says that they rarely spoke of literature, he cites several occasions when Joyce commented on the new writers. He apparently thought many were so obscure that they themselves didn't know what they were writing, whereas he could account for his every line. (Immediately overtaken by such immodesty, he added: "I may have oversystematized Ulysses.")[67] In addition, Joyce's tastes were clearly defined. He consistently praised Wyndham Lewis, Goldsmith, Mangan (as opposed to Swift), Henry James (and his influence on Proust), W. B. Yeats, Synge, and George Moore.[68] Ellmann's statement that they rarely spoke of literature thus seems to mean that they rarely spoke *at length* about *other* writers' literature. Yet Joyce must have discussed his own work with Beckett; these were among the most productive and trying years for Joyce. Regular installments of *Work in Progress* had appeared in *transition* and other magazines since 1927; sections were published in book form in New York in 1928; the French edition of *Ulysses* was published in 1929; the original was banned in the United States and Britain (and pirated versions were being sold); and Stuart Gilbert completed his book on *Ulysses* in 1930. Most likely, they discussed Beckett's work as well — specifically *Proust* and the pieces in *transition*.

That they discussed Joyce's writing is implicit in Beckett's contribution in *Our Exagmination Round His Factification for Incamination of Work in Progress*, the collection of twelve essays Joyce organized on *Work in Progress*. Even Joyce admitted that he had stood "behind those twelve Marshals [contributors] more or less directing them what lines of research to follow."[69] In any event, Beckett's "Dante . . . Bruno . Vico . . Joyce" (the periods indicate the number of centuries separating each writer from the previous one) was given the place of honor, appearing first in the volume.

The essay is interesting for its discussion of Joyce's Italian influences — whether or not Beckett took his lead from Joyce. (Beckett also connects his observations with Stephen's in *Portrait of the Artist As a Young Man*.) He begins with Vico's theory of "preordained cyclicism" — the recurrent cycles of social organization (Theocratic, Heroic, Human), language (hieroglyphic or sacred; metamorphic or poetic; and philosophical or abstract), and myth (literal to allegorical) — which he then connects with the "primal spontaneity" of language, myth, and human event in *Work in Progress*. Vico, in turn, had developed a great part of his theory from Bruno, who believed that all contraries are present in each other (and all coincide in God). That both Dante and Joyce invented a new language in response to the "threadbare" language of their time provides the starting point for Beckett's final comparison, although he focuses on Joyce's Purgatory as a unique realm of nondirection or multidirection, of "the absolute absence of the Absolute." He suggests that Joyce's divine comedy embraces an earthly realm of both heaven and hell, virtue and vice. The essay also anticipates *Proust*, revealing some of Beckett's earliest aesthetic judgments, many of which apply to his own later work.

Beckett begins with what have become two often-quoted statements: "The danger is in the neatness of identifications," and "Literary criticism is not book-keeping." He warns the reader not to look for abstract or systematized meaning in great writing. He also praises *Work in Progress* for its inseparability of form and content. Here, "form is content, content is form," with the result that the work is "not *about* something" but "*that something itself.*" Like life itself, Joyce's words evoke "an endless . . . germination, maturation, putrefaction, the cyclical dynamism of the intermediate."

Beckett also highlights the integrity of the artist, who is obliged to pursue his vision, regardless of the seeming incoherence of his work and the "dribbling comprehension" of a "decadent" or lazy audience. (One of *transition's* best-known essays concludes with the provocative statement: "The writer expresses, he does not communicate. The plain reader be damned.") In addition, Beckett discusses Joyce's "desophisticating" English, a language that has already been "abstracted to death." Although Beckett will forge his own very different style, this remark will apply to his own work as well, and is of interest in his later decision to write in French.

Finally, and regardless of Joyce's hand in the essay, Beckett indicates the import of the inner mental landscape as the subject and form of art, as well as his awareness of the artist's awesome task in forging a language to serve this function. As Beckett puts it, "when the sense is sleep, the words go to sleep." In addressing this last subject, Beckett may well have made an attempt to clarify related goals urged by the *transition* Verticalists and Revolution of the Word proponents. Form and subject in Beckett's later work are also unified, as conscious and unconscious thought patterns reflect what he later called the "excavation" of the deepest core of self.

That Beckett and Joyce discussed Joyce's writing is also implicit in Joyce's invitation to Beckett, at about the same time (1930), to translate his "Anna Livia Plurabelle" passage. Beckett had already verified some of the Greek-rooted words for *Work in Progress*, and it must have been flattering when Joyce invited him to do the French translation. One can also imagine Beckett's pleasure in discovering himself as part of *Work's* narrative, particularly when Joyce refers to Beckett as his "friend" and "brother" and expresses faith in Beckett's linguistic gifts: "Sam knows miles bettern me how to work the miracle. And I see by his diarrhio he's dropping the stammer out of his silenced bladder since I bonded him off more as a friend and as a brother. . . . He'll prisckly soon hand tune your Erin's ear for you." Finally, we know that in the later years, Beckett and Joyce not only read their work aloud for the other's criticism but that they committed each other's lines to memory.

Joyce, for instance, memorized and quoted for friends a passage from *Murphy* ("By closing time, the body . . . vomit"). Clearly responsive to the ambiguity of Murphy's accidental or suicidal death, Joyce then composed (in green ink) the limerick: "There was a young fellow called Murphy/who went for a breeze by the Surphy"; or "who breezed off for a whiff of the Surphy." [70] Beckett reciprocated with the acrostic "Home [Homo] Olga" ("Word Man").

If Beckett and Joyce did discuss their own, if not others' literature at some length, the possibilities regarding their conversations are limitless. As Joyce was fashioning the collective unconscious in *Work in Progress*—and telling Beckett: "I wished to invade the world of dreams" and "I have put the language to sleep"—they may have discussed the sleeping state as the great democratizer, that area of universal human activity, universal needs, and universal language, where all ages are one. [71] Beckett also "invaded" the world of dreams in his later work.

Joyce's ambivalence toward Freud was obvious to his friends. He frequently discussed psychoanalysis with them (including his analysis of their dreams, especially if they happened to be in therapy). Jolas reports that after their walks together, Joyce retained, from all the passersby, every "scrap of conversation [and] slip of the tongue—all the verbal grotesqueries and fantasies which he heard issuing in unconscious moments." In any environment, he was always "intensely conscious of the unconscious drama" within human experience. [72] Joyce also toyed with Freud's theories of verbal association in his *Exiles* notes, despite his insistence that Freud's symbols were "too mechanical." He even compiled his own analysis of Freud's *Wit and its Relation to the Unconscious*, as well as his own "dreambook," which consisted of his interpretation of Nora's dreams. At one point Adrienne Monnier asked him, "Why deny your indebtedness to Freud and Jung," to which Joyce playfully remarked that he had named his grandson after Freud's grandson. [73]

Perhaps, as Ellmann maintains, Joyce's frequent defensiveness toward psychiatry was really directed toward its pretentious scientific methodology. That is, even though he called Jung the "Swiss Tweedledum" and Freud the "Viennese Tweedledee," he acknowledged that he shared many of their discoveries. Interestingly enough, the superstitious Joyce believed that his name meant the same thing in English as "Freud" in German. But as Ellmann suggests, what most mystified Joyce (and, I would add, Beckett) was not the world of the unconscious but the world of logic. Ellmann's remarks would later apply to Beckett: "Joyce was close to the new psychoanalysis at so many points that he . . . disavowed any interest in it. 'Why all this fuss and bother about the mystery of the unconscious?' he asked. 'What about the mystery of the conscious?'" [74]

Indeed, to everyone's wonder, Joyce could follow Lucia's language as her mental state deteriorated; she spoke in a form over which he had control. Father and daughter were "like two people going to the bottom of a river, one falling and the other diving."[75] Beckett joined Joyce as a master artist of the unconscious—after his subsequent researches into and personal engagement with psychoanalysis.

70

What did Beckett and Joyce say about Ireland? Did Beckett know about Joyce's tribute to the Irish nationalist John O'Leary after he died in 1904, or about his tribute to Mangan? Did the two discuss the 1916 Rebellion and Joyce's disillusionment over how "politics" replaced the movement's earliest ideals?[76] Joyce apparently believed that the revolution had taken a "brutal, simplistic form of analysis, action, and then collapse."[77] Yet he deeply cared for those involved in the cause. "The oppressed are obliged to rebel," he had once said in a lecture in Trieste, and yet he remained a pacifist.[78] In terms of the specific events of 1916, Beckett and Joyce probably discussed the pacifist Francis Sheehy-Skeffington, shot in error by the British (see chapter 1). "Hairy Jaysus," as Joyce fondly called him, had been Joyce's good college friend; together they had published a twopenny pamphlet on social and cultural issues in 1901. (His widow, Hannah, was one of Joyce's Irish friends in Dublin with whom he retained a lifelong correspondence.)

As Beckett's father had taken the young Samuel in 1916 to see Dublin in flames—that event which long remained with Beckett—John Joyce's fierce devotion to the fallen Parnell had stirred the nine-year-old James to write a poem exalting Parnell, both as a lofty eagle and as Julius Caesar, betrayed by the Tim Healys and other Brutuses of the world. This so pleased Joyce's father that he had the poem printed and distributed it to his friends; he also sent a copy to the Vatican.[79] Joyce probably discussed with Beckett his own youthful worship of Parnell. To A. Walton Litz, the young Joyce strongly identified with Parnell and eventually shared many of his personality characteristics.[80]

In the biography, Ellmann describes Joyce's attitude toward Ireland as generally a balance between "bitterness and nostalgia." However, in a brief but rarely cited essay (1979), Ellmann leans toward the view of Joyce's many friends who insist that his writing was clearly political. "To say Joyce wasn't interested in politics comes from the simplistic idea that politics means voting in elections."[81] The substance and texture of Joyce's work, Ellmann continues, was always a response to the way the church and state activated the darker and joyless side of human behavior. It was an appeal to the innocence within human nature.

Joyce's earliest hope, in *Portrait of the Artist As a Young Man*, was for communal liberation through socialism, but this broad wish for human freedom remained in *Ulysses*, which, as Ellmann emphasizes, was completed at the same time the Irish Free State was born.[82] Joyce viewed *Ulysses*, like Ireland's great, new president, Arthur Griffith, as a mirror from which the state and individual could discover its true secular conscience. (Ellmann fleshes out Joyce's early admission to Budgen that if the politician could change the world through "persuasion," the artist could change it "through beauty.") Later, as Joyce's international political interests grew, his antifascist sympathies propelled him to social action as well. The international, polysynthetic dream language of *Finnegans Wake* reflected the universal, apolitical language of all people of all times. Joyce also privately aided at least a dozen Jews in their escape from the Nazis.[83]

He had always been interested in Jewish history—not just the gratuitous suffering to which Jews had been subjected, "the easiest of all prejudices to foment"—but its connection with the Jews' (and his own) special regard for the family.[84] The Jews' resistance to Christian revelation, he told Budgen, was a heroic sacrifice, which enabled them to be "better husbands . . . fathers . . . [and] sons." Joyce was especially proud to have "put Bloom on the map of European literature"; he had also once told Budgen: "There's a lot to be said for the theory that the *Odyssey* is a Semitic poem."[85] Ulysses had been his "favorite hero" since Belvedere; he had found Homer's subject "the most human in world literature"; this was, as he described it, "an epic of two [persecuted] races"—the Israelites and the Irish.[86]

Joyce even identified himself as a Jew in bondage during World War I, when he felt like a prisoner in Zurich: "The Talmud says at one point, 'We Jews are like the olive: we give our best when we are being crushed, when we are collapsing under the burden of our own foliage.'"[87] By this time, he had also dissolved his friendship with Oliver St. John Gogarty, in part because of Gogarty's anti-Semitism. Beckett later testified in a trial during which charges of anti-Semitism were brought against Gogarty.

Some critics, like Morris Beja and Suzette Henke, argue that Joyce's politics were manifest primarily in his language, a refutation of colonialism. Robert Martin Adams, for example, maintains that since his youth, Joyce despised English and the English, but because language remained precious to him, he chose to modify it radically.[88] Other scholars go to great lengths detailing Joyce's overt political convictions. Ellmann's student Dominic Manganiello addresses Joyce's hatred of Ireland's seven centuries of occupation. Manganiello points to the O'Leary poem "Et tu Healy" and concentrates on essays like "Home Rule Comes of Age" (where Joyce compares Parnell to the betrayed Christ); he discusses articles Joyce wrote as a journalist, in which he endorsed Sinn Fein, and argues that Joyce drew parallels between his own statements and Griffith's. Generally, Manganiello maintains that after Joyce's disillusionment in 1916, and then again in 1922 (when he endorsed Griffith's

ends, if not his means), wherever he resided he always bore the political bur-
dens of his native home (as well as those of his new land). In Zurich, during
World War I, for example, he aided the Allies by organizing productions of
English and Irish plays—even to Budgen, an act of cultural propaganda.[89]

Throughout his life, however, and regardless of the nature of his "politics," he retained at least two certainties. The greatest tyranny in his personal
life, as he put it, was "the Roman tyranny [which] occupie[d] the palace
of the soul," and, regarding world events, that he must remain a pacifist.
His explanation of the latter is fascinating, as it anticipates Beckett's future
poetic language: "The violence of birth and death," said Joyce, "was trau-
matic enough."[90] Another of Joyce's related statements similarly anticipates
Beckett's imagery (although Beckett speaks of the human condition, not specifically Ireland): "The Emerald isle is a field of thorns."[91]

Setting aside these larger political matters and the likelihood that Beckett
and Joyce discussed them, Joyce's more everyday experiences would have
been of interest to Beckett, even if they did not involve him directly. One
such pursuit was Joyce's zealous patronage of John Sullivan from 1929 to
1933. The Irish tenor from County Cork (McGreevy's birthplace) had a gift,
Joyce told Beckett, of "three dimensions."[92] Joyce made devious arrangements to ensure that all his friends heard the gifted Sullivan. On one occasion, he bought up tickets for *Guillaume Tell* and gave them even to his
nonmusical friends; he then jumped up during the performance, shouting,
"Thank God I have recovered my eyesight!" He finagled notices about Sullivan into the Paris, London, and New York newspapers, approached important impresarios on Sullivan's behalf, and tried to arrange for his appearance
in Covent Garden. He even managed to turn Sir Thomas Beecham's very
skilled ear to a Sullivan performance and beseeched George Antheil to com-
pose an opera for the tenor based on Byron's Cain and Abel drama.[93]

Other of Joyce's social and professional interactions probably had a
subtle but indelible effect on Beckett. When César Abin began his Joyce
sketch for *transition*, for example, Joyce asked that he be portrayed in a battered old derby with a star on the tip of his nose—as a reminder that
someone had called him a "blue-nosed comedian." (One thinks of Beckett's
Krapp here.) So, too, Adrienne Monnier at times referred to Joyce in his own
terms—as both the "Melancholy Jesus" and "Crooked Jesus," whose echoes,
both visually and substantively, fill *Godot*.[94]

A number of people who visited the Joyce flat became Beckett's close
companions, like the Russian Jewish émigré Paul Léon, who had fled the Bol-
sheviks in 1918 and who was, when Beckett met him, one of Joyce's closest
friends. Twelve years younger than Joyce, Léon was a man of many skills—
a lawyer and sociologist, a specialist in international jurisprudence, and the

author of a study on Irish Home Rule; he was also a sophisticated student of literature, philosophy, Greek, and Latin. He was known, in addition, for his clever humor and whimsy. Léon read nineteenth-century novels aloud to Joyce and helped manage his financial and professional affairs. He also shared his own writings with Joyce—many, on the subject of social justice. Since Beckett visited the Joyce home regularly, he probably heard them debate matters of social equity and saw them reading Joyce's galleys—with Léon, of necessity, spelling every word aloud.[95]

The Joyces invited Beckett to many social gatherings, including the unfortunate dinner mentioned above with Ezra Pound, at Les Trianons. This must have been an event Beckett long remembered, like the later legendary luncheon, "the Déjeuner Ulyssé," which celebrated the French translation of *Ulysses* and twenty-fifth anniversary of Bloomsday. A bus had been chartered to carry the guests to a village near Versailles, and on the return trip— with Dujardin, Valéry, Soupault, Romains, Fargue, Sylvia Beach, McGreevy, Giorgio Joyce, and Helen Kastor Fleischman (Giorgio's fiancée) aboard—the group decided to "ingloriously abandon" Beckett. He had been instigating stops along the way for one and then another nightcap.[96]

There were, of course, more comfortable social gatherings. Joyce's annual birthday parties were traditionally marked by singing, silliness, dancing, and drinking.[97] Beckett gave Joyce a walking stick on one birthday and the acrostic on another; since Joyce always remembered his friends' birthdays, we can only guess at what he might have given Beckett. Beckett may also have been invited to smaller gatherings with, say, Léon and his wife, Lucie Noel, or with Stuart and Moune Gilbert; the witty Englishman, retired from a judgeship in Burma, was at work (with Joyce's assistance) on his landmark introduction to *Ulysses*.

We know that Beckett became a member of Joyce's closest circle of friends—each of whom Joyce bet, six months before publishing *Finnegans Wake*, could not guess his new title. (Eugene Jolas did guess it, and Joyce paid him a hundred francs.) In the later years, Joyce actually depended upon Beckett's presence at social gatherings. Maria Jolas describes how, for example, at her Christmas party in 1939 at her home near Vichy, Beckett comforted Joyce, who had been drinking heavily because he feared that his son's marriage was failing. Joyce had a great affection for his daughter-in-law, but Helen had recently suffered a nervous breakdown whose aftereffects he feared. Jolas describes how "Sam had become a close friend and his presence at that moment of personal distress and general anxiety was particularly welcome."[98] A similar incident occurred the following Easter, less than a year before Joyce's death. Indeed, the fact that Beckett was then and long after Joyce's death considered as a family member is evident in the roles he performed.

He was best man at Stephen Joyce's wedding, and he was asked to handle the complicated possibility of moving Joyce's remains back to Ireland.[99]

As we recall some of Joyce's most severe professional disappointments, as well as these personal trials, we may consider the way in which Joyce shared them with Beckett and the subsequent effect they would have on him. As Maria Jolas repeats, given all of Joyce's friends and acquaintances, Joyce was "less guarded with Beckett than the rest."[100] Beckett would have a formidable time publishing his work, but Joyce endured rejection throughout his career. His early contract for *Chamber Music* had been lost, rewritten, and then broken by his publisher; *Dubliners*, in type and print, had been destroyed; *Ulysses* had been banned. Joyce's largest advance, for *Finnegans Wake*, was $3,000 from an American publisher and £400 from one in London. Once the work was published, he suffered not just humiliating reviews but vicious attacks on his life-style and family. Joyce's experiences may well have prepared Beckett for the trials of gaining publication and the reviews that followed.

Beckett and Joyce might also have discussed the paralysis an author feels when he loses control over his work—an issue of later concern to Beckett, particularly in the production of his plays. Samuel Roth had published, without Joyce's permission, expurgated editions of *Ulysses*. Such figures as Hemingway, Yeats, Gide, Eliot, Von Hofmannsthal, Unamuno, Mann, Maeterlinck, Croce, and Einstein signed petitions to protest this act of piracy. Even those who had expressed their reservations about the work, including E. M. Forster, D. H. Lawrence, and Virginia Woolf, signed. But Roth continued his publications. So too, after the trial and Random House's agreement to publish *Ulysses*, a serious rift occurred between Joyce and Sylvia Beach, who was not just Joyce's publisher but also his financial and often emotional mainstay. Beckett would have known about the issues that contributed to their falling out, including the complications of international copyright law, translation, and the fair appropriation of royalties.

Beckett would have borne witness to Joyce's great disappointment when people like Pound, Valéry Larbaud, H. G. Wells, and Wyndham Lewis told him that *Finnegans Wake* was a hopeless puzzle and a literary dead end. Even Harriet Weaver and Sylvia Beach had found it inscrutable. After Harry Crosby agreed to publish excerpts, there were other humiliating moments. Joyce asked Picasso for a frontispiece portrait and Julian Huxley and J. W. N. Sullivan for introductions; they all refused. The mathematician C. K. Ogden finally wrote the introduction, and Constantin Brancusi did the "portrait." To appease the publisher, he relinquished his realistic image for a curlicue, symbolic of Joyce's enigmatic evolution.[101]

Beckett probably met many of Joyce's other friends, like Brancusi, whose friends included the equally eccentric Marcel Duchamp. (Brancusi lived in seclusion with his white spitz dog, and whenever he was seen about Paris, he was inevitably accompanied by "Polaris"—even at films, where he always reserved the dog's seat in advance.) It was welcome news to the art world in 1928 when the U.S. Customs department recognized Brancusi's *Bird in Space*, evaluated at $600, as more than a piece of taxable metal. Adjudicated as a "work of art," the piece was allowed out of the country duty free, the first work of modern art to be so treated. This decision changed not only export law but Brancusi's life as well, since his 1920 work, like *Princesse X*, had been condemned as phallic and obscene. Brancusi had worked at his craft for nearly thirty years and had taken on a number of jobs in Paris in order to support his nighttime sculpting. He even sang at a Rumanian Orthodox church, although he was dismissed when the priest discovered the starving man eating the sacrificial bread. Beckett would have observed a great deal about artistic dedication from these people.

As we consider the extent to which Joyce shared his professional life with Beckett, we might also consider the degree to which the two men shared their personal or past lives. Did Joyce show Beckett the notebooks he compiled in preparation of his career as a journalist? Not only did Beckett shortly thereafter embark upon his own career as a journalist, but he later began keeping his own working notebooks.

Did Beckett know that as a child, Joyce had been distinguished not only for his "retentive memory" but also, perhaps surprisingly, as an excellent athlete (at Conglowes) and leader among his peers?[102] "Sunny Jim," as his family called him, had won cups for walking and hurdling and had taken a special interest in cricket. At Belvedere he had also pursued a precocious talent in foreign languages (Latin, French, and Italian). To what extent did Joyce speak about his college friends, now immortalized in *Portrait* and *Ulysses* (J. F. Byrne, as Cranley; Francis Sheehy-Skeffington, McCann; George Clancy, Davin; Oliver St. John Gogarty, Buck Mulligan)?

What did Beckett and Joyce share regarding their parents? Like Beckett's father, John Joyce often took his two eldest boys on long walks and was an inexhaustible storyteller. Did Joyce reveal what Ellmann calls his deepest wish (and, perhaps, Beckett's as well)—his mother's approval of his career? Ellmann also reports that Joyce's letters to Nora reveal his need for an intimacy even beyond that of husband and wife. While Beckett would not have seen these letters, he would have observed Joyce's greatest demand of Nora— and her willing compliance—that she share her every response to life with her husband. Joyce's wish for prenatal comfort from Nora is reminiscent of the same sentiment articulated by Beckett's later fictional characters: "O that I could nestle in your womb like a child born of your flesh and blood, be fed by your blood, sleep in the warm secret gloom of your body." If, as

Ellmann says, Joyce viewed himself as a weak, passive child surrounded by burly extroverts—a "Parnell or a Jesus among traitors," indeed, a Stephen Dedalus (with all the subtleties that that name evokes of Calvary)—Beckett must have intuited this. Could the imagery of crucifixion and martyrdom in *Waiting for Godot* have been associated with Joyce's self-image? [103]

The severity of Joyce's eye problems was a daily reality: "I saw him crying when he found he couldn't see to write," said Lucia.[104] Joyce underwent his tenth and eleventh eye surgeries during this time (1930). He surely discussed this with Beckett, who would later suffer serious eye ailments himself. Ellmann describes Joyce's "lugubrious" conversations with Thomas W. Pugh and with Aldous Huxley in 1929, the latter yet another victim of severe eye problems.[105]

Beckett was undoubtedly aware of Lucia's deteriorating mental state both through direct observation and through Joyce's comments. Joyce had apparently worried about his children's every physical symptom when they were young, and, as they grew older, he worried even more. Lucia may have been born on a charity ward (Nora was given twenty crowns when she left the hospital), but Joyce's attitude toward his two children was that they should be indulged in love. Always mindful of his being disciplined with a pandybat as a child, he often said: "Children must be educated by love, not punishment." He apparently wanted a "maternal" bond with his children, and he encouraged them, as Beckett told Ellmann, to speak up boldly to him; they never felt any fear toward their father.[106] Yet all his attention to Lucia could not avert her subsequent breakdown. Most of Joyce's friends report that as the years passed, Lucia's illness "tormented Joyce" and was "almost the only topic of [his] conversation." Said Gillet: "I fancied hearing the complaint of King Lear carrying Cordelia in his arms." [107]

We can only wonder at what point in his near-obsession with his daughter's condition Joyce was aware that Beckett was himself involved in her life disappointments. In fact, Beckett had romantically attracted the lonely Lucia, poignantly named after the patron saint of light and eyesight. She once said: "It means light, like Paris, the City of Light, you know." [108] He visited the Joyce apartment almost daily, and he escorted Lucia to several public events, restaurants, and the theater; however, he did not reciprocate her amorous feelings for him. Lucia was tall and slender, and she had a beautiful oval face with blue eyes that had a touch of strabismus, which gave her a slightly cross-eyed squint. She was also self-conscious about her spoken French. The Joyces had moved so many times that she had difficulty in mastering the language. She often slipped from English to French to Italian, and her idioms were often incorrect. However, she was full of life and, like her father, sang in several languages. She pursued her talents as a singer, pianist, and illustrator, and Joyce spent a great deal of time (and money) trying to help her career along. She had, for example, designed a set of capital letters in medieval style for each of his thirteen poems in Pomes Penyeach (one critic likened them to the Book of Kells), and Joyce was finally able to arrange their publication in Paris. Her design for "The Mime of Mick Nick and the Maggies" was published in the Hague.

Lucia pursued her interest in dance with even greater dedication. She practiced six hours a day, which Beckett encouraged, and was gifted with a lovely physical grace. At her last recital, when she failed to win first prize, the audience protested and beckoned her back on stage by calling for "l'Irlandaise," which, Beckett told Ellmann, greatly pleased her father.[109]

When Lucia attended parties, she would often impersonate Charlie Chaplin—in baggy trousers and with a cane. She even wrote an essay on Chaplin for a Belgian review. Perhaps Beckett and Lucia went to Chaplin films together and exchanged ideas about that hobo type Beckett had been sketching since his youth. His later tramp heroes would resemble the Chaplin figure, at least visually. At parties, Lucia also impersonated her other favorite hero, Napoleon.[110] Like her father—and Beckett—she seemed attracted to archetypal couplings like Dedalus and Bloom, Shem and Shaun, and Cain and Abel dimensions of human nature.

Lucia finally openly declared her feelings to Beckett, and he was compelled to tell her that his interests were in her father, not her. This clearly damaged Beckett's relationship with the Joyces, who then set about locating a suitable bridegroom for their daughter. Lucia's continuing decline virtually broke Joyce's spirit. Mary Colum writes: "Her malady grew tragically. I think it affected Joyce more than anything . . . in his life; perhaps it hastened his end." Beckett himself, for many years following, felt a deep guilt and sense of regret over not being able to love Lucia, for what he called his "inhuman feelings" toward her. However, in light of the more recent theories of schizophrenia as a genetically programmed illness whose time of onset may be environmentally influenced, it is possible that Lucia's breakdown may have actually been postponed, rather than exacerbated, by her several years of unrequited love for Beckett.[111]

According to Brenda Maddox, Beckett was irresistible to women, self-centered, and opportunistic. Maddox writes: "Beckett exuded sexual awareness. His pale green [actually, blue] eyes, high cheekbones and brooding intensity excited women and his shyness only inspired them to take the initiative." In describing his attitude toward Lucia, she writes: "[He] saw his literary future jeopardised by the unwanted attentions of the daughter of his idol." And citing Deirdre Bair, she asserts that Beckett was "emotionally retarded" and "clearly . . . not the marrying kind." Finally, viewing Lucia's entire predicament, she reports that Joyce confided to Beckett that Lucia's situation was due to a tooth infection.[112]

Although Lucia's collapse occurred in 1936, and Beckett's reconnection with Joyce took place at the end of 1937, Lucia had exhibited troubling signs during the entire period Beckett had known the Joyces. In 1929, she expressed a sense of abandonment when Giorgio fell in love with Helen, and she later became deeply disturbed when her parents formalized their marriage. Her behavior grew increasingly erratic and violent, both at home and in public. She had several temporary hospitalizations before 1936 and received various forms of treatment—psychotherapy, salt-water injections, and glandular medication. When she was allowed to return home she would not sleep in a bed, and her parents were regularly awakened by the police: regardless of the weather, she was found asleep in the garden. When she visited friends they had to remove the handles from gas taps, for fear she would commit suicide. She also disappeared from time to time.[113]

Whenever Lucia was hospitalized, Joyce wrote and visited her regularly. His letters reveal his inconsolable sadness: "My dear little daughter," he often began, "I am sure that . . . one fine day—and soon—the clouds will roll away. They are not storm clouds but only cloudlets." In another poignant letter, he wrote: "I see great progress . . . but at the same time . . . a sad note. . . . Why do you always sit at the window? No doubt it makes a pretty picture but a girl walking in the fields also makes a pretty picture." He continuously blamed himself for the ill fortune of both his children: "I am and have been an evil influence on my children." In what he called "a blind man's rage and despair," he pleaded, "Minerva direct me."[114]

After Lucia's permanent institutionalization in 1936, Beckett established what may have been his most intimate relationship with Joyce, when, as Peggy Guggenheim said, "Joyce loved Beckett as a son."[115] The two resumed their old activities; on some occasions they discussed the world situation. Joyce spoke of how the vile acts of intolerance promulgated by the Nazis were not new in the history of humanity. In Joyce's Letters, at least those involving the Brauchbar family, it is apparent that, whatever his personal adversities, Joyce considered it his ethical responsibility to help the Jews.[116]

Leon Edel reports that during his last days in Paris Joyce refused to believe that the Germans would reach the city, and, once they did, he refused to believe they would remain. Unlike most of his friends, he stayed in Paris until 1939—because Lucia was in a nearby institution. His only modification in life-style involved changing flats and then moving into a hotel (when Beckett helped).[117]

That Joyce well understood the world situation was obvious to his friends, although by now, and much like King Lear, he often found his private torment more consuming than the debacle surrounding him. At moments, he expressed his anger toward Chamberlain for trusting Hitler and signing the Munich Pact. He also condemned Mussolini's Italy for "putting the squeeze on France." Yet he retained an absolute faith in the French army, and at one point he publicly demonstrated his own heartfelt patriotism by leading hundreds of British and French soldiers in the singing of the *Marseillaise*.[118] As a former resident of Trieste—where Stanislaus's unpopular opinions had condemned him to a four-year internment in Austria—Joyce had obviously been familiar with the manifestations of fascist power. He had also been aware of a divided citizenry in Trieste, a city long torn between Austrian and Italian control.

Once war was declared, Joyce determined to lead his own family to safety, but this became increasingly complicated. Not only was Lucia institutionalized, but Giorgio's wife, Helen, had suffered the breakdown which necessitated her local hospitalization. Giorgio's insistence on remaining in Paris also worried Joyce, because Giorgio risked conscription into the French army or German arrest.

At the start of the war, Nora and Joyce left Paris for La Baule, in Brittany, in order to be near Lucia, where presumably she and the other female patients in her hospital were being transferred. But when the Joyces arrived, these plans had been canceled. Joyce's distress was consuming: "At the time of writing," he said in a letter of September 1939, "I have no idea where my daughter is—this after all my preparations to be near her!" His letters repeat his fear that "she must not be left alone in terror, believing she is abandoned by everyone in case of a bombardment." Thus, when Lucia was finally settled in a new hospital, Joyce went to stay with her, to protect her from the very sounds (of the bombs) he so deeply feared himself.[119]

Joyce had to assure the safety of his grandson as well, with Giorgio in Paris and Helen hospitalized. (Helen's brother eventually brought her back to the United States.) Nora and Joyce took the seven-year-old Stephen to the Saint-Géraud-le Puy–Vichy area, where Maria Jolas took him in; she had recently moved her school for American and French children there. Joyce and Nora found lodgings nearby, so they could regularly visit the child (during which times Joyce told the boy about the great adventures of Ulysses). The Joyces arrived at Saint-Géraud-le Puy on December 24, 1939, and remained there for nearly a year.

Joyce's life was one of continuing frustration. The arrangements he finally made to transfer Lucia to the area were derailed; he had had a falling out with his great friend Paul Léon (which was eventually mended); *Finnegans Wake* continued to be poorly received; his stomach pains, earlier attributed to "nerves," were increasing. (The perforated duodenal ulcer that took his life in 1941 was diagnosed as an ailment of at least seven years' duration.) Life in the village was also extremely difficult for this cosmopolitan man, who had long preferred living in large cities. As the months passed, it is likely that he observed the moral dilemmas created by the new Vichy regime. He undoubtedly also witnessed the incalculable sadness of the many refugees who fled their homes before and during the Occupation. The Nazis even occupied this little town for six days before accepting their proper jurisdiction a few miles away. As Joyce walked the streets, frail and exhausted, "the poor old man," as he was called, with dark glasses, a cane, and a now-oversize coat, he had yet another war to fight—the abundance of dogs (which he greatly feared) in the streets. For this he filled his pockets with stones.[120] (Here one thinks of Beckett's Molloy and the stones in his pockets.)

Still, he remained consumed with getting his family out of France and into Switzerland, their refuge during World War I. His Letters make abundantly clear his many aborted plans and subsequent frustrations: "We hardly know where we are going or when," Joyce wrote early on, and this lament persisted in his correspondence. He wrote both friends and authorities for assistance. At one point, the Germans finally granted Lucia an exit visa, but the Swiss refused Joyce's application—for various and unpredictable reasons. As Joyce summarized the situation: "We are aliens, then Jews, then beggars. What next, burglars, lepers?" He persevered from one agency to another: "Switzerland, having discovered that I am not a Jew from Judea but an Aryan from Eiren has [now] asked not only for ten references—already given— but a bank deposit and a guarantee of 500,000 French francs." [121] He wrote acquaintances both on the continent and in the United States for assistance. By the time the necessary funds were deposited, Lucia's visa had been revoked, and Joyce left France for Zurich without his daughter.

According to Budgen, Joyce's last days were spent in melancholic reflection—on the invasion of France, the plight of the fleeing refugees, and the Occupation of Paris.[122] In Zurich, he witnessed blackout exercises as bombs fell on the German-Swiss border. And his daughter remained in occupied France. Joyce's health deteriorated rapidly: he had arrived in Zurich on December 14, 1940; by January 13, 1941, he was dead.

Although little is published about Joyce and Beckett during this last period, we know from Joyce's Letters and from Maria Jolas that Beckett was invited to Joyce's last sacred family events. In one of his letters, Joyce wrote of his anticipation of Beckett's visit to Saint-Géraud for an always-important birthday celebration—this one for his grandson, Stephen. When Maria Jolas prepared her Christmas 1939 and Easter 1940 dinners, Beckett was also present. (Before the latter, Joyce considered going to Easter services with him.) Beckett also joined Joyce and Nora for a weekend in Vichy.[123]

These were all occasions when his presence was essential for his disconsolate friend. In the summer of 1940, before the Germans marched into Paris, Beckett joined in the mass exodus from the city and made his way to Vichy. This was the last time he saw Joyce.

Only six months before, Beckett had taken Joyce to the train station when he left his City of Light for the last time. One of the last things Joyce told him, in December, 1939, as Beckett reported to Ellmann, was "We're going downhill fast." [124]

Beckett later made frequently quoted comments distinguishing his work from Joyce's: "Joyce was a synthesizer. I am an analyzer," he said, as well as: "Joyce tends toward omniscience and omnipotence as an artist. I'm working with impotence, ignorance." [125] We can only wonder if any of these thoughts occurred to him during the early years. Both statements would seem to reveal conflicting assumptions regarding the artist's means and ends. *Synthesis, omniscience,* and *omnipotence* describe the vantage point of teleological authority. Indeed, to Joyce, in forging a moral-spiritual conscience through his writing, all experience could be accommodated into a single, virtually Dantesque vision. Joyce had, after all, told Beckett that reality was a paradigm, an illustration of a perhaps unstatable rule. This may be what Beckett had in mind when he said: "Joyce seemed to make no distinction between the fall of Satan and the fall of a sparrow. Contemplating life from this perspective turned it all to sad and rollicking farce." [126] In contrast, Beckett's terms *impotence* and *ignorance* imply the vantage point of an artist lacking both the form and knowledge with which to systematize experience.

Yet Beckett and Joyce have much more in common than Beckett's comments suggest. Indeed, Ellmann's characterization of Joyce [127] illuminates certain qualities Joyce and Beckett shared. Both gave heroic consequence to the common person; both made the ordinary extraordinary. Each removed humankind from its traditionally heroic backdrop and, however unsavory the new and true environment, each displayed the nobility of ordinary people transcending their own ingloriousness. In so doing, their style and content were in many ways complementary. For Joyce, historic, linguistic, and symbolic texturing set into motion a universe of dazzling verbal potential. Words not only provided an understanding of and connection with ultimate realities; they were a part of the very wonder of creation. They granted power: experience, as it attached to, separated from, and reattached to language, was eternally concrete and revelatory.

Beckett's verbal sparsity would, at first, simulate a sense of emptiness, dwindling energy, and silence. It would seem to be the sign of one's failure to understand the mystery operative both in and outside the mind. Words would appear to be the fetters of the hobo-hero-everyperson, and they would seem to immure one in a morass of dwindling energy and of "ignorance" and powerlessness—a continuous reminder of the illusion that one can understand or control mind, body, and the external world.

In a sense, Joyce was Beckett's Don Quixote, and Beckett was his Sancho Panza. Joyce aspired to the One; Beckett encapsulated the fragmented many. But as each author accomplished his task, it was in the service of the other. Ultimately, Beckett's landscapes would resound with articulate silence, and his empty spaces would collect within themselves the richness of multiple shadows—a physicist would say the negative particles—of all that exists in absence, as in the white patches of an Abstract Expressionist painting. Beckett would evoke, on his canvasses of vast innuendo and through the interstices of conscious and unconscious thought, the richness that Joyce had made explicit in words and intricate structure.

In their specific subject matter, they would also share the same human imperative—to journey toward identity and meaning—despite their radically different conclusions. Throughout Beckett's work—from his Dublin Belacquas to the Unnamables in jars, the mouth in Not I, and his paradoxical "Stirrings Still"—he too would exalt the quest, regardless of its illusory destination. Joyce's heroic aims and possibilities were more clearly (and traditionally) drawn.

Here the comparison ends, for Joyce's most forlorn Dubliners would often acquire insight, if only in the fragile meditations of their heart—even if that insight occurred too late for them to change their lives. The possibility that they could control their destiny, however, had they so chosen, always implied to Joyce that the self was capable of renewal—a great inspiration to the reader. For Beckett, such a victory would remain more complicated, as his heroes would struggle with the unreliable, sometimes treacherously misleading mind in a world that would remain entirely unfathomable. It would be Beckett's compassion for their unyielding perseverance, as well as the hard-won humor they would bring to it, that would elevate these apparently impotent souls to the status of tragicomic heroes. Ultimately, Beckett's work would portray a quest as exalted and sacred as any in the canon of literature.

FOUR

Jack B. Yeats

He was a great believer in Ireland and its destiny and its peasant
class: a somewhat unusual point of view for a man of his
breeding and generation; for the Yeats[es] were Irish Protestant
landlords. —JOHN W. PURSER, on Jack B. Yeats

Beckett returned to Dublin in the summer of 1930.
As stipulated by his commencement awards, after his two years of teaching at the Ecole he was to teach three more at Trinity and complete his
master's degree. Having spent two extraordinary years in Paris—gaining the
acquaintance of and publishing alongside the great artists of the time—he
moved into his rooms at the college and assumed his newly created position as lecturer in French and assistant to his former professor, Thomas B.
Rudmose-Brown. He also pursued his study of Descartes, Geulincx, Kant,
and Schopenhauer and took his master's degree in December 1931.

Beckett lectured on Balzac, Alfred de Musset, Alfred de Vigny, Flaubert,
Stendhal, Racine, and Bergson. He was "liked and admired" by his students,
as one colleague described them, a "crumb-picking" and "avid audience."
But given his previous two years among the avant-garde, Beckett found the
work of writers like Balzac lacking in the texture and "complexity" of great
art, as he had defined it in Our Exagmination and Proust. Their "preconceived
equations" lent their work the tidy "book-keeping" quality that was clearly
not to his liking. The "artistic disorder" and "state of flux" of a Rimbaud, as
he told his students, was decidedly superior.[1]

After a few terms, Beckett left. In his own words, he "behaved very
badly: I ran away to the Continent and resigned." Pilling reports that Beckett
"felt guilty for many years" for this moral breach of contract. But, as Beckett
explained, he could not tolerate the "hateful comedy of lecturing"—the "absurdity," the "indignity of teaching to others" what he did not know himself.[2]
While such sentiments anticipate his sense of "impotence" and "ignorance"
regarding the elucidation of "meaning," Beckett also said that in leaving
Trinity, he "lost the best." He long retained a deep "affection and gratitude"
toward the college and later made generous contributions to it.[3] In 1959,
the modest Beckett even returned to Trinity to accept an honorary degree—
clearly a public gesture of personal gratitude to his alma mater. (He did not
go to Stockholm to accept his Nobel Prize.)

Beckett had made some important friendships during this Trinity period. Georges Pelorson was the exchange lecturer from the Ecole Normale, and the two of them wrote a comic burlesque of Corneille's *Le Cid*, which they called *Le Kid*. When Trinity's Modern Language Society produced it at the Peacock, Beckett played the role of Don Diègue. He wore the bowler hat that his heroes later wore and that we now associate with several figures in his life—his father (who wore bowlers regularly), Joyce (in Abin's *transition* drawing), and Lucia's hero, Charlie Chaplin (who made his own *The Kid*). Pelorson became a frequent contributor to *transition* and other small French magazines and one of Joyce's acquaintances in Paris. In the late 1930s, Pelorson also became an instructor at Maria Jolas's bilingual school near Vichy and was a guest at Joyce's (and Beckett's) last Easter dinner at her home.[4]

Beckett's most important friendship during this period was with the painter Jack B. Yeats, the poet's younger brother, who was thirty-five years Beckett's senior. Thomas McGreevy introduced this "Cézanne of our time" to Beckett in late 1930, and Beckett was overwhelmed by Yeats's work. He immediately bought *Regatta Evening on Dublin Bay* and expressed his profuse gratitude to McGreevy for introducing them. McGreevy recalls Beckett's note to him: "Beckett was completely staggered by the pictures and though he has met many people through me, he dismissed them all in his letter with the remark, 'and to think I owe meeting Jack Yeats and Joyce to you!'"[5]

Hilary Pyle, Yeats's biographer, describes the painter as generally reserved, particularly reticent about his life, ceremonious, independent, and often given to silences. However, Pyle notes that Yeats could also be buoyant and extroverted and was capable of an irresistible puckish humor. He readily won affection from others.[6] Later a novelist and playwright, as well—described as a practitioner of the New Novel and Theater of the Absurd[7]—Yeats was for Beckett yet another Irish artist with whom to identify. Although the two shared a number of casual pursuits—many of which, like sports, went back to Beckett's youth—they had several more basic interests, including a deep concern and respect for the most disenfranchised of human beings. This they manifested artistically in remarkably similar subjects and settings. That both were talented in more than one art form may have also brought them together—an unusual quality but one that characterized several of Beckett's closest friends, including Joyce and McGreevy.[8]

Yeats, McGreevy, and Joyce already shared a deep regard for one another, personally and professionally. Joyce had bought two early Yeats paintings, and they were always on view in his apartment.[9] They also had a number of qualities in common. Like Joyce and Beckett (despite McGuinness's suggestion to the contrary), Yeats openly expressed his deep devotion to his father and the great influence he had had on his life. For many years after his father's death, he still introduced himself by saying: "I am the son of a painter."[10] By the time Yeats and Beckett met, Yeats, like Joyce, had also overcome a number of career adversities. A successful illustrator and traditional watercolorist, he had been forced to accept the fact that the camera was making his work obsolete; if he wanted to pursue the career of an artist, he would have to create new forms. This he did, during Beckett's childhood years, by turning to Irish subjects. Throughout his career, however, and like Joyce, McGreevy, and Beckett, Yeats had to sort out a complex, often ambivalent, attitude toward the Irish. He was undoubtedly the most politically active of these artists.

As a teenager Yeats had involved himself in Irish affairs.[11] After his family moved to London in 1887, when he was only sixteen, he was outspoken in the cause of Irish independence. In 1888, he attended organized meetings in Hyde Park to welcome T. D. Sullivan and the Irish members of Parliament released from prison after their sentences under the Crimes Act.[12] He left London religiously every year to attend the Sligo celebrations of the 1798 Uprising.[13] He even learned the Irish language, because he believed in the slogan "Tír gan teanga tír gan anam": "A country without a language is a country without a soul." Of his feelings toward the English, he told Lady Gregory: "You will never break the heart of the British empire. You cannot break pulp."[14] Nevertheless, by his mid-twenties, he came to feel acute pain over the inevitable sufferings incurred in warfare, and by the time of the Irish civil war and World War I, he was overcome by the grotesqueries and bloodshed of contemporary world events. (Some Yeats scholars believe it led to a breakdown.)[15] This attitude remained with him until the end of his life. *The Grief*, for example, an image conveying the costs of moral righteousness, was painted in 1957, the year he died.

Some of Yeats's most important earlier works focused on the British Massacre in 1914 (when the Rebels received German guns) and on the Easter Uprising of 1916. The artist's great distress with the moral contradictions inherent in war were evident: at the same time the Rebellion's leaders were prosecuting a local revolution, 150,000 of their kinsmen were fighting alongside the British in the Great War. Yeats's subsequent ambivalence toward the Rebels and Free Staters became apparent in paintings like *Bachelor's Walk* and *The Funeral of Harry Boland*. In these—indeed, in all his great works, *Yes We Will Home Rule*, *Communicating with Prisoners*, *Going to Wolfe Tone's Grave*, *On Drumcliffe Strand*, *We Are Leaving You Now*, *A Rose Dying*, and *The Public Orator* (the last, inspired by Padraic Pearse)—Yeats was fiercely idealistic, rather than traditionally "political," which we might say about both Joyce and the older Beckett (vis-à-vis the latter's World War II activities).

Yeats despised war under any circumstances. Pyle tries to explain his idealism: "To him, the Free Staters were [the empowered] middle-class, while the Republicans represented all that was noble and free. His patriotism had nothing to do with war or the practicalities of the situation but was rather a dedication to the perfect life . . . where no man was subject to another." [16] Brian O'Doherty similarly asserts that Yeats's vagrants and transients represented more than an attack on the bourgeoisie, that they represented more than stoical survival in the face of political oppression. To O'Doherty, Yeats's "tinkers, gypsies, sailors, circus performers, actors, travellers, tramps, jockeys, [and] gamblers" were reminders of prewar and innate human innocence: "The patriot on the run is a romantic figure like those other outsiders . . . the madman, the criminal, the clown and acrobat . . . all paradigms for a [lost] soul." [17]

In his lyrical monograph *Jack B. Yeats*, written in 1937 and not published until 1945, McGreevy initially applauds Yeats as the first painter in three hundred years to focus on the Irish as subject matter. To McGreevy, Yeats penetrated the Irish soul and reflected how, under every type of oppression—political, economic, and cosmic—the Irish could pursue the "true, good, and beautiful." He extols Yeats for capturing in his subjects that "trinity" which "constitutes the part of the kingdom of God that even profane philosophers allow to be within us." That is, "untramelled by outward mannerisms or privilege," Yeats's modest figures—laborers, tramps, and circus people—actually "delight in [their] own [earthly] potential for truth, goodness, and beauty." Ultimately, to McGreevy, Yeats captured the "consummate . . . spirit of his own nation"—"epicureans not hedonists," alive in the here and now, a society of heroic people with the most "primitive" virtues of courage, benevolence, and sincerity. McGreevy focuses on the "integrity of life" in Yeats's various hoboes and other descendants out of commedia dell'arte. Indeed, if one substituted a metaphysical for the political or economic focus in the following, one might be describing Beckett's future work: "[Yeats knew] like Velázquez . . . that paint can make rags as humanly beautiful if not as socially elegant as the brocades. And thus he . . . [expressed] the humanities in terms of an underdog, conquered people." [18]

In addition to his political and "trinitarian" concerns, Jack Yeats was, like Beckett and Joyce's friend Paul Léon, deeply committed to social justice. And, also true of Joyce, there was always an intimate connection between his lived experience and narrative subject matter. In 1905 Yeats embarked upon a project to establish better living conditions in Ireland. Joining a project sponsored by the *Manchester Guardian*—that is, pursuing traditional channels—he participated with his friend John Millington Synge in a venture to set up relief works and small industry within the congested districts of Connemara and Mayo. [19]

As Yeats and Synge traveled, both were overcome by the hopelessness of the sociopolitical situation, specifically by the extreme poverty in these districts. The shortage of just a few potatoes or fish, they observed, could easily result in starvation. Yeats painted numerous canvases after this trip and is said to have long recalled it to others, especially one instance which occasioned an unequivocal commitment to the Republican cause. A wealthy property agent had hurled a tenant and his wife into the street, and Yeats heard a voice say: "I swore by heaven, and I swore by hell, and all the rivers that ran through them, I'd be a Nationalist." Yeats deeply believed—and he published this conviction—that "No man can have two countries. A man must be part of the land and of the life he paints." [20]

Despite later differences with his poet brother, from that point on, Jack Yeats listened to Connolly and Pearse. Thus began his exaltation of the Uprising's leaders—an exaltation that was, all the same, soon tempered by the stubborn paradox that the Rebel's enemy at home was his brother's keeper in the trenches. (Like Beckett's painter friend Henri Hayden during World War II, Yeats painted relatively little during the Uprising and World War I.)

The vicious guerrilla warfare of 1919–20, fought by the Irish Volunteers (forerunners of the IRA) against the British, disturbed him even more. When civil war broke out in Ireland after the British left in 1922, the Republican forces defeated, and the South now a British dominion—with Ireland, in essence, still paying allegiance to the Crown—he became deeply disillusioned. As McGreevy explains, with partition established and imperial connection remaining: "The imperialists laid the final odium of moral defeat on the Irish themselves." [21] By 1929–30, Yeats abandoned the political and socially realistic images that had marked his early style. He not only created a new style but he also began his career as a novelist. During this period he and Beckett became friends.

In developing his new forms, Yeats first returned to sketches he had made thirty years earlier. From these, he worked toward an art that would convey not just his political ambivalence but the inherent contradictions of the human condition. In the process, his images grew increasingly complex and resistant to summary. In the early watercolors and oils, he had begun with a pencil or charcoal outline and worked toward recognizable, descriptive, local scenes in a matte finish. Now, experimenting with opacity and the diffusion of linearity, he started with a concrete image from his personal past but then released himself from his earliest associations with the image. Eventually, memory—the concrete experience—and the dream and free associative state became inseparable, [22] and he used the interplay of image and painterly texture to convey this complex condition of thought. Curiously enough, as removed as he had been from the Surrealists, Verticalists, and the other avant-garde movements on the continent, he evolved an aesthetic that in many ways echoed theirs.

In order to portray the past in the emotional context of the present, Yeats applied paint directly to the canvas (from the tube with his fingers, or with a palette knife). Then, as if working with a screen either rich with impasto or bare to the fabric, he sought to exteriorize the twilight area between fact and possibility, experience and illusion—experience as a product of conscious and unconscious response. He served his own ambivalence toward historical event by rejecting the singularity of statement implied in simple linearity. Like Joyce in his manipulations of dream language in Finnegans Wake, Yeats used paint to evoke the way experience and objects appear before they are categorized in the mind, as in Discovery, Grief, In Memory of Bianconi and Boucicault, Tirnan 'Og California, Palaces, and They Come, They Come, and many of his great "rose" paintings. He tried to capture the image whose source is pre-memory, the image that emerges out of the twilight zone of forgetfulness or the unconscious. Later Beckett analogically wrote in The Unnamable: "You must say words, as long as there are any, until they find me, until they say me strange pain strange sin." When Beckett later reviewed Yeats's novel The Amaranthus (1934), he praised the author for his complex, if difficult, evocation of "the amorphous"—the verbal equivalent of his painting techniques: "There is no allegory, . . . there is no symbol . . . there is no satire." Instead, there are the "series of imaginative transactions" in the "stages of an image."[23]

This is not to say that within his combination of bold new colors and dissolution of strict line and form the image was entirely lost. In many of his greatest works, like High Water, Spring Tide, Yeats retained his focus on the most modest but common human activities of surviving—revelry, boredom, hope, or despair, as in A Silence or The Sisters. The ephemerality of human experience remained his consuming theme. But humanity was now obliged to come to terms with itself in an environment free from external interference. His figures were subject to the indifference of nature or to forces beyond nature. One of his critics even viewed his people as "part of some kind of unspecified larger-than-social system, some kind of cosmos which makes men the butt of its jokes. . . . Nature is an ominous background or an illusion."[24]

One may argue that even in his early work, regardless of its social commentary, he had already captured the ephemeral nature of human activity. His figures were always people without roots—local circus characters, carnival tinkers, ballad singers, boxers, horse racers, travelers, and tramps. But since they were the product of a recognizable environment, one could claim (like McGreevy initially) that Yeats was the first painter of the Irish people as Irish in three hundred years. In this light, one could broadly align him (like the Joyce of *Dubliners*) with a more Naturalistic tradition: his subjects were the offspring of a specific external environment. But in the later works, Yeats created dramas without specific backgrounding; he painted images that lacked clearcut, single referents. Here was the human condition in its most authentic state: the self within the self. Conflict occurred in the private forums of being, where individuals do battle with the wild, uncompromising nature of an unknowable reality.

Perhaps Beckett saw this in Yeats's work when he exalted him as one of the most important of all painters.[25] Perhaps he saw how, as in all great art, Yeats's smallest passages were charged with human significance, and was intrigued by Yeats's artistic understanding of how experience exists only as a measure of individual perception. Beckett may have also felt a special affinity with Yeats's specific subjects, often clowns or war figures—the oppressed who *adapt* to forces over which they have neither control nor understanding. The extraordinary *Bachelor's Walk: In Memory*, for example, merges the themes of human adaptation and war. A flower girl, whose life work consists of selling mementos for the dead, stands with her back to the viewer; with her outstretched hand and arm, she throws a carnation into the air, as she hears of a young man's death. In that gesture, in displaying her own personal memorial, Yeats captures the profound humanity of despairing accommodation.

A later painting, *Tinkers' Encampment—The Blood of Abel*, which McGreevy considered Yeats's greatest work, portrays the world as a temporary camping ground. Its standing but distanced figures illustrate a line from the Missal at the Gospel for St. Stephen's Day (an interesting reminder of Stephen's namesake in *Portrait*): "All the blood that hath been shed upon the earth from the blood of Abel the just, even unto the blood of Zacharias . . . I say to you, all these things shall come upon this generation."[26] The image—of two lonely men on the verge of companionship or warfare, like Cain and Abel—recurred in many of Yeats's paintings—*Two Travellers*, *Men of the Plain*, *Men of Destiny*, and *The Top of the Tide*. It would find dramatic reexamination in many of Beckett's later works, as Beckett transposed into his dramatic rhetoric not just theme but linear design and visual texture from many artists.

Finally, one might suggest that in his late, most lyrical and metamorphosing images, Yeats accomplished goals similar to the Verticalists'. He reduced the artist's control of his universe to zero, aware of both the indeterminacy of meaning and self-knowledge at the same time that he accepted the interplay of conscious and unconscious thought. He realized that at best he could capture only "process" or, as his niece, W. B.'s daughter, Anne (like Beckett above), had said, he could recover only the "stages of the image."[27] Hence, his lonely vagabonds, torn between promise and regret, inhabitants of life-contemporaneous-with-death, were frequently painted at "twilight."

This was Yeats's visual expression of the life of words "half-said . . . and even quarter said,"[28] his expression of the human tragedy—in Beckett's words, the elemental "sin of birth" into "impotence" and "ignorance." This was humankind aloft on the isthmus between knowledge and powerlessness.

Jack Yeats's brother, the poet, commented on this use of twilight in a somewhat recondite fashion; he spoke of it as the source and subject of creativity: "The twilight between sleep and waking . . . alike in the stage and in the mind, between men and phantom, this perilous path as on the edge of a sword, is the condition of tragic pleasure."[29] Beckett seems to have understood the painter better. To Beckett, Jack Yeats had excavated those "perilous zones of being" in an effort to evoke that which eludes definition. Thus praising Yeats's literal and symbolic light, and appreciating his sense of the unverifiable nature of all our conclusions, Beckett said that Yeats brought light "to the issueless predicament of existence, reduc[ing] the dark where there might have been, mathematically at least, a door. The being in the street, when it happens in the room, the being in the room, when it happens in the street, the turning to gaze from land to sea, from sea to land, the backs to one another, and the eyes abandoning." In placing Yeats "with the great of our time, Kandinsky and Klee . . . Rouault and Braque," Beckett expressed his "wonderment" at Yeats's accomplishments: "What is incomparable in this great solitary oeuvre is its insistence upon sending us back to the darkest part of the spirit . . . and upon permitting illuminations only through that darkness." To Beckett, Yeats had tapped "the great internal reality which incorporates into a single witness dead and living spirits, nature and void, everything that will cease and everything that will never be." He had "submit[ted] to what cannot be mastered."[30]

Many considered Yeats's last works to be incomprehensible. Nevertheless, echoing Beckett's sentiments in Our Exagmination regarding artistic integrity, Yeats reveled in the public perception of his inscrutability: "I am the first living painter in the world. I have no modesty. I have the immodesty of the spearhead." In a more modest comment—one also appropriate to Beckett's future work—he said: "All painting to be painting must be poetry, and all poetry must be painting."[31] Always responsive to Yeats's art, Beckett kept his painting Morning with him throughout World War II. This, along with Regatta Evening and The Corner Boys, remained among his most valued possessions.[32]

After leaving Trinity, at the end of 1931—his second unhappy experience in teaching—Beckett visited his aunt Cissie Sinclair's family in Kassel, Germany. His cousin Peggy, about whom much has been speculated regarding Beckett's romantic attachment to her, had begun to show signs of the tuberculosis that would soon take her life.

Beckett returned to Paris in March 1932; he moved into the Hotel Tri-
anon, where Thomas McGreevy was living.[33] His stay in Paris, however, was
unexpectedly terminated in May, when the French president, Paul Doumer,
was assassinated. Beckett's papers were not in order, and because he lacked a
valid *carte de séjour* (similar to a green card), he was forced to leave the country. He returned home, or, more precisely, to Dublin. His family understood
his need for independent lodgings, and his father offered him the top floor
of his office—Beckett's "garret" living quarters for most of the next year.

Bair discusses Beckett's unhappiness throughout this period by saying
that his return to Trinity, particularly to his family, precipitated bouts of insomnia and pathological passivity, along with a number of psychosomatic
ailments.[34] Even if Beckett suffered from boils, cysts, and the other delicate
symptoms she enumerates at length, there is no current medical evidence
that any of these ailments are psychosomatic in origin.[35] There is no doubt,
however, that this must have been a very difficult time for him. As of the
spring of 1932, and at the age of twenty-six, he had no answers—for his parents, but perhaps, more important, for himself—regarding his career and
even his permanent place of residence.

FIVE

London

Men do not perish as a result of lost wars, but by the loss
of that force of resistance which is contained only in pure
blood.—ADOLF HITLER, Mein Kampf, trans. 1933

Now the day is over
Night is drawing nigh
Shadows of the evening
Steal across the sky.
—SABINE BARING-GOULD (author of "Onward, Christian
Soldiers"); epigraph to W. H. Auden, Age of Anxiety, 1947

Now the day is over,
Night is drawing nigh-igh, Shadows—
—SAMUEL BECKETT, Krapp's Last Tape, 1961

Beckett moved to London at the end of 1933, where
he remained for nearly three years.[1] Although accounts of his life there are
sparse, numerous momentous events help clarify why these were, as he put
it, "bad" years—"bad in every way"—"psychologically and financially."[2] Perhaps most critical was the death of his father in June 1933. Their relationship
was so close that William Beckett "carried his son's recent letters on his person until the day he died." And after he died, the bereft Samuel Beckett said:
"What am I to do now but follow his trace over the fields and hedges?"[3] For
many years following, Beckett tried to recover his father: "At night, when I
can't sleep, I do the old walks again and stand beside him . . . in the fields
near Glencullen."[4]

Beckett had already sustained a great loss in 1933 when his beloved
cousin Peggy died, only a month before his father. Her death remained a
lifelong sadness.[5] In addition, while geographically distant from Joyce—and
Beckett would undoubtedly have sought out any news about him—he must
have been deeply grieved to learn of Joyce's current tribulations. According to Ellmann, Joyce was, during this time, compelled to come to terms
with committing Lucia to a sanitorium. Also, nearly blind in his right eye
and with minimal vision in his left, he had been advised to undergo yet
another eye surgery. As Ellmann further reports, Joyce had become increasingly "obsessed" with the pornography trial of Ulysses, and his insomnia and
the stomach ailment that ultimately took his life grew more severe.[6]

Although any of these events might have been sufficiently grave to prompt Beckett's "crisis," he had yet other personal and professional problems.[7] After his difficult period at Trinity, he had returned to Paris, obviously to restore some order in his life. The years spent teaching at Belfast, the Ecole, and Trinity had left him, according to Harvey, with the feeling that a great deal of time had been wasted.[8] And even if he were uncertain that his future lay in writing, he had begun to establish a literary reputation in Paris. "Assumption," *Whoroscope*, and *Proust*, along with his translations, reviews, and poetry—and the recent publications of "Sedendo et Quiescendo" and "Dante and the Lobster"—had gained him a measure of recognition in elite artistic circles.[9] The forced move back to Dublin after Doumer's assassination must thus have been deeply disruptive. All the same (and despite what Bair insists was his increasingly pathological behavior), Beckett pursued his writing in Dublin, preparing most of the stories for *More Pricks than Kicks* and editing his poems for the eventual *Echo's Bones and Other Precipitates*.[10]

The death of his father, along with the lifelong sadness it brought him, precipitated new practical but sensitive problems. Had Beckett the wish or need to leave Ireland, he would necessarily have to impose upon his brother the entire burden of caring for his mother. He would also have to leave behind his debilitated and much-adored aunt Cissie and (part-Jewish) uncle Boss, both of whom, in 1933, had not only suffered their daughter Peggy's death but also escaped from Nazi Germany.

In addition—and of no small consequence in understanding this terrible period psychologically and financially—during the years Beckett lived in London, not only were there many "down-and-out-Irishmen," but *everyone* was down and out: it was the middle of the Depression. Beckett's "exile," in every circumstance, seems to have elicited his exquisite sensitivity to the suffering around him—in Foxrock and Trinity during the Irish Rebellion and civil war, in Belfast during its depression and religious conflicts, and in Paris and Roussillon during World War II.

During his stay in London, nearly three million people were unemployed and London had become a city of poor housing, ill health, and a widely demoralized population. Finally, this period also marked the Nazi ascension to power, and the London press was filled with Hitler's aberrant ambitions. It is highly unlikely that Beckett would have been insensitive to the spectre of fascism looming over the world.

Beatrice Glenavy's description of the insulated Dublin that Beckett left behind might well be applicable to the larger world he would observe during the next six or seven years. Speaking of Mussolini and Hitler, Glenavy remarked: "[As] two madmen [were] planning the death of millions of their fellow human beings, in Dublin, it was a time of memorable parties."[11]

Indeed, the terrible events which Beckett read about in London and later observed in France—and the way the democratic world reacted to them—might have indicated to him that Dublin was not unique in its indifference to escalating international suffering.

Beckett did survive his personal crisis in London. He underwent psychoanalysis, developed or renewed important and sustaining friendships, and read a great deal. He pursued a career in journalism with scholarly and literary reviews (on Rilke, Pound, O'Casey, Dante, McGreevy, and Jack B. Yeats), along with some translations, and he began his novel *Murphy*. His first collection of short stories, *More Pricks than Kicks*—some of which were reworkings of the unfinished *Dream of Fair to Middling Women*—and his cycle of thirteen poems, *Echo's Bones and Other Precipitates*, were also published during this period.[12]

Beckett also witnessed, during these London years, a transformation of the English cultural scene, particularly in the areas of newspaper reporting, radio broadcasting, dramatic acting, and painting—all of which may have been salubrious to his personal and artistic growth. While W. H. Auden and others were keeping a fearful vigil over encroaching international fascism, the schism between artists on the Left and Right was growing. The French Surrealists also arrived in London in 1935 to assist in the long-awaited celebration of the English Surrealists the following year. Their aesthetic, like that of their French counterparts, was heavily indebted to psychoanalysis—which Beckett was now experiencing firsthand. Equally important at the time and of obvious later consequence to Beckett, some of the greatest actors and directors in British stage history were establishing their reputations between 1933 and 1936. They brought to the stage a new acting and production style—with greater attention to the spoken word and the rhythms of body movement and gesture. Finally, Beckett had access to an important new technology. In 1933, the BBC began broadcasting, both from home and abroad, an unparalleled range of old and new plays, and these were performed by the best actors in the English-speaking world. The BBC also aired traditional and avant-garde music with world-renowned musical virtuosi, as well as vigorous debates on the most current social, moral, and philosophical issues. In short, the London years must have been a period of great intellectual, as well as emotional, growth for the twenty-seven-year-old Beckett.

The Depression in England lasted from 1931 until World War II, although unemployment was a major issue of British society throughout the interwar years.[13] Given Britain's decline in both industry and exports, the nation was preoccupied with the economic calamity at hand. Maintaining world peace and global disarmament, as promised by the Treaty of Versailles, lingered on everyone's mind, but these concerns were overshadowed by the problems of daily survival—employment, food, housing, and health insurance.

Cynicism toward government heightened—not only because of its advocacy of that "Great War" of little ideological rectitude—but because of its incompetence, if not conspiracy, in the present economic debacle. As one commentator put it, the politically powerful were clearly "inept" and possessed of a socioeconomic vision that could only be called "squalid."[14] A rather foolish Neville Chamberlain, for example, in his 1934 budget speech, boasted that the country "had gone from Bleak House to Great Expectations" (a statement that could only be matched by Herbert Hoover's 1929 prediction: "[This] has been a twelvemonth of . . . wonderful prosperity. . . . If there is any way of judging the future by the past, this new year may well be one of felicitation and hopefulness").[15] A resulting bittersweet, if not entirely cynical, detachment characterized the public's isolationism, toward both government at home and events abroad.

All the same, like the United States, England had become the beneficiary of an extraordinary number of technological advances. Radio, movies, transportation (including mass production of the car), and the proliferation of newspaper and book publishing had given birth to mass culture and the earliest stages of the global village. Advances in the pure and social sciences had similarly expanded the range of human possibility, particularly in the areas of nuclear physics, genetics, and the new psychology. Their promises were reminiscent of the Crystal Palace days: science, now under the new banners of Left or Right, could provide all the possibilities for humankind's self-fulfillment. The new scientific findings were also changing the "vision" of reality—or at least the lens through which one appraised it.

Through his ardent disciple Ernest Jones, Freud gained enormous currency in England during the 1920s and 1930s. Like Einstein in his theory of relativity, Freud questioned the concept of the fixed or absolute. Both Freud and Einstein challenged the concept that appearances (for example, human behavior or mass) were stable and constant—whether in terms of complex human motivation or the shifting intricacies of atomic configuration. The concept of "the relative" had such an impact upon current intellectual thought that even John Galsworthy, in the preface to Modern Comedy, facetiously applied it to God, country, and industry: "Everything now being relative, there is no absolute dependence to be placed on God, Free Trade, Marriage, Consols, Coal or Castle."

The importance of the subjective and irrational had long been expressed in the art of Paris, and, although Roger Fry had introduced the French avant-garde to the British, the latter were, on the whole, resistant to the new styles. E. M. Forster may have addressed the "beast" and "monk" in human nature, but he had retained traditional forms; similarly working within conventional genres, most postwar British writers, motivated by social and political issues, concentrated on class issues or the ravages of war. The same held true in the visual arts, where the devastation of modern warfare was the subject matter of Richard Nevinson, John and Paul Nash, and Stanley Spencer; Ben Nicholson and Barbara Hepworth were perhaps most stylistically innovative here. Many of the period's most talented writers and artists considered it their responsibility to galvanize the public to both the economic issues and the rise of global fascism. To many, finally, communism appeared the only solution. The outbreak of the Spanish Civil War, in the year Beckett departed from London, crystallized the (perhaps naive) overview of communism as the absolutely pure path (represented by the innocent Republicans) versus the evil direction taken by the totalitarian Franco (supported by Mussolini and Hitler).

Life in London, compared with Paris, limited the freedoms a young person like Beckett might indulge (and the social or literary circles in which he might indulge them). London of the early to mid-thirties may well have reminded Beckett, in important ways, of his youth and college days in Ireland and of his term in Belfast. If, during his happy childhood, he was dismayed by the plight of vagrants, the mentally ill, and the wounded veterans of World War I, and, later, by the poverty and discrimination in Belfast, then the sheer magnitude of destitution in Depression-era London must have affected him deeply. This may have been heightened, as it often is for sensitive children of privileged upbringing, by an acute awareness of the different fates that life bestows. "Remark that I might just as well have been in his shoes and he in mine. If chance had not willed otherwise," Beckett later wrote in *Waiting for Godot*. Beckett's external world, as much as his philosophical and personal introspections, molded his vision of human nature, and this crystallized after World War II in his outpouring of great work in 1946.

When Beckett arrived in London, the nation was suffering its third year of economic depression; these remained, as the British called them, "the locust years" or the "devil's decade." With half the population living at a standard inadequate to maintain healthy life, unemployment was recorded at nearly three million. Much of the nation was undernourished: official surveys at the end of 1935 cited 50 percent as "ill-fed" and 10 percent as "badly fed." Among the most striking events of 1933 were the organized hunger marches, which were brutally handled by the police. During one march, two thousand people invaded Whitehall with a petition of a million signatures to protest the 10 percent cut in unemployment benefits. Police charged with batons, injuring and arresting more than a dozen. At another dem-

Two Hundred Jarrow Men Step Out Bravely on Their Trek to London Carrying Town's Hopes With Them

BISHOP'S BLESSING FOR CRUSADE TO END UNEMPLOYMENT

Mayor and Clerk in Robes Lead Marchers to Boundary

BLITHE START WITH BAND PLAYING

HOPES, FEARS, LEAVE-TAKING, 'LAST-MINUTE JOKES—JARROW SAID GOOD-BYE TO-DAY TO THE 200 MEN WHO STARTED OUT GRAVELY ON THEIR 300 MILE TREK TO LONDON.

THEY STEPPED OUT WITH GOOD HEART ON THIS CRUSADE WHICH HAS FOCUSSED THE EYES OF THE COUNTRY ON THE TOWN WHERE UNEMPLOYMENT HAS HELD SWAY FOR SO LONG. IN THE VAN WERE THE MAYOR AND TOWN CLERK IN THEIR ROBES, MISS ELLEN WILKINSON, M.P., MRS. A. E. GOMPERTZ, REPRESENTING THE GOOD WISHES OF THE SOUTH SHIELDS LABOUR GROUP, PALMERS BAND, AND A NUMBER OF FRIENDS.

The enterprise was blessed by the Bishop of Jarrow before...

The hunger march from Jarrow to London became an emblem of widespread anger at the government's indifference to the poor. (National Museum of Labour History)

onstration, after a two-hour street battle, thirty people were taken to the hospital. Other marches were more subdued, such as one to Buckingham Palace, where old soldiers, wearing their medals, sang "Tipperary."[16]

The most memorable march originated in Jarrow, an industrial town in the northeast, where 80 percent were unemployed and the town had disintegrated to little more than a rubbish heap. The Jarrow crusaders walked for more than a month to London, picking up thousands of supporters en route. Doctors came forth and tended the ill; poor people interrupted the pilgrimage with donations of bread and margarine. When the Jarrow group finally arrived at Hyde Park, with banners, songs, and a petition signed by twelve thousand people, Prime Minister Stanley Baldwin refused to meet with them. Walter Runciman, president of the Board of Trade, appeared instead and reiterated the government's initial contention: "Jarrow must work out its own salvation." The Jarrow march became the decade's emblem of hopeless anger and despair.[17]

The marches had a great impact on England's university students, only a handful of years younger than Beckett. Oxford undergraduates spent weekends with indigents throughout Britain and organized marches on their behalf. In September 1934, for example, they protested the lack of safety precautions that had precipitated a mine explosion in North Wales, the worst mine disaster in twenty years, in which 264 men had been killed. Oxford and Cambridge began seminars on a variety of social problems, such as housing and illness.

Overcrowding and unsanitary slums were ubiquitous, despite the acts for slum clearance passed in 1930, 1932, and 1935. For a large number of people, including the seemingly permanently unemployed, there were also no insurance benefits, although the Unemployment Act of 1934 created an Unemployment Assistance Board. Under this new agency, applicants could gain assistance only after undergoing the most "stringent means"—or humiliation—of assuring they had no assets available. As Orwell wrote, noting the common fear that one's dole would suddenly be withdrawn: "The [Means] test was an encouragement to the tattle-tale and the informer, the writer of anonymous letters and the local blackmailer."[18] In a word, it stimulated a mild form of collaborationism and treachery, which Beckett would witness in its more aggressive and dangerous manifestations during World War II.

Despite these conditions, the British rarely questioned their deep-rooted national identity. As Orwell again wrote, musing on the resilient odd combination of disenfranchisement and patriotism in the English: "There is no question about the inequality of wealth in England. It is grosser than in any European country and you have only to look down the nearest street to see it. Economically, England is . . . two nations, if not three or four. But at the same time, the vast majority of people find themselves to be a single nation. . . . Patriotism [remains] stronger than class-hatred."[19] This kind of statement about English pride may have touched a delicate chord in Beckett, reminding him of having lived through the Irish Rebellion and riots and mayhem of Belfast as the son of a wealthy and Protestant Foxrock family.

Among other well-documented manifestations of the Depression, such as the drop in church attendance, breakup of marriages, and decline in birth rate, the death rate increased among families afflicted by long-term unemployment. In something of an understatement—and with shades of Engels and Franklin Delano Roosevelt—Harry Pollitt wrote: "The stark reality is that in 1933, for the mass of the population, Britain is a hungry Britain, badly fed, badly clothed and housed."[20]

Reaction took a number of forms. The poor were exploited by business: with "six people for every job . . . an employer could pick and choose among them . . . and there was always somebody who would do the same work for a little less money." [21] Oswald Mosley had another solution. Sixth baronet and Curzon's son-in-law, he had already withdrawn from the Conservatives in favor of the Labour party, but in 1932 he formed his own party, the British Union of Fascists. Presumably organized in protest against the twentieth-century robber-barons, his platform was that people must create "collectively their own police force to deal with the enemy and the exploiter." [22] Mosley's goal was a racially pure, essentially fascist state.

His meetings were organized around a number of "routines." To prove the dangers of free speech, for example, he would enact a drill where appointed hecklers would stand and shout, and then be punched by appointed fascist guards. (Women were slapped, not punched, by female guards.) Mosley would then deliver a homily on the need for fascist methods to preserve free speech. He also lectured regularly on modern decadence (the catch phrase Pétain later used), which he attributed to the "softness" of modern civilization. Mosley would return to a warrior, barbaric, atavistic spirit (his hero was Julius Caesar). For now, he lamented that "the aristocrat had become the financier; the warrior, the clerk; the doer, the talker." Before audiences of often twenty thousand (and he gave ten such talks a month), Mosley made such comments as: "If any country in the world attacks Britain or threatens to attack Britain, then every single member of this great audience of British Union would fight for Britain. But . . . we fight for Britain, yes, but a million Britains shall never die in your Jews' quarrel." [23] In July 1934, one of his supporters threw a four-year-old Jewish child through a plate-glass window, and the "blackshirt" was never criminally charged. Dressed in his tight black clothes from head to foot, with his face garnished by a Hitler mustache, Mosley continued to debate whether Jews should be castrated or banished to Madagascar. Harold Pinter was one of countless young Jewish children in London victimized by those under the Mosley spell. [24]

Mosley's was one reaction, but as Richard Griffiths documents, in *Fellow Travellers of the Right*, there were numerous other fascist organizations and many popular anti-Semitic magazines. Many had been published since the 1920s, including *The Patriot*, *The Jewish Domination*, and *The Nameless Beast*. Prominent personalities, like Emerald Cunard (the rebellious Nancy's mother) and the powerful Lord Rothermere, who owned the *Daily Mail*, openly supported their points of view. [25]

In addition, many newly formed Left groups such as the Artists' International and the Writers' International (both started in 1933), attracted numerous artists and writers; countless music, film, and theater groups also organized. The important socialist Left Book Club, associated with Victor Gollancz, Harold Laski, and John Strachey, was founded in 1936. Created to bring a concerned, unorganized segment of the population into contact with the labor movement, if not to cement a united front against fascism, the club sent its members a book each month. By definition, the books explored the nature of fascism, anti-Semitism, or racism. By the end of 1936, between 150 and 200 Left Book Clubs had organized throughout the country. With a membership of upward of sixty thousand in 1935, the club had one and a half million volumes in print by the end of the decade.[26] Numerous Left magazines were also being published, including the *Left Review*, the most aggressive of the journals, under the impetus of the Left Book Club. They included *New Atlantis*, *Albion*, *New Britain*, and *The Week*, and such writers as Bertrand Russell, Rebecca West, and Kingsley Martin contributed to them. People also took courses in the Russian language or traveled to the Soviet Union (for example, Shaw, Gide, and Lady Astor). Bair reports that in 1935, Beckett considered going to Moscow to study film with Eisenstein or Pudovkin.[27]

Albeit from differing political vantage points, many writers focused on the unemployed and assailed the sordid and hypocritical solutions thus far proposed—J. B. Priestley in *English Journey* and *Angel Pavement*, Walter Greenwood in *Love on the Dole*, and Graham Greene in *It's a Battlefield*. An angry young Greene wrote: "Laws were made by property owners. . . . That was why a fascist could talk treason without prosecution; that was why a man who defrauded the State in defence of his private wealth did not ever lose the money he gained." Many artists, if not official members of the party, expressed at least an *appreciation* of communism.[28] Even T. S. Eliot noted Marx's appeal, especially to the young. His *Waste Land* may have sounded the clarion call to the waste of the Great War and its subsequent impact on contemporary society—and Eliot did indeed turn to tradition, conservatism, and elitism in the end—but in 1932, he wrote: "No one who is seriously concerned can fail to be impressed by the work of Karl Marx. He is, of course, much more cited than read; but his power is so great, and his analysis so profound, that it must be very difficult for anyone who reads him without prejudice on the one hand, or without any definite religious faith on the other, to avoid accepting his conclusions."[29]

To understand the appeal of communism was not necessarily to adopt it, and many, like Eliot (Pound, Wyndham Lewis, and Roy Campbell), maintained the social imperative of "high culture"—the social function of literature, language, or literary criticism. Even D. H. Lawrence, in an entirely different vein, had fought against modern industrialism, acquisitiveness, and the debasement of human instinct—what he often assailed as the "tragedy of [modern] ugliness." For Lawrence, the instinctive life, rather than sociopolitical forces, was the foundation of spontaneity and individuality, which alone could restore the organic and functional community. There were, of course, many varieties of socialism, in addition to Marxism-Leninism. Clement Attlee, for example, advocated an idealistic form of party (Labour) socialism that would serve as a commonsense force to inspire idealism. Later in the decade, he wrote: "Every individual should be afforded the fullest opportunity for developing his or her personality . . . on moral grounds. The evils of our society were due to the failure to put into practice the principle of the brotherhood of man." [30]

Unambivalent "party" people were those like John Strachey, whose *Coming Struggle for Power* (1934), while condemning the noncommunist involvement of Eliot, Wells, Shaw, Proust, and Joyce, attracted many intellectuals to the Left. Although C. Day-Lewis was the only official communist among the Oxford group, Auden, Spender, MacNeice, and the others were deeply committed to the party's goals. Ronald Blythe explains the intellectual or poetic rebellion of what he calls these "humanistic pinks": "The Communist flirtation ran little risk of developing to the point of consummation. The intellectual Left and the small solid Red of the C.P.G.B. [Communist Party, Great Britain] were not made for each other"—not the least reason being the bourgeois roots of most of the writers. Blythe continues: "But they enjoyed and were cynically amused by the affair . . . and the emotional warmth it spread to the proletariat was stimulating and occasionally heady." The October Club at Oxford, formed to study communism, grew to three hundred members by 1933. At Cambridge, a Federation of Socialist Societies was also organized. Both universities published a number of popular revolutionary magazines.[31]

Although Auden later wrote—and this, in memorializing another poet–political activist, W. B. Yeats—"Poetry makes nothing happen," he, like MacNeice, Spender, Day-Lewis, and many others throughout the decade, professed to know "the way" to social equality, and they all committed themselves to an art that would show that way. Unlike Beckett at the time, many had traveled widely and seen fascism in its earliest stages (Isherwood, Auden, and John Lehman in Germany; Julian Bell, William Empson, and Peter Quennell in the Far East). Their art, however, focused on the death of liberal England. Auden lamented the derelict landscape racked with unemployment and depression, and, concluding with a line from Lenin, described Britain as "already comatose / Yet sparsely living," where people "hunger, work illegally / And [remain] anonymous" ("Our Hunting Fathers"). To Auden, these were the "massive and taciturn years, the Age of Ice." MacNeice (who had spent a fair amount of time in Dublin during Beckett's Trinity days), in the long *Autumn Journal*, focused on the human spirit in the face of government indifference: "Still they manage to laugh. / Though they have no eggs, no milk, no fish . . . / The human values remain." Spender's prose, as in *The Destructive Element*, as well as his poetry (*Vienna*), turned to the need for new belief to counter the contemporary socioeconomic disorder. For each of these poets, the *Left Review* (November 1934) reiterated the artist's obligation: "A writer's usefulness depends on his influence."

Even if Russian ideology provided "the answer," the communist movement in England remained modest, with only fifteen thousand members at the end of the 1930s. All the same, its goals seemed urgent and relevant, and anthologies like *New Signatures* and *New Count* appeared (1933); any member of the working class became the new hero, a cause célèbre. At least one historian observed that the most genuine expression of political feeling was in "the sympathy with the Negro cause," as demonstrated by Nancy Cunard's nine-hundred-page anthology *Negro*, published in 1934, to which Beckett contributed numerous translations.[32]

A great deal of theater and film was political as well. Auden and Christopher Isherwood's *The Dog Beneath the Skin* (1935) and *Ascent of F6* (1936) indicted England's deplorable social and economic conditions: "See the land you once were proud to own . . . / Smokeless chimneys, damaged bridges, rotting wharves, and choked canals." A number of American imports, like Eugene O'Neill's *All God's Chillun Got Wings*, with Paul Robeson, portrayed the working class or blacks as social victims; the latter were no longer to be the mere subjects of comic relief. Claire and Paul Sifton's *Age of Plenty* focused on social problems caused by mass unemployment; in 1935, in *Stevedore*, Robeson played the role of a revolutionary black leader of the working class fighting exploitation. Among the many theater groups producing Leftist plays were Group Theatre (which presented the Auden-Isherwood plays) and the Workers' Theatre Movement (with their successful *Ragged Trousered Philanthropists*); other agit-prop groups included the Rebel Players, Left Theatre, and Unity Theatre.[33] Many productions were censored and therefore forced into makeshift theaters—the beginning of the "fringe" theater.

Eisenstein's *Battleship Potemkin* was released in 1934, after years of censorship, and his *General Line* also appeared.[34] Kino (meaning "cinema" in Russian) sponsored numerous Russian and German films, like *National Hunger March* (1934) and *March against Starvation* (1936); the Workers' Film and Photo League, associated with Kino, was also organized, and additional films and documentaries about the working class followed, such as *Construction* (1935).

All of this is not to suggest that the artistic Right remained silent. Many Right book clubs like the Book Society propagated "Baldwin taste," with advocates including George Gordon, Hugh Walpole, and Clemence Dane, but they were not as successful (or vocal) as the Leftist organizations. F. R. Leavis at Cambridge and the Scrutiny group continued to focus on the social function of literature as a critique of mass civilization, but Leavis also maintained that "fine living" depended upon language and the standards of great literature. An anti-Marxist, while articulating the crisis of capitalism, Leavis called for social change through high culture. Like Eliot and I. A. Richards, his solution involved a transcendental critical sensibility and an extreme kind of cultural individualism. Many, like Leavis (Denys Thompson, Q. D. Leavis, C. L. Knight, among others), remained dedicated to the elitism of art and the unequivocal social responsibility of literary criticism. (Scrutiny had attacked Picasso, Joyce, Diaghilev, and Surrealism for their destruction of old values, charging that they had only replaced the sickness of modern life with iconolastic technique and style.) Nevertheless, although F. R. Leavis and diverse writers like Evelyn Waugh, Edith Sitwell, Julian Symons, Cyril Connolly, and John Betjeman would have been in the literary public eye during Beckett's London years, they did not elicit the fanfare of those on the Left—many of whom finally found a place to exercise their moral values—in the Spanish Civil War of 1936–39. Of the twenty thousand volunteers in the British Battalion of the International Brigade (not just writers), five thousand were killed and five hundred were seriously wounded. Many of those who returned did so disillusioned by the manipulative and devious communist behavior in Spain.

Bair argues that throughout this time, Beckett was obsessed with his divided consciousness and the need to understand his "prehistory."[35] He had presumably identified with one of Jung's remarks about a child patient who "had never been born entirely." After hearing this, according to Bair, Beckett began discussing his womb fixation, explaining, for example, that his troubled life was the result of an improper birth. Regardless of the accuracy and implications of Bair's statement, I would argue that it was during this London period that Beckett came to understand human behavior better, particularly the workings of the innermost mind. This may have occurred for any number of reasons, including his psychoanalysis, the job he took on at a mental hospital, his reading of Jung and Freud, his refocus on the Surrealists—all following upon his first-hand experiences with Lucia and James Joyce. In addition, his own recuperative powers and great insight clearly played a synthesizing role.

The events of the world—perhaps a reminder of his past—pushed him toward profound introspection. Beckett would have been aware of the fascists' threatened breakdown of all human value systems—and the remarkable indifference (or rationalizations) with which much of the world responded. Examples of unusual moral failure were apparent often in the local news. Beckett, an aspiring journalist, particularly as a cricket enthusiast, could have followed the 1933 cricket scandal when the British were accused of "unsportsmanlike" activity in Australia for using "body-line bowling" and fracturing the head of a batsman. This was as prominent a news event as the peculiar rash of murders (especially "trunk" and spousal murders) that occurred during 1934–35. In response to such events, as well as to the larger world situation, an undefined moral rootlessness seemed to touch people of all classes. Even the habitually blasé Noel Coward commented on this in his atypically dark comedy *Post Mortem* (written in 1931): "[There is] a sort of hopelessness which isn't quite despair, not localized for that."

World events reported in the daily press, particularly the abundance of alarming information coming out of Germany, would not have escaped Beckett's notice. Hitler was so proud of his activities in the 1930s that he encouraged foreign correspondents to write about his every accomplishment. Andrew Sharf and Robert Desmond, among other journalist-scholars, reveal how until "the final solution," the Nazis made no attempt to conceal their activities. Only then were reporters placed under surveillance, although their phone calls remained unsupervised, enabling them to transmit their reports verbally. Between 1933 and 1937, only nine reporters were asked to leave Germany; most stayed on, although some gathered their information and returned home before printing it.[36] During Beckett's London years, reporters were free to travel through Germany and even photograph the new nation. Hitler held many interviews, during which he assured audiences that he both "wanted no war" and "would be only too glad if nations which take such an enormous interest in Jews would open their gates to them."[37]

In 1933, daily news coverage in London would have made any thinking person aware of the complexity—if not hypocrisy and duplicity—of human nature, let alone the megalomania or savagery of human instinct. The fact that Beckett joined the French Resistance in its earliest days—and for the reasons he gave of fighting for his friends and not a nation—may be understandable in the context of the larger world in which he matured. To repeat Beckett's phrase, these were "bad years"—when, too often, passivity or detachment seemed the dominant national responses to obvious evils.

During Beckett's years in London, there were seven major dailies—the *Times, Daily Telegraph, Daily Herald, Morning Post, Daily Express, News Chronicle,* and *Daily Mail*—as well as three important Sunday papers, the *Sunday Times, Observer,* and *Manchester Guardian*.[38] Although London had been the home of the world's first news agency (Reuters, 1852), this was the period of burgeoning magazine and newspaper sales; every paper sponsored a major subscription drive; this was also the new age of the "foreign correspondent." Each paper had an editorial policy that attracted a specific audience, and hence each had a specific political position to maintain. Petty rivalries between newspapers—for instance, between the *Daily Mail* and *News Chronicle*—occasionally overshadowed the news. The *Daily Mail,* London's only pro-

Hitler paper, had an upper- and middle-class readership. With a policy dictated by owner Lord Rothermere until his retirement in 1937, the *Mail* both advocated British air armament and admired Hitler's retrieval of Germany from "Israelites of international attachments" (July 10, 1933). The newspaper paid homage to Hitler's "magnetic" influence and compared him to George Washington. The *Mail's* Ward Price was Hitler's favorite interviewer.

At the other political pole was the consistently anti-Nazi, conservative, and imperialistic *Daily Telegraph*. Owned by the Berry brothers (Sir William Berry, who ran the paper, became Lord Camrose), it was also read by the middle and upper classes. The *Telegraph* supported the British government, although its respectful but unpopular stance against appeasement made the paper less sympathetic to Neville Chamberlain than to Anthony Eden and Winston Churchill. It not only continuously condemned the subsequent Munich Conference but from the early years focused heavily on the concentration camps. Before he retired, owner Lord Camrose combined the *Telegraph* with the *Morning Post*, which also vocally opposed Nazism.

At times even more outspoken against the Nazis was the *Manchester Guardian*, which consistently and vigorously condemned Hitler's terrorism, his persecution of the Jews, as well as his installation of concentration camps. F. A. Voight was among the *Guardian* reporters who described the New Germany as beyond the pale of civilization. On July 14, 1932, Voight wrote: "[Hitler's] incredulous meetings [gather] a mob that lynches in imagination. . . . It makes [one] sick."

The *Daily Express*, read by people of all incomes but predominantly the lower middle class, was owned by Lord Beaverbrook and focused primarily on entertainment. Advocating isolationism, the *Express* contained little international news and was filled with political and social gossip and cartoons. It also covered subjects like food tariffs and public works. On its masthead was the slogan "There Will Be No War." The *News Chronicle*, a liberal paper owned by Lawrence Cadbury and edited by Gerald Barry, was also considered lightweight ideologically, although it flaunted its contempt of the *Daily Mail*, reporting, for example, on August 31, 1937: "There is nothing in modern politics — not even in German politics — to match the crude confusion of the Rothermere mentality as revealed in the Rothermere press. It blesses and encourages every swashbuckler who threatens the peace of Europe . . . and then clamours for more and more armaments with which to defend Britain, presumably against his lordship's pet foreign bully."

The *Daily Herald*, the Labour party newspaper owned by J. S. Elias, attracted the lower middle and working classes. Primarily concerned with industrial news and financial matters, it had little criticism of Hitler. The *Observer*, run by J. L. Garvin and the oldest of the Sunday papers, strongly advocated the growing sentiment that the Treaty of Versailles had been prejudicial to the French and anti-British as well. It also urged that England and Germany restore better relations; it simultaneously advocated British rearmament. Later, it welcomed the Munich Pact (January 1, 1939; March 1, 1939).

The Times was controlled by several people, including the Lord Chief Justice of England, the Warden of All Souls College, Oxford, and the president of the Royal Society, and it was edited by Geoffrey Dawson, who was succeeded in 1934 by Robert M. Barrington-Ward. Although it had its own internecine battles (between Dawson and Lord Milner, for example), the Times tried to maintain objective and thorough coverage, with specific consideration of the national and international implications of events abroad. By the early 1930s, the paper had gained a reputation as the official organ of the British government; many on its staff were friends and neighbors of Baldwin, Chamberlain, and Halifax. Most journalist-historians agree that "for the researcher today," the Times "remains the best and most complete source of reliable contemporary information about, and assessments of, events in Germany."[39] Reports in the Times provide a lens for viewing world events as Beckett may have read about them, particularly those occurring in Germany.[40]

That Beckett was interested in the Jewish plight is certain; as Richard Ellmann notes, forty years after the war the subject of Jewish suffering made Beckett weep.[41] That Beckett would have empathized with the Jews as a persecuted people even before his London days is also likely. In addition to his general "sensitiv[ity] to the suffering around him," his friend and hero James Joyce, who had forged an epic figure in the Jew Leopold Bloom, often spoke of himself as a Jew (see chapter 3). Joyce equated the Jews and Irish as persecuted peoples ("Israelite-Irish"). Beckett himself, during these years in London, had known the experience of ethnic discrimination. (He said: "They always know you're an Irishman. The porter in the hotel. His tone changes. The taximan says, 'another sixpence, Pat.' They call you Pat.")[42] In addition, Beckett's beloved uncle Boss, who was half-Jewish, felt sufficiently threatened by Nazi actions to leave Germany in 1933.

The details that follow were all plentifully recorded in the London Times and other newspapers and magazines and would have been available to Beckett in London, as they had been in Dublin. Attention focused not only on major national and international events but also on the unique totalitarian programs implemented by the Nazi state and the mounting persecution of the Jews. Although the information is well known, I ask the reader to imagine the response of someone with Beckett's sensibility — not just to the plight of the London poor but also to the vulnerability of victims across the world.

Hitler had become chancellor of Germany on January 30, 1933, and

CANADA'S BURDEN OF DEBT

MR. BENNETT'S PLAN FOR CONVERSION

PROPOSED LOAN COUNCIL

FROM OUR OWN CORRESPONDENT

OTTAWA, SEPT. 10

Mr. Bennett, the Prime Minister, in his second broadcast speech last night, dealt with the debt problem. Although phenomenal progress towards recovery had been made during the last two years, he said he could not see any real promise of permanent security until the awful burden of national debts was lightened.

It was the intention of Canada to pay all her obligations as long as possible, Mr. Bennett said, but even if direct taxation was increased—as he forecast—the question was whether the Dominion resources were great enough to meet domestic and foreign obligations, or whether there was in prospect a measure of business improvement which would help the Canadian people to carry an unreduced burden of debt without breaking their backs.

Creditor and debtor alike would agree that it would be "unwise, unprofitable, unpatriotic, and profligate to continue bearing a burden which might finally wreck us." The Government therefore had no alternative but to face the duty of undertaking a comprehensive revision of the whole national debt structure. The Government would invite the Canadian people to convert their holdings in Dominion, Provincial, municipal, and railway stocks at substantially lower rates of interest. There would be no more tax-free bond issues. Mr. Bennett explained that his plan contemplated the creation of a National Loan Council to supervise the refunding operations. The co-operation of the Provinces and the municipalities would be enlisted.

RELATIONS WITH U.S.

Turning to Canadian relations with the United States, Mr. Bennett hinted that with the present increase in the external debt a favourable trade balance with all other countries would be sufficient to enable the Dominion to meet her obligations to the United States unless Canadian exports to that country increased. The United States could not eat its Canadian cake and have it. He had high hopes that a desirable readjustment of trade relations with the United States would soon be achieved, but if the United States Government did not open their doors wider to Canadian exports it would not affect the honouring of Canada's pledge about her debt obligations.

The last part of Mr. Bennett's address dealt with the problems of unemployment and social security, and after discussing various phases of them he reiterated his 1930 declaration that he would end unemployment, and said, "I make it as sincerely now as I did then."

As one step towards this objective the Government accepted the principle that workers over 60 years of age should be withdrawn from the labour market, which would mean the retirement of 126,000 workers during the first year. This plan would be supplemented by auxiliary schemes for absorbing the unemployed by public works, afforestation, and housing schemes. Mr. Bennett also promised the extension of the benefits of the Farmer Creditors Arrangements Act to urban house owners, and declared that the action of educating and training boys and girls whose parents through unemployment were unable to train them properly would be tackled if his Government were returned.

FEDERAL LOAN FOR ALBERTA

SEPARATE SCHOOLS FOR JEWS

NEW GERMAN DECREE

FROM OUR OWN CORRESPONDENT

BERLIN, SEPT. 10

Herr Rust, the Minister of Education, has issued a decree designed to bring about "as complete a racial separation as possible" in German schools of all kinds from the school year 1936. Jewish elementary schools are to be established wherever there are enough Jewish children to make it possible. A minimum of 20 in a district is laid down as a guiding rule.

The decree, the full text of which has not yet been published, was issued by the Minister at a Press conference to-day.

The expert claimed that by signing it the Minister was taking actively in hand the fulfilment of an old National-Socialist demand. "Our aim," he said, "is the complete elimination of Jewry from German life; it is ineradicably clear and has already been carried out in various spheres by the officials' and hereditary farm legislation, &c."

Much, it is stated, has already been done by setting up special Jewish public and private schools for non-Aryan children belonging to the Jewish religion." But this is not enough. The fundamental point is not membership of the Jewish confession, but of the Jewish race." The racially foreign Jewish child is a foreign body in the class community of Aryan school children and teachers. His presence proves an extraordinary impediment in German-conscious National-Socialist instruction and renders impossible the necessary harmony, founded on race, between teacher, scholar, and the material of instruction."

Even in the higher schools, despite the limitation of admission under the first National-Socialist school law of 1933, Herr Rust finds that there is still a disproportionately high percentage of Jewish children of both classes, especially in big cities, and he proposes to take steps to remedy this state of affairs. In the new Jewish schools he intends to collect together all schoolboys and schoolgirls with either one or two Jewish parents. The so-called quarter-Jews, with only one Jewish grandparent, are to be exempted from the racial separation arrangement.

The President of the Reich Press Chamber has forbidden the public exposure and the sale of newspapers and periodicals which "entirely or in part, according to the title or the content, are addressed to the Jewish population." The Reich organizations of the German wholesale and retail newsagents are commissioned to supervise the execution of the ordinance.

This is the latest of the series of measures by means of which the Reich Chamber of Culture and its subordinate organizations have sought to banish "Non-Aryans" from even the farthest outskirts of "culture" and deprive them of their livelihood.

PUBLIC AND PRIVATE HOSPITALS

PRESIDENTIAL ADDRESS AT B.M.A.

FROM OUR CORRESPONDENT

MELBOURNE, SEPT. 10

In his presidential address at the British Medical Association's annual meeting to-day Sir James Barrett, of Melbourne, dealt with the hospital systems of Victoria, New Zealand, and Britain. He said that if hospitals were nationalized the medical profession inevitably would be

NAZI RALLY AT NUREMBERG

HERR HITLER AND HIS FORCES

A SPECTACULAR REVIEW

FROM OUR SPECIAL CORRESPONDENT

NUREMBERG, SEPT. 10

The seventh Nazi Party rally began at Nuremberg to-day. The same excellent weather which attended the last two national gatherings of the party ushered in this year's rally, and bright sunshine lit up the old city walls, which have been profusely decorated with swastika flags and garlands of fir branches.

Herr Hitler arrived this evening by air from Munich and drove through the streets, attended by his deputy, Herr Hess, General Göring, Dr. Goebbels, and other Nazi leaders. Although the crowds which cheered the Führer as he drove past were large, as yet only the vanguard of the vast Nazi army which the rally will mobilize has arrived, although contingents are reaching the town each hour, and thousands of the Labour Corps will be arriving in special trains throughout the night.

At the opening ceremony of the congress in the Town Hall, Herr Liebel, the Mayor, presented Herr Hitler with an imitation of the Imperial Sword, the possession of which had been for centuries the boast and pride of Nuremberg. In a brief reply, Herr Hitler thanked Nuremberg for the gift, expressing his appreciation of the efforts of the town to supply a dignified setting to the national congresses of the Nazi movement.

One noticeable characteristic of this year's rally is the great increase in the number of black uniformed special guards (S.S.). Altogether it is stated that the S.S. will number 20,000; About 13,000 of the special guards were employed to-day in lining the streets through which Herr Hitler passed and in forming cordons at the end of those streets immediately surrounding his hotel.

In an address to the German and foreign Press representatives this afternoon, Dr. Dietrich, the chief of the Reich Press Organization, described the foreign policy of the Nazi Party.

National Socialism he said puts forward the policy of co-operation between free and sovereign States with equal rights instead of the policy of the so-called collectivity of the victor States in the shadow of Versailles. The Geneva policy of an endless succession of ineffectual mammoth conferences which manage to keep in existence only by means of adjournments and procrastinations is one for which we wish to substitute the principle of direct negotiation between State and State, with immediate practical results, as in the case of the German-Polish treaty of friendship and the Anglo-German Naval Agreement. To the method of secret diplomacy we oppose the policy of frank speech and equality of negotiation between sovereign States. To the policy of the formation of blocs, the development of pact systems, and threatening military alliances in the form of pacts of mutual assistance, which only promise conflicts, we oppose the principle of pacts of non-aggression, the localization of conflicts, and thus the isolation of contestants, which increases the responsibility of statesmen in the interests of peace. Against the catchword of the indivisibility of peace we establish the practical peace policy of isolating war by removing in good time the essentials for war.

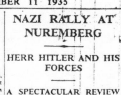

Nazi mass rallies and anti-Semitic policies received extensive news coverage.
(© Times Newspapers Limited, 1935)

formed his Nazi cabinet, which included Goebbels, Goering, and Himmler. The Reichstag was mysteriously set on fire in February, which was denounced as a communist plot, whereupon a slow-witted Dutchman was
"found guilty" and immediately decapitated. The London Times reported the
event both at the time and on the front page of its "Year in Review" issue as
the moment the Weimar Constitution ceased to exist. The occasion allowed
Hitler the opportunity, as the reporter put it, to "suspend" all the "articles of
the constitution referring to personal liberty, right of assembly, privacy . . .
and communications" (January 1, 1934). Hitler immediately established a
four-year plan to abolish unemployment, and he outlawed, among other
things, all other political parties, trade unions, free speech, and the free
press—in short, all civil liberties.

The first step to ensure Aryan superiority was a national boycott of Jewish goods and Jews in the professions. Planned as a "dress rehearsal for the
permanent boycott of Jews," the Times reported it as "completely effective"
(April 3). Hitler's overt goal was not to exterminate the Jews but simply to
harrass, humiliate, and ultimately expel them. An official department was
established to implement Jewish emigration, although the first concentration camps were built at Dachau, Oranienburg, Brandenburg, and elsewhere.
Numerous issues of the Times described the beatings and other cruelties in-
flicted in the camps. The newspaper soon began excerpting Mein Kampf, concluding its first installment with Hitler's statement: "With Jews there is no
bargaining—there is merely the hard, 'Either-or.' "[43]

Goebbels staged his first student book burning in 1933. Twenty thousand
"decadent, subversive or non-German" works by Jews and non-Nazis were
destroyed at Berlin University. The ceremony was repeated at universities
throughout the country. The Times detailed how in Berlin "20,000 'Marxist,'
pacifist, Jewish or other un-German books" were ritualistically destroyed
in the Opera Place. After each was set aflame—including books by Mann,
Heine, Marx, Freud, Arnold and Stefan Zweig, Schnitzler, and Remarque
(along with "writers such as . . . Ernest Hemingway and Jack London")—students were "shepherded" to the microphone, where they "recited an appropriate couplet," concluding with the chant " 'I consign to flames the writer
————.' " The article announced a new list of books compiled for libraries,
bookshops, and the general public on the themes of "Nordic Racial Purity"
and "Romanticizing War" (May 11, 1933).

At the end of the year, the German minister of education avowed that no
Jews had been admitted to German universities and that German Jews would
be banned from the 1936 Olympics. In addition, four hundred thousand
Germans were to be sterilized for hereditary defects. These "Nazi Eugenics"
were reported as follows: in the "400,000 cases [to be dealt with] . . . it was

explained that the Government was determined to stamp out heredity disease as the first step in its population problem" (January 9, 1934).

The London press also covered the menacing events transpiring in the rest of the world: Japan's occupation of northern China; Japan's and Germany's withdrawal from the League of Nations; and the terrible situation in the USSR, where starvation reached record levels. Anti-Nazi demonstrations occurred in Paris, New York, Buenos Aires, and Palestine. In London, on July 20, and again at the end of the year, thirty thousand people protested against Hitler's policies; here, as elsewhere in the world, many argued for economic boycotts.[44] Every response was significant, including de Valera's indictment of the fascists and Ireland's subsequent repeal of an import tax on matzohs to alleviate hardship for poor Jews.

Hitler had begun 1934 with a "blessing" to his nation. As cited in the *Times*, he said: "Remain firm and determined, faithful, and . . . disciplined. Know no other aim than to make Germany once again happy and therefore free, no other aim than to restore honour to the millions of our compatriots" (January 2, 1934). The *Times*'s retrospective provided these details:

> The brutal persecution of pacifists, Communists, political opponents, and the 600,000 German Jews was . . . defended on the ground that . . . these people had weakened Germany. . . . The nation must become racially self-conscious, politically and spiritually united, and turn its back on the political traditions of Western Europe. . . . In every branch of activity, interference and persecution were rife. The killing and maiming of political opponents, the filling of concentration camps, the settling of private feuds, went on . . . [with] little strife. . . . Democratic procedure had everywhere given way to the "leadership" principle. . . . The elimination of non-Nazi and Jewish elements was well underway. . . . The work of the "Enlightenment" goes on in the able hands of Dr. Goebbels . . . who has virtual control of the press, wireless, theatre, and film. Political unification having been achieved, nothing now stands in the way of the creation of a German education on the principles of its leaders. Some indication of the nature of those principles was given by extracts from his book *Mein Kampf* published in the *Times*. (January 2, 1934)

The year 1934 was marked by numerous Nazi bloodbaths, including the assassination of storm trooper Ernst Roehm and seventy-seven of his followers (who bore additional allegations of homosexuality). Roehm had been the leader of the Brownshirts, but his growing power and popularity threatened Hitler. After the murders of Roehm and his alleged traitor-colleagues, Hitler solidified his control within the party and Germany. The *Times*'s report of the German citizenry's response to the deaths was as troubling as the event itself: "The reaction in Munich . . . is one of uniform satisfaction.

[The event] seems to have acted as a lubricant in the cramped relations between one German citizen and another. German people in cafes and tram cars talked more freely than they have done for the last fifteen months, and in Munich at least the Chancellor seems to have won more whole-hearted supporters this week-end than he did during the last year" (July 2, 1934).

The Nazis continued their control of the arts. In 1933, they had banned Negro and Jewish music, condemned modern art (Gleichgeschäft), and closed the Bauhaus, after which thousands of artists emigrated (including Bruno Walter, Schoenberg, Klee, Kandinsky, and Mies van der Rohe). In 1934, the exodus of the film industry began, with Fritz Lang, Billy Wilder, Fred Zinnemann, and Douglas Sirk. Benjamin Franklin's speech from the Constitutional Convention was rewritten: "If immigration of Jews hadn't been restricted, Jews would have ruined the country." Even the Bible was rewritten: the psalms were revised, with nasty references to Jews; the Jewish prophets were replaced by Germanic leaders.[45] On July 10, the Daily Mail, England's largest daily, published an editorial in support of such policies.

Fascist fever was spreading. Italy and Ethiopia clashed at the Somali border. Mussolini tightened his control of the country's economic life. Anti-Jewish demonstrations took place in Lithuania. Arab pogroms began in Algeria; "green-shirt" activity emerged in Belgium. Father Coughlin organized the antidemocratic National Union for Social Justice in the United States. The Japanese continued their depredations in China.

Hitler continued to give interviews and invite reporters to his mass rallies. He even made a racial appeal to the British, via the Daily Mail: "Germanic nations such as ours ought to be friends by sheer force of natural instinct. The Nazi movement would regard war between Germany and England as a racial crime" (August 6, 1934). Yet Nazi propaganda released in Britain, as in the other democracies of the world, was immediately assailed; strikes and demonstrations continued, and German imports were banned. Churchill persistently warned Parliament about the German air menace.

Hitler's rhetoric dominated the news, as though he were determined to have the fiery incantation of his megalomaniacal designs take hold of the international, as well as the German spirit. When other nations came under his sway, their leaders pursued the same verbal and then physical tactics in elevating the "chosen" and humiliating the "defectives." As the Times reported, Hitler attributed his successful, "spiritual revolution" — "a miracle" he called it — to the "self-sacrifice" of his superior leaders. The New Germany was being "rescued by . . . their faith in National-Socialism." The old Germany had been governed by "pernicious . . . types who mocked heroism, beauty, belief, strength and health" — by Marxists and Jews who had "created a misalliance of capitalism and communism that nearly ruined Germany"

(January 31, 1934). Hitler also made speeches specifically to women during 1934, indicting female emancipation as a Jewish invention and insisting that a German woman's highest reponsibility lay in caring for her husband and children.

In 1935 the Saar basin south of Luxembourg (part of prewar Germany which had been turned over to France during the peace settlement) voted ten-to-one for reunion with Germany. Seeking to strengthen his position against France and Britain, Hitler blatantly denounced the Treaty of Versailles and its disarmament terms. To pacify Anthony Eden and others, he vowed not to expand his navy to a size larger than 35 percent of the Royal Navy, and this merely to protect Germany from communist Russia. But he then announced further conscription and established the Luftwaffe, appointing Goering Minister for Air.

Hitler's "racial purity" policies (often referred to as "ghetto legislation" by the Times) dominated the international news pages: "German fellow-countrymen! Do you know that the Jew violates your child, ravishes your wife, ravishes your sister, ravishes your betrothed, murders your parents . . . that Jewish physicians murder you slowly?" (August 16, 1935). The Nuremberg laws explicitly defined Jewish identity, deprived Jews of their German citizenship, and made intercourse between Jews and Aryans a capital offense. Himmler started the Lebensborn (life source) state breeding program. Young women of pure Aryan blood were encouraged to mate with SS officers for a future Nordic dynasty of blue-eyed, narrow-lipped blonds. In 1935, ten thousand German children, Hitlerjugend (Hitler youth), took a formal oath "to eternally hate the Jews."

In 1936, without military opposition, Hitler blatantly violated the Locarno Treaty by entering the demilitarized zone of the Rhineland. In the face of Germany's domestic and foreign policy, international participation in the Berlin Olympics served to legitimize Hitler's policies. The Times gave elaborate coverage to the magnificent Olympics and vividly described how, emblazoned within a circle of enormous swastika flags, Hitler ascended "to the dais from which Caesar was to accept the salutes of the athletes of 50 nations." One article was headlined "Olive Branch for Herr Hitler" (August 3).

Encouraged by their successes, Hitler and Mussolini, who was fresh from his own triumph over Ethiopia, met during the year. In accord regarding foreign policy, they formed the Rome-Berlin "axis"—to be joined later by Japan. Totalitarianism was on the upswing. Stalin escalated his purges; Franco and Mola led the army against the Spanish Republic. Headlines of the Spanish Civil War replaced German news for about two weeks in July. As the Times reported (July 18, 1936), because "direct news from Spain is sub-

AFTER HERR HITLER HAD REPUDIATED THE LOCARNO TREATY: FLOWERS FOR GERMAN TROOPS ENTERING DÜSSELDORF, IN THE DEMILITARIZED RHINELAND ZONE, AS "SYMBOLS" OF EQUALITY OF RIGHT.

Rhinelanders welcoming Nazi troops. Hitler invited foreign correspondents to cover his successes, and newspapers detailed his rise in power. (*Illustrated London News* Picture Library) ject to censorship, the political issues fueling the Spanish Civil War remain unclear." Articles detailed how both sides committed mass murders and acts of terrorism. "The Goth and the Vandal seem to have left abundant traces of their sojourn in Spain," wrote one reporter, adding prophetically: "Whatever the military outcome of the present struggle, ruthless dictatorship seems its inevitable consequence" (July 29).

The Jewish refugee problem in Jerusalem remained: Should the state be partitioned and what should be done with those who had "illegally" settled there? As the British considered allowing German Jews into Palestine, the Arabs delivered an order demanding an end to Jewish immigration, organized their first attack on British troops in Palestine, and instituted massive raiding and looting of Jewish and British buildings—after which the British declared martial law.[46] Anti-British riots then occurred in Egypt and Zanzibar. At the end of the year, an anti-Semitic party formed in Rumania. Ecuador was one of very few countries still offering land to the Jews.

Hitler's rallies provided the most vivid images of his messianic powers. Here he would counter the "degenerate" modern spirit by cultivating the superior German soul. Hundreds of thousands, bearing sacred torches, could chant in unison their devotion to their omnipotent leader. If "degenerate" artists had foolish notions about modern alienation (or what Jules Romains had called "atomization"), one could come here and relinquish any "struggle in the deserts of individualism." Here was one answer to the moral and socioeconomic disorder of the decades following World War I.

Notwithstanding the extensive reportage of world events, most people in England were preoccupied with the overwhelming shortages of food, rent money, and jobs. Pacifism and isolationism were underscored by the "Buy Britain" and "Support Britain" slogans that extended from the new tariff walls to popular new plays reinforcing "The Empire" (the title of a popular Hilaire Belloc play).

In early 1934 Beckett became a patient of Wilfred Bion, M.D., a Kleinian analyst from the Tavistock Clinic and specialist in paranoia and depression; Bion is today also considered an expert in group behavior and the collective mental life, although his psychoanalytic practice at the time consisted of shepherding patients through various stages of dream experience to self-knowledge.

To a man of Beckett's background, interests, and personality (including his superstitiousness), working with Bion must have seemed fortuitous. In addition to having the surname of the Greek pastoral poet (which happened to begin, like Beckett's, with the letter B), Bion was also of Huguenot descent, an outstanding athlete (particularly in swimming and rugby), and a quasi-exile. He had been born in India, transplanted to England as a child, and, despite wide travel, had never returned to India. He was also a strikingly handsome man with a bent toward philosophy and language and, like many of Beckett's friends, was said to be "a powerful and colourful personality who deeply affected all those who came into contact with him."[47] Bion had also spent a great deal of time with the philosopher H. J. Paton, the author of numerous works on Kant, justice, reason, perception, and time.[48] Bion's texts are sprinkled with references to Kant.

Deeply disillusioned over World War I, Bion had written an autobiography, The Long Week-End, 1897–1919, which concentrated on his youth and demoralization as a soldier.[49] (Nevertheless, like Beckett after World War II, he was decorated for his bravery, receiving the Distinguished Service Order and Légion d'Honneur.) Like Freud, Bion wrote several clinical works in an autobiographical style, and published more than a dozen books, some on group therapy, others on his unique method of psychoanalysis. During his long career in London, he became chairman of the Tavistock Clinic, as well as director of the London Clinic of Psychoanalysis and president of the British Psychoanalytic Society. Tavistock during his tenure was closely associated with Anna Freud, Ernest Jones, Melanie Klein (Bion's analyst), John Richman, and D. W. Winnicott, and it was here that Beckett heard Jung speak about the fragmented nature of the self.

Although Beckett had reservations about his analysis, he wrote McGreevy about his profound hope that it would help him.[50] Bion's main goal in analysis was to assist his patients in moving from what he called the "alpha" to the "omega" stage — the point of "Onement" or "O" — perhaps the origin of the o in "Godot."[51] The process was a probing of self aimed at personal integration — rather than cure. As Bion explained, analysis was self-revelatory. "Cure or improvement," he wrote, is both "irrelevant and undesirable." "Onement" involved a journey to the ineffable, absolute reality and unity of the fragmented self. Because it was a religious or mystical experience, one's knowledge of O could barely be translated into language. As various commentators have remarked, Bion was undoubtedly influenced by his childhood years in India: his use of terms like "omniscience" and "omnipotence" at the stage of Onement suggests an affinity with the nirvana of Buddhism, the wish for "absolute unification," a sense of the "fullness of the void" (or the womb?).[52]

Although this kind of mysticism recalls Jung, Bion's practical goal (his patients' "integration"), as well as his methods of analysis, was closer to Freud's. For both, dream analysis was essential, but memory and desire were alien to the process of discovery. Conscious or ordinary memory, as a by-product of sense experience, was inappropriate to the unconscious — that is,

THE GRID

	Defini-tory Hypo-theses 1	ψ 2	Nota-tion 3	Atten-tion 4	Inquiry 5	Action 6	... n.
A β-elements	A1	A2				A6	
B α-elements	B1	B2	B3	B4	B5	B6	... Bn
C Dream Thoughts Dreams, Myths	C1	C2	C3	C4	C5	C6	... Cn
D Pre-conception	D1	D2	D3	D4	D5	D6	... Dn
E Conception	E1	E2	E3	E4	E5	E6	... En
F Concept	F1	F2	F3	F4	F5	F6	... Fn
G Scientific Deductive System		G2					
H Algebraic Calculus							

Beckett's psychoanalyst, Wilfred Bion, created a "grid" that demonstrated the therapeutic stages to "O," or "Onement," the journey to ineffable unity of the fragmented self. (Jason Aronson, Inc. Mark Peterson on behalf of the estate of Wilfred R. Bion)

anxiety/emotion cannot be touched or smelled, nor is it a color. In addition, like memory, desire is an observing and confining tool. Unlike Freud, however, Bion believed that the analyst was as much affected by the patient-therapist transference as the patient. Both parties, he believed, should dispense with remembered details in their mutual effort to sustain an environment of faith.

As a part of Bion's therapy, and included in most of his books, was what he called his "grid"—an elaborate notational chart which indicated the various therapeutic stages one might take toward the O state. *A*, or alpha, for example, indicated when patients set aside memory in the gestation of dream formation; B, or beta, indicated their inability to use A properly, for in unsuccessfully dealing with memory and sense impressions, they might be led to feelings of persecution.[53] K indicated the words or analogies artists or great leaders might speak at having attained the O stage. (Bion regarded Jesus's words as metaphors to be concretized by Christianity, ultimately an innovative way of propagating a new integration of the self with the universe.)

Bion also supported many of Freud's specific clinical findings. He agreed, for example, that the language of the unconscious or of dream experience was the everyday speech of schizophrenics—that schizophrenics live in a continual dream state.[54] He also worked through Freud's tentativeness toward the life and death instinct in *Civilization and Its Discontents*, an idea similarly pursued by Melanie Klein and other Tavistock practitioners.[55]

Bion, however, challenged Freud's findings on group behavior by modifying Melanie Klein's theories; he spent a great part of his career questioning whether individuals in groups react primarily through emotion or intellect. Specifically, he challenged whether group responses were modeled on each participant's early family interactions (as Freud had suggested) or whether they were drawn from deeper, unconscious *individual* psychic needs. Bion also focused on verbal commmunication in groups—especially the displacement of emotion onto symbolic language in situations like panic. Just as ordinary language was inadequate in projecting the O state, it could only be symbolic in communicating a group member's response to communal stimuli.[56] Bion's focus on the deficiencies of language undoubtedly had an impact on Beckett.

Bion's prose—filled with highly erudite literary, historical, and Biblical references—also resonates with the paradoxes and refinements of his own thinking. He writes, for example, about the genesis of self-autonomy: "Traditions . . . in the [group] members . . . will determine their relations to one another, [which] approximates Plato's view that group harmony must be based on individual function." But, he adds, this "also has affinities with St. Augustine's view, in the 19th Book of *The City of God* . . . that a right relationship with [one's] fellows can only be achieved [when one] has regulated his relationship with God."[57]

What is of further interest here, given Beckett's college interest in the Unanimistes, is Bion's additional focus on what Jung called the collective unconscious. Jouve and the Unanimistes had assumed the existence of the collective unconscious, and they spoke of instinctual communication among group members. Romains went so far as to connect the unconscious with a pre-existing moral sensibility. (Pilling indicates that in 1934, Beckett was still thinking and writing about Romains.)[58] One wonders how Beckett's work with Bion affected his ideas about the Unanimistes and the collective unconscious: specifically, in the light of the emerging totalitarian history of the thirties, whether Beckett challenged Romains's inherent belief in "men of good will." Romains did, all the same, make clear that "spontaneity of the individual" remained imperative, which necessarily encouraged a "certain amount of anarchy as indispensible in order to avoid the demonical mechanism of society and to preserve the 'unanimous' life."[59]

In all likelihood, by 1933, Beckett had read Freud and Jung; both had published in the little French magazines during the 1920s. Harvey verifies that Beckett was familiar with Freud by at least the early 1930s, when he visited his friend Geoffrey Thompson's training hospital, and Pilling writes that during this time Beckett was reading everything he could get his hands on.[60] In 1935, Beckett attended the Tavistock lecture where Jung described the healthy unconscious as an unknown collection of fragmented selves to which the artist gives form in fictional characters. Jung also described the anatomy of unconscious process, again in healthy people, and how it expands or asserts itself in normal thought function through increasingly lightened circles of energy. The deepest part of the unconscious, the collective unconscious, occupies the darkest, smallest circle, he said. Schizophrenics, who function continuously in unconscious thought process, live, so to speak, in the realm of darkness. Beckett might well have been intrigued by the similarities of Bion's concept, with its light and dark metaphors, and the more mystical images of Dante, Plato, Schopenhauer, and Leibniz. When Beckett, years later, spoke of his own creative moments as mysterious and unconscious, he probably had Bion (the A stage), Jung, and even the Surrealists in mind. So too, his comment (in a review of Jack B. Yeats's poetry) "All poetry is prayer" would not have been alien to Jung or Jolas. *Murphy* seems an early example of Beckett's integration of Jung's and Bion's ideas.

Beckett lived in a furnished flat on Paultons Square in Chelsea before moving to 34 Gertrude Street. His Irish landlady, if Bair is accurate, was a "mother on draught"; she made homemade jam and tea and also made her piano available to him. However, as Ben-Zvi also reports, this was one of Beckett's most difficult periods: "I am deteriorating now very rapidly," he said. "I am quite convinced . . . that at this rate it is only a matter of a few years before a hideous crisis." As Bair would have it, Beckett could barely function: he could not sleep and his psychosomatic symptoms were increasing. She also suggests that in the absence of religious faith and incapable of finding any belief structure or rationale for being, both of which McGreevy had urged, he had become increasingly solipsistic. Yet, by her own admission, Beckett continued to see new and old friends—McGreevy, Jack B. Yeats, A. J. Leventhal, and Sean Kavanaugh. He pursued his studies, reading Schopenhauer, Nietzsche, George Eliot, Jane Austen, and Ben Jonson. He also began reading the Italians Manzoni, Machiavelli, Varchi, and Giusti, as well as books on film. He published reviews, visited the London galleries, and was particularly interested in the English Surrealists. As Pilling reports, Beckett was "often in contact with the artists and writers connected with the great Surrealist Exhibit in 1936." [61] In addition, for a year he was an attendant at Geoffrey Thompson's Bethlehem Royal Hospital, a mental health facility for the well educated—an experience, MacGowran reports, "that influenced him very much." [62]

Given his experiences in Paris, it is not surprising that Beckett remained interested in the Surrealist movement, which had been visible in Britain since the 1920s.[63] In 1920, Louis Aragon and Philippe Soupault had published in Ezra Pound's Little Review, and, through 1926, Pound published many Dadaists and Surrealists, including Breton, Eluard, Aragon, Soupault, Picabia, Tristan Tzara, and Man Ray. The first two issues of Ford Madox Ford's short-lived Transatlantic Review included Soupault and René Crevel; later issues published Tzara and Aragon. In 1924, after Nancy Cunard had become associated with the Surrealists via her affair with Aragon, she decorated her apartment with paintings by de Chirico, Tanguy, and Picabia and, in her own way, advertised the group on both sides of the Channel.[64]

It was not until 1934, however, that the English Surrealists gained a significant following. Although a small magazine out of Cambridge called Experiment had already published bits and pieces of Surrealist ideology, the critics initially looked upon the movement as one of naive, romantic disregard for Freud and a lame excuse for politics and social rebellion. In fact, the English Surrealists' main concern, like that of their French counterparts, was to exalt the dream as a creative source. In this alone could the mind lose self-consciousness and the tension that intrudes between mind and matter. However, to Herbert Read, the Surrealists had a social goal as well. Art, he wrote, "is the desperate act of men . . . convinced of the rottenness of our civilization." As Balakian had said of the French, these artists believed that humanity's inner resources might transform the world. Theirs was a "philosophy," via Marx, Freud, and Hegel, to "successfully [at]tune" the inner and outer worlds for an appreciation of the infinite possibilities within the most modest of experiences. To gain victory over ordinary existence, as Balakian explains, an acceptance of the absurd was as integral as an acceptance of the absolute: each could gain true meaning only in terms of the other. Interaction of the self and world—and the subsequent creation of metaphor (à la

Bion?)—became a victory over existence, a pathway to a "foolproof" unity of the self in the universe. Surrealism could thus advance a "credo" of hope based on faith in the potential capacity of the human mind to synthesize every possible element of dream and material reality.[65]

Transition had also been available in London, along with This Quarter and many other French little magazines, but in 1933, public arguments over the exotic new Surreal forms began. Peter Quennell's essay in the influential New Statesman and Nation was followed by Giacometti's "Poem in Seven Spaces" in New Verse, which, along with contributions from Eluard, Arp, Kenneth Allott, and Philip O'Connor, placed New Verse at the forefront of the Surrealist publications.[66] When Salvador Dali held an exhibition at the beginning of 1934, he provoked another cycle of controversial reviews in New Statesman, the art magazine Apollo, and, predictably, Eliot's Criterion.

Debate began over the so-called autonomy of rational functioning and the power of the unconscious over reason. One essay by Hugh Sykes Davies (editor of the Cambridge Experiment) addressed a subject familiar to Beckett— "Homer and Vico" (in New Verse, April 1934). Davies discussed Vico's opposition to Cartesian reason for a multifaculty psychology; he addressed how the mind operates in discrete areas of sensation, imagination, and intellect. He then analyzed myth and the primitive aspects of language in Homer.

Herbert Read, at about the same time, was gaining support as a major spokesperson of Surrealism. He described the new movement as the search for the reconciliation of reason and romanticism, organic and abstract experience, and his language was clearly Freudian. "Art," he wrote, "derives its energy from the id [and] is given formal synthesis and unity by the ego."[67] He tackled issues of will, order, and personality; chaos, emotion, and character; he spoke of "superrealism" versus "surrealism" and "romanticism" versus "classicism." Art, he maintained, could aspire toward the dialectical synthesis of imagination and reality, of organic and abstract form. Art could be a true expression of Marxist materialism and Hegelian dialecticism— without the mystical element. Read maintained that Surrealism was not a new movement but part of the continuing English literary tradition.

The year 1935 marked the turning point. The first manifesto, by David Gascoyne, was announced in Cahiers d'Art.[68] It exalted Breton's automatism, along with the principles of historical materialism articulated by Marx, Engels, and Lenin. Art, like life, maintained Gascoyne, must oppose any doctrine that justified capitalism. In 1935, Davies's Surrealist novel Petron was published and was favorably reviewed by Herbert Read. The manifesto and novel stimulated a great deal of further debate. But Gascoyne's Short Survey of Surrealism (November 1935) officially launched the movement. Gascoyne also announced Breton and Eluard's London visit for the opening of the International Surrealist Exhibition on June 12, 1936 — a show, which, one must assume, Beckett attended.

120

The organizing force of the Surrealist Exhibition, which displayed more than four hundred works from an international group of artists, was Roland Penrose, the wealthy poet-painter friend of Breton, Ernst, and Eluard. Penrose invited Breton to open the New Burlington Gallery officially, and he and his wife hosted the affair, both attired in green. (She even had green hair.) Dylan Thomas walked from salon to salon, serving boiled string ("weak or strong"); a lithe Dali-esque woman also wandered through the rooms wearing a white satin gown, long black gloves, and a rose veil over her head. In one hand, she held a model of a human leg filled with roses; in the other, she carried a pork chop. There were poetry readings and lectures. The physical concretization of emotional states, illustrated by the Surrealists' behavior, as well as their art, would echo through Beckett's work — for example, Nell and Nagg's situation in literal garbage cans (Endgame), Winnie's burial to her neck in sand (Happy Days), and the fact that the action of How It Is takes place in the mud.

In his talk entitled "Biology and Surrealism," Davies likened Surrealism to a kind of ubiquitous psychoanalysis:

> Surrealism is not a new style of painting, nor a new theory of art. It is concerned primarily with the condition of the human race. We propose an extension of our control over territories hitherto uncontrolled — the kingdom of the irrational within ourselves. And our purpose is this. As long as the world of dream and phantasy remains buried in the breast of each one of us, hidden, unseen, not understood, so long is it a potential danger. It is a private world, and when it invades the conscious life of any man who knows nothing of its strange shapes and images, he is helpless against it. He imagines that he alone in the world suffers from such feelings and such dreams. . . . We wish to make this impossible. We wish to make this private world public. We are to know one another's dreams, and to put an end to human loneliness in the face of this universal human situation.

Despite such optimistic yearnings, Davies admitted: "Not even the Surrealists claim that the human condition is a curable disease." [69]

Responses to the show appeared throughout the London journals and newspapers. In all likelihood, Beckett knew some of the personalities of the movement — Gascoyne, Humphrey Jennings, Roger Roughton, and Paul Nash — and Herbert Read was an old friend. Beckett may even have spent time with Breton and some of the others when they visited London for the show.

The continuing debate over Freud's definition of creativity and the Surrealists' response to it may have influenced Beckett's own creative work. *The Ego and the Id* (1927), published both by Leonard and Virginia Woolf at the Hogarth Press and by Bion's Institute of Psycho-Analysis, defined art as a (neurotic) rearrangement of psychic forces, specifically those of the super-ego and id. Freud's definition provoked Read's heated response to what he viewed as Freud's moralism; for Read, art represented the highest state of human expressiveness. In *Art and Society* (1936), Read later argued that art was inspired as well as collective. To Read, the "romantic" individual gesture was transformed in art into a larger, generic statement of universal social worth and application. As Surrealist art captured the collective unconscious, it could lead only to general human betterment. This issue of creative activity and social action as the product of psychic freedom or repression stimulated many books, not just about art but about any number of human endeavors, including Edward Glover's popular *War, Sadism, and Pacifism* and Christopher Caudwell's *Illusion and Reality*, which took Freud to task by means of a Marxist criticism of literature. W. R. Fairbairn's *Psychological Basis of Surreal Aesthetics* went so far as to investigate the similarity of Freud's and the Surrealists' dream images in the light of Melanie Klein's work with children's art.

With so many of Beckett's friends and acquaintances interested in the unconscious life—not just the French and British Surrealists (including Breton, who trained as a psychiatrist during World War I) but also James Joyce and, of course, Bion—Beckett probably gave serious thought to what Freud called "the psychopathology of everyday life" and the power of unconscious motivation. In addition, by the end of his two-year analysis, Beckett was once again discussing the nature of mental functioning with his psychiatrist friend Geoffrey Thompson, as the two visited the wards together and observed the language and behavior of the mentally ill. Given Bion's emphasis on symbolic language and dream analysis, as well as Beckett's own reading of Freud and Jung (and his experiences with Lucia Joyce), Beckett may well have been studying (or absorbing) the dream speech of the institutionalized patients. His later work would incorporate the paralogical functioning of primary-process thought.

Beckett had already begun *Murphy*, and writing this novel—as well as his therapy, job, reviews, study of Italian and English literature, and the pursuit of his friendships—comprised only a part of his day-to-day activities. If one assumes, unlike Bair, that Beckett was not living in a state of solipsistic anguish, other pursuits might have interested him—many of them cultural and free of cost. Quite possibly, in addition, given Beckett's earlier interest in sports, he may have enjoyed London's many amateur matches in cricket, bowling, boxing, croquet, rugby, and swimming.[70]

Beckett probably attended some of London's rich theater and musical offerings; during his Trinity days he had frequented the Dublin theaters and since childhood had displayed an interest and talent in music. While it is unlikely that nationalistic or Leftist plays of the time would have interested him, their relegation to unconventional theaters—later the home of much of the avant-garde—might have intrigued him. The fact that many plays of the period were censored might also have piqued his interest. His own short story collection *More Pricks than Kicks* was banned in Ireland in 1934 because of its title. Plays about Charles Stewart Parnell and Oscar Wilde were among those censored for sexual content.

The London stage during the 1930s offered the standard fare of mysteries, comedies, and musicals, plays by Harley Granville-Barker, John Masefield, Laurence Housman, James Bridie, J. B. Priestley, Noel Coward, and George Bernard Shaw. Coward's sophisticated wit and emotional ennui remained popular for audiences seeking escape, although for others involved in the economic crisis, *Cavalcade's* (1932) unabashed nostalgia for bourgeois Edwardianism seemed irrelevant, if not impertinent. During 1932–33, Priestley was welcomed as a writer of more significant stature. His first play, *Dangerous Corner*, with the new actresses Flora Robson and Marie Ney (directed by Tyrone Guthrie), was even placed in the tradition of the great Ibsen. *Eden End* (with Ralph Richardson and Beatrix Lehmann) was later touted as Chekhovian (1934).

The year 1933 was remarkable in British theater history for other reasons—even for those not pursuing politics as the staple of their cultural diet or for those following the new or established playwrights. The poetic dramas of Auden and Isherwood presented exciting innovations in language, and Eliot's *Murder in the Cathedral* was a stunning achievement. The stage was also enriched by the many imports of O'Neill, André Obey, and Jean-Jacques Bernard. Works by Pirandello, who won the Nobel Prize in 1934, were also revived.

Many actors in London at this time—gifted performers of both tragedy and comedy—became twentieth-century legends: John Gielgud, Laurence Olivier, Ralph Richardson, Charles Laughton, Robert Donat, Flora Robson, Peggy Ashcroft, Gertrude Lawrence, Celia Johnson, Edith Evans, Cathleen Nesbitt, Michael Redgrave, Alec Guinness, Beatrice Lilly, Hermione Gingold, Gracie Fields, and Sir Harry Lauder. The expansion of radio broadcasting had also caused a revival of music hall variety.

The years 1933–34 were also pivotal in English stage history because of the new production and acting styles initiated for the most part by Gielgud, and then Olivier, who returned to the stage after Gielgud's highly success-ful *Hamlet*. In 1933–34, Gielgud played in and directed many extraordinary successes, some of which Beckett might have seen, including *The Seagull*, *Richard II*, and his esteemed *Hamlet*. In 1934–35, Gielgud produced an impor-tant *Romeo and Juliet*, where he and Olivier alternated as Romeo and Mercu-tio. Old-style romance and sword-and-dagger panache, uninspired diction, and self-conscious, feigned emotion were replaced by simpler staging and a focus on the text—on slower and clearer diction and attention to gesture and carriage. With the focus on elocution and the use of voice came an em-phasis on the spoken word.[71] Beckett's production notebooks bear witness to his meticulous concern with details of staging, gesture, and diction. The distinctly new styles of acting may have alerted him to new possibilities in the dramatic-lyric form.

After 1933, when Tyrone Guthrie succeeded Harcourt Williams as di-rector of the Old Vic, he hired actors from film and the West End, such as Charles Laughton, Flora Robson, and Maurice Evans. The producer Henry Cass, from 1934–36, instituted three-week runs, giving actors an opportu-nity to play a greater variety of roles. During 1934, Beckett could have seen Laughton in *The Tempest*, *Macbeth*, *The Importance of Being Earnest*, and *Love for Love*.[72]

The BBC broadcast theater on radio, and because programmers were un-able to find good, original radio plays, they focused on Shakespeare, as well as traditional and contemporary works. This new style of programming, in-cluding plays from abroad as well as from London, was also inaugurated during the 1933–34 season. Presentations at the end of 1933 included *Macbeth* (with Ralph Richardson and Martita Hunt), *Coriolanus* (with Sybil Thorndike and Leon Quartermaine), and *The Wild Duck* (with Elisabeth Bergner). Produc-tions during 1934 and 1935 were equally impressive.[73] For musical comedy and comic revivals, BBC stars included Gertrude Lawrence, Josephine Baker, Marion Harris, and Eddie Cantor. These early BBC radio dramas and come-dies may have influenced Beckett's own later radio plays.

Radio was also unmatched as a cultural resource. In 1933 the BBC in-stituted talk shows that treated subjects like the twelve-tone scale, the dis-covery of induced radioactivity, and Joyce's *Ulysses*. In the same year the BBC launched a new kind of history program, "Twenty Years Ago," which was widely acclaimed for its reconstruction of the circumstances leading to World War I.

During Beckett's stay in London the city hosted numerous important art exhibitions in addition to the Surrealist show. A number of Old Masters shows in 1934 featured Dutch and Flemish painters including Holbein, van

Eyck, and Rembrandt, many of whom Beckett already admired. And if, as O'Brien states, Beckett spent a great deal of time in the National Portrait Gallery, he may have seen the museum's new acquisitions in August 1934: Hals's *Lady with a Fan*, Bellini's much-awaited *Portrait of Muhammad I*, and Hogarth's *The Graham Children*. Perhaps owing to Roger Fry's death, there were a great many postimpressionist shows at the end of 1934 and during 1935.[74]

Beckett had always enjoyed films, and these abounded in London. The great success of Alexander Korda's *The Private Lives of Henry VIII* gave a new seriousness to British filmmaking and provided Hollywood with new competition. Lighter fare included films by many of Beckett's favorites—Laurel and Hardy, the Marx Brothers, Buster Keaton, and W. C. Fields. By 1934–35, the English were also importing a greater number of avant-garde films.[75]

Numerous English, French, and Irish magazines were also plentiful at the time, some with essays by Beckett's old friends. In issue 35 of *Transition* (capitalized by this time), for example, were the provocative topics "Mutation in Language" by Marcel Brion, Ivan Goll, Theo Rutra, Philippe Soupault, and Beckett's good friend Georges Pelorson and "Experiments in Language Mutation" by Michaux, Eugene Jolas, and Pelorson. "The Subobject" and "New Roads to Modern Sculpture," in the same issue, were accompanied by glossy photographs of unusually high quality of works by Arp, Boccioni, Brancusi, and others. Given the social rivalries in Paris during the late 1920s, "Testimony against Gertrude Stein," by Matisse, Tzara, Maria Jolas, Braque, and André Salmon, would probably have fascinated Beckett.[76]

Some of the important books published during Beckett's residence in England, which Beckett may have been reading (if, indeed, he was reading everything he could get his hands on), included works by Jung, Freud, Malraux, Bergson, Carnap, Cocteau, Orwell, Eliot, and Jaspers. *The Brown Book of the Hitler Terror* was a bestseller, and in 1935, Penguin published its first ten paperbacks, each priced at sixpence, making many worthy titles more affordable.

Beckett left London shortly before Christmas and returned to Dublin, where he renewed several friendships and visited with his family. Although he took on odd jobs like tutoring and spent a period of time reading at the Trinity College library, he determined to complete *Murphy*, his first published novel (1938)—a funny book about a jobless young Dublin man who moves to London (to the same area in which its author had just lived) and who quests for the total separation (and control) of mind from body. Murphy works in a mental institution, where he yearns for the patients' "self-immersed indifference to the contingencies of the contingent world." They seem to have reached a Jungian or Bion-like state of Onement that unites all fragments—the "silence of the universe," where "light and dark [do] not clash, nor alternate, nor fade nor lighten." Murphy, however, who suffers from heart, foot, and neck problems, remains tied to personal and amorous relationships and is incapable of freeing himself from time and place. Bound to the flux, commotion, and light of ordinary experience, he resubjects himself to the accidents of the physical world, which conclude with his ashes strewn on a barroom floor amid sawdust and cigarette butts.

SIX

Germany and Prewar Paris

Politics too is an art, perhaps the most elevated art and the
greatest that exists, and we—who give form to modern
German politics—feel ourselves like artists to whom has been
entrusted the high responsibility beginning with the brute
masses, of forming the solid and complete image of the
people. —JOSEPH GOEBBELS

Beckett made a short trip to Dublin after leaving
London and then prepared for a journey through Germany—primarily to
Hanover, Munich, Berlin, and Dresden, with additional stops in Lübeck,
Lüneburg, Halle, Weimar, Hamburg, Würzburg, Regensburg, Nuremberg,
Leipzig, and Brunswick.[1] Of Beckett's mental state during this trip, Bair remarks that he was entirely preoccupied with his health and his difficulties
in publishing Murphy. He traveled, she reports, in a state of indifference to
the political events around him: "It [was] almost as though Beckett moved
through a phantom country in which he was the only occupant, paintings
were the only objects and museums and galleries the only buildings." Yet
Bair contradicts her own conclusions regarding Beckett's passivity and self-
absorption. He "was surprisingly social," she writes, and he met a number of
important artists like Kirchner, Ernst Barlach, and Schmidt-Rottluff; he also
met several art historians and critics, like Axel Kaun and Will Grohmann.[2]

On this extended trip, Beckett had more direct access to the actual political situation—through old and new friends. He had many opportunities to
observe the Reich's abominable treatment of the Jews. During the time he
spent with Grohmann, for example, he would have witnessed the Nazi ban
on Jewish cultural activities. Grohmann, a highly respected art historian,
had been dismissed from his Zwinger Gallery curatorship in 1933. He had
published widely, and his essays on the Surrealists had appeared in journals
including Cahiers d'Art during Beckett's London years. Grohmann's scholarship
on Klee, Kandinsky, Kirchner, Henry Moore, Willi Baumeister, and Braque
remains important to this day.[3] During Beckett's visit, Grohmann graciously
escorted his guest to private collections of works by Cézanne, Léger, Archi-
penko, Munch, and Nolde; he even invited Beckett to view his own important collection. Beckett must have been deeply flattered by his hospitality,
while keenly aware of Grohmann's plight.

What is one to make of this trip? Bair's contention that Beckett chose Germany by "process of elimination" does not seem credible. Amsterdam and Copenhagen, she writes, were too expensive; Spain was embroiled in war; and Italy would have interested him only for its art. Paris was unthinkable because of Beckett's alienation from Joyce. Yet Bair even admits that during Beckett's brief return to Paris in 1932 before President Paul Doumer's assassination, he had "moved once again into Joyce's circle."[4] Even with this contradiction, if economic (let alone political) comfort were Beckett's primary goals, Germany would surely have been among the last places for him to visit.

More likely, Beckett may have felt compelled to come to terms with Germany as a nation. He had long felt a sense of affection toward the country: he had spent considerable time there with his family, the Sinclairs. He had also had been introduced to some of the century's greatest art there, and German had been part of his concentration at Trinity. Perhaps this trip was a necessary means of verifying the increasingly terrible reports he had read about the moral descent of the German citizenry. Perhaps he had to see with his own eyes the condition of the civilization he had studied and respected.

According to physician and literary critic Gottfried Büttner (a long-time friend of Beckett's), the trip was, in part, a continuation of Beckett's education. He had begun his intense scrutiny of German culture and language and had closely studied Hölderlin, Fontane, Morgenstern, and Trakl; in addition, he had read Matthias Claudius, Ringelnatz, and the nearly forgotten Eduard von Hartmann, "who opened the debate on the notion of the subconscious." Deeply interested in painting, Beckett continued his art education; it was "a pilgrimage from one gallery to another throughout old Germany."[5]

Beckett may also have been interested in the Germany of the Surrealists. As Anna Balakian explains, the Surrealists were Germanophiles during the 1920s and 1930s until Hitler came to power.[6] They had reintroduced German literature to the French, and Breton was thoroughly fascinated with the "marvelous" country that had given birth to and nurtured Kant, Hegel, Feuerbach, and Marx. Up through 1935, while expressing his "antipathy" for Hitler, Breton continued to praise German culture, saying the Surrealists were heirs of this tradition which, Balakian remarks, should really have been called "European," not "German." (Breton's anti-Nazi position was more than nominal: before the International Surrealist Exhibition in Paris in 1938, he expelled Dali from the group because of his support of Hitler.)[7] Hegel had, after all, expressed his belief in the inner unity of contradictory phenomena and defined knowledge as the linking of thought and object. The Surrealists had also sought unity among contradictions—of the self and world, the concrete and the abstract.

Considering both these possibilities—the trip as an exploration of German culture and German behavior—what Beckett may have come to observe was a society held in thrall by a false idol in whose name all manner of brutality was rationalized as sacred. As he traveled from museum to museum, he may have also seen the dangers of an ideological aesthetic. Hitler and Goebbels, both frustrated artists, used art as a political instrument (as the epigraph to this chapter suggests), as a reflection of and means toward racial superiority and domination. Perhaps Beckett's awareness of this played a role in his later fashioning a literary form that was largely free of concrete place, person, and partisan political ideology.

Finally, as Büttner also suggests, perhaps Beckett visited Germany in an attempt "to describe and, if such a thing is possible, to come to terms" with the "desolate age." Schopenhauer ("one of the few that really matter," said Beckett) might have provided him with a framework for understanding the terrible world around him. *The World as Will and Idea* might have accounted for the perverse use of power that now dominated German culture—a quality, as Büttner puts it, that Beckett recognized in human nature, not just in German society. Pozzo, in *Godot*, later illustrated "the debased will, perverted into the naked exercise of power," just as Lucky demonstrated "automated, 'deteriorated thinking.'" Both characters represented "the monsters lurking in each and every one of us." Thus, while later writing *Godot*, this "tyrannical ghost" may "well have emerged from the depths of [his] memories."[8]

Büttner says of his long correspondence with Beckett that the letters revealed "what transpired in Beckett's psyche" as "he was searching for himself as a writer." This journey—in its many facets—not only revealed the "cultural catastrophe of the rising Nazi leadership in Germany and of the Fascists in Italy" but also helped, as Büttner puts it, in Beckett's clarification of his "world view" and provided another "pathway" to his "innermost self." Beckett's itinerary included visits to several cemeteries (in one of which his cousin Peggy Sinclair may have been buried). These visits, Büttner continues, reinforced his sense of human transience; but they also affirmed the wisdom of the ages—the advice of the Italian Leopardi, for example, whom Beckett also frequently quoted—regarding the stoicism necessary to meet the gloom of experience. In sum, the German journey, Büttner concludes, contributed to Beckett's "hard-won equanimity" and "admirable mastery of the [desolate] conditio humana of modern times."[9] It was clearly preparatory for the tests that would follow involving his physical and creative ability to survive.

We have assumed that Beckett followed Hitler's rise to power through the London press. In addition, he might have read some of the émigrés' books on German persecution, like the popular Brown Book of the Hitler Terror. Once in Germany, however, with his developing fluency in the German language,[10] he would have learned a great deal from the many available newspapers. More than a hundred publications circulated to more than four million people, including the most popular, the anti-Semitic weekly Völkischer Beobachter (VB). As John Hohenberg reports, Goebbels openly celebrated journalism for reinforcing the "efficacy of the monstrous lie." By 1938, continues Hohenberg, Hitler had refined this medium as a "weapon of war," publishing frequent and unambiguous pronouncements that he would settle old scores from the inequitable Treaty of Versailles with buckets of blood.[11]

In 1937, moreover, for visitors and citizens alike, it was punishable to possess a newspaper from any of twenty specified countries.[12] Beckett, the traveler and recent journalist, would surely have been aware of this brazen control of the press — not only as exemplified in VB but in its illustrated version, Die Illustrierte Beobachter. He must have also found it extraordinary that Nazi leaders published their own papers — e.g., Goebbels's Der Angriff (The Attack), a tabloid daily; Goering's Die Essener National Zeitung; and Himmler's Das Schwarze Korps; even the Hitler Youth had its own paper, Die Hitlerjugend. Public events Beckett himself witnessed or heard about would also have left a clear image of the status quo. He might even have found himself near one of Hitler's rallies, where two hundred thousand people typically gathered.

As Beckett traveled from city to city, he would have observed the strict enforcement of the Nuremberg laws. In 1937, discriminatory measures were extended to the most ordinary areas of daily life. Jews were banned from all national institutions, places of entertainment, parks, public baths, and health resorts. Jewish employment offices and rotary clubs were closed, and all Jewish youth groups were disbanded; B'nai B'rith organizations were similarly banned, which automatically terminated their work in hospitals, orphanages, and rehabilitation centers. Jews were even forbidden to play music by Beethoven and Mozart at Jewish cultural events, and they were allowed to patronize only Jewish-owned bookstores, which could not sell Aryan works. Kindergarten teacher Elvira Bauer wrote a new and popular Mother Goose consisting of forty-two illustrated pages of brute-like Jews poisoning handsome Nordics. The book was called Trust Not the Fox by Field or Pond, Nor Any Jew upon His Bond.

Beckett would have received first-hand reports of these and other examples of Jewish persecution from many people — acquaintances made during earlier trips, his half-Jewish uncle Boss, and new acquaintances like Willi Grohmann. His awareness of the extent of previous Jewish assimilation in Germany — thousands had fought in World War I and were leading artists, scientists, and intellectuals—may have made the Nazi depredations as incredible to him as they were to the many German Jews who thought that this, too, would pass.

When Beckett left England, British sentiment toward Germany was complex and ambivalent, similar to that in many other countries. Support for "appeasement" or neutrality vied with sentiment for intervention. Hitler had been diabolical in playing both individuals and nations (for example, the French and British) against each other. The issues at stake were the support of Czechoslovakia and Spain versus one's own need to keep the peace.

As Beckett traveled through Germany, Hitler's intentions grew increasingly more obvious. Repudiating all World War I guilt, he demanded the return of all former German colonies and the cancellation of all reparation payments. More important, despite his repeated pledge, "Peace is our dearest treasure," he began increasing arms production and conscription. When he announced the actual pursuit of lebensraum—more "living space"—his intent to go to war was clear. The nation needed more room, and his targets were Czechoslovakia and Austria.

Two events of 1937 left an indelible mark on the public consciousness. The first involved a declaration Hitler made before eight hundred district leaders in which he verbally sealed his last will and testament. Since he long believed that longevity was not in his genetic makeup, he demanded that his goals be accomplished no later than 1943–45. His speech contained no subtleties regarding the Jewish solution: "What can I get away with and what can't I?" he began. "I don't say 'Fight,'. . . I say 'I will destroy you.' "As John Toland reports, Hitler's last words left "no doubt that he meant to . . . kill the Jews, [and they] were drowned out by a spontaneous mass scream of blood lust."[13] The second event involved the simultaneous exhibitions of what Hitler regarded as decadent and distinguished art. Both shows were designed to encourage a "cultural cleansing" that would "end . . . the artistic stultification of Germany" and prepare for "a new vigorous flowering of art." The official, approved art was to be shown at Munich's House of German Art, the first public building commissioned by the National Socialist government—a Greek-style temple construction designed by Paul Ludwig Troost. There, Hitler would commemorate his favorite painters and sculptors, like Adolf Ziegler. In fact, although a selections committee was organized to scrutinize the fifteen thousand works submitted for the show, Hitler was disappointed with the panel's choices and personally selected the more than six hundred works that were finally exhibited.[14] The show was intended to promote a racially pure, racially ennobling volkisch art—art by and for Germans; it displayed images of rustic family life, pastoral scenery, and healthy, strong Germans participating in the joy of life; there were also portraits of

Hitler and other high officials, and mythological subjects that idealized the Volk as descendants, in beauty and spirit, of the great Greek and natural past. (When Troost's widow became aware of Hitler's criteria for the show, she immediately withdrew from the selections committee.)

In contrast, the "Degenerate Art" show (*Entartete Kunst*), which would subsequently travel to thirteen cities in Germany and Austria, was so designated to exhibit the hideous and disgusting work of the so-called contemporary masters. Hitler described these images as of "deformed cripples and cretins, women that can only elicit revulsion, men who are nearer to animals than humans . . . [and] children who, were they alive, must be regarded as cursed. . . . And this, the horrible dilettantes in our midst dare to present as the art of our time." [15] Such art, and its proponents, were to be purged from German culture. The Cubists, Dadaists, and Expressionists were also part of a foreign elitist conspiracy inspired by international Jewry and Bolshevism.

As such, the "degenerate" show would expose such "dangerous criminals" as Nolde, Barlach, Feininger, Corinth, Klee, and Grosz, as well as the confiscated paintings of Cézanne, Braque, Matisse, van Gogh, and Picasso. When the exposition opened, nearly all of the works, by 112 artists, were hung haphazardly, many without frames, crowded into seven rooms. Handwritten labels indicated the price of each painting (to indicate the waste of taxpayer money), and large captions on the walls displayed the critical judgments of Hitler, Goebbels, and others. Many paintings had comments pasted on them like "German Peasants Looked at in the Yiddish Manner" or "Thus Did Sick Minds View Nature." [16] Although the show was further subdivided into Negro, Marxist, and Jewish art, the largest group, including Kokoschka and Schmidt-Rottluff, was labeled "insane." To Hitler's chagrin, the "degenerate" show attracted five times more visitors than the exhibition of approved art.

Other local events of 1937 that might have engaged Beckett's attention related to the church—if only because the subject had been covered thoroughly in the London *Times* since 1933. By 1935, Hitler's appointees, Ludwig Muller and then Hans Kerrel, had instituted a reign of terror to force German Protestants into the Nazi mold. Although dissenting clergymen had been arrested and many churches were closed, Karl Barth and the Confessional Church remained highly vocal opponents. In early 1937, however, Protestant resistance crystallized under Martin Niemöller, as he adamantly pursued his anti-Hitler public sermons; Niemöller was then arrested and sent to a concentration camp.

Hitler's attitude toward the Catholic church was equally sinister. He continued accusing the clergy of treason and based arrests and convictions on trumped-up charges of illicit and perverse sexual behavior. Mocking and often disgusting cartoons appeared in the press. In 1937, Pius XI's encyclical letter "With Burning Sorrow" was smuggled into Germany and read aloud both within and outside the churches. Hitler's response was rapid: he closed the Bavarian Catholic schools.

Perhaps sensing that war was imminent,[17] Beckett left Germany and returned briefly to London and Dublin. In Dublin he testified against Oliver St. John Gogarty, who had been charged with anti-Semitic defamation by Harry Sinclair, his uncle Boss's brother. In order to discredit Beckett's testimony, the (unsuccessful) defending attorney ridiculed Beckett as a "blasphemer" who lived in the decadent city of Paris and authored books with titles like Whoroscope and More Pricks than Kicks. Following the trial, Beckett began extensive research on Dr. Johnson for a play about Johnson and Mrs. Thrale entitled Human Wishes. That Beckett subsequently spoke of playwriting as a "release" or "entertainment" may be understandable in the light of these recent experiences. He also learned that on Herbert Read's recommendation (and after forty-two rejections), Murphy had been accepted for publication. In the fall of 1937, he moved to Paris, which became his permanent residence.

Once settled in Paris, Beckett renewed his friendship with Joyce. He also renewed his acquaintance with Peggy Guggenheim, who, in Out of This Century, describes her romantic "obsession" with this "strange creature" Samuel Beckett. Given Beckett's superstitiousness, one might wonder if her first name, Peggy, added to his attraction to her, because it was the same as his cousin Peggy Sinclair's. Her reflections include anecdotal recollections of their subsequent affair, as well as observations regarding Beckett's artistic interests.[18] Guggenheim owned, with Herbert Read, the Guggenheim Jeune gallery in London, where she eventually exhibited, at Beckett's urging, Jack B. Yeats and Geer van Velde. Beckett, still interested in the Surrealists, also translated the preface to the Cocteau catalogue for Guggenheim's Surrealist show in 1938.

Guggenheim describes Beckett as "tall and lanky" with "tremendous" eyes that "never looked at any object but instead always seemed far off." She calls him excessively polite, rather awkward, and modest about his appearance. Her "Oblomov," Beckett apparently acknowledged his resemblance to Goncharov's inactive hero, who also lacked the willpower to get out of bed. Guggenheim also describes his silences and alternating warmth and distance, his odd mixture of eccentricity and puritanism. He was stern, moralistic, and conscience-ridden, would not indulge in good food or go out to "the right places," and was prudish in private matters. She nevertheless once returned to the flat and found him engaged with another woman. After Guggenheim expressed her distress, Beckett replied that "making love without being in love was like taking coffee without brandy." Guggenheim naturally assumed that she was the brandy in Beckett's life. Guggenheim also mentions Beckett's lingering guilt over not being able to love Lucia Joyce.[19]

On the night of January 7, 1938, an event occurred that has often been associated with Beckett's portrayals of the unfathomability of life. He had been walking on the avenue d'Orléans when he was held up by a pimp named Prudent. After Beckett refused to accommodate the criminal, Prudent stabbed him in the chest, and the wound was nearly fatal. Beckett subsequently saw Prudent at official headquarters and asked his assailant why he had chosen him. When Prudent replied, "Je ne sais pas, monsieur," Beckett did not press charges. Given the nature of the world he had been witnessing, Beckett may have felt that he had no special entitlement to freedom from attack or that random aggression was less evil than state-organized crime. The words "I don't know, Sir," are spoken by Godot's messenger in regard to the just nature of Godot.

Joyce was deeply concerned about Beckett's condition throughout his hospitalization; he visited him regularly.[20] The episode may have brought the two even closer to one another than they were previously; in a sense, Joyce had not lost a second child. But a second event related to Beckett's two-week stay in the hospital was of additional, immense importance. He was visited regularly by Suzanne Deschevaux-Dumesnil, a pianist at the Paris Conservatoire. Suzanne later became Beckett's wife.

Once recovered, Beckett renewed several other friendships—with Alfred Péron, the Jolases, Soupault, Nino Frank, Nancy Cunard, Brian Coffey, and Alan Duncan, among others. In the fall of 1938, he moved into the seventh floor apartment at 6, rue des Favorites, which he would occupy until 1961. Here, he wrote some poems that were published after the war and began translating Murphy into French with Péron.[21] Until this point, if Bair is correct, he retained "an obsessive need to know all that was happening in London and Dublin."[22]

Throughout this time Beckett would have also followed the news of Germany, as well as the frightening events in the other totalitarian nations. Virtually until the Occupation, the French public was given daily reportage of the atrocities occurring in Germany and elsewhere.[23] Even the little magazines—from the Dublin Review to La Grande Revue—detailed the international situation. One issue of Revue de Paris, which certainly would have interested Beckett, contained an essay on Mussolini's mental instability, alongside one on James Joyce, written by Beckett's friend Georges Pelorson.[24]

In 1938–39, although half the French papers in circulation since 1920 had ceased publication, thirty-one continued to function. Most important in terms of national influence were Le Temps, "the serious paper of record";

Le Figaro, read by moderates; *La Croix*, by militant Catholics; *L'Intransigeant*, by nationalists; *L'Action Française*, by monarchists; and *L'Humanité*, by socialists. (*Le Monde* did not commence publication until after the war, when *Le Temps* was appropriated by Charles de Gaulle in order to continue what had been "one of Europe's best dailies through World War II.")[25] Although the Rightist "Big Four" (*Le Petit Journal*, *Le Matin*, *Le Journal*, and *Le Petit Parisien*) had, until 1939, reached four to five million people, Leftist papers now increased in circulation: *Le Populaire* (socialist), *L'Oeuvre* (radical), *L'Humanité*, and *Le Soir* (communist).

As the *Times* of London served as a guide to world events that would have come to Beckett's attention during his residence there, *Le Temps* reflects material available to those living in France in 1938 and 1939. France had been intensely and publicly committed to a strong national defense. Its Maginot Line, a series of underground fortresses containing armaments and sufficient food for 150,000 people to survive a one-year siege, stretched 125 miles from Belgium to the Swiss frontier. Military service was compulsory, and France's army was five million strong. Despite Hitler's overt pugnacity, France believed itself to be well protected. In addition, *Le Temps* reported that Hitler had confirmed the complete disinterest of Germany concerning Alsace and Lorraine (September 14, 1938).

Front-page news reports covered the Japanese capture of Canton and Hankow, Mussolini's incorporation of Libya as a part of Italy, Franco's assault on Catalonia, and the ongoing Soviet purges. Headlines called attention to Germany's internal aggression against its Jews and external threats against its neighbors.

As Nazi rhetoric shed most of its ideological fervor and Germany's military goals came to the fore, Hitler took complete and uncontested control of the armed forces. He began his expansion of the Aryans to the "pure races" of other Nordic countries. On March 12, German armies entered Vienna, and Hitler proclaimed Austria a province of the Third Reich. The French and British protested, but neither nation took countersteps. Then, initiating the most widely covered news of the year, Hitler demanded that a part of Czechoslovakia, the Sudetenland, be ceded to Germany because of its large German population (reported in "Le Discours du Chancelier Hitler," September 14, 1938). After suspenseful negotiations with Daladier, Chamberlain, and Mussolini at Munich, Hitler agreed to renounce further territorial demands in return for the Sudetenland. Chamberlain returned home with his prediction of "peace in our time," but debate over the policy of appeasement dominated the newspapers for several weeks. Concern over continued peace was heightened, since immediately after Munich, Hitler called up 750,000 men for military service.

In November 1938, anti-Jewish activities in Germany ("L'Action Anti-juive en Allemagne" was one headline in Le Temps) became increasingly brutal. The most violent anti-Semitic demonstration occurred after seventeen-year-old Herschel Grynszpan shot Nazi Secretary Ernst vom Rath at the German embassy in Paris. Grynszpan had acted in response to the violence his parents had suffered in Poland. Although Le Temps's headline reported Goebbels's claim that anti-Semitic responses were spontaneous ("Les Manifestations Antisémitiques Furent Spontenées," November 13, 1938), the report the day before made clear that the "massacre" of Kristallnacht was well planned: on November 9 (the date usually cited; actually it began at 2 A.M., November 10), 1,400 synagogues, homes, and businesses were destroyed by the shattering of glass windows (hence, the name). An estimated 25,000 to 30,000 Jews were arrested, and scores were killed or committed suicide. A fine of one billion marks was then imposed on the Jews for the damage incurred, which was subsequently paid by insurance companies. This depleted the remaining financial resources of the Jewish community.

135

Following worldwide condemnation of Kristallnacht, the problem of international responsibility for emigrating German Jews became acute. Le Temps's headline noted great debate in the assembly on the problem of the Jewish refugees ("Un Grand Débat aux communes sur le problème des réfugiés israélites," November 23, 1938). Representatives from the Federal Representation of German Jews at the Evian Conference in July had urged that countries open their borders. France replied that it had no more space for refugees; Britain, that it had no suitable territory for permanent resettlement of large foreign groups; and the United States, that its existing immigration quota permitted only 27,370 Jews from Austria and Germany. Only Denmark, the Netherlands, Chile, and Brazil opened their borders without qualification.[26] Most Jews now had great difficulty finding refuge, and many incidents similar to the following occurred. As Le Temps reported, the S. S. St. Louis had left Hamburg for Cuba on May 15 with about one thousand German Jews. But on arrival, the refugees were turned away and President Laredo ordered the immediate departure of the ship. Another article, published the same day, described the same treatment given a ship from France (June 3, 1939).

Anti-Semitism escalated in Rumania, Poland, Yugoslavia, Hungary, Czechoslovakia, Egypt, Morocco, South Africa, and Libya. Italy continued expelling Jews; Mexico began debates about the Jewish problem. Le Temps's regular column "La Situation Internationale" published brief items on these events.

After Hitler crossed the Czech border in March and took the rest of that nation (Bohemia and Moravia), he turned his sights to Poland. Britain and France had given protective assurances to the Poles, just as they

LE TROISIÈME REICH CONTRE LES JUIFS

Une vague de propagande antisémitique va déferler sur l'Allemagne

La disparition des magasins israélites

Le rappel de M. Dieckhoff en Allemagne

Manifestation à New-York devant le consulat allemand

Le cardinal Verdier contre le racisme et l'antisémitisme

The French press closely followed Nazi policies against the Jews. (*Le Temps*)

had concluded mutual aid treaties with Rumania, Greece, and Turkey. The Anti-Comintern Pact signed earlier by Germany, Italy, and Japan against the Soviet Union was renewed in April 1939, and Hungary and what had become Franco's Spain had added their names to the pledge. In August—contradicting its avowed hostility toward Germany—the USSR negotiated a seven-year trade agreement and a ten-year nonaggression pact with Germany. This not only assured each nation's special territorial interests but also obviated the Anti-Comintern Pact. Communists and antifascists in countries the world over were staggered by Moscow's and Germany's alliance. On September 1, 1939, at 5:30 A.M., and in a new kind of land and air assault—a *blitzkrieg*

Increased Nazi violence against the Jews was documented daily, as in this front-page article. (*Le Temps*)

or "lightning war"—Germany attacked Poland and later divided the nation with its new partner, the USSR, at the Oder-Neisse line.

On September 2, Sweden, Denmark, Norway, Finland, and Iceland declared neutrality. On September 3, Britain, France, Australia, and New Zealand declared war on Germany. On September 5, the United States (re)declared its neutrality; on September 6, South Africa declared war, and Egypt severed all relations with Germany. On September 10, the British sent an Expeditionary Force of 150,000 to France, and Canada declared war on Germany. On September 16, the Red Army invaded eastern Poland; on September 27, Warsaw surrendered; on November 30, Russia invaded Finland.

In April 1940, Hitler invaded Denmark and Norway (and installed Quisling as head of Norway); in May, he invaded Holland, Belgium, and Luxembourg. Chamberlain resigned, and Churchill's coalition government gained power. At Dunkirk, the Allies barely avoided complete defeat when 224,585 British and 112,546 French and Belgian troops were evacuated to England in small boats. Not long thereafter, the German blitzkrieg broke through the French defenses with an ease that stunned both the French and the Germans. Within a short period of time, the Nazis penetrated deeply into French territory. In the face of this situation, the French submitted to an armistice and partial German occupation.

Hitler's goals were no secret during the thirties—or the twenties, for that matter—when he gained a name for himself after his failed attempt to overthrow the government in 1923 and subsequently wrote Mein Kampf (My struggle). We know that Beckett carefully studied Mein Kampf in 1942. Under suspicion, Suzanne was once followed back to their apartment, but when the Gestapo saw the book on the table, with Beckett's copious annotations, they did not arrest her. However, the date when Beckett first read the book is unclear. The London Times had published excerpts in 1933, Le Temps, in 1938. Although Mein Kampf was written during Hitler's nine-month imprisonment following the unsuccessful putsch, his megalomaniacal belief in his own messianic powers and the manifest destiny of his Aryan nation were blatant earlier. His first public statements against Marxism and Jews were made as early as 1919, in "Marxerei" and in a declaration regarding the "Jewish menace." This "alien race," as he put it, had been perpetuated through a "thousand-years' incest," and its "activities had produced racial tuberculosis among nations." Germany's "final goal," he insisted, "must unquestionably be the removal (Entfernung) of the Jews as a whole." [27]

Hitler's distorted sense of social Darwinism had given him confidence that it was only "natural" that war exist between the spiritually, physically, and emotionally superior (Aryans) and their unemotional, immoral, and physically defective inferiors. To Hitler, his ideology stood in the vanguard of scientific truth—the survival of the fittest. As he wrote in Mein Kampf: "[It is the] will of Nature for a higher breeding of all life [where] the stronger must dominate and not blend with the weaker, thus sacrificing its own greatness." [28] Once having achieved domination, accomplished only through a kind of Darwinian struggle or war, the "superior" victor was entitled to whatever lebensraum it desired—whether this meant the smaller Poland, the larger Soviet Union, or, indeed, the entire globe.

Throughout the 1930s and early 1940s, Hitler's plan proceeded with fanatical impersonality: his disciples were merely expelling a subspecies, as one might eliminate vermin. Those under his command—"good" family people, who were kind to their spouses, children, and dogs—had, from the start, acted matter-of-factly—barring Jewish games, requiring that Jews wear the yellow Star of David, and, later, affixing a J on Jewish passports. As events escalated, Jews were again, matter-of-factly, placed in separate domiciles. They were deprived of their businesses, properties, art, and jewelry. Such efficient orders continued to be imposed on what finally became an entirely depersonalized population.

It is my contention that Beckett did follow the events of the "bad" thirties—not only in London but also in Germany and the rest of the world. Given his experiences during this terrible decade, he must have gained a sense of the extraordinary cruelties people are capable of imposing on one another—through passive indifference as well as active deeds. "Was I sleeping while the others suffered?" he asks in *Waiting for Godot*.

I believe that, with the world shattering, Beckett's understanding of his own life thus far deepened, and he gained a new perspective on the Ireland of his youth during and after the Uprising and Great War, England in the throes of a devastating depression, and Nazi Germany in the pursuit of an ideology of unimaginable inhumanity. I believe the thirties were instrumental in Beckett's understanding of the potential dark underside of human nature and the insurmountable forces that impinge upon innocence, elements of life's "tragic" dimension. Beckett may have thought, as Hamm says in *Endgame*, "You're on earth, there's no cure for that!"

Although Beckett obviously did not see the full extent of the Nazi atrocities, his journey through Germany and the subsequent world events reported in the French press provided him with images of incredible moral depredation. His first-hand experience of the Nazi regime must have been crucial in his swift decision to resist the German evil actively, rather than accept it passively, when Hitler moved his troops into Paris in June 1940. Perhaps he thought, as Vladimir says in *Godot*: "Let us not waste our time in idle discourse! . . . Let us do something, while we have the chance! It is not everyday that we are needed. . . . At this place, at this moment of time, all mankind is us, whether we like it or not. . . . Let us represent worthily for once the foul brood to which a cruel fate consigned us!" If a positive and restorative capacity in human nature could be found in courage and camaraderie, this "tragicomic" dimension of the human experience would crystallize in the years ahead. Beckett's *Waiting for Godot* became for the post–World War II era what Eliot's *Waste Land* was for the post–World War I generation.

France

When the war began in Europe, Beckett was visiting
his family in Foxrock. As a neutral alien, he could have remained in Ireland.
Instead, he rushed back to Paris and, in the fall of 1940, joined the Resistance. As he told Alan Simpson: "I was fighting against the Germans, who
were making life hell for my friends, and not for the French nation." [1] Alec
Reid remarks of Beckett's war activities: "[Beckett] took no active part in affairs until the Germans occupied Paris. . . . Then the war suddenly became
something personal and with meaning. Like Joyce, Beckett had many Jewish
friends and he was incensed by the constant humiliations and maltreatments
to which they were subjected. He was enraged too at the repeated shootings
by the Germans of innocent people taken as hostages. . . . He couldn't stand
with his arms folded." [2]

Beckett may have seemed apolitical in the traditional sense of the term, [3]
but he clearly had powerful convictions regarding his moral obligations to
others. While his comment to Simpson indicates that he considered friendship a sacred responsibility, Reid's remark makes clear that Beckett felt compelled to stand up for the "innocent"—friend or not. Taken together, the
two statements reveal Beckett's inviolable personal belief system: he would
not accept the evil imposition of suffering on others with his "arms folded,"
whatever the personal risk. Beckett's "politics" transcended national bound-
aries. Like Thomas McGreevy, he might also have defined human decency
by saying: "Every place in which there are human beings matters." In this
sense, Beckett looked upon all of suffering humanity as his "friend."

One must believe, for example, that Beckett was deeply affected by London's frequent hunger marches and the indifference and exploitation with

which the starving and the ill were treated. Like other thoughtful and courageous people of the time, he may now have questioned the behavior of the leaders of the free world. Were they not abdicating, in a cowardly manner, their moral responsibilities to their friends in Ethiopia, Czechoslovakia, Spain, and China, as well as the forsaken Jews in Germany—all in desperate need of assistance against the demonic fascists? Hitler had not only been virtually granted permission to dismember democratic Czechoslovakia, but he had publicly announced his intention to destroy all the Jews in Europe. Where were the world's decent people when the fleeing refugees approached border after border? Indeed, after the stunning Russian-German pact and the French capitulation, could one be certain about any nation's ability to stand up for moral justice? How many additional members of the international community would adorn themselves with blue, green, brown, or black shirts to save their own hides?

Beckett may have dismissed his World War II activities as "boy-scout stuff," a typically modest response, but he was one of very few to join the Resistance as early as 1940. So, too, when he later took refuge in Roussillon, rather than cower in hiding, he fought with the maquis. After the war he joined a civilian rescue unit in Saint-Lô. Not until 1946 was he ready to begin his own "siege in the room" (an interesting word choice), one of prolific creativity.

If, however, as I have been arguing, Beckett was aware of the totalitarianism engulfing the world, just as if he possessed an unequivocal sense of right and responsibility—and if he was not the fragile, fragmented man that he is often portrayed as being—then his World War II activities should not surprise us. Since childhood he had had a mature sense of justice and an enormous sensitivity to suffering. From his earliest youth (the civil war in Ireland, the Foxrock hospitals for World War I veterans, the Dublin street beggars and homes for the insane), to his early manhood (the racial riots in Belfast), through the "bad years" in England, and in his most recent travels in Germany, he had seen humanity in economic, physical, mental, and spiritual distress. Until his death, he was pained at the slightest manifestation of human suffering, and he was never free from the memory of those who perished during the war.

Parenthetically, disturbing aspects of human nature were pervasive among those who confronted Hitler and his maniacal campaign. From their inception in 1940 through 1943, the umbrella organizations that fought the common enemy—the British Special Operations Executive (SOE) and de Gaulle's Resistance groups—were rife with political and personal dissension. The Gaullists were a complex, sometimes opportunistic mélange of difficult personalities. The distrust between them and their leaders, and even between

Churchill and de Gaulle, illustrates how personal vanity can influence the best and most noble. So, too, in the village of Roussillon, where Beckett spent the last two and a half years of the war, many people were more concerned with social standing than with ideals of right and national honor. In some ways, the multifaceted strife in France (and in English politics) was not unlike the complex internecine political struggles in the Ireland of Beckett's youth.

Nevertheless, in the midst of this, to borrow from W. B. Yeats, "a terrible beauty" was "born." From the chaos of the times emerged steadfast and dedicated heroes, those with "hearts with one purpose alone." They gathered, first, as outlaws in clandestine groups but then grew into a force that ultimately helped save France. These were ordinary people, not trained soldiers, and, like the people Yeats immortalized in "Easter 1916," they were writers, aristocrats, schoolteachers—people from many walks of life—who exchanged comfortable lives for the resurrection of freedom. Beckett was one of them.

Deirdre Bair has provided the most detailed discussion thus far of Beckett's experiences during the war. Historical scholarship about the period, however, puts some of her material in question.[4] She says, for example, that Robert Alesch, posing as a priest, exposed Beckett's Gloria group in Paris, although her sources connect Alesch only to agents in Lyons.[5] She fails to regard the seriousness of the underground activities, characterizing the agents as gossipy social groups.[6] Finally, she creates an eccentric image of Roussillon and Beckett's life there, attributing her information to the cultural historian Laurence Wylie, who vehemently denies any responsibility for what he calls her "fictions."[7]

Bair's generalizations about Beckett the man are perhaps most disturbing. She concludes, for example, that Beckett's war experience was a "tragic but unavoidable waste" and that in Roussillon he suffered his most serious schizoid break.[8] Bair acknowledges as her source of information on mental illness R. D. Laing, a psychologist of distinctly marginal views who achieved cult popularity when she was writing her book.[9] For Beckett, Bair reports, this was a time of mental disintegration, when he was plagued with psychosomatic symptoms and engulfed with guilt about his possessive and absent mother.[10] Perhaps Bair's most troubling judgment is that, given Beckett's psychic fragmentation, the war was a kind of ghostly experience in which he never truly functioned. After the war, she writes, it was relegated to the back of his mind as a separate, "idealized" state, distinct from the pain of his alternate, private reality.[11]

I would strongly contend that World War II was not "an unavoidable waste" for Beckett, but rather a time of immense, if difficult, personal and creative discovery and consolidation. I would further argue that, in addition to his having long read about — and observed — the escalation of world suffering, several abiding personal factors make it understandable if not inevitable that Beckett would take an active stance against the Nazis.

Beckett had spent years of his life studying literature and philosophy, just as he had immersed himself in the art of the moderns and ancients. He had also undergone psychoanalysis and spent a great deal of time with those exploring conscious and unconscious behavior — Joyce, the Surrealists, and the Unanimistes. He had also read Freud and Jung. For long periods of time, he had been separated from his family and from the intellectual and cultural community in which he had found his place. He had lost a number of people whom he most deeply loved — his father, his cousin Peggy, his uncle Boss, and Paul Léon, and he would shortly lose Joyce.

As a man of exquisite feeling and introspection, and as a survivor, Beckett, I believe, by 1940 was able to balance all the above: art and life, experience and ideology. He had come to terms with whatever differences might have separated him from his family. In the long process of maturing — particularly difficult when dealing with a well-loved and loving family — he had survived the strain of gaining his own autonomy. He had developed close relationships with people who encouraged his independence and artistic pursuits; he had sought out those who shared his high sense of moral integrity. In so doing, he had renounced Foxrock's Victorian values of financial security and traditional marriage and family, while retaining its fundamental commitment to virtue.[12] The war and its immediate aftermath gave Beckett an opportunity to become his own person: to put into practice the moral ideals he had been studying — and thus to integrate the values of both his childhood and adulthood. The war was an opportunity to confront, not merely contemplate, matters of human will, moral choice, and good and evil. The war also enabled Beckett to engage in activities requiring the kind of courage of which his father and uncles would have been proud. It allowed Beckett an arena in which to activate those values which he had always deeply held. And if, in the passage of these terrible years, he despaired over the unjust deaths of friends and acquaintances, his activities allowed him to pursue a kind of justice for them.

Ultimately, fighting an enemy of uncontested and categorical evil enabled Beckett to respond to a pain that he had carried since childhood — the experience of Ireland's civil war, which introduced him at a very early age to the depths of human suffering, further examples of which he was to witness repeatedly in subsequent years. As he told more than one person, he never forgot the day in 1916 when he saw O'Connell Street in flames. Now, in 1940, he would witness another nation torn apart — the French fighting the French, just as in Ireland, twenty-five years earlier, he had seen kinsmen fighting kinsmen. Bair's view of Beckett contradicts the picture of him that we see when the maquis marched in victory through Roussillon: "There stood Beckett at the front of the procession, carrying the flag."[13] One can only imagine the pride and relief that prompted such a rare gesture of public display. But given the complexity of the times and the man, and the lessons he had learned about potential good and evil in human nature, he remained, thereafter, entirely modest about his wartime experiences. His nephew, Edward Beckett, reports that his uncle never spoke about the war other than in very general terms.[14] Although Beckett may never have discussed the specifics of his World War II activities, the work of eminent Resistance scholars like Henri Michel indicates that members of the various Resistance organizations had common experiences. Whether one belonged to a Free French, SOE, Polish, communist, or occupational group—and many people joined more than one group—each organization retained its autonomy while it shared similar goals, activities, and rules of survival with other groups.[15] Thus, while Beckett's Paris group Gloria was funded by SOE's Prosper, it acted as an "independent dominion" and its "manner of conducting business was [its] own."[16] The same kind of independence was true of Etoile, with which Beckett was also associated. What remains of interest here is their common mission and the daily threats and consolations they shared.

Days before the German conquest in 1940, Beckett joined in the mass exodus from Paris and went south to the Vichy and then Toulouse areas for four months. (This was the last time he saw Joyce; see chapter 3.) When he returned to Paris, and following the arrest of his Jewish friend Paul Léon (who was subsequently tortured to death), he joined Alfred Péron in the Resistance. At first Beckett collected information (sometimes in code) regarding German troop movements, which he deciphered, classified, and typed before it was smuggled out to London; later on, he transferred the information to microfilm. In August 1942, after one of Gloria's members was tortured into a confession, Péron was arrested and the rest of the group faced imminent exposure. (Only thirty of eighty finally survived.) At 11 A.M., on August 15—Assumption Day—Péron's wife sent Suzanne and Beckett a telegram: "Alfred arrêté par Gestapo. Prière faire nécessaire pour corriger l'erreur" (Alfred arrested by Gestapo. Please do everything necessary to correct the error). By 3 P.M., they were gone, traveling mostly on foot and at night toward Roussillon, in the unoccupied zone in southern France. Jack MacGowran speaks of Beckett in flight as a "key man" for whom Nazi bullets were marked.[17]

Once in Roussillon, Beckett engaged in clandestine activities including setting up contacts between Resistance workers and picking up, hiding, and delivering ammunition for the destruction of railroad yards involved in transporting German supplies. Following the war, Beckett was decorated by Charles de Gaulle with the Croix de Guerre—for his "distinguished non-combatant activities." Beckett's medal, with a silver star, indicates specific acts of bravery "in divisional despatch," suggesting an alignment with a fighting unit, such as the French Forces of the Interior, which had, by that time, amalgamated members of the SOE, Resistance, and maquis.[18] He also received the Medaille de la Résistance. To both these honors, he responded with typical reserve and humility. After the war and a brief visit to his family, he intended to return to Paris, but his plans were necessarily suspended because of new restrictions on aliens. The resourceful Beckett then secured work with the Red Cross in Saint-Lô and returned to Paris after four months. Once back at his apartment, he began the prodigious outpouring of work for which he was to achieve an international reputation.

On the afternoon of June 14, 1940, the Germans entered Paris. In triumph, they proclaimed "das tausendjähriges Reich": the Reich will last a thousand years. Swastikas were mounted on the Eiffel Tower and public buildings; posters were attached to the kiosks reading "Trust the German soldier." Newspapers like *Le Matin*, *L'Oeuvre*, *La Victoire*, and *Paris-Soir* printed Nazi propaganda, and new, entirely German-inspired papers appeared virtually overnight: *Aujourd'hui*, *Dernières Nouvelles de Paris*, *La France au Travail*, *Temps Nouveaux*.[19] The French army was pulverized; in only five weeks it had suffered the worst defeat in its history. An estimated 95,000 were dead, with 250,000 wounded; 1.5–2 million were prisoners of war.[20] Civilians (among them, Beckett), numbering between 3.5 and 6 million, had been leaving the Paris area since June 9; they did not return until October.

On June 16, after presenting a plan for union with Britain and the withdrawal of French forces to North Africa, Prime Minister Paul Reynaud was defeated by his own cabinet. Marshal Pétain, chief of the new government in the southern spa town of Vichy, was mandated to request an "honorable armistice" from Hitler. Pétain had the support of his vice president, Camille Chautemps, and cabinet—Maxime Weygand (minister of national defense), Paul Baudouin (foreign affairs), François Darlan (navy), and the brilliant anti-parliamentarian Pierre Laval (famous for his early declaration that parliamentary democracy had caused the war and must "give way to an authoritarian, hierarchical, national and social regime").[21] Laval insisted that Britain was the real enemy, whereas Germany and Italy were France's true friends: "[France has been] nothing but a toy in the hands of England who . . . exploited us to ensure her own safety."[22]

Pétain, the nearly eighty-five-year-old Verdun hero and France's father symbol, addressed the French "state": "We must try to put an end to the fighting. Tonight I have contacted the enemy to ask if they are prepared to join us, as honorable soldiers, in seeking . . . the means whereby hostilities will be terminated."[23] According to the armistice of June 22, France would be divided into two zones. The occupied zone (including Paris) would incorporate both the English Channel and Atlantic coast areas (two-thirds of France, including the richer land of the north, west, and east); the unoccupied area would include the central mountains and the Rhône Valley. Alsace and Lorraine would be incorporated into Germany.[24]

On July 10, in a vote of 569–80 (with eighteen abstentions), parliament voted to abdicate its powers and support the new, authoritarian Vichy government. Former Popular Front leader Léon Blum and former Prime Minister Edouard Daladier were imprisoned, and Reynaud and Edouard Herriot were placed under house arrest. The French would pay the four-million-franc daily costs of the occupation army, surrender their weapons, disarm the great naval fleet, and retain only one hundred thousand soldiers (the Armée de l'Armistice) for the purposes of maintaining order. French prisoners of war would remain in captivity until the end of the war (which most people equated with the signing of the armistice).

In Vichy, as well as in the occupied area, degrees of personal acquiescence and resistance, like degrees of collaboration or "attentistes" (those who advocated a wait-and-see stance), would remain topics for historical debate. U.S. President Franklin D. Roosevelt dealt amicably with Vichy through November 1942; the Canadians also maintained a legation at Vichy, and although Churchill was "privately and publicly short with Pétain," he kept in touch with him through a number of unofficial missions.[25] At the Allied landing in Normandy, nonetheless, Pétain called upon the French to remain neutral, and Laval went so far as to call the landing "an act of aggression."[26] As late as August 1944, Vichy officials urged the United States to act as an arbiter, rather than a liberator, in Europe.[27]

What was Pétain—a victim or scapegoat?—a clever strategist of a "double game" for the sake of French survival, or a turncoat who enjoyed unlimited, near theocratic power? At his trial on July 23, 1945, the man who had led France to victory in 1918 maintained: "I spent my life in the service of France [and] on the most tragic day of her history, France turned to me once again. . . . When I asked for the armistice . . . I performed an act of salvation, [contributing] to the victory of the Allies. My Government was legally formed . . . recognized by all the powers of the World from the Holy See to the USSR."[28] Pétain continued, "Humoring the enemy made me suffer more than you . . . keeping France alive, though in pain. *What good would it have been to liberate ruins and cemeteries?*" The now ninety-year-old Pétain concluded by reiterating the official position: the Pétainists had established the foundations not only for de Gaulle's victory but for a virtuous, more "moral" France that would link its grand past with an even better new world: "[We continued] to honor the family, to prevent the class struggle, [to] safeguard the conditions of work in industry and on the land, . . . [to represent] a tradition which is that of France and Christian civilization." [29]

Some argue that Pétain gathered around himself a whole underworld of anti-Semitic, antiparliamentary agitators from the 1930s—the most extreme of whom carved out for themselves high positions in the fields of law and order and propaganda. [30] To Robert O. Paxton, what seemed to be Vichy's initial neutrality as "effective mediator" in "an increasingly fanatical world" was in reality a regime that instituted Nazi policy on its own. [31] Susan Zuccotti argues that the Nazis could not have pursued their objectives without the enthusiastic cooperation of the French. [32]

Paxton describes the instability of Pétain's cabinet: "Ministries came and went at speeds even more dizzying than at the worst moments of the Third Republic." The result was that Pétain alone remained in place: his signature became law, and with a brutal police force at his command, he pursued the relentless inhibition of public response. Disregard for law and order led to threats of retaliation and, finally, to an unremitting "witch-hunt" for "subversives." [33]

In the clutches of defeat, on June 18, 1940, Charles de Gaulle spoke to a depleted and demoralized nation. De Gaulle was little known—a career officer only recently named undersecretary of state for war, a maverick preoccupied with modernizing military weaponry and strategy. But he was a man driven by what he often referred to as a romantic and mystical vision of France's glory, and he saw the military as an essential accompaniment in France's march toward its glorious destiny. De Gaulle viewed Pétain's request for an armistice as anathema. France, he pleaded, must continue the fight.

Regardless of de Gaulle's righteousness and towering inspiration, one must remember that his challenge to the established Vichy government only exacerbated his (and any followers') criminal status. It was thus virtually by sheer force of will that he, with his symbolic Cross of Lorraine, ultimately became leader of the Free French. In his speech on June 18, he demanded the ultimate sacrifice from his countrymen: "Has the last word been said? Should all hope be abandoned? Is our defeat final? No! . . . We shall . . . prevail. . . . [I] call upon French officers and enlisted men. . . . I call upon French engineers and workers. . . . No matter what happens, the Flame of French resistance must not and will not be extinguished." [34] De Gaulle's summons was a challenge to the Vichy government, but it was sounded to a nation psychologically and materially unprepared to respond. The most powerful fighting machine in Europe had been devastated, the impregnable Maginot

Line of steel and concrete rendered useless.[35] Paris had been occupied by its historic enemy, and, not to be underestimated, the French remained haunted by the memory of the 1.5 million who had been massacred in World War I.

During the first weeks of the Occupation, German soldiers tried to win the goodwill of the French. They were not particularly aggressive; they even ran soup kitchens for hungry children — although no Jewish children were served.[36] However, it was not long before food and gasoline disappeared, apartments were commandeered, and unemployment increased precipitously. By the end of September, Jews were required to identify themselves officially as such. Almost immediately thereafter, Vichy passed its own anti-Semitic *Statut des Juifs*, and Jews were barred from public office and the professions. In July — again on its own — Vichy had begun its restrictions on foreign-born Jews: since 1880, many had escaped Eastern European persecution and settled in southern France; their future safety was thus already in jeopardy. During the same month, Vichy also acceded to the German decree that all dissidents be interned.

To many, France as a nation appeared to be Pétainist, in the most negative sense of that term. To others, support of Pétain meant support of France's very survival. There may never be sufficient documentation to establish the ethical motives of much of the French citizenry. While some cast their lot clearly with democracy (the Resistance) or with fascism, among those who claimed to accept Pétain for the sake of unity, moral intention remains problematic.

On the one hand, as Alexander Werth argues, there was throughout France a pervasive sense of humiliation, helplessness, and weariness, which Werth and others tie to a paradoxical "feeling of inferiority" and "a solidly-established sense of superiority" that had long characterized the French. With the Occupation, the myth of France's invincibility was shattered, and there emerged the very real possibility that France as a nation would vanish. The armistice, on the other hand, in promising the French their "place in the world" — and national survival — brought Pétain a great, if naive, following.[37] As a mediating power, France might be the connecting link between America and Europe, and it would at the same time have a role with the Axis powers. This was essentially a dream of "neutral France stepping forward as the sole remaining arbiter among the exhausted giants."[38] Even André Gide admitted: "I should rather gladly put up with . . . a dictatorship, which is the only thing, I fear, which might save us from decomposition. Let me hasten to add that I am speaking here only of a French dictatorship."[39]

Finally, there are increasingly less compassionate explanations regarding the French population. M. R. D. Foot, for example, views the French as sheer opportunists, arguing that "collaboration with victorious Germany was positively popular." Zuccotti examines in detail Paxton's statement that "the new regime . . . enjoyed massive support and elite participation."[40] Regardless of one's opinion on these complicated issues, immediately after the Occupation, France was no longer a *République* (use of the word was forbidden even on stamps and coins), and it appeared to be becoming a subsidiary power in Hitler's New Order in Europe.[41] In many ways, Pétain was not unlike Hitler at the end of January 1933. Pétain also summarily dismissed representatives of the people (its deputies, senators) and in their place brought forth Hitler's "leadership principle"—power centralized in the very few (himself and his coterie). From July 1940 through November 1942, the authoritarian "state" was "restored in its sovereignty." Restrictions on personal freedom were also clearly defined. Individualism was denounced. Pétain declared: "This individualism which the people of France treated as a major privilege is at the root of the troubles from which we nearly died. . . . There is no creative virtue in individualism. . . . Individualism receives everything from society and gives nothing in return."[42]

149

The dreaded Milice—the French version of the German SS that has been compared to the Black and Tans who disgraced the British in Ireland—was created later.[43] The Comité des Amis de la Waffen SS would also form (first known as the French SS Volunteer Grenadier Regiment and later as the Charlemagne Brigade)—French volunteers between twenty and twenty-five years old. But as early as July 1940, youth camps were established, and by January 1941, Vichy decreed that all Frenchmen under twenty (boys as young as fifteen were accepted) spend eight months in a camp modeled on Hitler Youth organizations. There, in their French blue shirts, the young Companions of France practiced fascist salutes and bugle calls and underwent indoctrination into zealous patriotism.[44] A comparable group for girls was formed later, and membership reached an estimated 25,000–50,000 in 1942.[45] Pétain and his cronies were all supportive of Hitler. Many rationalized that they were only protecting France from a worse fate (total occupation or the deportation of all able men to Germany for conscription) and were working to give the nation an influential position in a German-controlled Europe. But for some of Pétain's men, there is little doubt regarding their strong fascistic leanings.[46] The extent of Vichy's role in the "Final Solution"—specifically, knowledge of that "solution" and its active implementation—similarly remains debatable. However, an increasing number of documents indicate that Pétain and his cohorts were directly responsible for the deportation of thousands of Jewish adults and children to the camps.[47]

In response to this indictment, others reply that Vichy never intended to destroy the Jews, even if they were placed in concentration camps, which existed in France as early as 1940. That is, just as Pétain first refused to demand that Jews wear the yellow star, he only "sequestered" Jews from the economic, cultural, and political life of France, as he put it, for their own good.[48]

In the months following Pétain's new assumption of power and de Gaulle's call for French resistance, very few rallied to de Gaulle. A military tribunal had, after all, sentenced him in absentia to death. Anyone who joined him would have been similarly condemned. Not until June 1941 was a sizable Resistance forming. Many historians say, as Paxton does, that "their number . . . was minuscule, and it was to grow smaller still during the first year," June 1940 to May 1941.[49] But other scholars, along with dozens of memoirs, survey the widespread opposition of ordinary citizens.[50] In July 1940, for example, at least nine organizations were printing anti-Nazi propaganda, including the communist paper L'Humanité, which distributed 140,000 copies and was published ten times a month (for which ninety people were arrested). Action groups began carrying out sabotage activities—mostly burning German vehicles and cutting telecommunications wires. Severe reprisals for such minor offenses as defacing German posters were instantaneous. Rewards, beginning at ten thousand francs, were offered for names of offenders, and fines on entire towns were imposed for "acts of provocation." The fledgling Resistance was taking shape.

In October 1940, the Paris police announced the arrest of 871 people and the seizure of thirty-five printing presses. In November, massive student protests began. Members of the Sorbonne faculty, including many Jews, were dismissed, and classes in the New Order were instituted. Physicist-professor Paul Langevin was arrested for contributing to what became a popular campus pamphlet attacking Vichy (Université libre). Protests followed both at the university and on the Champs-Elysées. The official response was printed in Travail: "Just when Marshal Pétain is clearly explaining the policy of Franco-German collaboration, rumors and cunning underhand agitation are current in the Latin Quarter where judeo-masonic influences have been at work for some time."[51]

Despite the most recent order that such demonstrations cease, an estimated three to ten thousand people, with hundreds of flowers and badges of red, blue, and white, gathered on Armistice Day at the Etoile and then decorated Clemenceau's monument. Shortly thereafter, German troops made more than 140 arrests and killed at least five students. Despite such reprisals, small, independent groups continued to sabotage factories (by pouring sand into machinery, setting oil tanks on fire, derailing railway cars, and cutting telephone and telegraph cables). Those who were caught were killed instantly. At the end of the year, the Nazis posted throughout Paris a large announcement in red letters of the execution of one Jacques Bonsergent, a young engineer who was shot in the place of a friend who, according to Simone de Beauvoir, had not "bowed his knee" to German authority:

Warning
Jacques Bonsergent, engineer of Paris, having been condemned to death by a German Military Tribunal for an act of violence against a member of the German Armed Forces, was executed by shooting this morning.[52]

Life throughout France was becoming increasingly repressive. To Pétain, the "cult of ease"—what he saw as its depraved habits of using birth control, drinking socially, and even listening to jazz—had caused the nation's fall. Pétain envisioned his mission as that of stemming such "unbridled individualism." The restoration of church power, traditional education, the large family, peasant unity, and corporatism became Pétain's steps toward the "Travail, Famille, [and] Patrie" of the National Revolution. Problems regarding moral education, debated even before the Third Republic, were now scrutinized in the universities throughout France. Graduates of Beckett's Ecole Normale Supérieure, like Jean Jaurès and Léon Blum (also students of philosophy and literature), had, after all, been so "negatively influential" in Third Republic politics that "Albert Thibaudet christened the regime since the Dreyfus Affair as 'the republic of professors.' "[53] Faculty were now subject to loyalty oaths and staff purges.

In the occupied area, the best way of dealing with the present "decadence" involved targeting Jews and communists, but this called for special organization. Although in the early days, there were no signs of Himmler's *Einsatzgruppen* (extermination teams) in Paris—and the German High Command was initially opposed to Gestapo units in the French capital—Himmler bypassed the German military and quickly set up a small Gestapo unit in the Hotel Lutétia, on the boulevard Raspail (Beckett's friend George Reavey's favorite stopping place until then). Led by SS Major Helmut Knochen, Ph.D., the unit recruited many French outlaws and criminals into its service, and the powers of the German army and police expanded. The two divisions of the police consisted of the *Ordnungspolizei* ("Orpo"), organized to maintain order, and the *Sicherheitspolizei* ("Sipo"), the security police. Within the next two years, France built its own "slow death camps," like Vernet and Gurs (described vividly in Arthur Koestler's *Scum of the Earth* and André Schwarz-Bart's *The Last of the Just*). But even at the time, Resistance forces reported of these camps: "[The] recourse to violence and medieval torture became the rule. . . . Slow death camps served both as jails and as places of extermination."[54]

The "purification" of the nation proceeded with prodigious speed. The citizenship of more than 15,000 French citizens naturalized since 1927 was revoked (6,500 of them Jewish exiles from Germany).[55] Following Vichy's edict that all Jews declare themselves, identity cards were stamped "Juif." Anti-Jewish demonstrations were also whipped up in cities throughout the country. By the end of 1941, businesses were displaying black and yellow cards warning "Jüdisches Geschäft" (Jewish Enterprise); factories had fired Jews and foreigners, and most Jews were excluded from the civil and military services, the professions, and businesses. Jewish property, from land to artworks, was confiscated. In March 1941, Darlan appointed a very efficient central officer for Jewish affairs, Xavier Vallat, famous for his banter with an SS officer: "I am an older anti-Semite than you. I could be your father in these matters."[56] Resistance activities continued, nevertheless. Although workers were forbidden to strike, the French communist party organized one hundred thousand people in a two-week strike in northern France. Acts of sabotage proliferated.

General Hans Speidel, Hitler's Paris overseer, reported 54 Resistance activities in July 1941; 73 in August; 134 in September; and 162 in October; assassinations of German soldiers were becoming more frequent, and German retaliations—mostly against Jews or communists—were becoming more severe. Also in July, the first mass arrests occurred in Paris (of 3,600 Poles), with additional arrests of "foreigners" the next month. The October execution of German officers at Nantes and Bordeaux resulted in the massive retaliative shooting of random batches of prisoners. Pétain then made his famous announcement: "We have laid down our arms. We have no right to take them up to stab the Germans in the back." The next day, however, all over France, a five-minute strike honored the "martyrs." London, without effect, ordered that there be no further attacks on the German military.

In the fall of 1941, the Soviet Union, now at war with Germany recognized the Free French as the official government of France, which brought even larger numbers of communists into the Resistance. The British also recognized de Gaulle as the leader of the French government on September 23, 1941, and, on the following day, the Germans imposed a million-franc fine on Paris—a penalty for the five-minute "martyr" strike. In December, a week after the Japanese attack on Pearl Harbor, one hundred Jews were executed in Paris, one hundred "notable" Jews were arrested, and a billion-franc fine was imposed on the occupied zone.

The large-scale deportation of Jews in February 1942, which brought massive protests and reprisals, was shocking not only in its reality but in the diabolical strategies by which the Germans captured the Jews. The General Union of Israelites, for example, masqueraded as an emergency mutual aid program. Jews seeking assistance went to the Union, left their names, and were then picked up by the police.[57] The year 1942 was indeed a time of *Nacht und Nebel* (night and fog), the phrase coined by the German authorities for what became their dark and repulsive activities. By the end of the year, there were massive concentration camp internments in both northern and southern France.

At the beginning of May, SS Chief Reinhard Heydrich arrived in Paris, and SS Colonel Karl Oberg was appointed head of the police. The summer of 1942 was a grave turning point in the treatment of Jews, as Laval gained more power, and Pétain intensified Vichy's collaboration with the Nazis. The notorious racist Darquier de Pellepoix also became Commissar-General of Jewish Questions. Two days after Rommel's offensive in Libya, the Germans decreed that Jews (all wearing the yellow star) were forbidden to enter public buildings like libraries, movie theaters, and restaurants. Those who protested (or forgot) were executed. On June 1, Eichmann proclaimed the "Final Solution"—to be implemented throughout Europe—and 100,000 Jews were deported to Auschwitz from both French zones. In July and August 1942, Vichy deported 30,000.

After the middle of July, when de Gaulle's committee became France Combatante, activities against Jews escalated even further. Terrible raids in Paris and the suburbs occurred on July 16: all "foreign, stateless" Jews were arrested by the French police (with the cooperation of French authorities). Single persons without children were shipped to "primary centers" or local concentration camps like Drancy, three miles northeast of Paris; families with children (often separated from one another) were placed on city buses for Vélodrome d'Hiver ("Vel d'Hiv"), the sports arena south of the Eiffel Tower, where they were held for several days before being sent to their doom at Auschwitz. In all, 12,884 were arrested, including 4,051 children. By the summer of 1942, an estimated 26,000 Jews were similarly arrested.[58] Concentration camps in the south—for example, Saint-Paul d'Eyjeaux—looked like Drancy, Pithiviers, and other camps in the occupied area, with gray wooden barracks, high barbed-wire fences, and armed guards in watchtowers. By the summer of 1942, an estimated 26,000 Jews were incarcerated in French concentration camps in the unoccupied zone alone—again, for the crime of being Jews (for the sin of "being born," as Beckett evokes the human tragedy in *Godot* and Proust).

The first U.S. Air Force bombing of Germany occurred on July 29, 1942. The same day, the French and German police signed an agreement officially "harmonizing" their activities.[59] The Brigades Spéciales worked with the Gestapo in tracking down communists. On August 8, Vichy implemented the new "relève" proclamation, by promising 350,000 French workers to Germany; 120 protested and were executed. Because the work of the saboteurs had also increased, the "Oberg" proclamation declared that reprisals would now extend to the children and relatives of all terrorists. For the general population, a law, ironically entitled *Judenbeguenstigung* (Be kind to Jews), was in full effect. Lending a hand to Jews, in any way, was punishable by death.

> "*Dubito ergo sum.* I doubt, therefore I survive," the golden rule of the Resistance.
> —M. R. D. FOOT

By August 1942, Resistance groups were growing and lessons in clandestine warfare were in the making; Beckett had been in the Resistance since October 1940. The unique complexion of these groups—their specific responsibilities and accomplishments, and clear definition of who had to account to whom—remains unclear. Of the major movements, there were de Gaulle's Free French, organized in London and later called the Fighting French, the French communist party and Polish groups, and, later in the war, the maquis—the guerrilla units that organized in the mountains frequently to escape German conscription. The SOE—Churchill's organization, which he called the "Ministry of Ungentlemanly Warfare"—was of enormous significance in providing money, arms, supplies, and training facilities to de Gaulle's organization, as it developed its own elaborate underground operation. The larger mission of the SOE was to oversee all underground activities in the occupied nations. In addition, many clandestine groups formed within France which were unaffiliated with larger movements: some were Gaullists, some were not. Collections of religious people, students, peasants, teachers, factory workers, railwaymen, farmers, clergy, bankers, lawyers, doctors, and even debutantes and prostitutes—regardless of their politics— fought with a common honor and fierce dedication to destroy the enemy. This was to be a war of resisters—of ordinary people—as well as of armed forces. And ultimately it was these brave people who played a major role in recovering the French pride and integrity that had been forfeited during the German conquest.

Of those who volunteered during these early and lonely days, only a handful became part of France's oral or published history. At the time, nevertheless, events like the execution of Jacques Bonsergent (see above) might have been discussed (or witnessed) by any Parisian, including Beckett. Recalling Beckett's remark that he joined in the fight because he could not tolerate the brutality he had witnessed, I wonder if certain events might have recalled to him the courage of the Easter 1916 heroes. One occasion involved Etienne d'Orves ("Honoré"), a man of no particular fame or literary or oratorical talent, who, after being arrested, said to his fellow prisoners: "I have assumed full and total responsibility for everything we have done. I say I was the one who persuaded all of you to join my network. But when you are interrogated, conduct yourselves in a manner worthy of Frenchmen. Remember that you have had the honor of fighting for France. . . . A few of us will die. That is inevitable. May God allow us to die honorably! Good night, my friends, courage, and may God help you!"[60] Facing a firing squad, d'Orves and his men refused to be blindfolded or to have their hands tied; they stood at attention and prayed for their families and France. There are many erudite explanations as to why Beckett erased the specifics of time and place, as well as of person, in his work, but a simple explanation presents itself in the courage he witnessed in the seemingly most "ordinary" of humankind.

M. R. D. Foot attributes the inspiration of the Resistance throughout Europe (he defines "Resistance" as any group's struggle to be free of an occupying power) to a person still "within living memory": Michael Collins, military chief of the IRA during the troubles of 1916–1922. "The greatest resistance leader of the twentieth century" according to Foot, Collins understood the tactics of "irregular" warfare and the basic grammar of sabotage. "Irish resistance, as Collins led it," Foot continues, "showed the rest of the world an economical way to fight wars, the only sane way they can be fought in the age of [the] bomb." What Collins accomplished in Dublin, he goes on, "had a noticeable impact [on] British secret service method[s] . . . through two of [Collins's] junior but intelligent opponents, J. C. F. Holland and C. McV. Gubbins. . . . Both [men] saw the advantages, in economy of life and effectiveness of effort, of the Irish guerrilla they could not stem. And both determined that next time, if there had to be a next time, guerrillas should be used by the British instead of against them." Foot concludes that "Ireland from 1916 to 1921 was in a position . . . comparable to that of, say, France . . . during part at least of the war of 1939–1945, [and] the Irish movement for national independence was comparable to the . . . struggles of the French, the Dutch, the Yugoslavs, the Norwegians, the Poles, and so on." Foot even compares Collins and de Gaulle's great agent, Jean Moulin: "There were in fact similarities, sometimes close ones, between what Collins was doing and what—to take three disparate resisters to Hitler—Tito, Jean Moulin, and Bor-Komorowski were trying to do [in terms of] efforts and methods."[61] Although Foot admits that not many Europeans would have heard of Collins (and thus associated the French and Irish situations), Beckett could have done so.

A survey of these early Resistance activities must include the now-celebrated Musée de l'Homme group (the counterpart of Combat in the south). This group was not just the first to use de Gaulle's term résistance, but its membership included Alfred Péron, Beckett's close friend who involved him with the SOE-related Gloria movement. (Péron had by now spent time in the military, as a liaison officer with the British Eighth Army Corps.) A collection of ethnologists, professors, lawyers, librarians, and even Dominican priests, this "National Committee of Public Safety" (Résistance) was organized by Boris Vildé and Anatole Levitzky and met at the Palais de Chaillot. In the first issue of its clandestine newspaper, *Résistance* (December 15, 1940), it declared: "Resist! That is the cry that comes from the hearts of all of you, and the anguish caused by our country's disaster. It is the cry of all who are not recognized. . . . Unknown to one another . . . none of us has ever before participated in the quarrels of prewar political parties. . . . We are completely independent . . . and nothing else. We have but a single ambition, one passion, one desire: to restore an undefiled and Free France."[62] In February 1941, the organization was exposed by a German double agent, and, over the next few months, sixteen members were shot, six were decapitated, and others were deported and imprisoned. Although this particular group consisted mainly of friends, it would be followed by any variety of others—some collections of friends, others of strangers—all of which became the networks, or *réseaux*, of the organized Resistance.

Foot, in his landmark study of the SOE, places Beckett in one of the circuits loosely connected with the Prosper group. As Foot explains, these small circuits looked to Prosper's leaders, François Suttill and Armel Guerne, for "arms and money but not . . . orders." He continues: "They had enough of the fundamentals of clandestine work to keep to themselves," so that dealing with the leaders "through couriers and cut-outs, they were less prey for the Gestapo." He also notes, that "Some of Guerne's intellectuals, like Samuel Beckett," had the "intelligence and the security sense" to lie low. Elsewhere, Foot describes how Guerne (a Melville translator), second in command to Suttill (a poet), met regularly with the resisters at a black market restaurant near the Arc de Triomphe and at a café near Sacre-Coeur. Here they carefully enacted business—and sometimes played cards—despite the presence of Nazi waiters.[63]

Historians have immortalized the leading figures of the major resistance groups, although, as Foot puts it: "The full tale of French resistance is an epic, a Homeric study that still awaits its Homer."[64] André Dewavrin ("Colonel Passy") became the chief of de Gaulle's secret service, and Pierre de Vomécourt became "Lucas," the first secret agent of the F (French) section of the British SOE. De Vomécourt was connected with Beckett's group, as were Suttill and Guerne, who formed all the Paris groups connected with Prosper. Henri Frenay and Marcel Chevance, who met in Marseilles, also pledged themselves to the fight, and they organized Vérité, which joined with the Combat group in the unoccupied zone. Similarly, from Cannes came Corniglion-Molinier and Emmanuel d'Astier de la Vigerie, who later formed La Dernière Colonne, which eventually joined with Libération. Gilbert Renault-Roulier ("Rémy") ultimately founded the Confrérie de

Notre-Dame. Other relatively early contacts were made by Christian Pineau, Robert LaCoste, Pierre Brossolette, as well as Claude Bourdet, Robert de Menthon, Paul-Henri Teitgen, Georges Bidault, Rémy Roure, René Capitant, and Georges Loustaunau Lacau ("Navarre"), whose three thousand members of Alliance were known by the names of birds and beasts. (The Germans called Alliance "Noah's Ark.")[65] Details of these groups' early organization reveal how unskilled these future heroes were in the mechanics of secret warfare. Some of de Gaulle's earliest agents, for instance, who had adopted names of Paris metro stops (Maurice Duclos—not to be confused with the communist leader Jacques Duclos—was "Saint-Jacques"; Beresnikoff, "Corvisart"; Lagier, "Bienvenue"), were supposed to retain the initial of their real name. That they forgot to do so caused considerable confusion among their colleagues.[66]

Some people mentioned above had rallied to de Gaulle in London, when, with Churchill's support, he formed the Free French Committee on August 7, 1940. De Gaulle's initial hope was to organize a voluntary French force of naval, land, and air resources and employ whatever scientific and technical personnel he could collect. With Britain's support, the French would fight the "common enemy." "France is not alone," de Gaulle proclaimed; "she has a vast empire behind her. She can unite with the British Empire, which holds the seas and continue the struggle!"[67] Yet, not only had sufficient volunteers failed to materialize, but petty political rivalries between the British and French leaders interfered with their goals, as I shall discuss ahead.

Churchill had organized his own clandestine operations within the SOE. On July 19, 1940, he charged the entire SOE to coordinate all subversive and sabotage activities against the enemy and to "set Europe ablaze" (his earlier phrase, barked in response to Hitler's boast that he would conquer Britain after France, Holland, Belgium, Denmark, and Norway). The SOE had many clandestine London headquarters, but its French section met at 82 Baker Street, courtesy of Marks & Spencer stores. The F section, consisting mostly of French exiles in England, also played an important role in the Allied invasion of Normandy and southern France and in the Liberation. Just as de Gaulle's initial call for volunteers was barely answered—at least in terms of volunteers—Churchill's initial designs were similarly frustrated. Churchill wanted to take the offensive by air bombardment. "How wonderful it would be if the Germans could be made to wonder where they were going to be struck next!" he had said. He wanted to have a common front, a disciplined force, that would connect with the Allied forces throughout Europe. At the time, however, this was impossible, and sabotage and subversion became the next, most practical means of operation. The British mission was thus redefined: to effect "a reign of terror," to make "the lives of the German troops . . . an intense torment." Hugh Dalton, newly in charge of the SOE, stated: "We must organize movements in enemy-occupied territories comparable to the Sinn Fein in Ireland."[68]

The names of some of the SOE's early, great figures include C. McV. Gubbins, Maurice Buckmaster, and N. R. Bodington; early agents were de Vomécourt (about whom Foot says: "He did for F section's work in France what . . . Parnell [did] for home rule"),[69] Virginia Hall, Ben Cowburn, and Christopher Burney. Later heroes, all killed, include Charles Grover-Williams, Robert Benoist, Michael Trotobas, Gustave Bieler, and Brian Rafferty. Those perhaps better associated with code names or circuits — all finally executed as well — include Suttill ("Prosper"), Gilbert Norman ("Archambaud"), Jack Agazarian ("Marcel"), France Antelme ("Renaud"), and Noor Inayat Khan ("Madeleine"). In the F section were Paul Rivière ("Roland"), Michel Brault ("Miklos," "Jérome"), F. F. E. Yeo-Thomas ("Shelley"), Raymond Basset ("Marie"), André Jarrot ("Goujon"); colonels included George Starr ("Hilaire"), R. H. Heslop ("Xavier"), and the great Francis Cammaerts ("Roger"), about whom I shall say more, since, like some of the others mentioned above, Beckett is likely to have known him.

Until 1942, when the Germans (and Beckett) moved south, there was an obvious difference between resistance work in the occupied and southern areas. In the occupied zone, where one was subject to direct contact with the enemy, subversive activity was always risky. As a result, contrary to Bair's contention, groups tended to be smaller and more secretive. Some people worked in complete isolation, unaware that their neighbors or friends were similarly employed; others joined groups. Among the northern circuits established during Beckett's war residence in Paris were SOE's Prosper, the largest and most powerful network in Paris, Chestnut (also in Paris), Cinema (south of Paris and so named because its handsome leader, Emile-Henri Garry, resembled Gary Cooper), Autogiro (short-lived), Robin, founded by two wealthy Jewish businessmen, and both Tinker and Monkey-puzzle (which bridged the two zones). Later important groups included Scientist, Professor, Farmer, Musician, Donkeyman, Farrier, Stockbroker, and Sacristan. Other important groups from the occupied area, many formed during the early years and working in isolation, included Défense de la France, a collection of university students supported by a French industrialist. The Défense primarily stole German cars and printed the newspaper *Défense de la France* in the basement of the Sorbonne, and these were distributed to some hundred thousand people. Another group with a popular newspaper was Jean Lebas's L'Homme Libre, organized by the socialist mayor of Roubaix. Maurice Thorez and his deputy Jacques Duclos were among the leaders of this communist group, which concentrated on stirring factory strikes in the north; they later worked in maquis zones with the Franc-Tireurs et Partisans. Other organizations included Ceux de la Libération, Les Bataillons de la Mort, Le Mouvement National Révolutionnaire (the Trotsky-ite wing of the French socialists), L'Armée des Volontaires, and Socialisme et Liberté (Sartre's university group). Even though most of these defined them-selves in political or ideological terms, people from vastly different back-grounds and political persuasions became colleagues, with rapprochements that would have been unthinkable before the war—between communists and Catholics, freethinkers and believers. For all of these groups, operations and assignments were often similar. Michel, discussing how many people used multiple pseudonyms as they performed the same work for different organizations, speaks of the great difficulty of sorting out specific people and specific affiliations. One of the greatest Resistance heroes, in fact, Philippe de Vomécourt, volunteered in 1940 for both de Gaulle and Churchill, and both dismissed him because of his proposed guerrilla tactics.[70]

Thus, while the SOE's only requirements were that its non-French agents speak impeccable French and have a thorough knowledge of French culture (which resulted in a sophisticated membership), Beckett might as easily have worked for the Free French (although de Gaulle primarily, but not exclu-sively, enlisted French people) or any number of unaffiliated Paris groups. Both the Free French and SOE, for instance, sought people to send coded messages to London—which Beckett did—just as both relied on people in the south to handle ammunition at key railway sites, which Beckett later did in the Vaucluse. It appears at that point that he was working with the maquis, and his group may or may not have been connected with either Francis Cammaerts from the SOE, or Jean Moulin, de Gaulle's coordinating agent.

Nevertheless, requirements for service were similar[71] and matched Samuel Beckett's qualities. Resistance workers had to have character and courage; dedication to human dignity and respect for human rights; intelli-gence (for assimilating, condensing, and remembering information); emo-tional stability (flexibility, strong nerves, a quick wit); the ability to be silent and to be inconspicuous; resourcefulness (what could be called the novel-ist's eye for detail); a sensitivity to one's surroundings and an awareness of imminent danger; and respect for luck and even superstition. Fearlessness was also essential, for Gestapo "V-men" (*Vertrauensmann*) were continuously infiltrating these groups, and the Gestapo's offer of £5,000 or more for in-formation leading to the arrest of an underground worker became increas-ingly appealing to many among the hungry population.[72]

Maurice Buckmaster, in charge of the F section of SOE from 1941 until the end of the war, organized what he called his "Education for Cloak and Dagger."[73] Hundreds of thousands of copies of military intelligence officer

C. McV. Gubbins's pamphlet, "How to Use High Explosive," were distributed throughout the war. Gubbins also trained agents as radio operators (called "pianists") or for a variety of sabotage activities, such as railroad destruction; these people, in turn, trained other new members. Some information was passed by word of mouth—for example, the accepted rule that if a person were caught (and it was assumed that no one was invulnerable to torture), he or she was expected to say nothing for two days, even under duress of having teeth pulled one by one. The two days' delay would give companions time to escape. The best technique of remaining silent, they were instructed, was to count under one's breath, although the ideal goal was to emulate the bravest of prisoners, Jean Moulin, who never spoke at all when he was finally beaten to death. The optimal way to protect one's life—this was a fundamental rule —was to cultivate a life of privacy, since arrest inevitably meant discovery, which meant torture, which meant deportation, which meant death.[74]

Acts of sabotage could be as subtle as the imagination could contrive. One important tool, for example, was the fat hammer (in partnership with cunning creativity). With such an instrument, half an hour's work in a factory could destroy the optical glassworks that had taken six months to produce. Abrasive grease, which would actually wear out the parts it appeared to lubricate, was unparalleled for railway sabotage. Mismarking seals on goods and rewriting directions for trains or trucks might (as it once did) send a truckload of women's underwear to the German airfields.[75] Contrived incompetence, for instance, in typing, filing, or taking phone messages, was also a great weapon.

Certain agents concentrated on a plastic explosive that looked like and was packaged like butter. This could be smeared anywhere—on aircraft, a ship rudder, building, or helmet. Pocket incendiaries and tire busters were efficient devices for planned, very brief acts of sabotage—for example, when one was walking toward a more ambitious assignment. In telecommunications work, it was important that agents not just cut wires (which could be repaired) but that they destroy junction boxes, or better yet, jumble cables. Industrial sabotage took on an extraordinary range of possibilities. One SOE official report detailed thirty-seven operations that had required a total of three thousand pounds of explosive—almost all plastic—in the destruction of tanks, coal, electrical connections, ball bearings, artillery, cement, locomotives, wireless equipment, tires, oil refineries, copper, aluminum, textiles, alcohol, and lorries.[76]

Carrying forged papers was a complicated matter, for one needed at a minimum an identity card (with photo), work permit, ration card, tobacco card (whether or not one smoked), a permit to be in certain areas (if relevant, like a coastal or frontier zone), demobilization papers (for males), a license and insurance certificate (if one drove), and, after the summer of 1942, a medical certificate explaining why one had not been deported to Germany for labor.[77]

Dropping, recovering, and hiding supplies (among Beckett's tasks in the south) required absorbing a wide variety of information: details about drops of clothes and boots, as distinguished from small arms (which ultimately went to more than a million people), explosives (which serviced tens of thousands of demolitions), and even jeeps (loaded with machine guns).[78] Finding a safe hiding place was always difficult.

The abbreviations, codes, and code names to learn or decipher were vast. Most agents had a personal code—a name or series of numbers, or even a transposition key as long as a couplet or the quatrain of a poem. Coded messages might consist of four-letter phrases with alternating vowels and consonants, printed in columns with a prearranged meaning attached to each. AKAK FOUR DODO LONA, for example, meant "parachute at next opportunity for container-loads bren gun ammunition in magazines." These codes, explains one specialist, while gibberish to the Germans, "would obviously enough be surenciphered, not sent in clear." Other, more accessible codes, which Beckett might have known, included "Attila," the German invasion of Vichy France, begun November 11, 1942; "Dragoon" (originally "Anvil"), the Allied invasion of Vichy France, begun August 15, 1944; "Fortitude," the cover name for "Overlord," the Allied invasion of Northwest Europe, June 5–6, 1944; and "Jedburgh," the Anglo-Franco-American teams reinforcing the maquis during Overlord, June-September 1944. Abbreviations similarly used by agents sending messages to London included AI10, MOI(SP), or NID(Q)— all cover names for the SOE; D, for the decipher section of French Intelligence; W, for the interservice committee handling the most secret matters in London; and MI9, escape; MI19, refugees; XX, double-cross committee; DF, SOE escape section; and Y, wireless interception service.[79]

The following "props" were all the inventions of Colonel Elder Wills, who before the war was a scenic artist at the Drury Lane Theatre and a film art director.[80] Wills invented "invisible" ink, which appeared only under infrared light, and his microfilm documents were so small they could be sealed into tiny containers that could then be hidden in body orifices, on a matchstick (which was then marked by a tiny nick), or within toothpaste tubes or shoelaces. Wills's laboratory also created microdots no larger than a speck of dust that would fit on the lens of an eyeglass or watch face. Explosives were some of Wills's most imaginative creations—from the more obvious fountain pens, cigarettes, and nuts and bolts that squirted ammunition to coal lumps, logs, milk bottles, and bread loaves. Another impressive invention was his (explosive plastic and handpainted) horse, camel, mule, and elephant dung, which was used accordingly in western or northern Europe, or in Africa or the Far East. One drop in front of a parked SS car worked miracles.

So too the Free French and SOE worked out ingenious messages for their agents, and listeners to the BBC could hear phrases throughout the day like "Josephine wears a blue dress"; "Uncle Jacques has lost his umbrella"; "The cow will jump over the moon tonight." [81] Although listening to the radio was forbidden—with severe punishment on discovery—many hid their radios and then wrote down messages which were subsequently printed in hundreds of clandestine papers. If a Resistance agent were occupied on a given day, he or she "checked in" later with an assigned listener for messages.

There were, of course, translations for all these riddles. "Benedictine is a sweet liqueur" informed the tank turret manufacturers at Montbéliard that Harry Ree was a good agent. "I see green eyes everywhere" relayed to some of Xavier's saboteurs in the Ain that they would get an arms drop. "Is Napoleon's hat still at Perros-Guirec?" told the Breton resisters in touch with the Special Air Force that they should parade with their weapons in the village square at five minutes before midnight. [82]

By the spring of 1944, stations announced important news twice a month, on the first and fifteenth, and at 7:30 and 9:15 P.M., so that when D day approached, agents could be alerted. Thus, on the evening of June 5, when the call for action arrived, it was followed by an epidemic of explosions at railway stations and telecommunication centers, as well as by various sabotage activities throughout France, Belgium, and the Netherlands. The signal had been two lines from Verlaine's "Autumn Song." The first line— "The long sobbing of the violins of autumn"—indicated that the invasion date had been set. The second line—"Wound my heart with monotonous langour," broadcast amid jumbled phrases like "The doctor buries all of his patients"—signified that the attack would begin within forty-eight hours and that sabotage activities should begin simultaneously. [83] The Resistance carried out its duties meticulously.

Throughout this period of German brutality and heroic resistance, pettiness and competition over recruitment and governance continued in the British and French high command. Many French viewed the British as greedy imperialists who were harboring secret designs to rule France. The fact that the F section of the SOE was, for a time, even concealed from de Gaulle because some of his entourage were viewed suspiciously, later enraged the general. [84]

The British defended their position by questioning the very legitimacy of de Gaulle's role as "the Voice of France." Franklin D. Roosevelt never recognized de Gaulle as the undisputed leader of France, and Churchill did so only after the Resistance embraced him as such.[85] When not viewing the French agents "as a sideshow," the British viewed their organizers as political opportunists. "Leaders of the Resistance," they said, "assert their position [only] with an eye on the future."[86]

As to the truculent manner with which de Gaulle conducted himself, the general admitted in his Memoirs (1954) that his willfulness was calculated because his position was weak. De Gaulle had to be rude to the British in order to prove to French eyes that he was not a British puppet—a behavior which, the British complained, he "carried out" with "perseverence." But de Gaulle also believed that the British were making his groups into puppets, thus weakening their resolve.[87]

Compounding these conflicts were major disputes among the rank and file within each group. De Gaulle's agents bickered over whether in his exile he truly understood conditions in France. Some argued for, and others against, the right-wing conservatives in his entourage. While some thought de Gaulle was too authoritarian, others found him too weak. So too, the SOE endured its own internal conflicts. It faced constant criticism from the already established British War Office and Secret Intelligence Service (SIS) over issues of turfdom. Who, for example, controlled the propaganda agencies? The SOE was also seriously criticized for recruiting "longhaired civilians." Like the Irish volunteers in 1916 (and most of de Gaulle's Free French), its first members were "amateurs almost to the man"—lawyers, merchants, fashion designers, teachers, commercial artists, opera singers, chefs, barristers, debutantes, and even the leader of a Boy Scout unit.[88] Although top personnel like C. McV. Gubbins from military intelligence had devised a training program for intelligence, telegraphy, unarmed combat, and parachuting, the SOE's second tier of volunteers, like many of the Free French, were people from every walk of life who frequently had to teach themselves survival skills. To add to the confusion, the communists, already active in small groups, were also neglected or embraced—depending upon one's political convictions—and numerous other political, professional, and academic groups, with smaller memberships, had their own problems. Foot writes that rivalry between the nongaullist and Gaullist country section of SOE for France, for example, and between the British SOE, SIS, OSS, and other international organizations, like the FBI, GRU (Central Intelligence Directorate) and NKVD (People's Commissariat for International Affairs) "was no better or worse than the rivalries between Himmler's Sicherheitsdienst and Canaris's Abwehr."[89]

Rivalries between de Gaulle and Churchill also involved serious military decisions, like those taken in Mers-el-Kébir, Dakar, and Syria. With Britain essentially alone in fighting the Germans—and the sense that France was "willy-nilly" both at war and not at war (France had, after all, only concluded an armistice)—the British were compelled to protect their own interests. Thus, to avoid a potential sea invasion from German-occupied France, they virtually destroyed the main French ports, killing 1,300 sailors at Mers-el-Kébir. Between September 1940 and May 1941, Brest endured seventy-eight separate British air attacks; similar bombings of Le Hâvre reduced the population to 50,000. The land battle at Dunkirk in May 1940 destroyed 80 percent of its homes, and by November 1941, 60,000 of the 100,000 Dunkirk residents were living in basement shelters. Caen and neighboring Saint-Lô, where Beckett volunteered his services at the end of the war, were almost entirely destroyed by the Allies. In total, France's "friends," including the British, killed 60,000 and injured 75,000.[90] Although de Gaulle's outrage at events like Mers-el-Kébir was unremitting, he continued to work with Churchill for the good of France, but he also looked to France's colonial resources in Africa for support.

De Gaulle finally realized, in late 1942, that to be the acknowledged leader of his country, he needed the support of all the underground groups in France, in both the north and south, regardless of their sponsorship. Although many others had tried to amalgamate these various and scattered groups—including Buckmaster, Dewavrin, Brossolette, and Yeo-Thomas—de Gaulle's choice of Jean Moulin ("Rex," "Max") for this purpose was brilliant. By 1943, Moulin had successfully sorted out the seemingly inextricable tangle of political rivalries and formed the Conseil National de la Résistance (CNR).

Moulin, a former Chartres prefect, had begun his Resistance activities at a farm near Avignon the year before Beckett arrived; by 1942, his work was legendary. During the next year, he coordinated Resistance movements, labor unions, and political parties. He unified, for example, the existing three major southern Resistance groups into the Mouvements Unis de la Résistance (MUR). Henri Frenay, one of de Gaulle's first volunteers, had formed the important southern Mouvement de Libération Nationale, which later joined with another predominantly left-wing Catholic organization (Liberté); both subsequently went under the name of the Combat group. Even at the end of 1941, with its seven important leaders—Frenay, Bertin-Chevance, Claude Bourdet (of Vérité), F. de Menthon, P. H. Teitgen, Georges Bidault, and Rémy Roure (of Liberté)—its membership of liberal Catholics was estimated at between 20,000 and 40,000.[91]

The more revolutionary group in the south, with a more popular membership, had been Libération, led by Emmanuel d'Astier de la Vigerie—a group of communists, socialists, and trade unionists who wanted to mobilize the masses in industrial centers. D'Astier had already founded, with

Corniglion-Molinier and Cavaillès, La Dernière Colonne. Libération's press, under Georges Bidault, had produced 250 issues in eighteen months. Other groups included Father Chaillet's Témoignage Chrétien, which rescued Jewish children, and France d'Abord; important names from these groups included Jean-Paul Lévy, Pierre-Henri Teitgen, Yves Farge, and Gilbert Dru. Lyons, the capital of the southern Resistance, was home not just to Combat and Libération but also to Franc-Tireur and many of the groups mentioned above. SOE circuits in the south—also to be reconciled into de Gaulle's amalgam—included the active (and increasingly depleted) Wheelright, Acolyte, Acrobat, Stationer, Spruce, and, in Beckett's region, Jockey, Monk, Gardener, and Pimento.

After the Conseil National de la Résistance was formed, with Moulin in charge, the numerous militant organizations that had been supplied arms by the SOE were then amalgamated into the Armée Secrète, with SOE liaison officers a part of the organization. Various groups, including the Service d'Opération Aériennes et Maritimes (SOAM) and BIP (a propaganda section) were formed; Moulin was even able to bring the maquis into contact with several Resistance units. Although some groups thought this arrangement too political, and the communists often dissented, it was the best orchestration thus far. The umbrella organization that Moulin finally proposed was the Bureau Central de Renseignements et d'Action, consisting of political and nonpolitical people: soldiers, trade unionists, and church members—a diverse group united in its commitment to oust Hitler and support de Gaulle. Through the accomplishments of the bureau, also in 1943, three of the major groups of the occupied area became coordinated.[92] Libération Nord had had a membership that was largely Socialist, members of the Confédération Générale du Travail, and Catholic trade unionist. Its paper had circulated fifty thousand copies a week; by the Liberation, it had printed 190 issues. As early as 1941, the group had established contacts with both the British and Free French, but in 1943, it became a major part of the new amalgam.

Compared with Libération Nord, the Organisation Civile et Militaire was reactionary and militaristic. Its members were soldiers, civil service personnel, and professionals, as well as orthodox socialists. Having established a relationship with London in 1942, it had operated chiefly in Paris and its environs. Front National (FN), which had received financial support from London, ultimately built up additional networks in southern France. Large and both political and military, the organization espoused an ideology embracing that of the Popular Front; it also established numerous small units, like the French Women's FN, the Peasants' FN, Shopkeepers' FN, Lawyers' FN, Lawyers' FN, and so on.

On May 27, 1943, the Conseil National de la Résistance met with representatives from two trade unions, eight Resistance movements, and six old political parties, and passed a resolution canceling all the acts of Vichy and entrusting de Gaulle with management of the state. Moulin had recently been arrested and tortured to death, and de Gaulle, demonstrating that he was entirely bipartisan, chose Libération's Georges Bidault to take charge. At the same time, de Gaulle established the Comité Française de Libération Nationale (CFLN) in Algeria to bring together political and military leaders outside France. Until the Allied invasion, the CNR controlled the military; after D day, the CFLN did so; in the summer of 1943, liberation committees were set up in each department of France. Three days before the invasion, the CFLN changed its name to the Provisional Government of the French Republic.

By the time Beckett arrived in the south, the Germans had invaded the unoccupied zone (Operation "Attila," November 11), thus destroying whatever remained of the illusion that the south was safe. (At this point, all Jews — those who were not in hiding — were routinely picked up and killed or deported.) The Germans also geared up the recruitment of available French males for their factories, with the result that more and more young men joined the maquis. By this time, anyone involved in underground activity faced increased danger. If the earliest Resistance groups, especially in the south, had been "mere pinpricks" hardly noticed by the Germans, the situation now had clearly changed.[93] The Gestapo began arresting thousands of saboteurs for activities that in any way threatened Germany's economic and military productivity. Until the end of the war, every circuit, in the north and south, was in danger. At the same time, the American war machine was now moving to full capacity, and this, along with the German defeats in the USSR and North Africa, provided an added impetus to join the Resistance.

When the Allies landed in Normandy, Jean Luchaire, the foremost of the Parisian journalist-collaborators and now the leader of the French press, issued an official directive. It was the "duty" of all French citizens "to hate" both the English and the Americans, whom he referred to as "the enemy," and their maquis or Resistance partners. Vichy mobilized the Milice and called on all French citizens to join in the counterattack against the enemy: "Consider as enemies of France . . . those belonging to Resistance groups; attack saboteurs, parachutists and others; track down traitors who try to sap the morale of our units."[94] In response, members of the maquis, dressed as Milice, entered the offices of the Ministry of Information and shot the minister, Philippe Henriot. A twenty-million-franc reward failed to uncover their whereabouts. By this time, the maquis and all the underground armies of the Resistance, working with the Forces Françaises de l'Intérieur, had joined with the Inter-Allied forces under Dwight Eisenhower and were instrumental in the last efforts toward victory. Because of the maquis's continued sabotage of communications, for example, the Germans were incapable of bringing adequate forces to the Normandy beachheads. The maquis and Resistance, by their own efforts, freed one-third of France, including Paris.[95] Although many German troops had fled with the entire Vichy regime to Sigmaringen, in southern Germany, others remained behind. Supported by the Milice, they went up and down the Rhône valley in search of villages with Jews or members of the Resistance or maquis.[96] Seven hundred people, including 250 children, were killed at Oradour-sur-Glane. By D day, 30,000 Resistance and maquis had been executed; another 30,000 had been killed in battles with the enemy. Of the 115,000 deported to the Buchenwald, Ravensbruck, Dachau, and Mauthausen camps, and countless others deported for forced labor, only 35,000 returned.[97]

| Roussillon

Until 1942, Resistance activities in the south and occupied areas were different in terms of risk, if not of motivation. By November 1942, when Beckett arrived in Roussillon, the stakes had changed. As discussed in chapter 7, the Germans had not only marched into this previously protected zone, but the new STO compulsory labor law (proposed in 1942 but not passed until February 13, 1943) was demanding conscription of all males into German factories. Following its losses at the Russian front, Germany had drafted all its own young men into the military. Now there was a conspicuous need for additional factory workers in Germany. Former efforts had failed to entice the French into the relève—the voluntary enlistment program, where one French war prisoner was released for every three volunteers, each of whom also received a thousand-franc bonus. "They are giving their blood," the Germans had advertised; "Give your labor to save Europe from Bolshevism." By the end of 1942, membership in the southern Resistance had escalated.[1]

The STO law gave new meaning to the maquis—so named after the wild Corsican brush country that was originally a well-known hideout for outlaws. Until November 1942, only a few hundred guerrilla forces had organized in the mountains. After the STO law went into effect, however, an estimated 30,000–50,000 maquis came forth.[2] The Germans were actively rounding up French males on the streets, in schools, or in movies—anywhere—and reprisals for nonservice were predictable and severe. With the law demanding that all men born between 1920 and 1924 enlist—and with little response—it was only weeks before the Germans drafted all men between the ages of eighteen and fifty-five, in all the occupied countries.

Not all the students and peasants who then joined the maquis did so for strictly honorable reasons. German retaliatory measures and rumors of the imminent Allied bombing of German cities incited many to flee to the maquis to save their lives. If they were from French cities, they went to the country; if they lived in the country, they went to the mountains. The maquisards finally included a number of French and foreigners who primarily feared conscription—Alsatians, Lorrainers, Belgians, Danes, Poles, and Yugoslavs—as well as, of course, Jews and anti-Hitler Germans.

As a group, the maquis threatened the authority of the Resistance, for it considered itself a secret army, but in fact the maquisards lacked arms and military experience. They were mostly young, now-homeless, and often angry or embittered men who wanted to fight a real war. They stole whatever weapons they could; these farmers and peasants could make them out of pitchforks, knives, and other farm equipment. As a group they were fearless. They saw themselves as coordinating insurrectional operations, as preparing the country to take part in the Allied military operations on D day. Such fervor and anarchical structure worried de Gaulle and Moulin; they feared that the maquis were creating an armed force that would not wait until D day.

Christian Durandet, in *Les Maquis de Provence*, writes of their activities in the area during the time that Beckett lived in Roussillon and fought with them. Their different sabotage activities—some in Gordes, the local maquis center about three kilometers from Roussillon—sound like more violent versions of Resistance activities enumerated in chapter 7. He also insists that the maquis "were perfectly organized and functioned just like a regular army." He underscores the leadership of Jean Garcin, who never lost sight of their cause and often said, "The important thing is that we decide to remain French and to continue the struggle."[3]

Under Moulin's directive, the maquis was finally assisted by the Conseil National de la Résistance and Mouvements Unis de la Résistance, which provided food, clothing, forged papers, and ration cards. The Comités de Résistance Ouvrière connected the maquis with the Forces Françaises de l'Intérieur (FFI), which trained many maquisards as soldiers. As such, they came to be "the most hardened, if not the most experienced, part of the FFI."[4] The maquis's primary activities, however, remained the destruction of rails and the sabotage of German army regroupings. For example, immediately after D day, 180 German trains were derailed, railroad lines were cut; within three weeks, 3,000 railways became inoperative, necessitating German travel by land. At this point the maquis changed street signposts and destroyed vehicles so that the Germans were forced to travel by foot.

Francis Cammaerts ("Roger") was one of the most important leaders in the south, whose work, following Peter Churchill and Francis Basin, was essential in the final amalgamation of forces that occurred in 1943. Cammaerts had an interesting history, several aspects of which he shared with Beckett. A large, athletic, and strikingly fit man, he had been a schoolmaster in Belfast and a graduate of Cambridge. The bilingual son of a French father and British mother, he called himself a "civilian" before and after the war.[5] In fact, in 1939, he declared himself an official conscientious objector and for this had to perform involuntary agricultural work. Three years later, in 1942, at only twenty-six (and apparently after great soul-searching), he reversed his political position, deciding that the war against the Nazis was a just and necessary cause. He joined the SOE and devoted himself to setting up underground circuits throughout the south, including Beckett's area. Like Moulin, he then worked toward the amalgamation of the many scattered southern groups. His decorations—the Distinguished Service Order and Légion d'Honneur, among others—celebrated his valor in successfully organizing groups of ordinary artisans, laborers, farmers, and villagers within a vast geographical area. In the face of great danger, he had worked toward coordinating the activities of the SOE with these many diverse groups of the Resistance and maquis.

Cammaerts's main objective in the Avignon region was to dynamite key railway yards and to arrange the drop and pickup areas for explosives and supplies—tasks which Beckett also accomplished. Cammaerts is also credited with having successfully led a group of mountain maquis in assisting the Allies during Operation Dragoon, the invasion of Vichy, by turning the Germans' left flank in the Rhône valley and thus moving them out of the south,[6] an activity that was typical of Beckett's Roussillon-Gordes group. Finally, Cammaerts is associated with the Polish countess and beauty queen, Krystyna Sharbek ("Christine Granville"), also a distinguished Resistance fighter. Like the Countess Markiewicz, who defended Stephen's Green during the Irish 1916 Uprising, Countess Sharbek exchanged a comfortable and glamorous life to pursue her political ideals. She is particularly acclaimed for arranging escape routes for hundreds of prisoners out of Poland, Hungary, and Rumania, and for later parachuting into southern France for an assortment of dangerous activities.

Certain details of Beckett's—or anyone's—experience in the south from late 1942 until the end of the war are not commonly known. For example, both great and small events, including those outside France, were reported in newspapers that were passed from hand to hand and went from village to village, crossing from one zone to the other, and thus were available to an enormous population. Among the dozens of underground presses in the south were Libération, Combat, Franc-Tireur, Marseillaise, Résistance, Valmy, Défense de la France, L'Humanité, France Liberté, Le Coq enchaîné, France d'Abord, Cahiers du Témoignage Chrétien, and Pantagruel.

Four newspapers were available in Roussillon alone—Marseillaise (communist), Provençal (socialist), Méridional (conservative), and Dauphiné libéré (socialist);

in nearby villages, Beckett could also find, among many others, *L'Espoir* (socialist), *Rouge-Midi* (communist), and *Provence libérée*.[7] Fighting groups of the area also had their own papers — e.g., *Ceux de Maquis* — just as families of prisoners put together *Victoire* and *Aide*. The peasants published *La Terre*, *Le Paysan patriote*, and *La Résistance paysanne*. Professional people, such as scientists concocting Molotov cocktails and doctors signing false certificates to get young people out of obligatory service, produced newspapers as well, for they too fought with whatever resources they could collect and wanted their activities recorded.

With the maquis working primarily after dark, life for Beckett in Roussillon was often a mixture of uneventful days and dangerous nights. We are able to fill in some of the particulars of Beckett's environment during the last two-and-a-half years of the war from the extensive research of the French cultural historian Laurence Wylie. In *Village in the Vaucluse*, he broadly details life in Roussillon, and, of special significance to us, his statistics reflect the official census of 1946. This work, along with Wylie's subsequent publications, also drawing upon vast interview material and descriptions of the village's cultural, political, and social life before and after the war, provides useful, often fascinating information about Roussillon during the war.[8] Two books inspired by Wylie's work, both by Francis Berjot, have also been published on Roussillon.[9]

We begin with several facts and hypotheses — some more obvious than others. First, as one would expect, the mayor of Roussillon during the war was appointed by Vichy, and his principal goal was to maintain the peace. Second, the village was untouched by German raids, although neighboring villages as close as three to five kilometers away were marked as maquis areas and suffered the consequences of Nazi brutality. Finally, many Roussillians, including Beckett, engaged in maquis activity in these neighboring towns. One might assume that most of the population lived, at best, with a precarious sense of safety, and, at worst, with a continuous awareness of impending danger. In reality, neither was the case.

How the villagers viewed Beckett and how he presented himself publicly are intriguing questions. Although Beckett was, after all, a stranger in their midst, there were many refugees in Roussillon, from the poorer parts of the Italian and Spanish Alps, Alsace, and Belgium, and thus it is possible that the Roussillians thought he was one of these. But Beckett was not typical of the Roussillan refugees. He was an Irishman-become-Parisian Resistance agent, whose circuit had been exposed. As Jack MacGowran said, he was a marked man. Although Bair asserts the contrary, the villagers were entirely unaware that Beckett was a fugitive;[10] Beckett, however, is unlikely to have

dismissed his wanted status from his mind. In addition, despite Beckett's extraordinary linguistic skills—and he spoke only French during these years—
the local dialect was Provençal. Beckett's distinctive Parisian dialect might
have further intensified his self-consciousness as an outsider. The same might
be said of his awareness that he was a (neutral) Irishman in hiding: interestingly enough, he registered at the town hall as Samuel Beckett from Dublin,
England.

If Beckett lived with a precarious sense of safety, given the times and the
activities he performed, he must have experienced a combination (or alternation) of boredom and anxiety—that state of waiting and uncertainty he
later evoked in *Waiting for Godot*. Any day-to-day structured activity—a job in
Roussillon's shrinking wartime black-market economy, like any physical activity—would have been welcome. Resistance activity at night would also
give purpose to his life, as would his writing.

But this is only one supposition regarding Beckett's life in Roussillon.
Wylie's elaborately detailed information about the community, unexamined
thus far in connection with Beckett, suggests other alternatives and contradicts what Bair has written about Beckett and the village. For example, she
reports, typically, his psychological deterioration:

> Beckett suffered a very real breakdown in Roussillon—probably his most
> serious—one directly related to the schizophrenic form and content of
> much of *Watt*. . . . He made only minimal attempts to be part of life in
> the village . . . [and] was scathing in his denunciation of life in Rous-
> sillon and hated the circumstances that placed him there. He followed a
> bizarre schedule of strange ritualistic tramps throughout the countryside
> despite the ridicule of his fellow exiles and the taunts of the villagers. . . .
> To some . . . he seemed to be two persons. . . . He felt guilty that he wasn't
> with his mother every time a letter came from her. . . . Self-hatred and
> his instinctive reach toward self-preservation were at war within him,
> and they caused a split; a "center" failed to hold, so that fragments of
> himself seemed to fly off in so many directions that he was on the verge
> of total disintegration.[11]

I would reply that although Beckett may have experienced great pain during
this time—and for any number of reasons—he clearly had a resilient side
to him that channeled that energy into both Resistance and creative activity.
He did, after all, write *Watt* during these years, and this acted as a kind of
healing process. As he said, he wrote the novel "to get away from war and
occupation."[12] It was a means of "staying sane"—a means, one must add,
that indicates a cohesive, not a fragmented, center.[13] This period strength-
ened Beckett as both a person and an artist.

Wylie suggests, to begin, that Beckett was probably "quite comfortable" living in Roussillon. Josette Hayden, wife of the painter Henri Hayden and Beckett's friend in Roussillon, also implies this in her comment that, if Beckett chose to work in the fields, "he did so out of friendship with the peasants."[14] As Wylie explains, despite Beckett's Irish origins, the villagers would have been no more suspicious of him than of one another; they would have "taken to him" on an individual basis. Francis Berjot also refers to Beckett's "warm" treatment by the villagers.[15] More important, Beckett might have come to share—and this was especially pronounced during the war—what Wylie calls the villagers' strong sense of survival, of "débrous-sillement" or "système d"—their stoical accommodation in pursuing "life as usual" in the face of potential danger.[16] The endurance that characterized "système d" may have provided another important model in Beckett's grow-ing affirmation of human durability. But the Roussillians were motivated by self-serving and often petty concerns, as well. To understand them better, we shall survey the village's peaceful daytime appearance and then turn to its night world of maquis activity. The latter, however, was a subject that the Roussillians, like Beckett, were always reluctant to discuss.

Daytime Roussillon

The effects of the war . . . were relatively slight. No Germans or Americans came to the village, except for a patrol now and then which passed through without causing trouble. There was no fighting in the commune. There was no bombing. No French town could have been less molested physically.—LAURENCE WYLIE

The only Germans likely to have stopped in Roussillon would have been vaca-tioning officers.—ROBERT O. PAXTON

The village of Roussillon, between the valley of Coulon and the plateau of Vaucluse, is perched on a high cliff overlooking the Apt valley. Visible from all directions, the brilliant reds of the farms and village rise up out of a sparse olive green and light yellow vegetation. Roussillon is located only three to five kilometers from Goult, Gordes, Saint-Saturnin, and the larger market center of Apt—all maquis centers during the war. Orange and Carpentras to the north and Avignon and Cavaillon to the west are larger, somewhat more distant cities; they were centers of Nazi and maquis activity during the war.

Like the entire southeastern area of the Vaucluse, Roussillon is domi-nated by the six-thousand-foot Mont Ventoux ("windy mountain"), as well as the smaller Monts de Vaucluse and Montagne de Lubéron. Their eroded, sloping cliffs and spotty greenery give the scene a wild and primitive ap-pearance, although farms and small towns dot the region, and the Calavon River runs parallel to the two ranges.

Well known for its warm and constant sun, the Vaucluse has produced, over the years, prodigious crops of fruits and vegetables; in Beckett's time, Roussillon's crops were chiefly grain, potatoes, melons, tomatoes, apricots, asparagus, and truffles. The area has always been ideal for vineyards. The hills, with their southern slopes, provide maximum exposure to the sun; the rocky soil is unparalleled for holding the heat and reflecting it upward to the grapes.

The first thing Beckett would have noticed in approaching Roussillon was its brilliant coloration, its dramatic red cliffs and soil, which the local historians say inspired Bellini in his religious scenes.[17] ("There, everything is red," writes Beckett in *Godot*.) The magnificently shaped and brilliantly colored hills range in tone from light tan to a subtle variety of reds, the latter due to the extraordinary ochre deposits there, a unique mixture of claylike sand and iron oxide. The deposits have been called "the most important . . . in the world"; mining dates at least to Caesar's time.[18]

Beckett would have also noticed the beauty of his immediate surroundings, for the architecture throughout the village was distinctive.[19] The houses and shops, built of rounded stones (a protection against the heavy rains) and Roman roof tiles, were a combination of red and white; in the surrounding villages, they were red and gray. In Beckett's time, a number of the wealthier homes, as well as the old hotel on the place de la Mairie, retained ramparts from Roussillon's ancient past. Roussillon was a village of such natural beauty that streets like the strikingly geometrical rue de l'Arcade have continued to provide some of France's most widely circulated photo images.

Until recent years, the history of Roussillon was one of hardship and adaptation—a tale of recurring success and failure in an economy that relied alternately on agriculture and ochre mining. In 1801, the year of the first French census, the village was an isolated farming community. Due to a combination of factors—primitive farming techniques, sudden changes in weather, and animal and plant epidemics—harvests were poor and the standard of living, low. Improvements in transportation in 1850 allowed Roussillon to expand to a home industry collective. The town also began to cultivate and sell silk to the larger cities of France. The old village houses, in fact, which Beckett would have seen, retained rooms with rows of holes about two inches wide and one inch deep that once held the silk trays. Farmers, in addition, began to cultivate garance, a root that produced red dye used for coloring cloth.

In 1870, a series of disasters occurred: the severe winter temperatures froze many crops, including the olive trees; the manufacture of artificial dye made the garance industry obsolete; and a vine disease destroyed the vineyards. By 1890, about a fifth of the population of nearly 1,500 moved and left 79 of the village's 349 houses vacant. (These came to be inhabited by a growing collection of strangers who arrived in Roussillon during the next century, including the maquis.) At the turn of the century, outsiders constituted 10 percent of the population.

During the nineteenth century, ochre mining had been limited, but by 1901 it became more extensive because of more efficient machinery, as well as an expanding market. For several years, the area actually supplied the world market with this precious source of pigment for paints: by the start of World War I, 56,000 tons were exported a year. The war, however, cut off the Russian market, and by 1916 all the foreign markets closed. Production ceased, and the village population dropped to nine hundred. After the war, ochre mining began again, and by 1929, it reached prewar levels. Nevertheless, the Depression curtailed the building industry severely and there was little need for house paint. Once more, ochre production dropped precipitously. By the start of World War II, the foreign markets were again closed; at the end of the war, the United States had begun manufacturing a synthetic ochre. This, along with the village's declining population—fewer than 250 of its now 400 houses were occupied—occasioned a return to farming. In their typical spirit of survival, the farmers began shipping their fruits, vegetables, and wines to northern France, which finally provided them with a manageable standard of living.

After the war, a villager, Elie Blanc, formed the Carrefour Literary and Artistic center, and the town began to sponsor cultural events—art exhibitions, concerts, dance, and theater. Painters seemed naturally drawn to the extraordinary coloration and lighting effects here, but the area also gained residents from political and artistic circles—Fernandel, Darius Milhaud, Bernard Buffet, André Roussin, Max Juvénal, Jean Giono, Jean Marais, Jacques Laurent, Frédéric Mistral, and Claude Rich.[20]

In 1967, the cultural community began dispersing to other areas, and the region between Monts du Vaucluse and Lubéron, "the Golden Triangle," became primarily a tourist attraction for people of many backgrounds. Although a number of celebrities remained or subsequently moved here—for example, the biographer Jean Lacouture—the town was different from what it had been both before the war and in the late 1950s and 1960s. Neither a small farming community nor a cultural center, Roussillon still produced wine, for example, but imprimaturs from newly built or renovated châteaux (or from vintners and enologists) replaced the simple wine makers of Beckett's day. Tourism had become and remains a major source of income.

There are, all the same, qualities of Roussillon which neither time nor tourism can change. The region has the purest air in France (which led to the postwar construction of the Observatory of Saint-Michel and, later, France's

guided missile launching area). And despite the noisome Calavon River—
due to the sulfa preservative disposed there from Apt's candied fruit industry (which dates back long before the war)—Roussillon has always been an
unusually healthful city, untouched in Beckett's time by many of the diseases
such as typhoid, smallpox, and dysentery that invaded the other villages. As
primitive in its technology as in its appearance, Roussillon also remained,
until its cultural renaissance, largely unchanged by modern inventions and
conveniences. The farmers may have replaced their sickles and *araires* (wheel-
less plows) with scythes and horse-pulled reapers, but even these were a
dated technology. Through the early 1950s, there was also very little in the
way of modern plumbing and electricity. It was typical to see open sewers
and privies throughout the village, as well as the use of "night soil" as fer-
tilizer; animal excrement was also visible throughout the streets. Yet Roussillon maintained its reputation as particularly healthful. As the locals put
it, the mistrals swept illness away. These powerful winds—which, according to Roussillon tradition, blew in multiples of three, for three, six, or nine
days at a time—are a part of the unchanging aspect of Roussillon which
Beckett would have experienced. The awesome mistrals bent to one side the
old houses, olive trees, and even the cypresses that dot the flat streets outside the town.

The areas where Beckett might have walked and spent his time—many
now filled with tourist buses and parking lots—were rich and varied in their
coloration and smells: areas of pine, oak, and olive trees, of mushrooms,
wheat and asparagus fields. His house, still referred to as "la maison Beckett,"
was located at one end of the village, on the road to Apt. (Beckett lived next
to the local leader of the maquis, who became the mayor after the war.)
At the opposite end of the town, at the highest point of the hill, near the
old château and in the direction of Saint-Saturnin, was "la maison de Miss
Beamish"—the woman who invited Beckett to Roussillon. In Beckett's time,
many of the old buildings and major socializing areas were at the Place de la
Mairie. The Café de la Mairie, which sold wine, tobacco, and stamps, was a
meeting place for both villagers and outsiders and was well patronized for
its pastis, Raphaël-citron, and Noilly cassé. It was also a *foyer* for the lonely
and poor, a place to watch or play belots or to share the many newspapers
that were always available.

Probably of interest to Beckett were Roussillon's Paleolithic caves, brilliantly decorated with ochre designs; the long-functioning Pont Julien,
which carried the Domitian Way across the Calavon River; and the Pérreal
hill site where, before Caesar's time, the Barbarians engaged the Romans.[21]
More recent antiquities, also picturesque, included one or two of the re-

Beckett's house in Roussillon, located next to that of the head of the local maquis.
(Courtesy B. Roullier)

maining windmills, now wingless and abandoned, on top of the hills, as
well as the *bories*, the primitive huts constructed of overlapping stones.

As unusual as Roussillon might seem for a man accustomed to large
cities, certain qualities of the village may well have reminded Beckett of
the Ireland of his childhood; the sparse mountainous areas of the Vaucluse
may have recalled the paths he had walked with his father. ("With closed
eyes, I walk those back roads," he would say in later years.) Roussillon, like
the Dublin hills, was a natural setting of unique coloration, extraordinarily
clear air, and remarkable ruins. Perhaps these reminded Beckett of the ruins
in Clonmacnois County, or the special retreats of his youth, like the ancient
church and graveyard at Tully, or the cromlech at Glen Druid. Roussillon's
quarries could have recalled what O'Brien calls Glencullen's "music of the
stone-cutters' hammers," just its windmill could have recalled the windmill
in Feltrim.[22]

Roussillon may have also stirred negative associations. As Wylie describes
it, the town was filled with the kind of gossip and provincialism that characterizes many villages or suburbs, like Beckett's own Foxrock. Although

most historians and sociologists consider village life, by definition, as fixed and stable, Wylie discovered that Roussillon had an unusually mobile population. Only a few families remained from generation to generation to lend the village any sense of permanence.[23] All the same, the Roussillians were very much like other small-town people in taking fierce pride in family and in resistance to innovation. They contented themselves with day-to-day responsibilities, and their lives rotated around the crops, making ends meet, the marriage of a child, health, and recreational activities. Habit was a great comfort (or "deadener," as Beckett writes in *Godot*), for it provided a sense of identity and gave them a clear concept of their limits. As Wylie summarizes: "Imagination . . . [is] the quality that the people . . . lack most seriously, the imagination to grasp abstract goals beyond their concrete experience. . . . A person can live with himself. He sees himself in the perspective of time and nature. He thinks it is important to 'see things as they are.' . . . He knows that his knowledge and experience are limited. . . . He has a clear concept of his roles in life."[24] Even in their eccentricities, the Roussillians were in accord. A superstitious community, they employed, for example, a *guérisseur*, or healer, from whom they received medical advice and secret health cures. Every family swaddled its newborn's legs for months at a time to keep the infant's legs straight.

The Roussillians were also unusual in lacking any suspicion regarding strangers, but this, Wylie explains, was due to their equally unusual need for privacy. In fact, their contradictory need for privacy and community respect, along with their near-compulsion to gossip, did more to destroy the solidarity of the village during the war than the threat of German conscription or German brutality. The war may have brought scarcities and the black market, but, however one acted, one finally had to be secretive, or turn the other cheek, or become unnecessarily judgmental. "You should have been here before the war," the villagers told Wylie. "We got along better. There was a dance every Saturday night, and we were always visiting back and forth with each other over a cup of coffee. Now everyone stays at home."[25]

Before the war, when their main pastime was gossip (and gaining public honor), one's allegiances were clear: "If you are neither *brouillé* [quarreling] nor *bien* [getting along] with a person, you have little to do with him." The war created choices and thus suspicion, judgment, and secrecy. Pro-Nazi and pro-American posters were scattered throughout the city (and remained in view long after the war ended, until the rains washed them away). To some, Pétain was a hero; to others he was a villain. The black market also produced a deep sense of anxiety, for one often had to risk one's reputation or become the accuser. Honor and survival—these were often at odds. All in all, "it seemed that no one could do anything without arousing the antagonism of someone else." [26]

Roussillon politics before and after the war remain interesting. Although the villagers had surely worried about their children on the front and their family and friends in Germany (six Roussillians were killed and fifteen taken as German prisoners over five years), their wartime lives were filled with the rituals of daily responsibility. Even the allegiances of those who took political sides were less intense than their abiding concern with what their neighbors thought. A fierce sense of independence reinforced their collective identity, and this ultimately took precedence over individual differences. Thus, when Roussillon was liberated, and Beckett's neighbor (the former head of the local maquis) became mayor, he was told by the Comité d'épuration to arrest a group of collaborators (including the former Vichy mayor, town clerk, principal grocer, baker, and several wealthy farmers); his angry response was, "This is our business." This hostility toward any kind of intrusion, including the government's, continued long after the war. The villagers believed that politics was just propaganda and of no interest to them: "All sides have thrown it at us since '39—we don't pay attention to any of it any more." They had had "years of being pulled one way by the Third Republic and another by the Vichy Government, one way by the radio of Occupied France and another by the BBC, one way by the pro-German posters and another way by pro-American posters." [27]

It is therefore of note that, while Wylie lived in Roussillon in 1950 and "ask[ed] questions about every aspect of life . . . no one should mention Beckett!" Wylie adds: "I suspect there is a message in that." Only after subsequent visits and repeated interviews did he learn, "Yes, there was an Englishman named Beckett who lived here," who had his own house—"a very middle-class house—at the edge of the city." No one, however, openly acknowledged knowing that Beckett was a writer, that he was Irish ("he registered, after all, from 'Dublin, England' "), and that he had been involved in the Paris Resistance.

Given this kind of community, Wylie strongly believes that Beckett would not have lived in hiding; he would never have felt the need to do so. Instead, he would have been part of whatever community he wished to join—had those people liked him. And if he preferred to remain apart from the village, no one would have taken note of this. All the same, through consultation with many of the surviving older population during a 1992 visit, Wylie compiled a list of those with whom Beckett "was clearly or likely to have been a friend." The farmer Aude, for example, "not a bookish but a charming man," gave or sold Beckett vegetables and employed him to do odd jobs like pick grapes, melons, and vegetables. Aude, incidentally, was one of Wylie's best friends who only in later years mentioned Beckett. In addition, Beckett "had to have known Aimé Bonhomme, head of the communist party and in the maquis," and the now-famous Bonnelly (later a candidate for City Council), mentioned in *Waiting for Godot* ("We worked in the harvest at Bonnelly's farm in Roussillon").[28] Wylie also believes that Beckett knew the athletic Marc Grangeon, who tried but failed to form a soccer team, and a man named Roche, who, before the war had been a radio operator on a boat.

One of Beckett's "great friends was Miss Beamish," Wylie continues, rumored to be "a cousin of Winston Churchill," a writer who lived in the magnificent old house on top of the hill near the ancient château. Miss Beamish told Wylie, when he tracked her down in Nice after the war, that she had invited Beckett to Roussillon: "Yes, indeed, all foreigners had to move to the interior from the coast. He and I knew each other vaguely, and so I asked him to come here." According to the townspeople, after living in the small hotel Escoffier, Beckett moved to his "nice, little house" at the entry to the town. Others who probably knew Beckett include the Russian painter Eugène Fidler, who also came to Roussillon during this period; the moviemaker Jean-Charles Taccbella, Francis Berjot, and René Bruni. Elie Blanc, founder of the Carrefour art center and a resident composer for the prewar Roussillon orchestra, speaks of his personal relationship with Beckett and states that Beckett began planning *Godot* there.[29] Finally, according to Wylie, Beckett knew Jean David (the mayor), the communist Icard (in the maquis with Bonhomme), as well as the families connected to Aude and Icard (Lanson, Hector, Guilini, Appy, and Paulette Aude Icard), Lucien Maillet, Adrien Madon, and "Georgette," who took over Maman Jeanne's restaurant and who knew everyone.

It is difficult to estimate the extent to which Beckett was involved with the villagers, but as Josephine Hayden has said, if he worked as a farmer, he did so because of his friendship with the peasants, adding: "He loved the open country. He walked a lot over long distances, and he didn't mind working in the fields." [30] Beckett probably would not have joined the villagers in their popular boar hunts because of his love of animals, although one wonders if he might have sampled their famous thrush dish, *pis oiseaux*. Perhaps he joined in the farmers' favorite rainy-day activity of traveling from one vineyard to the next in order to taste the wines and also attended their concerts (although after a while they ceased entirely). In 1940, about twenty Roussillians had formed *L'Echo de la Limergue*, a horn orchestra, which also had an accordionist and violinist. They performed their own compositions and

some that the local priest Father David had composed. These local trouba-
dours even sold their songs in the other villages.

Whatever Beckett's interest in these occurrences, there were certain elements in Roussillon's everyday manners that must have touched a deep chord
in him, for they became incorporated, if dramatically transformed, in his
subsequent writing. The villagers' approach to childrearing, for example,
echoes in Vladimir and Estragon's relationship in *Waiting for Godot*. Roussillon
children were not permitted physical altercations; instead, they were *encouraged* to threaten, insult, and humiliate each other verbally. Combined with
this verbal outlet for hostility (or insecurity) was the Roussillians' practice
of humiliating, belittling, and physically discomforting their children — by
which they trained them to be stoical (which may remind us of the relationship between Pozzo and Lucky in *Godot*). Parents instructed children to walk
at an early age, for example, and steadfastly refused to pick them up; they
similarly trained them to play outdoors throughout the winter with uncov-
ered knees. Later, in school, children were often shamed by being isolated
and then mocked or criticized by their peers. The children obviously "enjoy[ed] singling out an individual and shaming him," observes Wylie, but
they also "all got along together better than an equivalent group of children
in this country."[31] By age four, most accepted their role as docile and were
courteous to their often-insulting superiors. In short, although they rarely
fought, they expressed themselves with "telling effect." As Beckett witnessed
this, he may have learned a great deal about the hostility and violence in
even the most "innocent" of humanity and the adaptations possible, regardless of one's humiliations.

Finally, to truly understand how the Roussillians "got on with their
lives" to the extent that their town appeared "relaxed," one has to return
to their stoical "système d."[32] First, they believed that not everything was
under the eye of Hitler or his surrogates; second, they added to this prem-
ise their practice of *débrouillardise*: their absolute conviction that there was a
way to "wrangle" anything. Vichy may have made the rules, but instead of
fighting them, one made one's way around them. The point was "to learn to
live with the life around you, without suffering too much." Wylie explains
further: "After all, the French are not a people to be flattened; they are very
much like the Irish in that sense."

In their communal solidarity and petty envies, in their need for group
respect and the demands they placed upon their children — among other
matters — the Roussillians may have reminded Beckett of his childhood in
Foxrock, both in a positive and negative sense. Perhaps, through an unpredictable twist of fortune, Beckett's stay in Roussillon was a blessing of sorts,

whereby he came to terms with unfinished matters of self-definition. That is to say, this may have been a propitious time for Beckett to further hone his own "système d," but for clarification of this, we must turn to Roussillon after nightfall, the province of the maquis and the Resistance.

Roussillon at Night

An outlaw is braver than a soldier, because he acts for himself. —LOUIS ARAGON

Ami, entends-tu	Friend, can you hear
Le vol noir des corbeaux	The flight of the ravens
Sur nos plaines?	Over our plains?
Ami, entends-tu	Friend, can you hear
Les cris sourds du pays	The muffled cry of our country
Qu'on enchaîne?	In chains?
Ohé! Partisans,	Ah! Partisans,
ouvriers et paysans,	Workers and peasants,
C'est l'alarme.	The alert has sounded.
Ce soir l'ennemi	This evening the enemy
Connaîtra le prix du sang	Will learn the price of blood
Et les larmes.	And of tears.

—MAURICE DRUON's "Song of the Partisans"

Another side of Roussillon may have served Beckett well. The village was a natural hideout for someone on the run. Thirty-five miles from Avignon, it was accessible only by car or bike. Up through the early 1950s, the only public transportation available was a bus at 8 A.M. on Thursdays. Even before the war, the area was known as an escape from civilization. Through the Depression, it offered a "return to nature," for "personal renewal." [33] In 1935, François Morénas founded the first youth village for nonconformists here, which he named "Régain," after a Jean Giono novel (1930) framed within this idyllic world. Simone de Beauvoir speaks of her late 1930s visit to the Mont Ventoux area with "a rucksack on her back." [34] René Bruni, in "Roussillon and the Intellectual from 1936," also discusses the "rediscovery of the village" at that time, when it was nicknamed "Delphes-la-Rouges." [35] During the war, the area became a refuge for many escaping the German conscription law.

Survival in Roussillon was not difficult. One could raise goats (for milk and cheese), harvest grain (for bread), and cultivate the local berries (for fruit and jelly). More important, free housing was available in one of the many houses built during the 1850s that were now unoccupied and unowned.

The old, deserted windmills also sheltered refugees, and, for fast concealment, there were many abandoned quarries in the cliffs, whose entries were marked by black holes left from the stone erosion.

To be sure, as Wylie says, "the townspeople knew the maquis were all around, settling old accounts with friends and enemies, and blaming them on the Germans and Vichy." Trying to pinpoint them "would have been like using a sieve to hold water." If, in fact, they were organized, he continues, it was as much through the friendship system as the Fighting French or SOE. An assemblage of young locals and strangers, the maquis roamed the villages at night armed with machine guns and in search of supplies and food. While most people contributed voluntarily, those who refused were eventually forced to give "their fair share." As a result, to some, "the maquis were a pile of bandits; to others, they were a group of patriots."[36]

Although there was resistance activity in Apt, Saint-Saturnin, and Goult —three to five kilometers from Roussillon—the center of maquis activity was in Gordes, five kilometers away. Also situated on the top of a hill with a magnificent castle that is now the Vasarely Museum, Gordes's old houses descended in a patternless maze of little paths and winding streets, making the village an ideal hiding place. On one occasion, after the Germans traced the maquis to Gordes, the Germans brought tanks and artillery to the top of the hill and opened fire, destroying many houses and a large part of the terrain (which has since been rebuilt). This occasion, like the loud denunciations and public executions in Saint-Saturnin, did not overtly concern the Roussillians, who continued to look the other way—toward their proper and paternalistic Vichy mayor, who would keep the peace. Most knew, all the same, that one Alsatian in their midst was maquis, as was Beckett's next-door neighbor, as was another villager who adopted numerous orphans. During the day, these maquisards pursued their lives of habit and obligation; at night, they arranged their "rendezvous" for private business. The townspeople did not live in a state of fear, explains Wylie. First, they were scattered. Second, and more important, they had their prosperous and caring Vichy mayor, who knew most of them personally and who was committed to keeping things quiet.

Several incidents reported to Wylie reveal the nature of the maquis's activities. On one occasion, the maquis learned that the Germans were sending a column to the area. They also knew that the only way to get from one side of the Lubéron mountains to the other was through the narrow Combe passage, a hundred-yard-long road winding through the rock. The maquis waited on top of the hills, and when the Germans reached the middle of this narrow path, they dropped ammunition and destroyed the column. They were never caught.

The second report relates to the day the victorious maquis marched into Roussillon, following the Allies' landing in the south. The maquis had been liberating all the small villages, and the Germans had fled the area. This momentous occasion — the Liberation — Berjot writes, was "more joyously celebrated than any other event in history."[37] The townspeople heard the sound of drums and great fanfare, and, as the heroes approached from Apt, so Wylie was told, they entered the village with Beckett at the front of the procession, carrying the flag.

Not every village had Roussillon's unique and mobile population; nor did everyone operate according to a "système d." However, the history of Le Chambon, another town in the south, and its leader (André Trocmé) were so similar to Roussillon's and Beckett's that they deserve mention. Moreover, since the town was near one of the southern concentration camps, Saint-Paul d'Eyjeaux, its activities would probably have been communicated to other villages via the many underground newspapers, if not by word of mouth. It is therefore likely that Beckett would have known of Le Chambon — a Protestant town whose entire population, according to Philip Hallie, was involved in the protection of hundreds of Jewish children.[38]

As Hallie chronicles the life of this village from the end of 1942 to 1945 (the years Beckett lived in Roussillon), he explains how every person was dedicated to nonviolence — to the motto "Human life is precious," with the corollary that every citizen felt the moral obligation to oppose peacefully any activity that threatened life. This was apparently the religious commitment the pastor, André Trocmé, had inspired in the entire community. But the town was unique in a way that might have particularly intrigued Beckett, given his Protestant and Huguenot background. (Beckett was always proud of his Huguenot roots.)[39]

In a country that is less than 1 percent Protestant, Le Chambon had been a stronghold of Protestants for more than four centuries. In fact, its population of three thousand during the war included only one hundred Catholics. Hallie goes so far as to suggest that "The history of the Protestants in France . . . prepared them for a certain kind of resistance," which he then explains historically. "Farther south in France," he writes, "the revocation of the tolerant Edict of Nantes in 1685 had produced, in time, the bloody battles between the government and the Camisards, the Huguenots deep in the south of France . . . [who] resisted the . . . government . . . by quietly refusing to abjure their faith. . . . This was . . . the resistance of exile."[40] While Beckett's "faith" and "exile" were hardly of the religious sort which inspired the Chambonnaise, Beckett's writing reverberates with their conviction that death is the ultimate absurdity.

Le Chambon's leader might also have interested Beckett. Both Beckett and Trocmé came from wealthy families whose ambitions they rejected. Like Beckett at an early age, Trocmé experienced a kind of civil war, during World War I. Son of a German mother and a French father, he saw his mother's countrymen killing his neighbors on the streets of his Protestant town of Saint-Quentin. He grew up to become apolitical and a pacifist.

Under the leadership of Trocmé and his assistant, Eduard Theis, the Chambonnais thus pacifically pursued a "kitchen struggle" against the Nazi menace. They welcomed into their homes French or assimilated German or Austrian Jews, as well as Jews from Eastern Europe. Some Jews stayed in Le Chambon, but most were moved to different villages or conducted across the Alps into Switzerland. Most daringly, Le Chambon families took all the refugee children into their homes and raised them as their own.

Albert Camus coincidentally spent the year 1942 in the region of Le Chambon, where he began The Plague. As Hallie observes, similarities between the village and novel are clear.[41] Both center around a leader (Dr. Rieux/Trocmé) dedicated to saving lives because of his awareness of the absurd horror of death. In the face of the nonrational destruction of life—the plague/the Nazis—each organized a city into defiant resistance.

Many years after the war, the aged Trocmé wrote about the "meaning" of his activities during that time and concluded that "without knowing it," he had "joined Sartre and Camus, who were unknown at this time."[42] He spoke of the simple way he had pursued life intuitively—only now understanding that in a meaningless universe, one can act only according to conscience.

Beckett's experiences demonstrated this as well (although he reached his own conclusions perhaps in the reverse manner of Trocmé). Beckett had been a devoted student of philosophy, but for the remainder of his life he maintained that he was no philosopher. Beckett would never reach the certainties of Plato, Aristotle, the Stoics, Kant, or even his contemporaries Camus and Sartre. Nor would he demonstrate the kind of religious faith that had moved the pastor Trocmé. Beckett had, nevertheless, demonstrated the highest values of moral commitment. If, as the philosophers had taught him, virtue is dependent upon character and action, rather than the product of an a priori state of being or "meaning," then Beckett's actions throughout the war were exemplary. Although under no immediate threat himself, Beckett repeatedly put his life in danger to battle the enemies of human decency.

Working in the fields by day and writing and fighting by night, Beckett's activities argue for an inner state of cohesion, rather than fragmentation. They indicate an increasing sense of self-confidence, purpose, and consolidation of self. His ability to live up to his creative aims in Watt and his ethical ideals in the Resistance bear witness to this consolidation.

NINE

Saint-Lô

Despite the relief and jubilation of the Liberation, France was to face yet another battle—in terms of political, economic, and social survival. Of the political situation, Henri Michel writes: "[After the Liberation] political forces were thrown completely into confusion; the Right suffered from having supported Vichy, and temporarily disappeared from the political scene; by failing to play an active part in the Resistance, the Radical Socialists lost their pre-eminent position; . . . the big Roman Catholic party . . . drew members from these two discredited parties; the Socialists merely took up their pre-war position. New factors [included] the discovery of the strength of the Communist party and the continuing support for de Gaulle among the general public."[1]

Even the staunchest of patriots posed a threat to de Gaulle. Since 1943, civilian authority had been in the hands of de Gaulle's provisional government, with local power in the Departmental Liberation Committees. The transfer of power to follow, however, was as frightening for many as it had been in 1940, when it passed from the defeated Third Republic to Vichy. De Gaulle was suspicious of the many political groups that now sought his favor; he was suspicious of the maquis, many of whom were busy settling their own scores. For a time, he refused to take authority from Pétain, whose camp was also seriously divided. Since the last months preceding the Liberation, France resembled a "state [in] civil war—except that this kind of civil war involved hatred and suspicion within each of the two major camps." By the Liberation, the number of Frenchmen killed by Frenchmen was estimated as between 4,500 and 120,000.[2] It is not surprising that Beckett left Roussillon without signing out properly.[3]

Estimates of French war casualties vary but are generally reported as follows: 250,000 soldiers died or were missing in action; 760,000 civilians had been deported to Germany; 80,000 Jews were killed. Over the four-year occupation, Germany employed within France the equivalent of 5.2 million man-years—solely for its own economic or military interests. France had also been Germany's largest supplier of foreign manpower in the relève.[4] The Germans had levied inflated "occupational costs" on the nation, equivalent in 1940 to 10.9 percent of the estimated French national income; the figure rose to 36.6 percent in 1943, at least ten times the actual cost of the military occupation.[5]

Although the casualties of World War I exceeded those of World War II, France faced new and grievous problems. It seemed as if the very institutions of the nation had been shaken. Everything had to be rebuilt—from the near-extinct economy to the sense of French national identity. The problems of physical repair seemed insurmountable: 1,800,000 buildings had been damaged (442,000 beyond repair), and many great cities, including Rouen, Le Hâvre, Caen, and Brest, were in ruins. Virtually no main railroad bridge remained intact. Only 2,900 of the 17,000 prewar locomotives were in working condition. Agricultural and industrial systems were similarly crippled, and the land was devastated. (Enormous areas had served as mine fields.) Furthermore, farm labor was nowhere to be found, and few horses and tractors were available. The wheat, grape, and sugar crops had been reduced to a bare minimum. Food, coal, steel, and cement—all the necessities for survival—were also wanting, along with the systems to bring them to the nation. Although billions of francs were ultimately invested in restoring the country's physical and industrial structures, the present appeared grim. For at least five years afterward, with a rising debt and without any certainty of repayment, and with a drastically lowered standard of living, along with the precarious political stability of the emerging Fourth Republic, an enormous insecurity took hold of the nation. To many, France's very survival seemed questionable.[6]

The subsequent Epuration ("cleansing") was, like the Nuremberg trials, a psychological and moral necessity. There was a profound need, particularly for those in the Resistance, to arraign the war criminals, the collaborators. And, as one scholar put it, "distinctions between 'German victory' collaborators and 'French survival' collaborationists were no longer made. Support for Vichy and support for Hitler came to the same thing. The francisque [Pétain's blue and gold badge of honor, the Gallic axe and marshal's baton] was by now as detested as the swastika."[7]

There were two different stages of the Epuration. Before the Liberation, for two or three weeks, summary executions were carried out by the maquisards as "appropriate" acts of war. These sometimes sadistic reprisals against the Pétainists were acts of rough justice, often marked by tremendous haste, brutality, and individual vindictiveness.[8] Of the estimated 5,000–10,000 assassinations of collaborators by the Resistance, most occurred during this time.[9] After the Liberation, de Gaulle set up official trials in order to prevent the lynchings and massacres, but even members of the FFI continued with these illegal practices and were arrested. Throughout, there were also punishments which, to many, appeared excessive, such as the imprisonment of Maurice Chevalier and Sacha Guitry for entertaining French prisoners of war in Germany.

The results of de Gaulle's judicial reform disappointed many. Proportional to the population, there were fewer arrests in France by February 1945 than in Belgium, Holland, and Norway. Only 574 death sentences were imposed on the 7,053 persons tried.[10] Ordinary people who had "served France" under the Vichy government were not penalized; women who had consorted somewhat too generously with the Germans merely had their heads shaved. Such statistics—and the "rationality" of the trials—seemed, to many, to represent an endorsement of the pro-collaborationists. Pétain, Laval, and Maurras, of course, paid for their misuse of power, but Maurras, despite his ruthless support of the Nazis, was sentenced only to life imprisonment. Pétain, who had admitted, "Laval and I are one," at the time Laval affirmed his complete support of Germany, was also given life imprisonment. Laval tried to maneuver his trial into a political controversy when he pretended the role of an *attentiste*; but, like Brinon, Darnaud, and Buchard, he was sent before a firing squad.

By 1949, only 2,071 had been sentenced to death (in addition to the 2,329 who were sentenced in absentia); 768 executions were actually carried out. Within the French armed forces, 3,035 officers were dishonorably discharged; 2,635 retired (involuntarily); approximately 5,000 civil servants, including eighteen magistrates, were dismissed; seven bishops were quietly removed. In all, 39,000 prison sentences were handed down.[11]

When de Gaulle first returned, he inspired the nation's confidence. There was a tacit agreement to treat Vichy as if it had never existed: the de facto authority of Vichy was declared null and void by ordinance. On the day of the Paris Liberation, in fact—an event which de Gaulle insisted that he lead (it had been four years since he had been in France)—he was asked if he would proclaim the reestablishment of the République, to which he replied in the negative. "Why should I?" he said; "The Republic has never ceased to exist."

De Gaulle strove to restore France's independence with internal reforms. The coal mining industry was nationalized; the press and radio were transformed into public services; a series of quotas established government control of foreign trade. Freedom of the unions was also restored, and a social welfare program was instituted. De Gaulle also worked to establish international security—including a rapprochement with Italy and stable relations with Russia.[12]

Despite these efforts, controversy continued regarding the extent to which Vichy policies and personalities were still functioning after the Liberation. De Gaulle appeared to be inciting new antagonisms and exacerbating old ones. He knew, for example, that the Resistance, with its series of political and social reforms, wanted political power, so he proceeded to disband it. With his eye clearly focused on unifying the country through a new government and strong presidency, he rejected the numerous political parties that wanted a strong voice in the new government. His quarrels with the Allies continued. Not having been informed about the invasion at Normandy until hours before it occurred and subsequently not being invited to the meeting at Yalta were two of the "insults" that he endured for the sake of his nation. However, the divisions between Left and Right had become so deep that he resigned only sixteen months after the August 1944 liberation, expecting that "his" people would call him back. This call did not come for twelve years, when France faced yet another war crisis—a potential civil war in Algeria.

These complex political issues again suggest difficulties of alliance and solidarity—even in the face of victory. Such matters would not have passed without attracting Beckett's thoughtful attention.

After leaving Roussillon, and in May 1945, Beckett returned to Ireland; he had not seen his family for five years. He intended to return soon thereafter to his apartment in Paris, where Suzanne awaited him, but restrictions had been placed on resident aliens, due to the severe shortages in France. Beckett then volunteered to help the Irish Red Cross build a hospital in the town of Saint-Lô in Normandy.

It is frequently assumed that Beckett took on this job because it provided easy access to Paris.[13] There are, however, additional factors to consider—both in terms of Beckett's volunteering and his subsequent activities in Saint-Lô. Beckett had been in Ireland for three months before leaving with the Red Cross, and while Bair says that this was a spontaneous decision (he "went directly . . . to volunteer" after a physician-friend suggested it),[14] I would suggest otherwise. Beckett was not an impulsive man, and the war continued outside of Europe. While back in Ireland, he would again have been reading the daily newspapers—with their reports of both the ongoing battles in the Pacific and the grave conditions within the liberated nations. The bombings in France may have ended, but the problems of France's recovery were just beginning.

The Saint-Lô hospital was a project arranged by both the Irish and French

Red Cross. In Dublin, more than a few people would have been interested in the project, for although Ireland had been neutral during the war, its media were filled with various campaigns enlisting Irish aid for their European brethren. On one radio broadcast, according to Eoin O'Brien, Thomas J. McKinney, director of the Red Cross unit, began: "It is imperative that Ireland help France, her neighbor and friend."[15] The people of Dublin were already involved in a number of activities to assist the French—for example, taking in two hundred French children suffering the effects of war.

Most Dubliners would have been keenly aware of the devastation suffered by Saint-Lô, as it had been well reported in the press. The Irish Times called the Allied invasion "possibly the most momentous epoch in [humankind's] annals." The newspaper closely documented Saint-Lô's "heartrending ordeal." Not a day passed without increasingly gruesome details: "The ground for miles shook with the intensity of the barrage"; "savage artillery action" was delivered through the "ruthless use of men"; "7,000–8,000 tons of bombs" were involved in "the surprise blow" at Saint-Lô, with "mammoth air assaults twice as big" as any previous attacks "in the annals of the war in the sky."[16] These terrible reports were frequently accompanied by a complex ambivalence toward the necessities of victory: "Friends of France throughout the world—and what civilised man is not a friend of France?—continue to deplore, although they can do nothing to prevent, her long drawn-out sufferings. The plight of her people is sorrowful. When the Allies landed in Normandy . . . the Norman countryside was . . . a land flowing with milk and honey." In the course of the successful invasion, Saint-Lô had become a city "set on fire by tons of serial bombs dropped on the town since D-Day and tons of artillery hurled into it . . . a ghost town."[17]

The London Times, also read by many in Dublin, had treated with equal thoroughness the transformation of the once-beautiful Saint-Lô into a city of death and rubble and frequently published images of inexpressible human despair. After Churchill's three-day visit to the the front, the Times reiterated that "the biggest force of heavy bombers ever used"—"more than 3,000 aircraft"—had been deployed at Saint-Lô. Newspapers throughout the world reviewed the situation as "breathtakingly grotesque," a funeral pyre where "smoke is coming out of the beaten earth, [with] grim fighting raging everywhere."[18]

In 1945, during the month before Beckett departed for Saint-Lô, the Irish press was filled not just with continuing war news but with the seemingly eternal debate over Ireland's status with Britain. The question of the Irish "republic" seemed particularly newsworthy, and discussions of partition and commonwealth were commonplace.[19] Having just lived through Vichy's fateful renunciation of France as a "république," one may well assume Beckett's interest here. De Valera's unbending position raised timely questions regarding a nation's (or individual's) responsibility to take a moral stance in wartime. De Valera had said repeatedly: "Rights here do not arise from British law. . . . In the last European war, we were neutral, . . . [with] anxieties from both sides. The only attitude we could take up was that we would defend our territory against any power that came in to attack."[20]

Additional international news in the Dublin press highlighted the events leading to Japan's surrender and the trial of the Vichy leaders. "Appeals of Mercy for Pétain" (July 31) included former U.S. ambassador to Vichy William Leahy's "tribute" to Pétain (August 1). The Irish Times also disclosed a letter Pétain had written to Hitler, which, as reported, "constituted in itself a military alliance" (August 7). Several articles argued that Pétain had refused to use French fighters to defend Paris against RAF raids in 1941 (August 9). The trial of Laval was also well covered, following his attempted escape to Spain (August 1). The article "Laval Thought Germany Would Win" appeared in the same issue as Beckett's review "MacGreevy on Yeats" (August 4).

The ebb and flow of political power continued to be reported: Churchill's resignation and the victory of the Labour party and Clement Attlee (July 27); the accusations against de Gaulle for his "dictatorial ambitions" (July 31); King George's overtures to formalize socialism by bringing British banks under public ownership and nationalizing the coal industry and health insurance (August 16). So, too, the persistent blaming and face-saving, even in the most urgent matters, was made public: articles on who was responsible for Pearl Harbor (with Harry S Truman blaming Admirals Kimmel and Stark, August 30). The vagaries of human conscience and memory were also well indicated. According to one survey in France, the large majority of those interviewed said they would have voted against the 1940 armistice with Germany (July 27). Another article concerned the financial burden in having to feed German war prisoners (August 17).

The war could hardly have been, as Bair contends, "a tragic but unavoidable waste" during which Beckett "fritter[ed] away" his time; nor could it have been an event that later receded from his mind, as she also claims.[21] Names and events in the news—ranging from those who acted with megalomaniacal grandiosity during the war to those who were now modestly helping the disenfranchised—would surely have reminded him of his own experience of the last several years. A day did not pass without major news attention to, at one extreme, Hitler and Eva Braun's supposed appearance in Argentina (July 18) or, at the other extreme, Ireland's clothing drive for the poor with tuberculosis (August 22)—that disease which had taken so many people close to Beckett and which he would once again encounter in Saint-Lô, where he would lose yet another close friend, Arthur Darley.[22]

I believe that the same altruistic impulses that had motivated Beckett's earlier Resistance activities prompted him to join the ranks in Saint-Lô. Although he performed the most menial and boring of tasks, the important element is that everything he did was in the service of rebuilding and healing. In addition, the radio announcement he wrote in 1946 reveals that he felt a deep sense of national pride in joining his Irish kinspeople in an active contribution to the war effort.

Bair reports that Beckett's initial activities at Saint-Lô were satisfying, but the chores became "time-consuming" and frustrating: "He went back and forth to Paris, which only added to his frustration . . . waiting for various decisions to be made in various bureaucracies. Even more galling, he discovered that the 'store-keeper' part of his title was meant literally. . . . He . . . often found himself working seven days a week with no respite from the constant good cheer of the Irish staff, the recalcitrance of the German prisoners . . . and the abject misery and sickness of the patients." Although Beckett continued to assist the Red Cross even after he returned to Paris, he did this, Bair claims, only to relieve his guilt "about abandoning his post before the work was completed." [23]

This explanation seems to me both unkind and unlikely. It seems more probable that Saint-Lô provided Beckett with an opportunity to continue his activities in the service of humanity. Saint-Lô was a logical extension and perhaps consummation of his prewar and wartime experiences. Beckett seems to have been determined to battle suffering—whether combating an evil invading force or alleviating the destruction caused by friendly fire.

He would now become a healer, an active participant in the restoration of one of the postwar ruins of the world. He would again wear the uniform of the medical assistant, the orderly's dress, which he had worn more than ten years before when he worked at a London mental hospital. Indeed, at this time in history, the world might well have seemed a madhouse without walls. In addition, as a one-time Irish "exile" now working with an Irish group in France, Beckett could connect his past with the nation that would become his future, permanent home.

Finally, the Saint-Lois illustrated the combination of human misery and human resilience, the absurd victory, that Beckett would shortly write about. The townspeople had achieved liberation through unspeakable suffering. They had sustained the bizarre paradox of a relatively peaceful, if humiliating, enemy occupation, followed by a destructive, if liberating, victory. Gratitude at salvation—freedom gained at the cost of incomprehensible despair—would be an ingredient of Beckett's future tragicomedy—a gloss, perhaps, on Lucky's "lucky" relationship to the brutal Pozzo in *Godot*.

Ultimately, Beckett's experience in Saint-Lô provided him with a long-awaited equanimity in a larger, metaphysical sense. It gave him a sense of balance, of what in *Godot* he would call the "tears" and "laughter" of the world—the black-comic alternation of elation and despair that is the individual's lot, as well as the nature of history.

Joyce, through Stephen Dedalus in *A Portrait of the Artist As a Young Man*, defines Aristotle's "pity" in the tragic emotion as "the feeling which arrests the mind in the presence of whatsoever is grave and constant in human sufferings and unites it with the human sufferer." He then defines the accompanying "fear" in tragic emotion as "the feeling which arrests the mind in the presence of whatsoever is grave and constant in human sufferings and unites it with the secret cause." Joyce's clear distinction between "pity" for the "sufferer" and "fear" for the "cause" might well have been the terms of reference with which Beckett long identified. But Saint-Lô, I suggest, also provided him, in concrete terms, with a living example of the human capacity both for destructiveness and for stoical forbearance, courage, humanity, and even humor in the face of brutal forces. It must also have stirred resonances within him of what he had first seen as a youth in Dublin and Belfast, and, as an adult, in London, Germany, and wartime France.

Beckett's activities in Saint-Lô, as described by those who worked with him, attest to those attributes of the man described in the introduction—his generosity, kindness, sense of responsibility, and modesty. His own comments, when he later reflected on this period, tell us much about the conclusions he had reached thus far concerning his life's experiences. In his 1946 radio speech, "The Capital of the Ruins," he specifically celebrated the dignity of mere survival in a "contingent" universe.

> I doubt if anyone who ever ducked bullets and shells in the hedgerows, waded through the mud on foot, and scrambled over the hedgerows never knowing when he might find himself looking into the muzzle of a German tank gun, will look back on those days with any remembered feeling other than of the deadly unrelenting fatigue and danger. Except when the Germans counterattacked, there was so little result to show for so much suffering; just a few hedgerows gained, each one just like those already behind and those still to take. . . . For most, it had been a thankless, disheartening battle, wrecked by the . . . losses . . . [of] sometimes nearly all.—Archival report of U.S. Armed Forces in Saint-Lô

> We are all born mad. Some remain so.—SAMUEL BECKETT, *Waiting for Godot*

Saint-Lô is thirty-one miles west of Caen and south of what have come to be known as Utah and Omaha beaches. Originally known as Briovère, the city was renamed after its most prestigious resident, Lauto or Lô, a sixth-century bishop, received sainthood. To the extent that the town had a cider mill in the northeast and paper mill in the northwest, one might have called it industrial, but it was primarily a trading center for the surrounding agricultural areas which produced beef cattle, dairy products, and fruit. With a population of about twelve thousand, it had had a long and turbulent history. Fortified by Charlemagne, it had been attacked by the Vikings, by Plantaganent English kings, and, during the Reformation, by reactionary French Catholics. These invasions were clearly insignificant compared to that of 1944. In fact, after the war, the French nicknamed Saint-Lô "Capital of Ruins," the title Beckett later used for his radio address. Since few towns in Europe had suffered such cataclysmic destruction, Saint-Lô received worldwide news coverage.[24]

Although I do not know how aware Beckett was of the following events, they provide background of the Red Cross mission and indicate the contingencies of human event and motivation—even in the supposedly well-planned strategies of military management. Furthermore, I would suggest that, once in Saint-Lô, Beckett would have learned some of the local history, details of which would have been reminiscent of the vanities and victories of those in power both in occupied and unoccupied France, as well as in Ireland during the Irish Uprising.

Saint-Lô had been targeted as a key area during the Normandy invasion because its location offered the Allies a jumping-off point to other areas. The Allies mounted attack after attack, from the beginning of June, through a severe siege from July 11 through July 19, until their final successful assault, July 25 and July 26. It was then that the "milk and honey" landscape, also renowned for its scent of apple blossoms, was transformed into a world of rubble and unburied bodies. Nevertheless, the Allies' military victory unhinged the entire west end of the German line, permitting the Allied breakthrough to Marigny and St. Gilles, which destroyed the German Seventh Army; after this, the Allies moved on to Brittany.

Operation Cobra, the air attack, was marked by the same kind of military intrigue and last-minute changes in strategy that characterized the larger Operation Overlord—all planned to distract the enemy (although it often accomplished a certain degree of confusion among the Allies). Although to many at the time the military goal was rational and straightforward, recent analysts have found it less so. James A. Huston points out that while Saint-Lô may have been a German communications center, there was no need, strategically or tactically, to proceed with destruction of such magnitude. There was no German air force there, he argues, and, since the Allies had yet to move into ground operations when the enormous bombardments began, there was no need to protect infantry forces. The devastation accomplished, he insists, was excessive if not irresponsible. That is (and as the Saint-Lois would surely have agreed), the maneuvers taken here were in total disregard of the most basic ethical guidelines of war. Huston cites Saint Augustine's "Conditions of Just War," which is based on the assumption that military actions can be condoned only if they are necessary for the restoration of justice: violence must be a *last* recourse toward the reinstatement of justice. Huston maintains that the use of saturated, rather than pinpoint bombing in Saint-Lô was the most significant evil there, and the results of the destruction that followed clearly outweighed any anticipated advantage. He concludes that with the French ultimately suffering more then the Germans or Allies, there was no advantage gained whatsoever.[25]

This was clearly not the position taken by the military.[26] The *Armed Forces in Action* report argues to the contrary, insisting that the bad weather limited air power, just as the hedgerows limited tank efficiency. Most of the significant fighting, it maintains, came down to the infantry's pushing ahead inch by inch within the hedgerows.[27] An air attack became essential.

Regardless of hindsight evaluations and recriminations, the Allied forces had a well-defined goal: to break open the entire Normandy front by attacking this narrow area, whose topography and location were unique. Set low in the Vire Valley, Saint-Lô, with its hills to the east and west, offered important access to the entire area. "On a map, [Saint-Lô] resembled a hub of a bicycle wheel, with eight major roads radiating from its center."[28] From the hills, one could even oversee the highways that led to other German units and their supplies.[29] The other key factor for targeting Saint-Lô concerned its hedgerows. These, along with their enclosed small fields, had been protecting the Germans from assault and had thus allowed them time and space to build important communications networks.

The hedgerows seemed impenetrable. Walls of earth and stone supported entangled bushes, brambles, vines, and trees, and they were three to five feet thick and four to ten feet high. As such, they provided the Germans immunity to artillery and mortar. Safely entrenched in their foxholes (which were covered with logs and earth) and always well armed, the enemy could keep watch overhead and know that, in the event the Allies attempted a ground attack, the turf above was filled with mines and booby traps. Finally, within the hedgerows were pastures that could always become citadels for army regrouping — either for organizational or strategic purposes. The Germans had already built an elaborate underground tunnel (called the Acropolis), where for two years they had been constructing hospital facilities; they could store all the food and arms they needed in these enclosures.[30] The entire area, eight square miles laced by nearly four thousand tough and deep-rooted trees, remained a formidable danger zone.

Allied victories were often tallied according to how many hedgerows were conquered. As the *New York Times* reported: "[Another] advance of 1,500 to 2,000 yards [and] Hill 122, just south of the forest, has been seized. Once two other hills—112 and 92, a little farther south—are in American hands, our infantry will dominate the surrounding country and the way will be open for a direct attack on Lessay and the area to the south" (July 13). *Stars and Stripes* claimed that fighting here was as hard as the first landings on the toughest beaches. To "advance three hedgerows" was a "sizable, bitterly contested advance." [31]

The beginning of the campaign, however, had black comic elements. On July 4, 1944, after the Americans performed a special Fourth of July holiday salute, the 111th Field Artillery of the Twenty-ninth Division began its siege. Using an early tactic that was common on the Second Front, the Allies dropped artillery shells stuffed with propaganda (written in German) and filled with timed fuses so they would burst high in the air and scatter. Their first goal was to demoralize, not kill, the enemy. Some of the leaflets read:

YOUR LEADERS HAVE PROMISED YOU:
That the Atlantic Wall is closed without gaps.
WE HAVE BROKEN THROUGH. . . .
That the German Luftwaffe is invincible.
IT HAS DESERTED YOU. . . .
WE, HOWEVER, PROMISE YOU: . . .
That your sacrifice in the sector of St. Lô is
    as senseless as that of your comrades on the Cotentin Peninsula.
That you can save yourselves, for yourselves and Germany, if you will see
    in time—
WHO LIES? WHO SPEAKS THE TRUTH?

The Germans retaliated with their own barrage of leaflets—appeals to the soldiers' sexual instincts. Images of scantily dressed women in the arms of happy male civilians were captioned: "[This is what you] would be doing [at] home instead of in the Army." [32]

Warfare followed—alternating gunfire and cease fires. Then the planes, artillery, tanks, and bulldozers (necessary to clear the rubble) arrived, along with the great human losses—for all but the Germans, who remained safe in the hedgerows. Any Allied troops also mired in the marshes and hedgerows were, at best, at a stalemate with the enemy. In addition, many lives were being lost as troops moved forward from the beaches.

Allied headquarters' response was carpet bombing, to be followed by a massive ground offensive. As the war chronicler Joseph Sullivan describes the situation, the bombing was accomplished only after deep rivalries were articulated not just between the high command but among the fighting men as well. Clear lines of authority were confused; unanticipated complexities arose regarding the combining of both air and ground forces. Field Marshal Montgomery, for example, was called weak and lacking in drive; Trafford Leigh-Mallory was considered unqualified for directing strategic air forces. Bombardiers, who had been assigned their own independent air missions, considered their "new diversion" to support the ground forces as "tragically wasteful." In the midst of battle, commanders threatened resignations.[33]

Because a straight line of highway northwest of Saint-Lô could serve as a check line for high altitude bombers, the next problem concerned whether there should be parallel or perpendicular bomb deployment. The bombs were to saturate a rectangular area one by five miles just south of the Saint-Lô–Periers Road. More than 1,500 heavy bombers entered in three waves (each fifteen minutes long, with bombs falling at the rate of one per second), with five minutes in between. "The target area would be pounded with elemental fury, saturated with 50,000 general purpose and fragmentation bombs."[34] The bombs spread fires everywhere, at the same time that the Germans' gas supplies, now also in flames, burned everything in sight.

Dissension then arose regarding how far the ground troops should and could safely move to assure proper followup measures, and as poor weather conditions continued, there were inaccurate range sightings and accidental bombings. On the evening of July 24, General Omar Bradley anticipated the possibility that if the back-stabbing did not stop, amid the confusion in orders, "it could develop into much more than another military setback"— the resignation of "Monty," "perhaps Ike . . . and my own."[35]

The gross errors in bombing had a profoundly demoralizing effect.[36] The regimental history of the 120th Infantry reports: "Huge flights of planes [arrived] in seemingly endless numbers. . . . Fascinated, we stood and watched this mighty drama. . . . Then came that awful rush of wind—that awful sound like the 'rattling of seeds in a dry gourd.' . . . The earth trembled and shook. Whole hedgerows disappeared and entire platoons were struck, huge geysers of earth erupted and subsided leaving gaping craters." On July 25, 111 men of the Seventh Corps were killed by the Eighth Air Force, while the Germans remained, still sheltered in the hedgerows, and the blame-calling among the generals continued. The final result was reported in the official archives of the U.S. Army: "The bombing caused an estimated 700 German casualties and 601 reported American casualties. In view of the fact that only 37 planes bombed north of the bomb safety line, it seems safe to assume that the disproportionately small number of German casualties was due to the fact that they were well dug in, whereas only a small fraction of the American troops had dug foxholes."[37]

The story of those who bore the brunt of the destruction—the Saint-

Lois—is similar to that of many others throughout France and the other occupied nations, who of necessity suffered the ravages of both the enemy and the Allies. In the case of Saint-Lô, with the innocents killed by the Allies—even in the service of annihilating the enemy—military or practical logic was seemingly at odds with ordinary common sense. If Hitler's campaign against the Jews was an example of human barbarism, the invasion in Saint-Lô was one of human absurdity.

Responses to the Saint-Lois' "liberation" were equally absurd: this is a "story of tears and blood. . . . In the collective memory of the French, the liberation will remain synonynous with the joy and hope that marked the following period" (emphasis added).[38] Press photographs captured old women with young orphans standing amid ruins, all of them throwing flowers to the liberating troops that had just destroyed their homes and families—the kind of material Jack Yeats might have painted. Numerous photographs ironically illustrated the "victories" during the last hours of warfare: house-to-house fighting when "face to face and only a few feet apart, the two groups shot it out in the street. [On one occasion,] four . . . Germans had been killed, one wounded, and the remaining one captured, while three Americans were killed, and one wounded."[39]

Saint-Lô was charred and broken, every landmark now ash: homes, shops, the city hall, prefecture, hospital, theaters, hotel, prison, asylum for the insane, and finally, the great church, Notre Dame, which had taken three-and-a-half centuries to build. Beneath the ruins were the dead and maimed. The town had become, in great part, a living cemetery. In such a world the survivors struggled to go on.

Even a year afterward, bodies were still being removed from the debris, and three thousand people were living among the ruins. A local correspondent likened Saint-Lô to "an upturned dustbin" where life began again, almost incredibly, after the holocaust: "Life started again in spite of the deadening atmosphere . . . in spite of the dust . . . darkness . . . [and] the mud which is everywhere."[40]

Reconstruction continued for ten years. Along with the Irish came the Swiss, and their Don Suisse project distributed clothing, shoes, furniture, and other essentials; they later organized a nursery, kindergarten, and sewing school.[41] So, too, the Americans came to assist the French with the continuing reconstruction. The hospital became a major facility in the area.

In the beginning, when Beckett was there, clearing away the debris by hand unearthed dead bodies and unused mines. Even though this lengthy and difficult task was eventually accomplished, for the next ten years deep cavities in the earth remained next to the newly constructed apartments and shops. And many people continued to live in prefabricated barracks next to

Beckett (*front, second from left*) joined the Red Cross in Saint-Lô to help rebuild one of the postwar ruins of the world. (*The Irish Times*)

the cavities or gravesites. The city still retained the look of a "temporary military post" or of a "temporary town around a dam-building project." It took fifteen years to complete major reconstruction, at a cost of more than ten billion francs.[42]

Reviewing Beckett's involvement with the Irish Red Cross, Eoin O'Brien says that in August 1945, an advance party was sent from Dublin to survey the situation. This included Beckett's physician-friend, Alan Thompson, later elected President of the Royal College of Physicians in Ireland and now director of the project. (They remained in close contact until Thompson's death in 1974.) The advance party also included "Mr. Samuel Beckett, Quartermaster [and Storekeeper]-Interpreter."[43] Equipment and supplies followed for the hundred makeshift wooden huts that were used for the hospital facilities; flowers and trees were also planted. The patients were all survivors of the bombings and concentration camps, and all of them suffered from tuberculosis, dysentery, and other diseases of wartime.

Soon the supplies arrived—174 tons of equipment, including six ambulances, a utility wagon and lorry, and medications like penicillin and blood serum.[44] Beckett's first tasks included picking up supplies and driving staff to and from various destinations—generally, doing whatever was called for, all of which he performed with enthusiasm and generosity. Harvey speaks of his meeting new arrivals from Ireland at Dieppe and driving them through Rouen to Saint-Lô.[45] O'Brien describes how, when Beckett went to greet new volunteers, he would arrive in his large Ford V-8 utility wagon and present them with enormous bags of plums, grapes, and pears. The staff's personal facilities were rudimentary: there was electricity, but no running water, and little in the way of entertainment. Their life was their work, and they worked until they had built a facility that could handle 200 outpatients and 115 inpatients.[46]

When more supplies arrived, Beckett worked alongside both local laborers and German POWs on loan from the French government. There were about one thousand such prisoners, and they sorted, stacked, and made stock cards for the 250 tons of supplies that had been received. The prisoners were treated respectfully, given the same kind of uniform that Beckett wore, and sometimes they attended the unit's occasional recreational events, like picnics at the beach. One of the attending physicians, James Gaffney, describes Beckett's general caring and good nature: "[Beckett] is a most valuable asset to the unit—terribly conscientious about his work and enthusiastic about the future of the hospital; [he] like[s] a game of bridge and in every way [is] a most likeable chap, aged abut [sic] 38–40, [of] no religious persuasion; I should say a free thinker—but he pounced on a little rosary beads which was on a stall in Notre Dame to bring back as a little present to Tommy D. It was very thoughtful of him." [47]

"The Capital of the Ruins"

After Beckett returned to Paris—the time of his great creative "siege"—he wrote the radio speech "The Capital of the Ruins" (June 10, 1946). The speech was occasioned by Dublin press coverage of France's ostensible lack of appreciation of the Irish effort in Saint-Lô.[48] Beckett's intention was reconciliatory, to praise both the French and Irish. However, his decision to make a public statement—exceptional for this man—and the nature of that statement deserve close inspection, for Beckett is atypically explicit in his personal and philosophical reflections. We know, in retrospect, that the end of the war marked a major turning point in his life; in this speech, Beckett went beyond the Saint-Lô experience to express a vision derived from his entire life thus far. He would later say that he wrote from "impotence" and "ignorance," but there is a sense here of his own wisdom and self-confidence. Perhaps for just this moment Beckett experienced a sense of "knowing" and a conviction of his own courage. Perhaps these were to be the foundation for his retreat to "the room," during which he engaged the world of his imagination. Beckett was forty when he wrote the speech.

In this beautiful and moving statement, Beckett exalts both the comfort to be drawn from the inward human capacity to surmount circumstances of the utmost gravity and the sustenance to be given and gained in moments of camaraderie. He also sets forth several articles of faith which will resonate throughout his great works to come.

The first is his awareness of the human capacity to endure the caprices of circumstance: "What was important was not our having penicillin . . . [but] the occasional glimpse obtained, by us in them [the patients] and, who knows, by them in us . . . of that smile at the human condition as little to be extinguished by bombs as to be broadened by the elixirs of Burroughes and Welcome, the smile deriding, among other things, the having and not having, the giving and the taking, sickness and health." The "smile deriding . . . the having and not having" would become, in *Waiting for Godot*, that which enables humanity to face the fact that "The tears of the world are a constant quantity." The smile also enables the consolation one derives from the corollary truth that "the same is true of the laugh."

Beckett's second point would seem to be that while the material universe is "provisional" and ephemeral, acts of mundane generosity are not: "The hospital of wooden huts and its gardens between the Vire and Bayeux roads will continue to discharge its function, and its cured. 'Provisional' is not the term it was in this universe become provisional. It will continue to discharge its function long after the Irish are gone." Beckett would seem to be extolling the human impulse to give of oneself to the suffering. It is this that is a steadfast thread in the human fabric, an aspect of life that is not provisional. Implicit in this remark is Beckett's contrast between the abiding nature of the human spirit and the transitory trappings of worldly power, between the permanence of generosity and the impermanent edifices of the material world. Also implicit here is his faith, as he again writes in *Waiting for Godot*, that regardless of circumstance, humanity will "represent worthily the foul brood to which a cruel fate has consigned us."

In perhaps his most optimistic statement, Beckett declares that the act of giving uplifts the giver as well as the recipient: "Those who were in Saint-Lô will come home realising that they got at least as good as they gave." This may be our salvation as we await Godot.

Beckett would proceed to evoke artistically increasingly sparse human habitations, and his worlds and its figures would seem to pale in comparison with, say, James Joyce's grand invocations of human possibility. But Beckett, perhaps more so than Joyce, had come to understand the limitations imposed upon the individual by powerful and eternally unpredictable inner and outer forces—the limits posed by the absurdity of the human condition. In this remarkable radio speech, Beckett defines what we come to intuit in his later work as life's redeeming virtues. The individual's fate may be provisional, and the course of history may be provisional, but the "smile" that derides the conditional is not. Its source is in the human spirit, and from this come healers of a moment—those who build hospitals, those who dance a jig, and those who would entertain a reader. The hospitals, like the dancers and the names of fictional characters, will fade, just as the names of the ordinary Irish or French patriots will be forgotten—but the spirit that moves them will not.

Finally, as a man of specific place and origin—always rooted in this world and certainly not an artist-would-be-god or an unworldly aesthete—Beckett stresses that the Irish in Saint-Lô demonstrated the best part of human nature, that quality that seeks to heal or console, rather than to dominate or desolate. With evident Irish pride he adds: "I think that to the end of its hospital days, it will be called the Irish Hospital, and after that the huts, when they have been turned into dwellings, the Irish huts."

At the end of the speech, revealing what was perhaps for him the crucial wisdom that would direct his future work, he adds: "I may perhaps venture to mention another [possibility], more remote but perhaps of greater import . . . the possibility that [those in Saint-Lô] . . . *got indeed what they could hardly give, a vision and sense of a time-honoured concept of humanity in ruins, and perhaps even an inkling of the terms in which our condition is to be thought again.* These will have been in France" (emphasis added). The willingness to give of oneself to the suffering is not only an abiding part of human nature. It is also the very means through which one can gain an "inkling" of the mystery of the human condition.

When Beckett wrote this speech, he had already resigned his post at Saint-Lô and was settled in Paris. This speech was thus one of his earliest postwar writings. Indeed, his earlier remark about the endurance of the Irish spirit and his final reminder that these lessons will have been consummated in France reconcile the land of his origin with the land of his destiny.

In addressing "our condition . . . to be thought again," Beckett braces himself for the great creative task now facing him.

Beckett was not a fragile and reclusive man set apart from the real world. He was a sensitive and courageous man, marked by and responsive to the world around him. Every city he lived in, every friend he made, every painting he studied, and every writer he read—all became a part of the man and part of his art. Brother fighting and consoling brother, the individual seeking meaning and sustenance from within and without, the capacity for humor which enables the spirit to transcend the harm that human nature and the human condition impose—these would be "thought again" in the works to come.

Notes

Introduction

Notes to epigraphs: As reported by Israel Shenker in *Words and Their Masters* (New York: Doubleday, 1974), p. 198. "Humanistic Quietism [a review of Thomas McGreevy's *Poems*]," *Dublin Magazine* 9 (1934): 79. As cited in Alec Reid, *All I Can Manage, More Than I Could* (Dublin: Dolmen Press, 1968), p. 15.

1. E. M. Cioran, "Encounter with Beckett," *Partisan Review* 43 (1976): 280.

2. Stated by his London publisher, John Calder, in "Beckett—Man and Artist," *Adam: International Review* 35 (1970): 337. Reid describes another of Beckett's frequently cited qualities, his "genius for companionship"—that ability to make others comfortable through the "instinctive recognition" of their needs. "The Reluctant Prizeman," *Arts* 29 (November 1969): 68.

3. Deirdre Bair, *Samuel Beckett: A Biography* (New York: Harcourt Brace Jovanovich, 1978), pp. 448–450, verified by Herbert Blau scholar L. B. Peskine in personal correspondence, June 20, 1992.

4. Personal conversation, August 17, 1967.

5. Personal conversation, November 12, 1987.

6. Rick Cluchey called Beckett a "saint," in personal conversation, July 9, 1991. Five of Beckett's directors, at a forum at New York University, October 24, 1991, spoke at length of his kindness. Public expressions of affectionate gratitude from Beckett's directors date back to Beckett's earliest productions. See Alan Simpson's *Beckett and Behan and a Theatre in Dublin* (London: Routledge & Kegan Paul, 1962) and Calder's *Beckett at 60: A Festschrift* (London: Calder & Boyars, 1967). Jonathan Kalb cites pertinent material involving Walter Asmus, Herbert Blau, Pierre Chabert, Ruby Cohn, Jack MacGowran, Alan Schneider, and others in *Beckett in Performance* (Cambridge: Cambridge University Press, 1989), pp. 264–270. See also Linda Ben-Zvi, *Women in Beckett* (Urbana: University of Illinois Press, 1990), where actresses, including Billie Whitelaw, discuss their professional relationship with Beckett; Martha Fehsenfeld and Dougald McMillan, *Beckett in the Theatre* (New York: Riverrun Press, 1988); S. E. Gontarski, ed., *On Beckett* (New York: Grove Press, 1986); and Lois Oppenheim, *Directing Beckett* (Ann Arbor: University of Michigan Press, 1994).

7. Bair, *Samuel Beckett*, p. xi.

8. Despite Beckett's public silence, his nephew Edward Beckett told the author

(April 9, 1992) of his uncle's displeasure with the book. See Richard Ellmann, *New York Review of Books*, June 15, 1978, 3; Hugh Kenner, *Saturday Review* 5 (August 1978): 46; Martin Esslin, *Encounter* 52 (1979): 49–55; John Calder, *Journal of Beckett Studies* (Spring 1979): 74–79. Since its spring 1990 issue, *The Beckett Circle* has periodically listed Bair's errors.

9. Martin Esslin, *The Theatre of the Absurd* (New York: Doubleday, 1961), p. 11. *New York Times*, September 17, 1961, sec. 2: 1. See also May 6, 1956, sec. 2: 1. Another frequent description of Beckett emphasized his "paradoxical combination of a Frenchman's fundamental 'commitment' to life and an Irishman's basic good nature." See Alan Schneider, "Meeting with Beckett: A Personal Chronicle," *Chelsea Review* (Autumn 1958): 3.

10. "The Point Is Irrelevance," *Nation*, May 14, 1956: 325.

11. "It's This Way?" *Newsweek*, February 24, 1964: 93.

12. Israel Shenker, *New York Times*, May 6, 1956, sec. 2: 1. *Village Voice*, March 1, 1962, 1.

13. Beckett has frequently been quoted as recalling his birth: "I have a clear memory of my own fetal existence." John Gruen, "Samuel Beckett Talks about Beckett," *Vogue* 127 (February 1970): 108. See also Nino Frank, *Il Mondo*, trans. Ciccio, *Introductory Bulletin* (November 1955): 5. Since Gruen reports that Beckett said this, critics have frequently quoted Gruen. Beckett presumably remarked: "Even before the foetus can draw breath it is in a state of barrenness and of pain," p. 108. In his beautifully illustrated (and conceived) book, Eoin O'Brien cites Irish locales in Beckett's writing illustrative of Beckett's birth memory, for example, in *Company*: "You were born on an Easter Friday after long labour. Yes I remember. The sun had not long sunk behind the larches. Yes I remember." *The Beckett Country* (Dublin: Black Cat Press; London, Faber & Faber, 1986), p. 1.

14. Bair, *Samuel Beckett*, p. 144.

15. Bair, *Samuel Beckett*, pp. 327–328.

16. In addition to the references cited below, I am indebted to Cathleen Culotta Andonian, who provided more than one hundred leads to biographical information. *Samuel Beckett: A Reference Guide* (Boston: G. K. Hall, 1989). Some of the biographical details in the present book were originally documented in my doctoral dissertation, "Dialectic of the Beast and Monk: The Dramas of Samuel Beckett" (University of Wisconsin, 1966).

17. James Knowlson, *Samuel Beckett: An Exhibition* (London: Turret Books, 1971), pp. 20–21.

18. Andrew Kennedy, *Samuel Beckett* (Cambridge: Cambridge University Press, 1989), p. 4. Knowlson, in *Samuel Beckett: An Exhibition*, dismisses the idea that Beckett's Dublin of the 1920s and 1930s had an impact upon his writing: "It would be quite futile to attempt to illustrate aspects of the setting or of the city of the region, since this would throw no light whatsoever upon the actual world in which Belacqua and Murphy (with some difficulty) live and move" (p. 20). Lawrence E. Harvey says of Beckett and World War II: "No doubt the break in normal existence occasioned by the war served to accentuate [Beckett's] passage from youth to middle age." See *Samuel Beckett: Poet and Critic* (Princeton: Princeton University Press, 1970), p. 350.

19. See Daniel Bell, *The End of Ideology* (Cambridge: Harvard University Press, 1988), pp. 35–36.

Chapter 1. Ireland

Note to epigraph: Jack MacGowran, "MacGowran on Beckett [interview by Richard Toscan]," *On Beckett: Essays and Criticism*, ed. S. E. Gontarski (New York: Grove Press, 1986), p. 223.

1. Lawrence E. Harvey, *Samuel Beckett: Poet and Critic* (Princeton: Princeton University Press, 1970), p. 154. According to Deirdre Bair, May was from landed gentry. *Samuel Beckett: A Biography* (New York: Harcourt Brace Jovanovich, 1978), p. 7.

2. Eoin O'Brien, *The Beckett Country* (Dublin: Black Cat Press; London: Faber & Faber, 1986), p. 3. See first chapter for a detailed discussion of the Foxrock landscape. Dorothy Coote Dudgeon, in Colin Duckworth, "Beckett's Early Background: A New Zealand Biographical Appendix," *New Zealand Journal of French Studies* (October 1980): 65. Future references will be cited as Duckworth.

3. Vivian Mercier, "Ireland/The World: Beckett's Irishness," in *Yeats, Joyce, and Beckett: New Light on Three Modern Irish Writers*, ed. Kathleen McGrory and John Unterecker (Lewisburg, Pa.: Bucknell University Press, 1976), p. 148.

4. Bair, *Samuel Beckett*, pp. 16, 22–23, 12–13.

5. Among the many who contradict Bair's description of May are Beatrice Glenavy, *Today We Will Only Gossip* (London: Constable, 1964). Glenavy emphasizes "the kindness of May Beckett's heart" (p. 48). As Harvey writes in *Samuel Beckett*, Beckett's mother may have been more austere and religious than his father, a pillar of strength and security during the inevitable crises of family life, but she was "no less tender and affectionate" (p. 147).

6. Dudgeon writes: "It is [in] the intention of providing an appendix, even a corrective, . . . that the following account is offered." See Duckworth, "Beckett's Early Background," p. 59.

7. Beckett also spoke of religion as "irksome" and of no comfort in times of sorrow. See Tom Driver, "Beckett by the Madeleine," *Columbia University Forum*, 4 (1961): 21–25, reprinted in Lawrence Graver and Raymond Federman, *Beckett: The Critical Heritage* (London: Routledge & Kegan Paul, 1979), p. 220.

8. Duckworth, "Beckett's Early Background," p. 63.

9. Mercier, "Ireland/The World," pp. 148–149. See Barry McGovern's similar remarks regarding Beckett's later friends and divided loyalties. "Seanchaí," *New Theater Review* 1.4 (1988): 10. Throughout *The Irish Tradition* (New York: Oxford University Press, 1969), Mercier speaks of Beckett as having made expatriation into a way of life. An interesting discussion of Beckett's use of Irishness is Sighle Kennedy's "Spirals of Need: Irish Prototypes in Samuel Beckett's Fiction," in McGrory and Unterecker, *Yeats, Joyce, and Beckett*, pp. 153–166.

10. Duckworth, "Beckett's Early Background," p. 64.

11. Harvey reports that Beckett had recurrent nightmares about this. *Samuel Beckett*, p. 298.

12. Alec Reid, "The Reluctant Prizeman," *Arts* 29 (November 1969): 64.

13. Beckett's profound grief at his father's death is discussed in chapter 5. O'Brien is rare among scholars in noting that Bill encouraged Beckett's intellectual interests, *Beckett Country*, p. 8. Harvey, *Samuel Beckett*, p. 154, remarks that "Beckett admired throughout the years his parents' life," despite its overly organized and bourgeois nature.

14. Numerous scholars and actors repeat this. McGovern, for instance, says: "He was born in a fine house of loving parents." See "Seanchaí," p. 10; many also cite Beckett's recollection of "that dreadful man," who "asked me if I'd had an unhappy childhood,

and was so disappointed when I told him, No, I'd been very happy and was fond of my parents." See also Harvey, *Samuel Beckett*, p. 154, and Reid, "Reluctant Prizeman," p. 64.

15. MacGowran, "MacGowran on Beckett," p. 223.

16. O'Brien, *Beckett Country*, p. 359, note 20.

17. Reid, "Reluctant Prizeman," p. 64.

18. O'Brien, *Beckett Country*, p. 358, note 11. Reid, "Reluctant Prizeman," p. 65, has him classified as a "medium heavyweight."

19. Harvey, *Samuel Beckett*, p. 154.

20. James Knowlson, *Samuel Beckett: An Exhibition* (London: Turret Books, 1971), pp. 20–21.

21. O'Brien, *Beckett Country*, p. 119. Reid summarizes Beckett's Portora days: "He was outstanding, and was regarded as an independent, if not indeed a rebel, in a class that contained half a dozen future Scholars of Trinity," in "Reluctant Prizeman," p. 65.

22. Duckworth, "Beckett's Early Background," p. 57.

23. O'Brien, *Beckett Country*, pp. 20, 24–29, 112, 350 note 43, 351, note 67.

24. Duckworth, "Beckett's Early Background," p. 60; O'Brien, *Beckett Country*, p. 214.

25. Duckworth, "Beckett's Early Background," pp. 61–62.

26. O'Brien, *Beckett Country*, p. 225.

27. MacGowran, in Gontarski, *On Beckett*, p. 223.

28. John Pilling, *Samuel Beckett* (London: Routledge & Kegan Paul, 1976), p. 1.

29. He discussed this with Sam Ben-Zvi, an Israeli, in the context of their shared experience of civil war and made the cryptic comment: "You can't go home again." This was told to the author by Linda Ben-Zvi, December 22, 1989.

30. Glenavy, *Today We Will Only Gossip*, p. 87.

31. Paul Johnson, *Ireland: Land of Troubles* (London: Eyre Methuen, 1980) and Sheila Lawlor, *Britain and Ireland, 1914–45* (Dublin: Gill & Macmillan, 1983). Other books on these questions include Edgar Holt, *Protest in Arms: The Irish Troubles, 1916–1923* (London: McClelland, 1960); Nicholas Mansergh, *The Irish Question, 1849–1921* (Toronto: University of Toronto Press, 1965); Dorothy Macardle, *The Irish Republic* (New York: Farrar, Straus & Giroux, 1965); Eric Strauss, *Irish Nationalism and British Democracy* (New York: Columbia University Press, 1951); George William Russell [A.E.], *Ireland and the Empire at the Court of Conscience* (Dublin: Talbot Press, 1921); Francis P. Jones, *History of the Sinn Finn Movement and the Irish Rebellion of 1916* (New York: P. J. Kennedy, 1917); Patrick S. O'Hegarty, *A History of Ireland under the Union, 1801 to 1922* (London: Methuen, 1952); W. B. Wells, *A History of the Irish Rebellion of 1916* (Dublin and London: Maunsel, 1918); and Nora Connolly O'Brien, *The Unbroken Tradition* (New York: Boni & Liveright, 1918).

32. Lawlor, *Britain and Ireland*, p. 9.

33. Quoted in Macardle, *Irish Republic*, p. 163.

34. Quoted in David Greene and Dan H. Laurence, eds., *The Matter of Ireland* (London: R. Hart-Davis, 1962), p. 107. Glenavy, not only a friend of Beckett's aunt Cissie and uncle Boss Sinclair, but of G. B. Shaw, notes, in a lighter vein, Shaw's fondness for certain street ballads, including the following (sung to the tune of "Yankee Doodle"): "De Valera had a cat / Who sat upon the fender, / Everytime she heard a shot / She shouted 'No surrender.'" *Today We Will Only Gossip*, pp. 127–128.

35. J. J. Lee, *Ireland, 1912–1985: Politics and Society* (Cambridge: Cambridge University Press, 1989), p. 30.

36. Redmond Fitzgerald, *Cry Blood, Cry Erin* (London: Barry & Rockliff, 1966), p. 65.

37. F. X. Martin, *Leaders and Men of the Easter Rising: Dublin 1916* (Ithaca: Cornell University Press, 1967), p. 132.

38. Even revisionist historians, reexamining the quality of support given the Rebels, as well as their tactics, reluctantly admit that Pearse and his followers foresaw their roles as sacrificial figures. Lee first argues that people of every class, both Catholic and Protestant, repudiated the Rebellion. Then he suggests that the Rebels' "martyrdom" was a pragmatic justification for their mismanagement of affairs. *Ireland, 1912–1985*, pp. 18–20, 26, 28, 30, 37, 41. See *The Modernisation of Irish Society, 1848–1918* (Dublin: Gill & Macmillan, 1973), as well as Ruth Dudley Edwards, *James Connolly: The Triumph of Failure* (Dublin: Gill & Macmillan, 1981); F. S. L. Lyons, *Culture and Anarchy in Ireland 1880–1939* (New York: Oxford University Press, 1980); Desmond Fitzpatrick, *Politics and Irish Life, 1913–21* (Dublin: Gill & Macmillan, 1977); and the less vitriolic Peter De Rosa, *Rebels: The Irish Rising of 1916* (London, Bantam, 1990).

39. Quoted in Lee, *Ireland, 1912–1985*, p. 26.

40. See, for example, Lawlor, *Britain and Ireland*; Fitzgerald, *Cry Blood, Cry Erin*; Kevin B. Nowland, *The Making of 1916* (Dublin: Stationery Office, 1916); and Thomas M. Coffee, *Agony at Easter: The 1916 Irish Uprising* (London: Macmillan, 1969).

41. Quoted in R. M. Fox, *James Connolly: The Forerunner* (Tralee, Ireland: Kerryman, 1946), pp. 162–163.

42. Quoted in Desmond Ryan, *The Man Called Pearse* (Dublin: Maunsel, 1919), pp. 117–118.

43. Connolly's writings are filled with such statements—e.g., "No agency less potent than the red tide of war on Irish soil will ever be able to enable the Irish race to recover its self-respect"; "I stand over all my acts and words. When I was a child of ten I went down on my knees by my bedside one night and promised God that I should devote my life to an effort to free my country. I have kept that promise." See Desmond Ryan, *James Connolly: His Life, Work, and Writings* (Dublin: Talbot Press, 1924), and O'Brien, *The Unbroken Tradition*.

44. Fitzgerald, *Cry Blood, Cry Erin*, p. 90. Desmond Fitzgerald, addressing the reason why more people did not initially "rally to the Republic" makes a parenthetical observation that relates to Beckett's Resistance activities. "The Rebels lacked popularity," Fitzgerald begins, because although their goals may have been just, their means were often unsavory; so too, he adds: "the maquis were unpopular in many French villages for exactly the same reason."

45. Lee, *Ireland, 1912–1985*, p. 29, is incorrect in saying of the Rising that "No detailed newspaper reports appeared until early May."

46. Richard Ellmann, *James Joyce* (New York: Oxford University Press, 1959; rev. ed., 1962), pp. 62, 704. Sheehy-Skeffington was Joyce's close college friend. This will be discussed further in chapter 3.

47. Quoted in Johnson, *Ireland: Land of Troubles*, p. 149.

48. Quoted in Coffey, *Agony at Easter*, pp. 14, 18.

49. D. G. Boyce, *Englishmen and Irish Troubles* (London: Jonathan Cape, 1972), p. 57.

50. Even the *Times*, November 30, 1920, wrote of "the nightmare of terror by which [the Irish] are cowed and tortured." See also Boyce, *Englishmen and Irish Troubles*. On the other hand, O'Brien, *Beckett Country*, p. 65, discussing the retaliative measures taken by the Free State against its adversaries, mentions the Noel Lemass grave site, a political memorial that children of Beckett's generation knew. Lemass was abducted and killed, and his body was dumped in the Glencree area.

51. Glenavy, *Today We Will Only Gossip*, pp. 90, 105–106.

52. O'Hegarty, *History of Ireland*, p. 90.

53. Glenavy, *Today We Will Only Gossip*, pp. 83, 112–113. O'Brien tells of the unjust trial and publicity given the retaliatory execution of a local gardener. *Beckett Country*, p. 650.

54. Verified at the library, August 5, 1991. Books deposited under the terms of the Industrial and Commercial Property Act were largely religious. See also *National Library of Ireland*, ed. R. I. Best (Dublin: Stationery Office, 1927).

55. *Dublin Magazine* (June 1924): 82. See also A. G. S., *A Subject Bibliography of the First World War* and *The Subject Index to Periodicals* (London: Library Association), published yearly through the 1920s. The latter divided books into these classifications: theology, philosophy, history, politics, economics, science, science and technology. The category "war" was further broken down into ethics, economics, inevitable causes, and human nature.

56. Wilfred Owen, "The Parable of the Old Man and the Young," *The Collected Poems of Wilfred Owen*, ed. C. Day-Lewis (New York: New Directions, 1964), p. 42.

57. Paul Fussell, *The Great War and Modern Memory* (New York: Oxford University Press, 1975), p. 35. See also H. Stuart Hughes, *Consciousness and Society: The Reorientation of European Social Thought, 1890–1930* (New York: Alfred A. Knopf, 1961); George A. Panchias, ed., *Promise of Greatness: The War of 1914–1918* (New York: John Day, 1968); Roland N. Stromberg, *An Intellectual History of Modern Europe* (Englewood Cliffs, N.J.: Prentice-Hall, 1975); and Theodore Ropp, *War in the Modern World* (Durham, N.C.: Duke University Press, 1959). One of the best introductions to the War remains A. J. P. Taylor's *The First World War* (London: Hamish Hamilton, 1963).

58. Joseph Wood Krutch, *The Modern Temper* (New York: Harcourt, Brace & World, 1956), p. 11.

59. Frederick Hoffman, *The Twenties* (New York: Free Press, 1962), p. 275.

60. Kenneth C. Bailey, *A History of Trinity College, Dublin, 1892–1945* (Dublin: The University Press, 1947), p. 64.

61. Bair, *Samuel Beckett*, p. 36.

62. Bailey, *History of Trinity College*, pp. 42–43. In 1923, the administration worked out a compensatory mechanism to account for its enormous loss of rental income — large sums of defaulted monies on which the college depended — subsequent to the land purchase legislation.

63. Bailey, *History of Trinity College*, p. 77. Bailey, p. 80, writes: "The backbone of instruction" in the four "classes of Laud's Statues — Junior and Senior Freshmen, and Junior and Senior Sophistes — consists of in the Freshman year": elementary mathematics (arithmetic, algebra, trigonometry), mathematical physics (statics and dynamics), logic, English, Latin, and Greek. English courses included the first two books of *Paradise Lost* and *Areopagitica*; selections from Dryden, Pope, Swift, Addison, Gray, Goldsmith's *Traveller* and *Deserted Village*; Johnson's *Lives* of Addison, Pope, and Swift; *Macbeth*; and some of Bacon's *Essays*. Latin works included speeches by Cicero, two books of Horace's *Odes*, one of Livy's, one Terence play, the fourth and sixth books of the *Aeneid*, and the Greek studies were comprised of Demosthenes, Euripides, Herodotus, Plato, Sophocles, and Homer. The Sophistes' program typically consisted of English, mathematical physics, ethics, logic, astronomy, and an additional course of study, such as two foreign languages, experimental sciences, or natural sciences.

64. Vivian Mercier, *Beckett/Beckett* (New York: Oxford University Press, 1977), p. 35.

65. Knowlson, *Samuel Beckett: An Exhibition*, p. 52.

66. See the bibliography in Virginia Williams, *Surrealism, Quantum Philosophy, and World*

War I (New York: Garland, 1987), pp. 304–320. Williams also discusses the "unprecedented" direct contribution of many scientists (some subsequent Nobel laureates) who were systematically employed to develop advanced war machinery—including James De War, Ernest Rutherford, W. H. Bragg, Paul Langevin, Marie Curie, Walter Nerst, Fritz Haber (pp. 6–7).

67. Bailey, *History of Trinity College*, chapter 9.

68. Bailey, *History of Trinity College*, p. 92.

69. See *Freeman's Journal* and *Irish Times*, October 15, 1923: 4 and 7, respectively.

70. Kenneth and Alice Hamilton, *Condemned to Life: The World of Samuel Beckett* (Grand Rapids, Mich.: William B. Eerdmans, 1976), p. 19. MacGowran, in McGrory and Unterecker, *Yeats, Joyce, and Beckett*, p. 173.

71. Roger Little, "Beckett's Mentor: Rudmose-Brown: Sketch for a Portrait," *Irish University Review* 14 (Spring 1984): 40, a special Beckett issue, ed. Maurice Harmon.

72. See, for example, *Dublin Magazine*, March 1924: 721–729, for his essay on Provençal poetry. His poems were also published there in July 1924: 1045–1046. See the August 1923 issue for his essay on the history of French literature.

73. Reid, "Reluctant Prizeman," p. 65.

74. *Irish Times*, October 6, 1923: 15.

75. Dawson Byrne, *The Story of Ireland's National Theatre: The Abbey Theatre* (Dublin: Talbot Press, 1929); Lennox Robinson, *Ireland's Theatre: A History, 1899–1951* (London: Sidgwick & Jackson, 1951); Gerald Fay, *The Abbey Theatre: Cradle of Genius* (London: Hollis, 1958). Knowlson, *Samuel Beckett: An Exhibition*, p. 23.

76. Bair, *Samuel Beckett*, pp. 41, 43.

77. Mercier, *Beckett/Beckett*, p. 38, referring to the unpublished "Censorship in the Saorstat [Free State]," as quoted by Harvey, *Samuel Beckett*, p. 415.

78. Seamus Deane, "Irish Poetry and Irish Nationalism," in *Two Decades of Irish Writing*, ed. Douglas Dunn (Chester Springs, Pa.: Dufour Editions, 1975), p. 8.

79. George Steiner, *Language and Silence* (New York: Atheneum, 1967), pp. 12–54, 4. Like Hugh Kenner in *The Stoic Comedians: Flaubert, Joyce, and Beckett* (Boston: Beacon, 1962), Steiner creates his own genealogy. James Atlas has an interesting discussion of Steiner's point in "The Prose of Samuel Beckett," in Dunn, *Two Decades*, pp. 186–196.

80. *Dublin Magazine* 1 (March 1924): 683. The *Irish Book Lover* is almost entirely devoted to Irish literature.

81. Samuel Beckett, "Recent Irish Poetry," *Bookman* 86 (August 1934): 235–236 (under the pseudonym Andrew Belis).

82. Carlos Fuentes, as quoted in Dunn, *Two Decades*, p. 6.

83. Bair, *Samuel Beckett*, pp. 42, 52.

84. McGovern, "Seanchaí," p. 10.

85. As quoted in Little, "Beckett's Mentor," p. 39.

86. See Bailey, *History of Trinity College*, pp. 93, 107.

87. Pilling, *Samuel Beckett*, p. 2.

88. Liam De Paor, *Divided Ulster* (Harmondsworth: Penguin, 1950); David Harkness, *Northern Ireland since 1920* (Dublin: Criterion, 1983); J. C. Beckett and R. E. Glasscock, eds. *Belfast* (London: BBC, 1967). See also St. John Ervine, *Craigavon: Ulsterman* (London: Allen & Unwin, 1949), and Michael Hopkinson, *Green against Green* (Dublin: Gill & Macmillan, 1988).

89. De Paor, *Divided Ulster*, p. 113.

90. Paddy Hillyard, "Law and Order," in *Northern Ireland: The Background to the Conflict*, ed. John Darby (Belfast: Appletree Press, 1983), pp. 34–35.

91. Michael MacDonald, *Children of Wrath* (Cambridge: Polity Press, 1986), p. 8. Also see J. Bowyer Bell, *The Secret Army: The IRA, 1916–1970* (New York: John Day, 1970), and D. W. Harkness, *The Restless Dominion* (New York: New York University Press, 1970).

92. MacDonald, *Children of Wrath*, p. 59.

93. Darby, *Northern Ireland*, p. 22.

94. *Belfast Star*, April 13, 1928. See also *Irish Times*, April 13, 1928: 11 and March 10, 1928: 8.

Chapter 2. Paris, 1928

Note to epigraph: Cited in John Pilling, *Samuel Beckett* (London: Routledge & Kegan Paul, 1976), p. 3.

1. Maurice Nadeau, *The History of Surrealism* (New York: Macmillan, 1965), p. 44. Would-be critic Leon Trotsky, in Paris in 1916, commented: "One of the results of this war is to have reduced art to bankruptcy." Gilles Neret, *The Art of the Twenties* (New York: Rizzoli, 1986), p. 35. Just as war had destroyed everything, the Dadaists set out to destroy art. Marcel Duchamp's *Mona Lisa*, with its Dali-esque mustache, assured the spectator that this was no longer an objet d'art; Francis Picabia's nonfunctional machines did the same.

2. Even the look of Paris in certain quarters, with its mixture of the old (in design) and new (in building materials), bespoke the contemporary impulse to sweep aside the outworn mentality of the prewar period. Auguste and Gustave Perret designed classical buildings in glass, metal, and concrete. Le Corbusier's Voisin Plan for rebuilding the city in pristine and functional angular forms was widely discussed. See André Salmon, "Letter from Paris," *Apollo* 9 (January–June 1929): 41, and J. Porcher, "Chronique d'Architecture moderne," *Gazette des Beaux-Arts* 2 (July–December 1929): 45–60. For overviews of the period discussed in this chapter, see William Wiser, *The Crazy Years: Paris in the Twenties* (New York: Atheneum, 1983); Hugh Ford, *Published in Paris: A Literary Chronicle of Paris in the 1920s and 1930s* (New York: Collier, 1975); Noel Riley Fitch, *Sylvia Beach and the Lost Generation* (New York: W. W. Norton, 1985); Ernest Hemingway, *A Moveable Feast* (New York: Scribner's, 1964); Malcolm Cowley, *Exile's Return* (New York: Viking Press, 1961); Morley Callaghan, *That Summer in Paris: Memories of Tangled Friendships* (New York: Coward-McCann, 1963); Gertrude Stein, *The Autobiography of Alice B. Toklas* (New York: Literary Guild, 1933), and *Paris France* (New York: Scribner's, 1964); Roger Shattuck, *The Banquet Years* (New York: Vintage, 1968); Samuel Putnam, *Paris Was Our Mistress* (New York: Viking Press, 1947); Joseph Barry, *Right Bank, Left Bank, Paris and Parisians* (New York: W. W. Norton, 1951); Sylvia Beach, *Shakespeare & Company* (New York: Harcourt, Brace, 1959); and Edmund Wilson, *The Shores of Light: A Literary Chronicle of the Twenties and Thirties* (New York: Farrar, Straus and Young, 1952).

3. "Beckett Across the Arts" has been a subject of discussion at the Modern Language Association for many years. See Lois Gordon, "Beckett Across the Arts," *The Beckett Circle* 15 (Spring 1993): 5. At the International Beckett Festival at The Hague, April 8–18, 1992, James Knowlson and many others addressed this subject.

4. Galleries bordering the Luxembourg Gardens displayed the postimpressionists, later acquired by the Jeu de Paume or Louvre. Gaston Diehl, *The Moderns* (New York: Crown, n.d.), pp. 105–107.

5. On the war and Surrealists, see Virginia Williams, *Surrealism, Quantum Philosophy, and World War I* (New York: Garland, 1987), pp. 13, 53. See also Frederick Karl, *Modern and Mod-*

ernism (New York: Atheneum, 1985), pp. 357–360; Jacqueline Chénier-Gendron, *Surrealism*, trans. Vivian Folkenflik (New York: Columbia University Press, 1990), pp. 3, 30.

6. André Breton, "What Is Surrealism?" in *The Modern Tradition*, ed. Richard Ellmann and Charles Feidelson, Jr. (New York: Oxford University Press, 1965), p. 602.

7. Enoch Brater discusses Beckett and Paris's cultural life (the world of Dali, Vertov, Cocteau, Tzara, Anouilh, and Aurenche) and how, for example, Buñuel's films influenced *Happy Days*, *Molloy*, and *Not I*; he observes that *Film* and *Murphy* are set in 1929. See "The Origins of a Dramatic Style," in *Beckett in Context*, ed. Enoch Brater (New York: Oxford University Press, 1986), pp. 3–10. For a discussion of the exhibitions, see *Fantastic Art, Dada, Surrealism*, ed. Alfred H. Barr (New York: Museum of Modern Art, 1947).

8. Speaking of the total autonomy of art, Kandinsky said that painting should arise from "inner necessity," which should determine form and color. Intuition, he continued, was the key to comprehending and representing the universe, and he compared his findings to recent scientific advances. The artist, he asserted, "test[s] matter again and again . . . finally [to] cast doubt upon that very matter which was yesterday the foundation of everything, so that the whole universe rocks. The theory of electrons, that is, of waves in motion, designed to replace matter completely," he concluded, "overturned all notions of normal process." Quoted in C. H. Waddington, *Beyond Appearance* (Cambridge: MIT Press, 1961), pp. 67–69.

9. Pilling, *Samuel Beckett*, p. 4.

10. See Ford, *Published in Paris*. Among the extraordinary range of writers publishing were Stein, D. H. Lawrence, Djuna Barnes, André Gide, Paul Valéry, Anaïs Nin, Jules Romains, Katherine Anne Porter, Thomas Wolfe, Ezra Pound, Hemingway, John Dos Passos, Fitzgerald, T. S. Eliot, Thornton Wilder, William Carlos Williams, Stuart Gilbert, Berenice Abbott, Arthur Symons, Liam O'Flaherty, Jean Cocteau, T. F. Powys, Countee Cullen, Henry Miller, Aldous Huxley, Laura Riding, Havelock Ellis, and Richard Aldington.

11. Wiser, *Crazy Years*, p. 220. Pilling reports that Beckett stayed up half the night playing the flute and that Beckett admitted to him that he "slept through the Ecole" and did little research there, *Samuel Beckett*, p. 5.

12. Wiser, *Crazy Years*. Vivian Mercier, *Beckett/Beckett* (New York: Oxford University Press, 1977), p. 38. Deirdre Bair, *Samuel Beckett: A Biography* (New York: Harcourt Brace Jovanovich, 1978), p. 159. Bair, who had access to the Beckett-McGreevy letters, uses them frequently to argue for Beckett's mental deterioration. She rarely includes specifics, such as their possible exchanges regarding common interests in art, Ireland, family, or even war.

13. Thomas McGreevy, *Jack B. Yeats: An Appreciation and an Introduction* (Dublin: Victor Waddington, 1945), pp. 4, 5, 6.

14. Beckett had also been exposed to art on his vacations either with the Sinclairs or traveling on the continent; he had also spent a significant period of time looking at art as an undergraduate (see chapter 1). Most of the Paris exhibitions, which were well advertised in the little magazines at the time, are catalogued at the Metropolitan Museum of Art in New York.

Apollo, 9 wrote of Hayden ([January–June 1929]: 111), "This obstinate seeker, who did not desire too early a success . . . is beginning to receive full justice." Hayden had debuted in 1910, and subsequently painted his famous *Baigneuses dans la Calanque*. But now, a "good classical [mind] made a happy union . . . with specialized mathematics" and attracted him to Cubism. This, with mention of his Renoir-like light, and his notable absence of figures, was the focus of critical discussion at the time.

15. See John Rewald, *Cézanne* (Paris: Albin Michel, 1939). Claude Roger-Marx, *The Arts* 16 (September–May 1928): 9–11. André Salmon, "Letter from Paris," *Apollo* 10 (January–June 1929): 43; see also W. Suida, *The Arts* 3 (January–June 1930): 83.

16. Contributors included Kay Boyle, Archibald MacLeish, Soupault, Desnos, Tselit-sieff, Ernst, Rilke, Larbaud, de Chirico, Leon-Paul Fargue, Fearing, Tanguy, Man Ray, Laura Riding, Masson, Schwitters, Berenice Abbott, Marinetti, Yvor Winters, Antheil, Alexander Blok, Eluard, and Horace Gregory.

17. Putnam, *Paris Was Our Mistress*, p. 226. *transition* 15 (February 1929): 11–16; *transition* 16–17 (June 1929): 242–253; 268–271.

18. *transition* 15 (February 1929): 15.

19. *transition* 18 (November 1929): 15. This ad appeared in virtually every edition of *transition* from 1927 to 1930.

20. *transition* 16–17 (June 1929): n.p.

21. *transition* 21 (March 1932): 222–223.

22. *transition* 19–20 (June 1930): 14–19. See also Jung, "Psychology and Poetry," pp. 23–34.

23. *transition* 22 (February 1933): 195.

24. *transition* 19–20 (June 1930): 23–45. See Beckett's "Future Reference," pp. 342–343; Jolas's "The Dream," pp. 46–47.

25. *transition* 21 (March 1932): 105–145. Although Beckett was in London by this time (see chapter 5), he continued publishing in Paris.

26. For surveys of Surrealism, see: Anna Balakian, *Literary Origins of Surrealism* (New York: King's Crown Press, 1947); David Gascoyne, *A Short Survey of Surrealism* (London: Cobden-Sanderson, 1935); Georges Lamaitre, *From Cubism to Surrealism in French Literature* (Cambridge: Harvard University Press, 1947); Nadeau, *History of Surrealism*; Marcel Raymond, *From Baudelaire to Surrealism* (New York: Wittenborn & Schultz, 1949); Chénieux-Gendron, *Surrealism*; and Mary Ann Caws, *The Poetry of Dada and Surrealism* (Princeton: Princeton University Press, 1970). In addition to these and the manifestos cited thus far, see Breton's "Les Vases communicants" and Eluard's "Les Dessous d'une vie où la pyramide humaine." See also *Surrealism*, ed. Herbert Read (New York: Praeger, 1971) for essays by Breton, Davies, Eluard, and Hugnet.

27. S. E. Gontarski, ed., *On Beckett: Essays and Criticism* (New York: Grove, 1986), pp. 3–4.

28. Anna Balakian, *André Breton: Magnus of Surrealism* (New York: Oxford University Press, 1971), p. 4.

29. Lionel Trilling, "Freud and Literature," *The Liberal Imagination* (New York: Viking Press, 1950), pp. 52, 160–180.

30. Putnam, *Paris Was Our Mistress*, p. 62. See also Nadeau, *History of Surrealism*, p. 205.

31. See Lois Gordon, "*Krapp's Last Tape*," *Journal of Dramatic Theory and Criticism* 5.1 (1990): 327–340. "Surrealism," quoted in Ellmann and Feidelson, eds., *The Modern Tradition*, p. 604.

32. "Objective Chance: Divination," reprinted in Nadeau, *Surrealism*, pp. 272–273.

33. For a discussion of this, see Judi Freeman, *The Dada and Surrealist Word-Image* (Cambridge: MIT Press, 1989), pp. 36–57.

34. Surrealist techniques appear in Beckett's earliest work—most noticeably, the use of hermetic symbols in stylistically free forms. The unnamed "Woman" in "Assumption" is very much like Breton's mysterious woman, Nadja. She provides a good answer to Breton's opening question: "Qui suis-je?" as she represents both the "merveilleux" and

214

chance. When she reappears and infuses new life within Beckett's young man, she allows him to experience the gamut of Surrealist contradictions: he can discover his own bestial and angelic nature; the savage and innocent potential inherent in both concrete and abstract experience; and the rewards and taboos, fantasied and real, afforded and suppressed, by the bourgeois world.

35. Caws, *Poetry of Dada and Surrealism*, p. 15. In addition to *Literary Origins*, see Balakian's *Surrealism: The Road to the Absolute* (New York: Dutton, 1959), where, on pp. 37–49, she makes summary statements like: "If the absolute is not understood as the subjective perpetuation of perfected human experience after death, how will the poet convey 'the substance of nothingness'? . . . The infinite therefore is the plane of reality in which combinations that we might call absurd . . . are accepted as possible. . . . [The Surrealists] enlarge and maintain the domain of the absolute from this very same type of cult of the absurd" (pp. 43–44). She again maintains that "seeing" was no longer considered a receiving process but an interchange between subject and object (p. 14).

36. Beckett considered traveling to Moscow in the early 1930s in order to study film (see chapter 4).

37. Quoted in Neret, *Art of the Twenties*, p. 23.

38. To this assertion Balakian adds: "They endured their nihilism not with tears but with a mocking smirk." *Literary Origins*, p. 92.

39. Letter to Cunard reprinted in Enoch Brater, *why beckett* (New York: Thames and Hudson, 1989), p. 25. Also published but not mentioned above was "Che Sciagura," *T.C.D.: A College Miscellany* 36 (November 14, 1929): 42.

40. Ford reports Cunard's earliest impression of Beckett: "He is a man of stone, you think until he speaks and then is all warmth, if he be with someone sympathetic to him. He is very self-assured in a deep, quiet way, unassuming in manner, and interested in mankind. . . . One would not call him aloof but very self-contained. If you think he is looking slightly severe, this may be because he is assessing what has just been said, and his laughter and ease of manner are frank and swift. He is enchantingly Irish, and . . . on first seeing him, I thought there was just a touch here of the silhouette of James Joyce." *Published in Paris*, p. 277.

41. Wiser, *Crazy Years*, pp. 160–163. See also Ford, *Published in Paris*, pp. 253–289.

42. West's review in the *Daily Telegraph*, cited by Alec Reid, "The Reluctant Prizeman," *Arts* 29 (October 1969): 67.

43. Wiser, *Crazy Years*, p. 220. Fitch, *Sylvia Beach*, p. 378.

44. See Putnam, *Paris Was Our Mistress*, pp. 78–79, 165 ff., 227–229, and Nadeau, *History of Surrealism*, pp. 233–316. On Matisse, Neret, *Art of the Twenties*, p. 40.

45. Bair, *Samuel Beckett*, pp. 78–79.

46. See Putnam, *Paris Was Our Mistress*, p. 166.

47. Paul Johnson, *Modern Times: The World from the Twenties to the Eighties* (New York: Harper Colophon, 1983), pp. 7, 8.

48. Wiser, *Crazy Years*, p. 183.

49. She died when her long scarf was caught in a car as it drove off. At her own expense, she had rented the Metropolitan Opera to raise funds for France during the War, and she gave up her chateau in Neuilly so it could serve as a hospital. See Wiser, *Crazy Years*, p. 192.

50. As Wiser, *Crazy Years*, and others observe (see note 2), the bistros, like the Select, La Rotonde, and Dôme, were barometers of fame and notoriety.

51. For some of the many books that recall these events, see note 2.

52. Wiser, *Crazy Years*, p. 197.

53. Wiser, *Crazy Years*, p. 197. See Richard Ellmann, *James Joyce* (New York: Oxford University Press, 1982), as he describes Stein's resentment toward Joyce with statements like "Who came first, Gertrude Stein or James Joyce?" (pp. 528–529). Even Hemingway knew that "if you brought up" Joyce's name more than once at Gertrude Stein's salon, "you would not be invited back" (Wiser, *Crazy Years*, p. 48).

54. Wiser, *Crazy Years*, p. 198.

55. Peter Buckley, *Ernest* (New York: Dial Press, 1978), p. 131.

56. Wiser, *Crazy Years*, p. 202.

Chapter 3. James Joyce

Notes to epigraphs: "A Message from Samuel Beckett," in *James Joyce: An International Perspective 1982* (Totowa, N.J.: Barnes & Noble, 1982), p. vii; Richard Ellmann, "James Joyce: In and Out of Art," *Four Dubliners* (Washington, D.C.: Library of Congress, 1986), p. 77.

1. Richard Ellmann, *James Joyce* (New York: Oxford University Press, 1959; rev. ed., 1982). Although I cite three additional Ellmann sources, most Ellmann material here is drawn from from the biography, hereafter referred to as JJ. Early Joyce scholars also drew on the following brief portraits: Herbert S. Gorman, *James Joyce: His First Forty Years* (Folcroft, Pa.: Folcroft Press, 1924; rev. ed., 1969); Seon Manley, ed. *James Joyce: Two Decades of Criticism* (New York: Vanguard Press, 1948); Louis Gillet, *Claybook for James Joyce*, trans. Georges Markow-Totevy (London: Abelard-Schuman, 1958); Kevin Sullivan, *Joyce among the Jesuits* (New York: Columbia University Press, 1958); Harry Levin, *James Joyce: A Critical Introduction* (New York: New Directions, 1941); Marvin Magalaner and Richard M. Kain, *Joyce: The Man, the Work, the Reputation* (New York: New York University Press, 1956); Maria Jolas, ed., *A James Joyce Yearbook* (Paris: Transition Press, 1949); Philippe Soupault, *Souvenirs de James Joyce* (Paris: Charlot, 1945); Lucie Léon, *James Joyce and Paul L. Léon: The Story of a Friendship* (New York: Gotham Book Mart, 1948); Richard M. Kain, *Fabulous Voyager: James Joyce's "Ulysses"* (Chicago: University of Chicago Press, 1947); Stanislaus Joyce, *My Brother's Keeper*, ed. Richard Ellmann (New York: Viking Press, 1958); Sylvia Beach, *Shakespeare and Company* (New York: Harcourt Brace, 1959), as well as the *Letters of James Joyce*, vol. 1, ed. Stuart Gilbert (New York: Viking Press, 1957; rev. ed. 1966). Volumes 2 and 3, ed. Richard Ellmann (New York: Viking Press), appeared in 1966.

Post-Ellmann studies, with interesting, often brief, biographical material include Bernard Benstock, *James Joyce: The Undiscover'd Country* (New York: Barnes & Noble, 1977); C. H. Peake, *James Joyce: The Citizen and the Artist* (Stanford, Calif.: Stanford University Press, 1977); Chester A. Anderson, *James Joyce and His World* (London: Thames & Hudson, 1967); Robert Martin Adams, *James Joyce: Common Sense and Beyond* (New York: Random House, 1966); Peter Costello, *James Joyce* (Dublin: Gill & Macmillan, 1980); A. Walton Litz, *James Joyce* (New York: Twayne, 1966), and *The Art of James Joyce* (New York: Oxford University Press, 1961); and the excellent Morris Beja, *James Joyce: A Literary Life* (Houndsmills, England: Macmillan, 1992).

2. See Gisèle Freund and V. B. Carleton, *James Joyce in Paris* (London: Cassell, 1965), p. 72. Gillet, *Claybook*, p. 93. Freund and Carleton, *James Joyce in Paris*, p. 85.

3. C. P. Curran, *James Joyce Remembered* (London: Oxford University Press, 1968), p. 94. Joyce arranged for Stanislaus to teach in Trieste; helped his sister set up a movie theater;

after a brother-in-law's suicide, he contributed toward the support of his sister and nieces.

4. See Curran, *James Joyce Remembered*, pp. 101, 73; *Letters*, 2: 311.

5. Padraic and Mary Colum, *Our Friend James Joyce* (Garden City, N.Y.: Doubleday, 1958; rev. ed., Gloucester, Mass.: Peter Smith, 1968), p. 134. Joyce humorously commented to Frank Budgen that Jesus Christ was not a perfect man: "He was a bachelor and never lived with a woman . . . surely one of the most difficult things a man has to do" (*James Joyce and the Making of "Ulysses"* [New York: Harrison Smith & Robert Haas, 1934; rev. ed., Bloomington: Indiana University Press: 1968], p. 186). On whether he had left the church, see Beja, *Literary Life*, p. 9.

6. Joyce, *Brother's Keeper*, p. 107.

7. He actually viewed "the greater part of any talent [he might] have" as springing from "an extravagant licentious disposition." *Letters*, 1: 312. In *Letters*, 2: 191–192, Joyce distinguishes the sexes: "A woman's love is always maternal and egoistic. A man, side by side with his extraordinary cerebral sexualism and bodily fervour (from which women are normally free), possesses a fund of genuine affection for the beloved."

8. *Letters*, 2: 311.

9. Sullivan, *Joyce among the Jesuits*, p. 59; nevertheless, Joyce told Budgen, his artist-friend: "To get the correct contour . . . you ought to allude to me as a Jesuit." Ellmann, *JJ*, p. 27.

10. Stanislaus Joyce, *The Complete Dublin Diary of Stanislaus Joyce*, ed. George H. Healey (Ithaca, N.Y.: Cornell University Press, 1962), p. 3. In *My Brother's Keeper*, speaking of Joyce's so-called abandonment of the church, Stanislaus writes: "Nothing could be farther from the truth. . . . There was never any crisis of belief. The vigor of life within him drove him out of the church" (pp. 130, 153). See also p. 238.

11. *Letters*, 3: 188, one of countless illustrations of Eugene Jolas's description of Joyce's "will of steel." Jolas, "My Friend," p. 4.

12. Ruby Cohn, *Back to Beckett* (Princeton: Princeton University Press, 1973), p. 14. Jack MacGowran "secretly believes" that the fact that "Joyce hadn't been given the Nobel Prize made [Beckett] feel that he was not entitled to it." See Kathleen McGrory and John Unterecker, "An Interview with Jack MacGowran," in *Yeats, Joyce, and Beckett: New Light on Three Modern Irish Writers*, ed. Kathleen McGrory and John Unterecker (Lewisburg, Pa.: Bucknell University Press, 1976), p. 174.

Note to epigraph: Eugene Jolas, "My Friend James Joyce," in *Two Decades of Criticism*, ed. Seon Givens (New York: Vanguard Press, 1963), p. 3.

13. Richard M. Kain, "An Interview with Carola Giedion-Welcker and Maria Jolas," *James Joyce Quarterly* 11 (Winter 1974): 95–96.

14. Frank Budgen, "James Joyce," *Two Decades of Criticism*, ed. Seon Givens (New York: Vanguard Press, 1963); Mary Colum, in *Our Friend*, pp. 78, 101, 116; Curran, *Joyce Remembered*, p. 92.

15. Gillet, *Claybook*, p. 100; Ellmann, *JJ*, p. 713 (on Beckett's report); Mary Colum, in *Our Friend*, p. 101.

16. Magalaner and Kain, in response to Gorman, *James Joyce*, p. 5. Freund and Carleton, *Joyce in Paris*, p. 107.

17. Ellmann, *JJ*, p. 6.

18. Cited in Frank Budgen, *Myselves When Young* (New York: Oxford University Press, 1970), p. 187; Levin, *James Joyce*, p. 9.

19. Padraic Colum, in *Our Friend*, p. 127; the occasion of "Come in" actually involved Beckett's notetaking. See Ellmann, *JJ*, p. 649. Joyce frequently admitted the autobiographi-

cal nature of his work. In *Letters*, 2: iii, he writes: "The order of the stories [in *Dubliners*] is as follows, [first] . . . stories of my childhood."

20. Quoted in Beja, *Literary Life*, p. 63.

21. Ellmann, *JJ*, p. 104. Yeats saw in *Chamber Music* "the most remarkable new talent in Ireland today"; when *Ulysses* was attacked, he called it "a work perhaps of genius." Ellmann, *JJ*, pp. 99–100, 104. Joyce always denied any seriousness to the statement that he told Yeats he was too old to influence him. Jolas, "My Friend," p. 15.

22. Quoted in Beja, *Literary Life*, p. 113, who also cites J. F. Byrne, *Silent Years* (New York: Farrar, Straus and Young, 1953), p. 53, on Joyce's "highly emotional" moments: "I had never before . . . seen anything to approach the frightening condition that convulsed him. He wept and groaned and gesticulated in futile impotence as he sobbed out to me the thing that had occurred. Never in my life have I seen a human being more shattered."

23. See McGrory and Unterecker, "Interview with Jack MacGowran," p. 182; Gillet, *Claybook*, p. 105, reports that Joyce thought that his own "special gifts" were genetically imbalanced in Lucia.

24. Ellmann, *JJ*, p. 611.

25. Peggy Guggenheim's phrase in *Out of This Century* (New York: Anchor Books, 1980), p. 144.

26. William Wiser, *The Crazy Years: Paris in the Twenties* (New York: Atheneum, 1983), p. 224.

27. Alec Reid, "The Reluctant Prizeman," *Arts* 29 (November 1969): 66.

28. Noel Riley Fitch, *Sylvia Beach and the Lost Generation: A History of Literary Paris in the Twenties and Thirties* (New York: W. W. Norton, 1983), p. 78.

29. Budgen, *James Joyce and the Making of "Ulysses,"* p. 37, reports that Nora said: "What is all this about Irish wit and humor? Have we any books in the house with any of it?" Joyce once said to Padraic Colum: "Isn't it extraordinary that none of my family read anything I write?" See *Our Friend*, p. 129.

30. "On first seeing him, I thought there was just a touch here of the silhouette of James Joyce," said Nancy Cunard. Hugh Ford, *Published in Paris: A Literary Chronicle of Paris in the 1920s and 1930s* (New York: Collier, 1975), p. 277. Childhood similarities will be discussed below.

31. He literally feared that his eyes would be attacked; he told Italo Svevo that the Irish would "drive a knife into [his] heart." Quoted in Beja, *Literary Life*, p. 44.

32. Jolas, "My Friend," p. 9. On his meeting with McGreevy, see Curran, *Joyce Remembered*, p. 108.

33. Fitch, *Sylvia Beach*, p. 324.

34. As told to Gillet, quoted in Ellmann, *JJ*, p. 645.

35. Although Joyce had written Pound that he planned to spend three months in Ireland to complete *Ulysses* (*Letters*, 2: 468), the Maunsel incident remained a deep wound. First, Maunsel had demanded that large portions of *Dubliners* be excised or rewritten and that Joyce contribute £1,000 toward publication. After Joyce consented to pay 60 percent of the cost of the first thousand copies, Maunsel disregarded all previous agreements. Joyce left Dublin with one printed copy; the book was published two years later in London, eight years after it had been completed. See Gorman, *James Joyce*, p. 38; Padraic Colum, in *Our Friend*, pp. 58–70; Gillet, *Claybook*, p. 97; Beja, *Literary Life*, pp. 36–39; Ellmann, *JJ*, pp. 320–338.

36. Mary Colum, in *Our Friend*, pp. 110, 134–135.

37. On meeting Beckett and other Dubliners, see Wiser, *Crazy Years*, p. 219. On return-ing to Ireland, Ellmann, *JJ*, p. 704.

38. Stuart Gilbert, in "Selections from the Paris Diary of Stuart Gilbert, 1929–34," *Joyce Studies Annual*, ed. Thomas F. Staley and Randolph Lewis (Austin: University of Texas Press, 1990), p. 10. For his comment on the carpet, see *Letters*, 1: 268. Joyce continually ex-pressed his wish to return to Ireland, to complete there, for example, *Finnegans Wake*. See Ellmann, *JJ*, p. 101, and *Letters*, 2: 468.

39. Mary Colum, in *Our Friend*, p. 127; see letter to Eliot, January 1, 1932, in *Letters*, 1: 311, where Joyce speaks both of his repeated promises to his father to return "but an in-stinct which I believed in [that] held me back from going, much as I longed to."

40. Curran, *Joyce Remembered*, p. 100.

41. Joyce, *My Brother's Keeper*, p. 238; Ellmann, *JJ*, p. 734. Joyce told Mrs. Sheehy-Skeffington that when he died the word "Dublin" would be found on his heart. Quoted in Beja, *Literary Life*, p. 44.

42. Curran, *Joyce Remembered*, p. 66. See also Budgen, *James Joyce and the Making of "Ulysses,"* p. 20.

43. Many studies indicate that supportive friendships are likely to improve frustrated family relationships. See Alice Miller, *The Drama of the Gifted Child*, trans. R. Ward (New York: Basic Books, 1981), and Heinz Kohut, *How Analysis Cures* (New York: W. W. Norton, 1982).

44. Ellmann, *JJ*, p. 648. See Budgen, "James Joyce," p. 20.

45. Padraic Colum, in *Our Friend*, pp. 101. Jolas, "My Friend," p. 3, also describes how Joyce avoided all abstract and esoteric conversation.

46. Curran, *Joyce Remembered*, p. 88.

47. Ellmann, *JJ*, p. 615n.

48. Curran, *Joyce Remembered*, pp. 26–27, 36–37, recalls that when the young Joyce be-came intolerably hungry, he would ask friends to bring him home for dinner. Beja, in *Literary Life*, quotes Joyce on profanity: "I never say that kind of thing . . . though I write it"; Mary Colum, in *Our Friend*, pp 16, 134, 140 (also on his verbal propriety). Budgen, *James Joyce and the Making of "Ulysses,"* p. 192, on his harmless expletive, adds that he "rarely talked of perversity," p. 186. Brenda Maddox, in *Nora: A Biography of Nora Joyce* (London: Hamish Hamilton, 1988), is mainly concerned with discussing Joyce's roving eye and what she calls Joyce's "dirty letters," poems, and thoughts.

49. See Budgen, *James Joyce and the Making of "Ulysses,"* pp. 14, 188. See also Mary Colum, in *Our Friend*, p. 88, and Curran, *Joyce Remembered*, p. 88.

50. Budgen, *James Joyce and the Making of "Ulysses,"* p. 190; Jolas, "My Friend," p. 3.

51. Cited in Kain, "Interview with Carola Giedion-Welcker and Maria Jolas," pp. 94–122.

52. Ellmann, *JJ*, p. 648. Wiser, *Crazy Years*, p. 220.

53. Curran, *Joyce Remembered*, pp. 44–45; Ellmann, *JJ*, pp. 131, 771 note 67.

54. Mary Colum, in *Our Friend*, p. 141. On his musical interests, see Padraic Colum, in *Our Friend*, pp. 34, 120, and Gilbert, in Staley, *Joyce Studies Annual*, p. 7.

55. Gilbert, in Staley, *Joyce Studies Annual*, p. 7.

56. Leon Edel, *James Joyce: The Last Journey* (New York: Gotham Book Mart, 1948), p. 21.

57. Budgen, *James Joyce and the Making of "Ulysses,"* pp. 177–182.

58. Budgen, *James Joyce and the Making of "Ulysses,"* p. 182.

59. Gillet, *Claybook*, pp. 108, 110.

60. For example, Hemingway and Joyce once lived within a few feet of one another, at 74 and 71, rue du Cardinal Lemoine. See Wiser, *Crazy Years*, and Ford, *Published in Paris*.

61. As cited by Jolas, "My Friend," pp. 10–11.

62. Beach, *Shakespeare and Company*, intro. James Laughlin (Lincoln: University of Nebraska Press, 1991), p. 43.

63. Richard Ellmann, *Samuel Beckett: Nayman of Noland* (Washington, D.C.: Library of Congress, 1986), p. 28.

64. Ellmann, JJ, p. 648. Of Joyce's interest in Aquinas and Dante, see pp. 63–64.

65. Padraic Colum, in *Our Friend*, pp. 32, 51; Jolas, "My Friend," p. 14.

66. Ellmann, JJ, p. 648.

67. Ellmann, JJ, p. 702.

68. Padraic Colum, in *Our Friend*, pp. 95–100.

69. *Letters*, 1: 283. Joyce also helped Gilbert in writing his guide to *Ulysses*, as he had helped Gorman earlier.

70. James Knowlson, *Samuel Beckett: An Exhibition* (London: Turret Books, 1971), p. 29.

71. Ellmann, JJ, p. 546.

72. Jolas, "My Friend," pp. 13, 15.

73. Cited in Padraic Colum, in *Our Friend*, pp. 88.

74. Ellmann, JJ, p. 490. See also *Letters*, 1: 16, Ellmann, JJ, p. 436.

75. Ellmann, JJ, pp. 679, 650.

76. Dominic Manganiello, *Joyce's Politics* (London: Routledge & Kegan Paul, 1980), p. 23.

77. Seamus Deane, as quoted in Morris Beja, "Political Perspectives," *Joyce and Paris 1920 . . . 1920–1940 . . . 1975*, ed. J. Aubert and Maria Jolas. Papers from the Fifth International James Joyce Symposium (Paris: Editions du CNRS, 1979), p. 167.

78. Manganiello, citing Joyce's 1907 lecture "Ireland, Island of Saints and Sages." *Joyce's Politics*, p. 8.

79. Edmund L. Epstein, "James Augustine Aloysius Joyce," *A Companion to Joyce Studies*, ed. Zack Bowen and James F. Carens (Westport, Conn.: Greenwood Press, 1984), p. 9. See also Ellmann, JJ, p. 33.

80. Litz, *James Joyce*, p. 21.

81. Richard Ellmann, "Joyce and Politics," *Joyce and Paris*, pp. 31–32. See also *The Consciousness of Joyce* (New York: Oxford University Press, 1977), where, in his concluding chapter, pp. 73–95, Ellmann develops his thesis that Joyce's politics and aesthetics were one.

82. Ellmann, "Joyce and Politics," p. 31. To Ellmann, Joyce, in *Ulysses*, associated the church with false idealism, sentimental love, cruel morality, and rule by terror; the state, with the occupation of Ireland, at the mercy of brutal materialism and the misuse of power.

83. See Budgen, *James Joyce and the Making of "Ulysses,"* pp. 187–188, 23, and Ellmann, JJ, p. 709. Epstein, in *Joyce and Paris*, discusses *Finnegans Wake* as overtly political, p. 26.

84. Maria Jolas, cited in Beja, *Joyce and Paris*, p. 115.

85. Budgen, *James Joyce and the Making of "Ulysses,"* pp. 23, 170.

86. Beja, *Literary Life*, p. 64.

87. Manganiello, *Joyce and Politics*, p. 148.

88. See note 77 regarding Beja and Henke, participants in the political symposium cited; Adams, *James Joyce*, p. 4.

89. Manganiello, *Joyce and Politics*, pp. 13, 23, 42–43, 139–141, 148; Budgen, "James Joyce," pp. 22–30. W. B. Yeats, Edmund Gosse, and George Moore instigated Joyce's production of the plays. He received £100 from the Privy Purse and organized the English

Players on behalf of the Allied cause. The point was to convince the Swiss that it was more pleasant and profitable to be on the side of the Allies than of the Germans.

90. *The Critical Writings*, ed. Ellsworth Mason and Richard Ellmann (New York: Viking Press, 1959), pp. 173, 104.

91. Quoted in Magalaner, *Joyce: The Man*, p. 20. See also "Ireland, Island of Saints and Sages," in *Critical Writings*, pp. 153–174, and Manganiello, *Joyce and Politics*, p. 148.

92. Ellmann, *JJ*, p. 620.

93. See *Letters*, 1: 287, 289–293; 3: 203, 414, 619–627.

94. Jolas, "My Friend," pp. 8–9 (on the drawing), and Ellmann, *JJ*, p. 489 (citing Monnier).

95. See Lucie Léon, *James Joyce and Paul L. Léon: The Story of a Friendship* and "James Joyce: Centennial Celebration," a 1982 television documentary produced by Séan O'Mordha, with Richard Ellmann as consultant, for Radio Telefis Eireann, 1982, aired on local affiliate National Public Television, February 2, 1992. Léon later risked his life for Joyce when, at the beginning of the Occupation, he returned to Joyce's apartment to rescue some valuables the landlord had put up for unauthorized auction. However, like yet another of Joyce's close friends, Louis Gillet, Léon was eventually taken by the Nazis. Beckett saw him the day before he was arrested and begged him to leave Paris, but Léon felt compelled to remain there while his son took his baccalaureate exam. (Freund and Carleton, *Joyce in Paris*, p. 102).

96. Ellmann, *JJ*, pp. 615–616.

97. Curran, *Joyce Remembered*, pp. 90–91.

98. As quoted in Gluck, *Beckett and Joyce*, p. 39.

99. This never took place; only a change in cemetery plot occurred in 1966, so Joyce and Nora, who had died in 1951, could be buried together.

100. Maria Jolas, in "James Joyce: Centennial Celebration."

101. See Nathan Halper's "Joyce and Brancusi" and "The Brancusi Portrait," both in Manganiello, *Joyce and Politics*, pp. 69–75, 76–78. See also Jolas, "My Friend," p. 6; *Letters*, 1: 279.

102. See Joyce, *My Brother's Keeper*, pp. 40–41, 47, 55, unsurpassed as a repository of information regarding James Joyce's childhood. See also Bruce Bradley, S.J., *James Joyce's Schooldays* (Dublin: Gill & Macmillan, 1982), and Peter Costello, *James Joyce: The Years of Growth* (New York: Pantheon, 1993).

103. Ellmann, *JJ*, pp. 129, 292, 293 (on the letters), 193 (on Joyce's association with Parnell).

104. As quoted in Colum, *Our Friend*, p. 137.

105. Ellmann, *JJ*, p. 622. It was also always of interest to Joyce that de Valera had eye problems.

106. Ellmann, *JJ*, pp. 434, 293, 371. Sylvia Beach reports Joyce's regret that he hadn't had ten children (like his father). *Shakespeare and Company*, p. 43. See also Ellmann, *JJ*, pp. 485; 787 note 5.

107. Gillet, *Claybook*, p. 105.

108. Padraic Colum, in *Our Friend*, p. 137.

109. Ellmann, *JJ*, p. 612. "L'Irlandaise" was, Bair reports, the name that Beckett used in the Resistance (*Samuel Beckett*, p. 311).

110. Ellmann, *JJ*, p. 611.

111. Mary Colum, in *Our Friend*, p. 141. Joyce's letters are filled with self-recrimination,

"a blind man's rage and despair," *Letters*, 1: 367. Guggenheim, *Out of This Century*, p. 149 (on Beckett's guilt). On recent theories, see William T. Carpenter, Jr., and John S. Strauss, "The Prediction of Outcome in Schizophrenia IV," *Journal of Nervous and Mental Disease* 179 (September 1991): 517–525, cited in *Harvard Mental Health Letter* 8 (January 1992): 6–7, and 9 (November 1992): 6–7. See also Heinz Kohut, *Analysis of the Self* (New York: International Universities Press, 1973).

112. Maddox, *Nora*, pp. 334, 336, 350, 432. Maddox also considers other possibilities for Lucia's illness, like Joyce's incest with her or "the bad luck of the Irish," because Ireland has three to six times the schizophrenia rate of most Western countries.

113. For a summary of how Lucia's illness progressed, see Mary Colum, in *Our Friend*, p. 118, and Beja, *Literary Life*, pp. 113–119.

114. *Letters*, 1: 382, 341; the letter imploring Lucia not always to sit by the window is quoted in Beja, *Literary Life*, p. 117. *Letters*, 1: 367, 346.

115. Guggenheim, *Out of This Century*, p. 144.

116. E.g., *Letters*, 1: 402. This letter is dated September 11, 1938. Given Beckett's subsequent involvement in the Resistance, these conversations could be very revealing. The publication of Beckett's letters, edited by Martha Fehsenfeld and Lois Overbeck, will provide more information regarding these matters.

117. Ellmann, *JJ*, p. 728.

118. Ellmann, *JJ*, pp. 727–728, 709, 150. See also Padraic Colum, in *Our Friend*, p. 150.

119. *Letters*, 1: 407; Ellmann, *JJ*, p. 702.

120. Ellmann, *JJ*, p. 730.

121. See, e.g., *Letters*, 3: 484–506, 451; and 1: 414–420, 495.

122. Budgen, "James Joyce," p. 25.

123. *Letters*, 3: 465–467. Ellmann, *JJ*, pp. 731–732.

124. Ellmann, *JJ*, p. 741.

125. Presumably told to Israel Shenker, *Words and Their Masters* (New York: Doubleday, 1974), p. 198, reprinted from "Moody Man of Letters," *New York Times*, May 6, 1956, sec. 2: 1, 3.

126. Ellmann, *JJ*, p. 551. Cited in Ellmann, *Samuel Beckett: Nayman of Noland*, p. 102.

127. Ellmann, *JJ*, pp. 6–7.

Chapter 4. Jack B. Yeats

Note to epigraph: John W. Purser, *The Literary Works of Jack B. Yeats* (Gerrard's Cross, England: Colin Smythe, 1991), p. 5.

1. A. J. Leventhal, "The Thirties," in *Beckett at 60: A Festschrift* (London: Calder & Boyars, 1967), p. 10. See his essay "Dante . . . Bruno . Vico . . Joyce," discussed in chapter 3, and S. E. Gontarski, Martha Fehsenfeld, Dougald McMillan, "Interview with Rachel Burrows," *Journal of Beckett Studies* 11–12 (1989): 7.

2. Cited by Enoch Brater, *why beckett* (New York: Thames and Hudson, 1989), p. 28. John Pilling, *Samuel Beckett* (London: Routledge & Kegan Paul, 1976), p. 7; Richard N. Coe, *Samuel Beckett* (New York: Grove Press, 1964), p. 12.

3. Alec Reid, "The Reluctant Prizeman," *Arts* 29 (October 1969): 67.

4. Richard Ellmann, *James Joyce* (New York: Oxford University Press, 1982), p. 731.

5. Quoted in Hilary Pyle, *Jack B. Yeats* (London: Routledge & Kegan Paul, 1970), p. 146. The letter is dated December 22, 1930.

6. Pyle, preface, *Jack B. Yeats*, n.p.

7. Marilyn Gaddis Rose, *Jack B. Yeats: Painter and Poet* (Frankfurt: Peter Lang, 1972), p. 22.

8. Beckett at one time wanted to be an artist and was "a very brilliant musician" who played "classics brilliantly on the piano," said Jack MacGowran, in Kathleen McGrory and John Unterecker, "Interview with Jack MacGowran," in *Joyce, Yeats, and Beckett: New Light on Three Modern Irish Writers*, ed. Kathleen McGrory and John Unterecker (Lewisburg, Pa.: Bucknell University Press, 1976), p. 175.

9. Joyce owned *Porter Boats* (the River Liffey) and *Salmon Leap, Leixip* (Dublin Bay). Gordon S. Armstrong, *Samuel Beckett, W. B. Yeats, and Jack Yeats: Images and Words* (Lewisburg, Pa.: Bucknell University Press, 1990), p. 160.

10. Pyle, *Jack B. Yeats*, p. 3. Nora A. McGuinness portrays Yeats as a narcissistic, lonely man, distanced from his father, like a person traveling in life "without a ticket." *The Literary Universe of Jack B. Yeats* (Washington, D.C.: Catholic University of America Press, 1992), pp. 1–12. Purser, in *Literary Works*, sets out to "correct" McGuinness on his first page.

11. In addition to the other biographical studies cited, see *Jack B. Yeats: A Centenary Gathering*, ed. Roger McHugh (Dublin: Dolmen Press, 1971); Douglas N. Archibald, *Jack B. Yeats* (Lewisburg, Pa.: Bucknell University Press, 1974); T. G. Rosenthal, "Jack Yeats," in *The Masters*, vol. 40 (London: Knowledge Publications, 1966); Marilyn Gaddis Rose, "The Sterne Ways of Beckett and Jack B. Yeats," in *Irish University Review* 2 (1972): 164–171, and "Solitary Companions in Beckett and Jack B. Yeats," *Eire-Ireland* 4 (Summer 1969): 66–80. See especially Beckett's "Hommage à Jack Yeats," *Les Lettres Nouvelles* (April 1954): 619–620. For an excellent selection of his work, see James White, *Jack B. Yeats: Drawings and Paintings* (London: Secker & Warburg, 1971).

12. Pyle, *Jack B. Yeats*, p. 33.

13. Thaddeus O'Sullivan, "Jack B. Yeats: Assembled Memories, 1871–1957," television documentary, produced by Margaret Williams and Arbor International for Radio Telefís Eireann, 1981, aired on local affiliate National Public Television, March 1991.

14. Pyle, *Jack B. Yeats*, p. 118.

15. See, e.g., McGuinness, *Literary Universe*, p. 54; Pyle, *Jack B. Yeats*, p. 119.

16. Pyle, *Jack B. Yeats*, p. 119.

17. Brian O'Doherty, "Jack B. Yeats: Promise and Regret," in *Jack B. Yeats: A Centenary Gathering*, p. 81.

18. Thomas McGreevy, *Jack B. Yeats: An Appreciation and An Introduction* (Dublin: Victor Waddington, 1945). See pp. 6, 9, 16, 15, 8, for the citations in the text.

19. According to Gordon Armstrong, Synge, born the same year as Yeats and also the son of a Protestant middle-class family, was plagued by guilt for having defied his mother by becoming an artist. This trip was Synge's attempt to effect social change in a "professional," traditional fashion, rather than through art—as in a play like *The Playboy of the Western World*. Armstrong, *Samuel Beckett, W. B. Yeats, and Jack Yeats*, p. 176.

20. O'Sullivan, "Assembled Memories." See note 13 on the recollection. Jack B. Yeats, *Modern Art* (Dublin: Cuala Press, 1922), p. 4.

21. McGreevy, *Jack B. Yeats*, p. 25.

22. Pyle, *Jack B. Yeats*, p. 128. On p. 136, Pyle briefly discusses Beckett's interest in Yeats's dream worlds.

23. Samuel Beckett, "An Imaginative Work," *Dublin Magazine* 11 (July-September 1936): 80–81.

24. Rose, *Jack B. Yeats*, p. 36.

25. As reported by Pyle, preface, *Jack B. Yeats*, n.p.

26. Quoted in McGreevy, *Jack B. Yeats*, p. 35.

27. Quoted in Armstrong, *Samuel Beckett, W. B. Yeats, and Jack Yeats*, p. 165.

28. Pyle, *Jack B. Yeats*, p. 136.

29. William Butler Yeats, "The Tragic Theatre," in *Essays and Introduction* (New York: Macmillan, 1961), p. 245.

30. "Two Pieces by Samuel Beckett," in *Jack B. Yeats: A Centenary Gathering*, p. 73.

31. Quoted in Armstrong, *Samuel Beckett, W. B. Yeats, and Jack Yeats*, p. 124.

32. Pyle, preface, *Jack B. Yeats*, n.p.

33. Brater, *why beckett*, p. 29.

34. Deirdre Bair adds that he had begun staying in bed "lying rigidly in a fetal position facing the wall." *Samuel Beckett: A Biography* (New York: Harcourt Brace Jovanovich, 1978), pp. 135–136.

35. See the definitive work on psychosomatic disorders of Harold I. Kaplan and Benjamin J. Sadock, *The Comprehensive Textbook of Psychiatry V*, vol. 1 (Baltimore: Williams & Wilkins, 1989), verified by psychiatrists specializing in psychosomatic disorders at the Columbia College of Physicians and Surgeons and the Albert Einstein College of Medicine.

Chapter 5. London

1. According to Ruby Cohn, *Back to Beckett* (Princeton: Princeton University Press, 1973), p. vii. See also Vivian Mercier, *Beckett/Beckett* (New York: Oxford University Press), p. 31, and Linda Ben-Zvi, *Beckett* (Boston: Twayne Publishers, 1986), n.p. Pilling and Harvey, on the other hand, speak of Beckett's spending two years in London, from 1933 to 1935. See John Pilling, *Samuel Beckett* (London: Routledge and Kegan Paul, 1976), p. 8, and Lawrence E. Harvey, *Samuel Beckett: Poet and Critic* (Princeton: Princeton University Press, 1970), p. 170. The (projected three-volume) publication of Beckett's letters, edited by Martha Fehsenfeld and Lois Overbeck, will clarify many of these problems.

2. John Fletcher, *The Novels of Samuel Beckett* (New York: Barnes and Noble, 1964), p. 38.

3. Harvey, *Samuel Beckett*, p. 154. Beckett wrote these lines shortly afterward: "the fairy tales of Meath ended, / So say your prayers now and go to bed / your prayers before the lamps start to / sing behind the larches / here at these knees of stones / then to bye-byes on the bones" ("Serena II," p. 155).

4. From a 1955 letter to Susan Manning, quoted in Enoch Brater, *why beckett* (New York: Thames and Hudson, 1989), p. 10.

5. Pilling speaks of this as perhaps the "most crucial of all" in Beckett's early life sadness, *Samuel Beckett*, p. 1. His uncle Boss died of tuberculosis thereafter.

6. Lucia's irrational behavior had even escalated to violent displays and announcements that each young man who visited her father had seduced her. See Richard Ellmann, *James Joyce* (New York: Oxford University Press, 1982), pp. 665, 667. Some of Joyce's other problems are discussed on pp. 663, 664, 667.

7. According to Mary Manning Howe, Beckett had a nervous breakdown at this time. See Brater, *why beckett*, p. 35.

8. Harvey, *Samuel Beckett*, p. 222.

9. "Sedendo et Quiescendo" and "Dante and the Lobster," originally planned as part of the unfinished *Dream of Fair to Middling Women*, appeared in 1932: the former, in *transition*

21 (March 1932): 13–20; the latter, in *This Quarter* (December 1932): 222–236. See also "Assumption," *transition* 16–17 (June 1929): 268–271; *Whoroscope* (Paris: Hours Press, 1930); and *Proust* (London: Chatto and Windus, 1931).

10. Bair, *Samuel Beckett*, pp. 170–173, and chapter 7. An example of her commentary is: "[Beckett] had unleashed torrents of anger and venom he felt toward his mother. . . . Thompson feared Beckett was on the edge of total incapacitation. . . . The night tremors became so severe that Beckett could relax only if Frank slept in the same bed, to hold and calm him when he was in the grips of nightmarish terror" (pp. 174–175).

11. Beatrice Glenavy, *Today We Will Only Gossip* (London: Constable, 1964), p. 159.

12. In *Bookman* 87 (Christmas 1934), he published several pieces: "Ex Cathezra," a review of Pound's *Make It New*, p. 10; "Papini's Dante," a review of *Dante Vico* by G. Papini, p. 14; and a discussion of Sean O'Casey's *Windfalls*, "The Essential and the Incidental," p. 111. His review of J. B. Leishmann's translation of Rilke's poetry appeared in *Criterion* 13 (1934): 705–707. *Dublin Magazine* 9 (July–September 1934) included reviews of McGreevy's poetry (pp. 79–80) and Jack B. Yeats's novel *The Amaranthus* (pp. 80–81). He also published *More Pricks than Kicks* (London: Chatto and Windus, 1934); *Echo's Bones and Other Precipitates* (Paris: Europa Press, 1935); both the story "A Case in a Thousand" and article "Recent Irish Poets" (signed as "Andrew Bellis") in *Bookman* 76 (August 1934): 235–236; and poems "Home Olga," *Contempo* (February 15, 1934): 3, and "Gnome," *Dublin Magazine* 9 (July–September 1934): 8. *Murphy* was published by Routledge in 1938.

13. Many add that other than unemployment, the General Strike of 1926 was of paramount, lingering importance: in an environment of falling wages and rising unemployment, the government and employers had tried to lower wages even further—to improve Britain's competitive market. For excellent introductions to the British Depression, see Ronald Blythe, *The Age of Illusion: Glimpses of Britain between the Wars, 1919–1940* (New York: Oxford University Press, 1983); A. J. P. Taylor, *English History, 1914–1945* (New York: Oxford University Press, 1965); Arthur Marwick, *The Expansion of British Society and Britain in Our Century* (London: Thames and Hudson, 1984); C. L. Mowat, *Britain between the Wars* (London: Methuen, 1956); Keith Laybourn, *Britain on the Breadline* (Gloucester: Alan Sutton, 1990); and Noreen Branson and Margot Heinemann, *Britain in the 1930s* (London: Panther, 1973).

14. Blythe, *Age of Illusion*, p. xii.

15. Quoted in Lois Gordon and Alan Gordon, *The Columbia Chronicles of American Life, 1910–1992* (New York: Columbia University Press, 1995), p. 182.

16. Joseph Whitaker, ed., *An Almanac: 1934* (London: Wm. Clowes & Sons, Ltd., published annually). On these hunger marches and official surveys, see Blythe, *Age of Illusion,* Julian Symons, *The Angry Thirties* (London: Eyre Methuen, 1976), Laybourn, *Britain on the Breadline,* Martin Green, *The Children of the Sun* (New York: Basic Books, 1976).

17. Ellen Wilkinson, *The Town That Was Murdered* (London: Gollancz, 1939), pp. 236, 246. See also Laybourn, *Britain on the Breadline*, pp. 140–142, and Blythe, *Age of Illusion*, pp. 155–173.

18. From George Orwell's *Road to Wigan Pier*, quoted in Blythe, *Age of Illusion*, p. 161. See Arthur Marwick on the "stringency means" test, *Expansion of British Society, 1914–1970* (London: Macmillan, 1971), p. 77.

19. George Orwell, "England Your England," *Inside the Whale and Other Essays* (Harmondsworth: Penguin, 1974), p. 73.

20. Alan Hutt, introduction, *The Condition of the Working Class in England* (London: Lawrence, 1933), p. xii. See Laybourn, *Britain on the Breadline*, for detailed charts and analyses of these factors.

21. Introduction, Symons, *Angry Thirties*, n.p.

22. Robert Skidelsky, *Oswald Mosley* (New York: Holt, Rinehart and Winston, 1975), pp. 309–310. See also Blythe, "Thugs, Trunks, and Things," in *Age of Illusion*, pp. 174–187.

23. Quoted in Skidelsky, *Oswald Mosley*, p. 440. See also Blythe, *Age of Illusion*, p. 177.

24. See Lois Gordon, *Harold Pinter: A Casebook* (New York: Garland, 1990), p. xxix.

25. Richard Griffiths, *Fellow Travellers of the Right* (London: Constable, 1980). See also Taylor, *English History, 1914–1945*, pp. 33–35, 170.

26. See "The Left Book Club in the Thirties," in *Culture and Crisis in Britain in the Thirties*, ed. Jon Clark et al. (London: Lawrence and Wishart, 1979), pp. 193–207. They included R. H. Tawney's *The Acquisitive Society*, Leonard Woolf's *Barbarians at the Gate*, André Malraux's *Days of Contempt*, George Orwell's *Road to Wigan Pier*, Arthur Koestler's *Spanish Testament*, W. H. Thompson's *Civil Liberties*, and C. R. Attlee's *The Labour Party in Perspective*.

27. Bair, *Samuel Beckett*, p. 204. The historian Arthur Marwick actually compared the Jarrow marchers, with their sashes and lapel badges, to the proud proletariats of an Eisenstein film (Marwick, *Britain in Our Century*, p. 87).

28. See Eric Hobsbawn, *Industry and Empire* (Baltimore: Penguin, 1969); Mowat, *Britain Between the Wars*; and Branson and Heinemann, *Britain in the 1930s*.

29. *Criterion* 11 (April 1932): 467–468.

30. Quoted in Mowat, *Britain between the Wars*, p. 94.

31. Blythe, *Age of Illusion*, pp. 110–111, 119–120.

32. Green, *Children of the Sun*, p. 279. Before contributing to Cunard's *Negro* (Paris: Hours Press, 1934), Beckett had written the poem "From the Only Poet to a Shining Whore. For Henry Crowder to Sing," for Cunard's *Henry Music*, published for Cunard's musician lover, Henry Crowder.

33. In 1934, they presented Friedrich Wolf's *Sailors of Cattaro*; John Wexley's *They Shall Not Die*; and in 1936, Montagu Slater's *Stay Down Miner* (with music by Benjamin Britten). For a good history of this, see André van Gyseghem, "British Theatre in the Thirties," and Jon Clark, "Agitprop and Unity Theatre: Socialist Theatre in the Thirties," both in Clark et al., *Culture and Crisis in Britain in the Theater*, pp. 209–218 and 219–239, respectively.

34. See Ralph Bond, "Cinema in the Thirties: Documentary Film and the Labour Movement," and Berg Hogenkamp, "Making Films with a Purpose: Film Making and the Working Class," in *Culture and Crisis*, pp. 241–256 and 257–269, respectively.

35. Bair, *Samuel Beckett*, p. 209.

36. See Andrew Sharf, *The British Press and Jews under Nazi Rule* (London: Oxford University Press, 1964), pp. 7–9, 80–87, and Robert Desmond, *Crisis and Conflict* (Iowa City: University of Iowa Press, 1980), pp. 420, 457. See also Desmond's *The Press and World Affairs* (New York: Appleton, 1937) and *Tides of War* (Iowa City: University of Iowa Press, 1982).

37. See *Daily Telegraph*, May 6, 1933, and *New York Times*, July 10, 1933, quoted in Milan Hauner, *Hitler: A Chronology of His Life and Time* (London: Macmillan, 1983), p. 94.

38. Among many excellent press histories, see John C. Merrill, *The Elite Press* (New York: Pitman, 1960); Merrill and Harold A. Fisher, *The World's Great Dailies* (New York: Hastings House, 1980); Franklin Reid Gannon, *The British Press and Germany, 1936–39* (Oxford: Clarendon Press, 1971); John Hohenberg, *Free Press/Free People* (New York: Columbia University Press, 1971); and Anthony Smith, *The Newspaper: An International History* (London: Thames and Hudson, 1979). See also George Thomas Kurian, ed. *World Press Encyclopedia*, vol. 2 (New York: Facts on File, 1982).

39. Gannon, *British Press and Germany*, p. 74.

40. Since page numbers in the *Times* differ in early and late editions, and it is impossible to ascertain from microfilm which edition was recorded, they have been omitted here. References to other newspapers are either cited directly or from secondary sources like Sharf, Desmond, Gannon, and the major journalists listed below. Most of the occasions cited were covered by the *Times*. For chronology of events, see: Hershel Edelheit and Abraham J. Edelheit, *The World in Turmoil: An Integrated Chronology of the Holocaust and World War II* (New York: Greenwood Press, 1991); Hauner, *Hitler: A Chronology*; Robert Goralski, *World War II Almanac, 1931–1945* (G. P. Putnam's Sons, 1981); Malvin Walker, *Chronological Encyclopedia of Adolf Hitler and the Third Reich* (New York: Carlton Press, 1978); Michael Zalampas, *Adolf Hitler and the Third Reich in American Magazines, 1923–1939* (Bowling Green, Ohio: Bowling Green University Popular Press, 1989); and Yitzhak Arad, *The Pictorial History of the Holocaust* (New York: Macmillan, 1990). See also Raul Hilberg, *The Destruction of the European Jews* (New York: Holmes and Meier, 1986); N. H. Baynes, *The Speeches of Adolf Hitler, April 1922–1939* (Oxford: Oxford University Press, 1942); Gilbert Martin, *The Holocaust: A History of the Jews of Europe during the Second World War* (New York: Holt, Rinehart and Winston, 1985); *Encyclopedia of the Holocaust*, ed. Israel Gutman, 4 vols. (New York: Macmillan, 1990); *The Catastrophe of European Jewry: Antecedents-History-Reflections*, ed. Gutman and Livia Rothkirchen (Jerusalem: Yad Vashem, 1976); and Lucy S. Dawidowicz, *The War Against the Jews, 1933–1945* (New York: Holt, Rinehart and Winston, 1973).

41. Richard Ellmann, *Samuel Beckett: Nayman of Noland* (Washington, D.C.: Library of Congress, 1986), p. 10. His longtime friends Dr. and Mrs. Gottfried Büttner discussed this with the author, April 9, 1992.

42. Quoted in Cohn, *Back to Beckett*, p. ix.

43. "The Meaning of 'Help'" described how black boot polish was poured on to the raw flesh of beaten men, who were then forced to scrape themselves clean (September 19, 1933). The *Mein Kampf* excerpt appeared July 24, 1933.

44. The title "The Moral Isolation of Germany," July 20, 1934, reveals a motif in many of the *Times*'s editorials. See also March 24–26, 1934, and October 17, 1934.

45. This was enthusiastically reported in the anti-Semitic *Liberation*, February 2, 1934; see Zalampas, *Adolf Hitler and the Third Reich*, p. 35.

46. A four-month strike, during which Tel Aviv Arabs stopped selling goods to Jews, was covered from March through July 1936, when the bombings began. See the *Times*, July 20, 1936.

47. Bion's obituary in the *Times*, November 15, 1979, 18.

48. See H. J. Paton, *The Moral Law or Kant's Groundwork of the Metaphysic of Morals* (London: Hutchinson University, n.d.); *In Defense of Reason* (London: Heinemann, 1951); *The Categorical Imperative: A Study in Kant's Moral Philosophy* (Chicago: University of Chicago Press, 1948); and *The Modern Predicament: A Study in the Philosophy of Religion* (New York: Macmillan, 1955). Paton was particularly concerned with adapting Christian, specifically Anglican, doctrine to the changing intellectual currents of the modern age.

49. W. R. Bion, *The Long Weekend, 1897–1919*, ed. Francesca Bion (London: Free Association Books, 1986).

50. Bair, *Samuel Beckett*, pp. 197–198.

51. In some of his works, he uses only the Greek letters; in others, he spells them out. See W. R. Bion, *Learning from Experience* (New York: Basic Books, 1962), and *Elements of Psycho-Analysis* (New York: Basic Books, 1963); "Onement" and "O" are also frequently capitalized.

52. In the introduction to *Second Thoughts: Selected Papers on Psycho-Analysis* (London:

Heinemann, 1967), Bion continued to explain that the content of dreams was neither pathological nor regressive. It could indicate things to come and could be integrative. Like Rank, Bion believed that dreams could even be pre-verbal and pre-natal.

On terms, see Salomon Resnik, *The Theatre of the Dream*, trans. Alan Sheridan (London: Tavistock, 1987), p. 207. See the following on Bion: *Bion and Group Psychotherapy*, ed. Malcolm Pines (London: Routledge & Kegan Paul, 1985); *"Do I Dare Disturb the Universe": A Memorial to Wilfred R. Bion*, ed. James S. Grotstein (Beverly Hills, Calif.: Caesure, 1981), and Leon Ginsburg et al., *New Introduction to the Ideas of Bion* (Northvale, N.J.: Jason Aronson, 1992).

53. See Bion, *Second Thoughts*, pp. 5–6, 24–33, 38–42, and chapter 9.

54. "The patient who cannot dream cannot go to sleep and cannot wake up. Hence the peculiar condition seen clinically when the psychotic patient behaves as if he were in precisely this state." *Learning from Experience*, p. 51.

55. Bion, *Second Thoughts*, pp. 36ff. See Resnik, *Theatre of the Dream*, pp. 361–362, for a discussion of this.

56. See Bion, *Second Thoughts and Experiences in Groups* (New York: Basic Books, 1961), as well as *Attention and Interpretation: A Scientific Approach to Insights in Psycho-analysis and Groups* (New York: Basic Books, 1970).

57. Bion, *Experiences in Groups*, pp. 173–174.

58. Pilling, *Samuel Beckett*, p. 4. See "Ex Cathezra," *Bookman* 89 (1934): 10, where, reviewing a collection of Pound's criticism, Beckett praises Pound for "stating among other facts . . . that Romains is Unanimism, and a poet of importance."

59. Quoted in André Maurois, *From Proust to Camus: Profiles of Modern French Writers* (New York: Doubleday, 1966), p. 258.

60. Harvey, *Samuel Beckett*, p. 266; Pilling, *Samuel Beckett*, p. 4.

61. Bair, *Samuel Beckett*, pp. 191, 258, 197–198, and Ben-Zvi, *Samuel Beckett*, p. 15 (on his mental state). Pilling, *Samuel Beckett*, p. 8 (on the Surrealists).

62. Whitaker, *Almanac*, 1934, p. 474 (on Bethlehem Royal Hospital). Jack MacGowran, "MacGowran on Beckett [interview by Richard Toscan]," in *On Beckett: Essays and Criticism*, ed. S. E. Gontarski (New York: Grove, 1986), p. 223 (on Beckett's working there).

63. Useful studies of Surrealism in England include: Paul C. Ray, *The Surrealist Movement in England* (Ithaca: Cornell University Press, 1971); David Gascoyne, *A Short Survey of Surrealism* (London: Cobden-Sanderson, 1935); Herbert Read, *Art Now* (London: Faber & Faber, 1933), and *Surrealism* (London: Faber & Faber, 1936); as well as *this quarter* 5 (September 1932). Notable articles include Hugh Sykes Davies, "Sympathies and Surrealism," *New Verse* 20 (April-May 1936): 15–21, and Charles Madge, "A Surrealism for the English," *New Verse* 6 (December 1933): 14–18.

64. William Wiser, *The Crazy Years: Paris in the Twenties* (New York: Atheneum, 1983), p. 163.

65. Ray, *Surrealist Movement*, p. 76. Herbert Read, as quoted in Marwick, *Expansion of British Society, 1914–1970*, p. 82. Anna Balakian, *Surrealism: The Road to the Absolute* (New York: Noonday Press, 1959), pp. 11, 108–109.

66. See especially *The New Statesman and Nation* (August 26, 1933): 131, as well as *New Verse* 6 (December 1933): 14–18.

67. Herbert Read, "Psychoanalysis and the Critic," *Criterion* 3 (January 1925): 214–230.

68. *Cahiers d'Art* 10 (1935): 112.

69. Quoted in Ray, *Surrealist Movement*, p. 146.

70. During his first year there (one of record sunshine) hiking, or "ramblin'," became

a fad; outdoor activity, physical health, and strenuous exercise became the nationwide response to the German and Russian concentration on physical fitness.

71. The new acting style spread beyond the West End, even to the Shakespeare Memorial Theatre at Stratford-on-Avon, reopened in 1933. (The former one had burned to the ground in 1926.) See Ruth Ellis, *The Shakespeare Memorial Theatre* (London: Winchester, n.d.); Roger Wood, *Shakespeare at the Old Vic* (London: A. and C. Black, 1958); Audrey Williamson, *Theatre of Two Decades* (New York: Macmillan, 1951); and Lynton Hudson, *The English Stage, 1850–1950* (London: George G. Harrap, 1951). For a summary of important performances during this period, see Hal Burton, *Great Acting* (New York: Hill & Wang, 1967); for thoroughness, see J. P. Wearing, *The London Stage, 1930–1939*, 3 vols. (Metuchen, N.J.: Scarecrow Press, 1990).

72. Maurice Evans acted in another extraordinary series, opposite many other great talents.

73. These included Gielgud's *A Midsummer Night's Dream* and *The Merchant of Venice*, as well as *Loyalty, The Skin Game*, and *The Sea Gull*. The BBC's radio production of *Three Sisters* was especially successful.

74. Eoin O'Brien, *The Beckett Country* (Dublin: Black Cat Press; London: Faber & Faber, 1986), p. 139. Of likely interest to Beckett in 1935 were Dürer's *Portrait of his Father* at the National Gallery, and Memling's *Man with the Pink*, and rarely seen works by Van Dyck and Jan Provost at the Knoedler. The year was also important for the Great Siennese Art show, which exhibited seven Sassetta panels and Tiepolo's *Diana and Endymion*.

75. Although Beckett would probably have seen experimental films earlier in Paris, like Eisenstein's *Potemkin* and *October* (*Ten Days that Shook the World*) and Lang's *M*, the British were now producing more of their own, including *Shipyard* (Paul Rotha), *Tell England*, and *Dance Pretty Lady* (Anthony Asquith).

76. See *Transition* 35 (1935).

Chapter 6. Germany and Prewar Paris

Note to epigraph: Quoted in *Assault on the Arts: Culture and Politics in Nazi Germany*, exhibition catalog, New York Public Library, February 27–May 28, 1993 (New York: New York Public Library, 1993), p. 1.

1. As with the period Beckett spent in London, dates of this trip are reported differently. Ruby Cohn, *Back to Beckett* (Princeton: Princeton University Press, 1973), p. ix, Vivian Mercier, *Beckett/Beckett* (New York: Oxford University Press, 1977), p. 31, Linda Ben-Zvi, *Beckett* (Boston: Twayne, 1986), n.p., and Deirdre Bair, *Samuel Beckett* (Harcourt Brace Jovanovich, 1978), pp. 241ff, place Beckett in Germany from late 1936 until the middle of 1937. John Pilling, *Samuel Beckett* (London: Routledge and Kegan Paul, 1976), p. 8, and Lawrence E. Harvey, *Samuel Beckett: Poet and Critic* (Princeton: Princeton University Press, 1970), p. 170, date the trip between 1935 and 1936. The publication of Beckett's letters may resolve these differences.

2. Bair, *Samuel Beckett*, p. 245.

3. Beckett often met people while traveling with whom he retained a long relationship. Following this German trip, for example, Beckett and Axel Kaun continued a long correspondence. For Grohmann's overview of modern art from Die Brücke through Braque and Picasso (in their Cubist periods), see *Cahiers d'Art* 10 (1935): 45–47; for his essay on Miró, see p. 38; see *Cahiers d'Art* 9 (1934) for his commentary on Jawlenski.

4. Bair, *Samuel Beckett*, pp. 241,143.

5. From Gottfried Büttner, "Some Aspects of Beckett's Cultural Relations with Germany," paper presented to the "Beckett and Biography" meeting at the Samuel Beckett Festival in The Hague, April 9, 1992, which I chaired. My quotations are from a photocopy, courtesy of the author. A summary appears in the festival program, p. 12. Citations refer to Büttner's paper and comments at the meeting.

6. Anna Balakian, *Surrealism: The Road to the Absolute* (New York: Noonday Press, 1959), p. 103. I draw on her excellent summary, pp. 103–108.

7. Philip L. Cottrell, *Events* (New York: Oxford University Press, 1992), p. 95.

8. Büttner, "Some Aspects," note 8.

9. Büttner, "Some Aspects," note 8. Beckett met a Dresden family during this trip named Pozzo. A friend of Beckett's for many years, Büttner has over 160 letters "from the great man." In April 1992, Büttner said they would not be part of the projected *Collected Letters*.

10. Harvey writes (*Samuel Beckett*, p. 170) that from previous visits to his family he had "picked up some German"; longer stops now "enabled him to consolidate" his knowledge of the language. Büttner, however, reported to me, in April 1992, that Beckett's German at this time was "impressive."

11. John Hohenberg, *Free Press/Free People* (New York: Columbia University Press, 1971), pp. 241–242.

12. John Desmond, *Crisis and Conflict* (Iowa City: University of Iowa Press, 1980), p. 405.

13. John Toland, *Adolf Hitler* (New York: Doubleday, 1976) p. , 413.

14. *Assault on the Arts*, p. 6.

15. *Assault on the Arts*, p. 8. Milan Hauner, *Hitler: A Chronology of His Life and Time* (London: Macmillan, 1983), p. 119. See also Toland, *Adolf Hitler*, pp. 414–416, and N. H. Baynes, *The Speeches of Adolf Hitler, April 1922–1939* (Oxford: Oxford University Press, 1942), pp. 584–592, as well as the elaborate history regarding the materials on display at the "Culture and Politics in Nazi Germany" exhibition at the New York Public Library, February 27–May 29, 1993. See note to epigraphs.

16. Toland, *Adolf Hitler*, pp. 414–416.

17. See Ben-Zvi, *Beckett*, p. 15.

18. See Peggy Guggenheim, *Out of This Century* (New York: Anchor-Doubleday, 1980).

19. Guggenheim, *Out of This Century*, pp. 140–144, 148–152, 155–156.

20. Pilling, *Samuel Beckett*, p. 10.

21. He also published "Ooftish" and "Denis Devlin," a review of Devlin's *Intercessions*, in *transition* 27 (April-May 1938): 33, 289–294, respectively.

22. Bair, *Samuel Beckett*, p. 298.

23. Certain journalist-historians refer to the "venality" of the French press after the Occupation, insisting that members of the media were bribed by the Germans. Most agree that from 1914 until 1939, the French press was one of the world's most liberal institutions. See Hohenberg, *Free Press*, p. 227, and Charles R. Eisendrath, "France," in *World Press Encyclopedia*, ed. George Thomas Kurian (New York: Facts on File, 1982), vol. 1, p. 341. After 1939, the combination of flattery, bribery, threat, and even worse coerced reporters to be "gentle" to the Nazis, so that their reportage "lulled" the public into a false sense of security. Hohenberg includes the British and American press here as well. Desmond, *Crisis and Conflict*, p. 431, goes so far as to speak of the French "readiness to accept pay-

ment and shape . . . policies . . . by both the French and Italian governments." See J. W. Freiberg, *The French Press* (New York: Praeger, 1981). There are few published studies of the French press during this period.

24. "James Joyce et le Livre de l'Homme," *La Revue de Paris* 17 (September 1939): 227, which also contained Maurice Montabré's "L'Evolution psychologique de Mussolini," 14–44. From the wide variety of magazines published, see also *La Revue Universelle* 74 (July 1938), Jean de Beaulieu's "Barbey d'Aurevilly et Trébutien," pp. 63–72, and Gonzague de Reynold's "Où Va L'Europe?" pp. 385–408; see also Roland de Marès, "La Guerre en Europe: La Tragédie Polonaise," in *La Revue de Paris* 19 (October 1939): 388–396, which also contained Marie de Chambrun, "Lorsque je voulais être chanoinesse," pp. 361–387. *Europe* published many articles on the Jewish situation and appeasement in volumes 189, 191, and 192 (September, November, and December 1938). In all, the "barbarism" of contemporary events was well documented for the French public.

25. Eisendrath, "France," pp. 341–359. See also Desmond, *Crisis and Conflict*; Hohenberg, *Free Press*; and Freiberg, *French Press*. See also Merrill, *The Elite Press*, pp. 32–43.

26. Goralski, *World War II Almanac*, p. 68.

27. Hauner, *Hitler: A Chronology*, p. 17. See also H. Rauschning, *Hitler Speaks* (London, 1939), and Baynes, *Speeches of Adolf Hitler*.

28. Hitler, *Mein Kampf*, p. 285. All citations are to the Ralph Manheim translation (Boston: Houghton Mifflin, 1971).

Chapter 7. France

Notes to epigraphs: Albert Guérard, *France: A Modern History* (Ann Arbor: University of Michigan Press, 1959), p. 423.

1. Alan Simpson, *Beckett and Behan and a Theatre in Dublin* (London: Routledge & Kegan Paul, 1962), p. 50.

2. Alec Reid, "The Reluctant Prizeman," *Arts* 29 (October 1969): 68.

3. According to James Knowlson, at the International Beckett Festival at The Hague, April 11, 1992, Beckett's sole overt "political" stance was in support of animal rights. Yet contrary to Knowlson's claim, Beckett was actively involved in the advocacy of individual rights—e.g., protesting against Arrabal's arrest, actively supporting the Polish dissident-exile Adam Tarn, and dedicating *Catastrophe* to the imprisoned Václav Havel. While Eoin O'Brien reminds us of Beckett's 1937 reply "UPTHEREPUBLIC" to "The Question—Addressed to Writers and Poets of England, Scotland, Ireland and Wales," the question was "Are You for or against the Legal Government and the People of Republican Spain?" *The Beckett Country* (Dublin: Black Cat Press; London: Faber & Faber, 1986), p. 67. Reid argues that although Beckett refused to "align himself with any political party . . . as far back as 1937 he associated himself with a group of British writers in their support of the Spanish Republican government in their opposition to the Fascist insurrection of General Franco." See "Reluctant Prizeman," p. 69. Beckett did refrain from signing numerous political documents, like the *Manifestes de Cent Vingt-et-un*, written by Sartre, supporting the FLN in Algeria and signed by 121 intellectuals, including many of his friends (see also Simpson, *Beckett and Behan*, p. 64). He refrained from joining specific political organizations, but throughout his life he played an active role in political campaigns regarding human free-

dom. In the 1960s, he was one of the British authors who forbid the sale or performance of their work in segregated South Africa.

4. Deirdre Bair, *Samuel Beckett: A Biography* (New York: Harcourt Brace Jovanovich, 1978), pp. 308ff. She refers, for example, to Beckett's underground connections in terms of various *réseaux*, a term ordinarily associated with de Gaulle's French groups. Beckett was, in fact, affiliated with Gloria, loosely connected with the British SOE, not de Gaulle's organizations. For specific mention of Beckett in the SOE, see Foot, *SOE in France*, note 3; see also M. R. D. Foot, *SOE: An Outline History of the Special Operations Executive, 1940–1946* (London: BBC, 1984) for further details regarding these groups.

5. Bair, *Samuel Beckett*, p. 317; See E. H. Cookridge, *Set Europe Ablaze* (London: Pan Books, 1965), pp. 97–98.

6. "Friends and neighbors were burning to get involved; each person seemed to bring in someone else. . . . Secrecy broke down. There were actually sections [in Paris where] groups met and compared notes." Bair, *Samuel Beckett*, p. 309.

7. Laurence Wylie, C. Douglas Dillon Professor of French Civilization at Harvard and an internationally recognized authority on Roussillon, made this denial in personal conversation, May 16, 1992.

8. Bair, *Samuel Beckett*, p. 336.

9. R. D. Laing, *The Divided Self: An Existential Study in Sanity and Madness* (Harmondsworth: Penguin, 1969).

10. Bair, *Samuel Beckett*, pp. 326–328.

11. Comparing his life to a Dutch painting, Bair writes: "The war was part of his background, the idealized landscape, the necessary contrast accentuating the main figure, whose brooding, introspective eyes seem to stare with alarming relevancy while still hinting upon unreal, private time and place" (*Samuel Beckett*, p. 320).

12. Beckett and Suzanne lived together for more than twenty years before marrying, and then only for purposes of Beckett's estate.

13. Wylie, in personal conversation, May 16, 1992. Bair, *Samuel Beckett*, p. 334, writes of this occasion: "[The maquis marched] along the road in a file, singing the *Marseillaise* at the top of their lungs and brandishing their rifles. To the rear and on the outside of their phalanx, Beckett marched without a rifle, his head bowed, grimly serious and silent. The war was over, and he was grateful but he had no time for wine and celebration. Two years was long enough, and he wanted to get back to living his own life on his own terms."

14. Personal correspondence, August 2, 1992.

15. Henri Michel, *Histoire de la Résistance en France* (Paris: Presses Universitaires de France, 1972), p. 32. See also his *Bibliographie critique de la Résistance* (Paris: Sevpen, 1964); P. J. Stead, *Second Bureau* (London: Evans, 1959); Edward Spears, *Assignment to Catastrophe*, 2 vols. (London: Heinemann, 1947); Rémy [Gilbert Renault-Roulier], *The Silent Company*, trans. L. C. Shepherd (London: Barker, 1948); John F. Sweets, *Choices in Vichy France: The French under the Occupation* (New York: Oxford University Press, 1986); Patrick Howarth, *Special Operations* (London: Routledge, 1955); and Vincent Brome, *The Way Back* (Cassell, 1957).

16. Foot, *SOE in France*, p. 319.

17. Kathleen McGrory and John Unterecker, "Interview with Jack MacGowran," *Yeats, Joyce, Beckett: New Light on Three Modern Irish Writers*, ed. Kathleen McGrory and John Unterecker (Lewisburg, Pa.: Bucknell University Press, 1976), pp. 173–174.

18. The fact that Beckett received the Croix de Guerre reinforces that he worked for the SOE, since de Gaulle created the Ordre de la Libération specifically, but not exclu-

sively, for the Free French. See Robert Werlich, *Orders and Decorations of All Nations* (Washington, D.C.: Quaker Press, 1974), p. 134; "Medals," *Encyclopedia Britannica*, 1973 ed., p. 64; and Guido Rosignoli, *Ribbons of Orders, Decorations and Medals* (New York: Arco Publishing, 1977), p. 86.

19. Frida Knight, *The French Resistance* (London: Lawrence and Wishart, 1975), p. 54. According to Simone de Beauvoir, *Temps nouveaux* blamed intellectuals like Gide and Cocteau, along with any number of writers, teachers, and Jews, for bringing about France's downfall. See *The Prime of Life*, trans. Peter Green (New York: World Publishing, 1962), p. 375. Some of the most notorious of the journalist-collaborators who were later tried as war criminals included Georges Suarez, Robert Brasillach, Jean Luchaire, and Paul Chack; the prominent Drieu la Rochelle committed suicide while awaiting trial.

20. The Air Force reported 892 planes downed, with 1,495 crew killed, wounded, and missing. See *Nazi Europe* (London: Cavendish House, 1984), p. 359, and for more specific statistics, Chris Cook and John Paxton, *European Political Facts, 1918–84* (New York: Facts on File, 1986), p. 242, and Robert Goralski, *World War II Almanac: 1931–1945* (New York: G. P. Putnam's, 1981), p. 421.

21. Arthur Marwick, *War and Social Change in the Twentieth Century* (New York: St. Martin's Press, 1974), p. 188.

22. *Nazi Europe*, p. 356.

23. Quoted in Claude Chambard, *The Maquis*, trans. Elaine P. Halperin (Indianapolis: Bobbs-Merrill, 1970), p. 2.

24. In addition, the departments of the Nord and Pas-de-Calais were placed under German military supervision in Belgium; a large area in northeast France was declared a "prohibited zone," and German farmers were settled there while French refugees were banned.

25. M. R. D. Foot, *Resistance: European Resistance to Nazism, 1940–1945* (New York: McGraw-Hill, 1977), pp. 235–236.

26. Robert O. Paxton, *Vichy France: Old Guard and New Order* (New York: Alfred A. Knopf, 1972), p. 326. David Littlejohn, *The Patriotic Traitors: A History of Collaboration in German-Occupied Europe, 1940–1945* (London: Heinemann, 1972), p. 274.

27. Paxton, *Vichy France*, p. 301.

28. Paxton, *Vichy France*, p. 47, cites Pétain's last proclamation in August 1944, when the retreating German armies carried him off to the Hohenzollern castle at Sigmaringen: "If I could not be your sword, I tried to be your shield."

29. Quoted in Alexander Werth, *France, 1940–1955* (New York: Henry Holt, 1956), pp. 15–16. See Simone de Beauvoir, *Prime of Life*, p. 398: "Never before . . . had I known what hatred really was. . . . Pétain's speeches had a more inflammatory effect on me than Hitler's, and while I condemned all collaborators, I felt a sharply defined and quite excruciating personal loathing for those of my own kind who joined their ranks—intellectuals, journalists, writers. . . . Fear, rage, and blind impotence: these were the foundations on which my life now developed." See also Littlejohn, *Patriotic Traitors*, pp. 205–206.

30. Knight, *French Resistance*, p. 82.

31. See Paxton, *Vichy France*, pp. 82, 308, and Michael R. Marrus and Robert O. Paxton, *Vichy France and the Jews* (New York: Basic Books, 1981).

32. Susan Zuccotti, *The Holocaust, the French, and the Jews* (New York: Basic Books, 1993). See also Stanley Hoffmann, *In Search of France* (Cambridge: Harvard University Press, 1963) and "Collaboration and Vichy France," *Journal of Modern History* 40 (September 1968); Richard I. Cohen, *The Burden of Conscience: French Jewry's Response to the Holocaust* (Bloomington:

Indiana University Press, 1987); and Jacques Adler, *The Jews of Paris and the Final Solution: Communal Response and Internal Conflicts, 1940–1944* (Oxford: Oxford University Press, 1987).

33. Paxton, *Vichy France*, pp. 199, 200. Between June 1940 and 1941 alone, there were four ministers of foreign affairs, five of the interior and of education, and six of industrial production.

34. Quoted in Chambard, *Maquis*, p. 3.

35. See Louis Snyder, *The War: A Concise History, 1939–1945* (New York: Julian Messner, 1960), p. 95.

36. Paxton (*Vichy France*, p. 238) states that "during the early days, the German occupation forces' behavior was unusually good for an occupying army."

37. Werth, *France, 1940–1955*, pp. xv–xix, xx. Werth explains, for example, how France had never recovered from its sense of failure and devastation following World War I. In a pithy essay in the *New York Times*, August 15, 1993: sec. 7, pp. 12–13, Patrice Higonnet writes: "Until quite recently, the French saw their History much as Michelet had presented it 150 years ago, as an alternation of France triumphant . . . and France martyred." Higonnet explains Vichy's anti-Semitism—and possibly the nation's: "Vichy's leaders . . . had their own homegrown reasons for persecuting Jews, ranging from xenophobia and the sudden shock of defeat to lingering rancor about the Dreyfus case of the 1890s to a century-old traditionalist, rural and conservative distaste for a republican, secularized, modernizing and urban Jewish minority that was mainly of eastern European origin." Stanley Hoffmann, in "The Effects of World War II on French Society and Politics," addresses the question of whether or not the unintentional cooperation of Vichy and the Resistance brought about a more dynamic, technocratic business and political leadership from new anti-individualist and interventionist practices.

38. Paxton, *Vichy France*, p. 290.

39. *The Journals of André Gide*, quoted in Paxton, *Vichy France*, pp. 33–34. Paxton explains that the new regime was anything but a cabal; rather, it enjoyed mass support for various political and social reasons.

40. Foot, *Resistance*, pp. 237, 239. See Paxton, *Vichy France*, p. 5, and note 32.

41. Philip P. Hallie, *Lest Innocent Blood Be Shed* (New York: Harper & Row, 1979), pp. 88–89. See also Paxton's *Vichy France* and Marrus and Paxton, *Vichy France and the Jews*, for a comprehensive discussion. Individual works cited below also focus on the demise of the republic.

42. Werth, *France, 1940–1955*, p. 38.

43. Foot, *Resistance*, p. 237. In *SOE in France*, p. 120, Foot describes the Milice as gangsters and sadists, recruited from the "scum of the jails, brutalised of the most brutal, cream of the offal."

44. Hallie, *Lest Innocent Blood*, p. 99.

45. Littlejohn, *Patriotic Traitors*, pp. 236–237, and Paxton, *Vichy France*, p. 162.

46. They ranged from all-out collaborators like the ex-communist Doriot, the ex-socialist Déat, "Ambassador" Brinon, Hérold Paquis (head of German radio in Paris), Jean Luchaire (head of the Paris *collabo*), and Pierre Drieu la Rochelle, to Darlan and Laval (with his memorable "I am hoping for a German victory, because otherwise Bolshevism will spread everywhere" and "An American victory would be a triumph for the Jews and Communism"). Louis Darquier de Pellepoix remains one of Vichy's most deranged and powerful officials. Pétain's heterogeneous political tendencies are apparent in the broad spectrum represented by his followers, including fanatical right-wing fascists (like Darnand); Action Française royalists and anti-Semites (Maurras, Darquier de Pellepoix); and

those with fascist tendencies with typical *ancien combattant* and good middle-class outlooks (La Rocque); there were also the church hierarchy and "classical" right (conservative, clerical) and the radical socialists. See Werth, *France, 1940–1955*, p. 51.

47. See especially Zuccotti, *The Holocaust, the French, and the Jews* and other books cited in note 32, most of which follow Marrus and Paxton's landmark *Vichy France and the Jews*. See also André Kaspi, *Les Juifs pendant l'Occupation* (Paris: Les Belles-Lettres, 1992) and Anne Grynberg, *Les Camps de la honte: Les internés juifs des camps français, 1939–1944* (Paris: La Découverte, 1991).

In summer 1992, one of the most bitter controversies appeared in the press regarding Hitler's reliance upon French officials to carry out the Final Solution. The case involved Vichy's order to round up ten thousand Jews for the camps. A simple enough task, so the authorities assumed, they decided to excuse children under eighteen if their parents had already been deported, as well as children under five (with their parents). When the quota could not be met, these exceptions were canceled. According to the attorney prosecuting the case, the many thousands "sent East from unoccupied France were the only Jews lost in the Holocaust who came from a place without any Germany military presence." See Richard Bernstein, "French Collaborators: The New Debate," *New York Review of Books*, June 25, 1992, 12; Zuccotti, and others cited in note 32.

48. Hallie, *Lest Innocent Blood*, p. 41.

49. Paxton, *Vichy France*, pp. 226–227. Paxton speaks of how de Gaulle was left "high and dry . . . nearly alone, even by his colleagues, few of whom joined him in London" (p. 42).

50. For a close chronology of events, see Knight, *French Resistance*; Paxton, *Vichy France*, and Marrus and Paxton, *Vichy France and the Jews*; Foot, *Resistance*; Werth, *France, 1940–1955*; Alfred Cobban, *A History of Modern France* (London: Cape, 1965); Marcel Baudot et al., *The Historical Encyclopedia of World War II* (New York: Facts on File, 1977); *Chronology of the Second World War* (London: Royal Institute of International Affairs, 1947); Andre Baufré, *1940: The Fall of France*, trans. Desmond Flower (London: Cassell, 1965); Robert Goralski, *World War II Almanac: 1931–1945* (New York: G. P. Putnam's Sons, 1981); Hershel Edelheit and Abraham J. Edelheit, *The World in Turmoil: An Integrated Chronology of the Holocaust and World War II* (New York: Greenwood Press, 1991); *Encyclopedia of the Holocaust*, ed. Israel Gutman, 4 vols. (New York: Macmillan, 1990); Jean-Pierre Azéma, *From Munich to the Liberation* (New York: Cambridge University Press, 1984); and Milan Hauner, *Hitler: A Chronology of His Life and Time* (London: Macmillan, 1983). Additional sources include some cited in chapter 5, note 40.

51. Quoted in Knight, *French Resistance*, p. 40.

52. Quoted in de Beauvoir, *Prime of Life*, p. 378.

53. Paxton, *Vichy France*, pp. 146–233, p. 157.

54. Chambard, *Maquis*, p. 36. See also Michel Garder, *La Guerre secrète des services Spéciaux Français, 1935–45* (Paris: Plon, 1967), p. 38; Ernst von Salomon, *The Captive*, trans. James Kirkup (London: Weidenfeld and Nicolson, 1961).

55. Paxton, *Vichy France*, p. 171.

56. Quoted in Paxton, *Vichy France*, p. 178.

57. Chambard, *Maquis*, p. 39.

58. Hallie, *Lest Innocent Blood*, p. 105. See also Claude Lévy and Paul Tilliard, *Betrayal at the Vel d'Hiv*, trans. Inea Bushnaq (New York: Hill and Wang, 1969) and Christopher Burney, *The Dungeon Democracy* (London: Heinemann, 1945).

59. Knight, *French Resistance*, p. 228.

Note to epigraph: Foot, *Resistance*, p. 110.

60. Quoted in Chambard, *Maquis*, from Barry Wynne, *No Drums . . . No Trumpets* (London: Barker, 1961), p. 11.

61. "The IRA and the Origins of SOE," in *War in Society*, ed. M. R. D. Foot (London: Paul Elek, 1973), p. 68. On "irregular warfare," see Peter Paret and John W. Shy, *Guerrillas in the 1960s* (London: Pall Mall, 1962). Foot, *War in Society*, pp. 68, 61.

62. Quoted in Chambard, *Maquis*, p. 31. See also G. Tillion, "Première Résistance," *Bulletin du Musée de l'Homme* (May 1958): 6–7.

63. Foot, *SOE: An Outline History*, p. 319, and *Resistance*, pp. 11–19. Foot, *SOE: An Outline History*, p. 138.

64. Foot, *SOE in France*, p. xvii.

65. Foot, *Resistance*, p. 241. See also Michel, *Histoire de la Résistance en France*.

66. Chambard, *Maquis*, p. 5.

67. Cookridge, *Set Europe Ablaze*, pp. 77–78.

68. Cookridge, *Set Europe Ablaze*, pp. 15, 17 (on Churchill), 18 (on Dalton).

69. Foot, *Resistance*, p. 163.

70. Michel, *Histoire de la Résistance en France*, p. 32. Cookridge, *Set Europe Ablaze*, pp. 78–79.

71. See Foot, *SOE in France* and *Resistance*; E. H. Cookridge, *They Came from the Sky* (New York: Thomas Y. Crowell, 1967), and *Set Europe Ablaze*; Michel, *Histoire de la Résistance en France*; Stead, *Second Bureau*; Rémy, *Silent Company*; Howarth, *Special Operations*; Brome, *The Way Back*; and Philippe de Vomécourt, *Who Lived to See the Day* (London, 1961). See also sources cited in note 15.

72. See Foot, *Resistance*, pp. 15–16, 18–19, 20. See "Who Resisted," pp. 11–21.

73. Buckmaster devoted himself primarily to finding out about the industrial enterprises in occupied France. After training new members, he would parachute them into France, in preparation for the Liberation. See Cookridge, *Set Europe Ablaze* and *They Came from the Sky*, as well as Foot, *SOE in France*, for extensive discussions of his activities.

74. Foot, *Resistance*, pp. 89, 122.

75. Foot, *Resistance*, p. 44. See also pp. 22–69, and *SOE in France*, pp. 40–60; Cookridge, *Set Europe Ablaze*, pp. 65ff.

76. Foot, *SOE in France*, pp. 505–517.

77. Foot, *Resistance*, pp. 96–97.

78. Foot, *Resistance*, pp. 124–125.

79. Foot, *Resistance*, pp. 109, 112, xv–xix; Foot, *SOE: An Outline History*, pp. viii–xvi.

80. Cookridge, *Set Europe Ablaze*, p. 37.

81. Foot, *Resistance*, pp. 105–110; Cookridge, *Set Europe Ablaze*, pp. 96–97.

82. Foot, *Resistance*, pp. 108–109.

83. Douglas Botting, *The Second Front* (New York: Time-Life, 1978), p. 93.

84. See Foot, *Resistance*, p. 146, whose terminology is even stronger: "We [were] regarded as a gang of wily imperialistic oaves, seeking our own profit and our neighbours' downfall from behind a screen of honeyed words" (p. 146). Pp. 247–248.

85. By this time, de Gaulle had also captured Brazzaville, so that the greater part of French Equatorial Africa went to him; shortly thereafter, the Cameroons, the French colonies on the Pacific and Indies, also helped his status. See William L. Langer, *Our Vichy Gamble* (New York: Knopf, 1947).

86. Cookridge, *Set Europe Ablaze*, pp. 33, 265.

87. Cookridge, *Set Europe Ablaze*, pp. 33–34.

88. Cookridge, *Set Europe Ablaze*, p. 32. Cookridge, *They Came from the Sky*, pp. 3, 4.

89. Foot, *Resistance*, p. 248.

90. Marwick, *War and Social Change*, pp. 185, 85–86.

91. Frenay, who originally wanted a group devoted to neither military nor intelligence activities (de Gaulle's and Churchill's focus), had pursued a more ideological, if not mystical, idea of revolution. See Michel's chapter "Resistance in the South," in *Histoire de la Résistance en France*.

92. See Werth, *France, 1940–1955*, and Cookridge, *Set Europe Ablaze*. Michel's *Histoire de la Résistance en France* is a landmark study of this subject.

237

93. Cookridge, *Set Europe Ablaze*, p. 80.

94. Littlejohn, *Patriotic Traitors*, p. 274.

95. Guérard, *France: A Modern History*, p. 422.

96. Hallie, *Lest Innocent Blood*, p. 238.

97. Werth confirms these figures from SHAEF, in *France, 1940–1955*, p. 168. They vary from scholar to scholar. Paxton, for example, relies on Gordon Wright's "Reflections on the French Resistance," *Political Science Quarterly* 77 (September 1962): 49, and reports strikingly lower figures.

Chapter 8. Roussillon

1. See Alexander Werth, *France, 1940–1955* (New York: Henry Holt, 1956), p. 138, and Henri Michel, *Histoire de la Résistance en France* (Paris: Presses Universitaires de France, 1972), p. 23.

2. Studies of the maquis include Claude Chambard, *The Maquis*, trans. Elaine P. Halperin (Indianapolis: Bobbs-Merrill, 1970); George Millar, *Hoaned Pigeon* (London: Heinemann, 1945); and Anne-Marie Walters, *Moondrop to Gascony* (London: Macmillan, 1946). Many of the works on the war cited previously devote significant attention to this subject.

3. Christian Durandet, *Les Maquis de Provence* (Paris: Editions France-Empire, 1974), pp. 35, 222 (my translation).

4. Werth, *France, 1940–1955*, p. 164.

5. E. H. Cookridge, *They Came from the Sky* (New York: Thomas Y. Crowell, 1967), p. 74. Cookridge, and Foot, in *Resistance*, treat Cammaerts' activities in detail; most work on the SOE calls him instrumental in both the formation and success of the Resistance in the south.

6. Foot, *Resistance*, p. 252.

7. Laurence Wylie, *Village in the Vaucluse* (Cambridge: Harvard University Press, 1974), pp. 213–214.

8. I am deeply grateful to Professor Wylie for his enormous contribution to this chapter, as well as his extended kindness in discussing its possible implications for Beckett during this time. I am especially grateful to him for pursuing my questions regarding Beckett with the older Roussillon villagers during his recent trips there.

Wylie lived in Roussillon during 1950–51 and spent significant periods of time there subsequently. See also the three reprints of *Village in the Vaucluse*, with updated introductions, as well as Laurence Wylie, "Roussillon, '87: Returning to the Village in the Vaucluse," *French Politics and Society* 7 (Spring 1989): 1–26.

9. Francis Berjot, ed. *Roussillon: Un Village de Provence: Histoire et Souvenirs*, preface by Simonne and Jean Lacouture (Apt, France: Archipal, 1992), and Francis Berjot, *Roussillon: Le Temps Retrouvé* (Mas du Sacré-Coeur, Marguerittes, France: Equinoxe, 1992). The first is a series of essays on the geological, historical, cultural, and archaeological history of

Roussillon, with essays on specific landmarks and products associated with the town. The second is an annotated photograph collection.

10. See Deirdre Bair, *Samuel Beckett* (New York: Harcourt Brace Jovanovich, 1978), p. 333. Bair cites Wylie as her major source regarding Beckett in Roussillon, pp. 685–686, but Wylie told me on several occasions that Bair "has badly misused [my] material." No one, for example, thought of Beckett as a fugitive.

11. Bair, *Samuel Beckett*, pp. 327–328.

12. John Fletcher, *The Novels of Samuel Beckett* (London: Chatto and Windus, 1964), p. 59.

13. Lawrence E. Harvey, *Samuel Beckett: Poet and Critic* (Princeton: Princeton University Press, 1970), p. 222. Harvey adds that writing *Watt* was a way "to keep [his] hand in" (hardly the response of a deeply disturbed man, as Bair would have it).

14. James Knowlson, *Beckett: An Exhibition* (London: Turret, 1976), p. 44.

15. Berjot, *Roussillon: Le Temps*, p. 75. Berjot connects the villagers' warmth to Beckett's reference in *Godot* to Roussillon: "We worked in the harvest at Bonnelly's farm in Roussillon. . . . Everything is red down there."

16. Personal conversation, May 19, 1992. John F. Sweets observes: "The French are . . . masters of the système 'd', to 'get by,' or to improvise." *Choices in Vichy France: The French under the Occupation* (New York: Oxford University Press, 1986). Since most of the cultural, economic, and demographic information on Roussillon during the war derives from Wylie, in conversation or correspondence, most of the citations refer to other sources (also derivative of *Village in the Vaucluse*).

Notes to epigraphs: Wylie, *Village in the Vaucluse*, p. 27. Robert Paxton, telephone conversation with the author, May 2, 1992.

17. Berjot, *Roussillon: Un Village*, p. 11.

18. Jacques Talbotier, "L'ocre et Roussillon," in Berjot, *Roussillon: Un Village*, p. 165.

19. Christophe Huet, "L'architecture du village," cited by Talbotier, in Berjot, *Roussillon: Un Village*, p. 201.

20. Berjot, *Roussillon: Un Village*, pp. 206–208. After the war Vasarely and Chagall went to Roussillon, along with Georges Marchais, the sociologist Georges Gurvitch, and Raymond Aron; in the 1980s, Jean Lacouture and even François Mitterrand bought property in the area. See "Roussillon, '87."

21. For interesting discussions of the "Prehistoric Epic," see Jean Bourguignon, "L'Epoque préhistorique," and Berjot, "Roussillon, son histoire," both in Berjot, *Roussillon: Un Village*, pp. 17–20 and 21–31, respectively.

22. Eoin O'Brien, *The Beckett Country* (Dublin: Black Cat Press; London: Faber & Faber, 1986), p. 312. O'Brien documents these at great length, pp. 59, 227.

23. Wylie showed me records dating back to the first of such official town documents.

24. Wylie, *Village in the Vaucluse*, pp. 336–338.

25. Wylie, *Village in the Vaucluse*, p. 27.

26. Wylie, *Village in the Vaucluse*, pp. 200, 28, 29.

27. Wylie, *Village in the Vaucluse*, pp. 210, 213–214.

28. This line in Beckett's *Godot* was modified in the English version. Wylie compiled this list during his July 1992 trip to his Roussillon home. The conversation with Aude cited was Wylie's first indication of Beckett's association with Roussillon.

29. See Berjot, *Roussillon: Un Village*, p. 206.

30. Knowlson, *Samuel Beckett: An Exhibition*, p. 44, quoting an interview from a Radio Bremen television program.

31. Wylie, *Village in the Vaucluse*, pp. 87, 50.

32. Robert Paxton, telephone conversation with the author, May 2, 1992.

Note to epigraph: As cited in Chambard, *The Maquis.*

33. Most of the material on modern Roussillon comes from Wylie's "Roussillon, '87," as well as the three updated prefaces in the 1964, 1974, and 1979 editions of *Village in the Vaucluse.* See also Berjot's work, as cited in the text.

34. Simone de Beauvoir, *The Prime of Life*, trans. Peter Green (New York: World Publishing, 1962), p. 297.

35. Berjot, *Roussillon: Un Village*, p. 206.

36. Wylie, *Village in the Vaucluse*, p. 29.

37. Berjot, *Roussillon: Le Temps*, p. 71.

38. Philip P. Hallie, *Lest Innocent Blood Be Shed* (New York: Harper & Row, 1979).

39. John Pilling, *Samuel Beckett* (London: Routledge & Kegan Paul, 1976), p. 1.

40. Hallie, *Lest Innocent Blood*, p. 167. See also pp. 97, 132–133.

41. Hallie, *Lest Innocent Blood*, pp. 248–249.

42. Hallie, *Lest Innocent Blood*, p. 257.

Chapter 9. Saint-Lô

1. Henri Michel, *The Second World War*, trans. Douglas Parmee (New York: Praeger, 1975). See also Philip Williams, *Politics in Post-War France: Parties and the Constitution of the Fourth Republic* (London: Longmans, Green, 1954); Maurice Duverger, *The French Political System* (Chicago: University of Chicago Press, 1958); Gordon Wright, *The Reshaping of French Democracy* (New York: Reynald & Hitchcock, 1948; 1952); François Goguel-Nyegaard, *France under the Fourth Republic* (Ithaca: Cornell University Press, 1952); Dorothy Pickles, *France between the Republics* (London: Contact Publishers, 1946); Robert Aron and Georgette Elgey, *The Vichy Regime*, trans. Humphrey Hare (New York: Macmillan, 1958).

2. Robert O. Paxton, *Vichy France: Old Guard and New Order* (New York, Alfred A. Knopf, 1972), p. 331.

3. According to Laurence Wylie, personal conversation, May 19, 1992, just as one "signed in properly," one signed out.

4. Paxton, *Vichy France*, p. 366.

5. Arthur Marwick, *War and Social Change in the Twentieth Century* (New York: St. Martin's Press, 1974), p. 186.

6. Albert Guérard, *France: A Modern History* (Ann Arbor: University of Michigan Press, 1959), pp. 435, 436–437.

7. David Littlejohn, *The Patriotic Traitors: A History of Collaboration in German-Occupied Europe, 1940–1945* (London: Heinemann, 1972), p. 288.

8. Guérard, *France*, p. 434.

9. Littlejohn, *Patriotic Traitors*, p. 289. See also Bertram M. Gordon, *Collaborationism in France during the Second World War* (Ithaca: Cornell University Press, 1980).

10. Guérard, *France*, p. 434. These figures vary. Paxton reports that during the more formal procedures, 124,750 were tried; 767 were executed, with 38,000 sentenced to some kind of prison term. Thousands were expelled or demoted in public service (*Vichy France*, p. 329). Littlejohn's figures are lower (see *Patriotic Traitors*, p. 288).

11. Littlejohn, *Patriotic Traitors*, pp. 288–290.

12. Michel, *Second World War*, pp. 803–805.

13. As Enoch Brater more kindly explains: "This was merely a ploy, [Beckett] said modestly at the time, to get him back to his Paris apartment" (my italics). See why beckett (New York: Thames and Hudson, 1989), p. 44.

14. Deirdre Bair, Samuel Beckett: A Biography (New York: Harcourt Brace Jovanovich, 1978), p. 342.

15. Eoin O'Brien, The Beckett Country (Dublin: Black Cat; London: Faber & Faber, 1986), p. 384, note 8.

16. Irish Times, July 4 and 5, 1944, respectively. Here, and in the following, all references are to front-page articles. Irish Times, July 4, 14, 19, 1944.

17. See Irish Times, July 12 and 18, 1944.

18. See The Times (London) from July 4–20 and July 24–26, particularly the photos of July 14, 1944. See also the Times (London) July 26, 1944. Irish Times, July 27, 1944.

19. On July 18, 1944, de Valera insisted that only the Irish should determine the constitutional status of their country: "We are an independent republic, associated as a matter of our external policy with the states of the British Commonwealth." He continued: "If anyone still persists in maintaining that our state is not a republic, I cannot argue with him, for we have no common language." On July 20, 1944, the front page of the Irish Times was once again set in bold print with de Valera's insistence that Ireland was "A REPUBLIC . . . WITH ONLY ONE HEAD OF STATE."

20. One of the fullest accounts of this sort had been published in the Irish Times, July 20, 1944.

21. Bair, Samuel Beckett, p. 336.

22. See O'Brien, Beckett Country, p. 386, note 45.

23. Bair, Samuel Beckett, pp. 343, 344. By Christmas most of the Irish staff had arrived; furthermore, Beckett had been separated throughout this period from Suzanne, who was awaiting his return in Paris.

Note to epigraph: St.-Lô (7 July–10 July 1944): Armed Forces in Action Series (Nashville: Battery, 1984), p. 125.

24. See indices of major papers in New York and London, for example. For discussion of Life magazine's treatment of Saint-Lô's burial of an "Unknown Soldier" (the "Major of Saint-Lô") and of local poetry, such as Joseph Auslander's "Incident at Saint-Lô," see Frederick Ruge, Rommel in Normandy, trans. Ursula R. Moessner (London: Presidio, 1979), p. 75.

For detailed chronologies and discussion of events on and following D day, see St.-Lô; Ruge, Rommel in Normandy, and the following sources: D-Day, ed. The Army Times (New York: G. P. Putnam's, 1969); Carlo D'Este, Decision in Normandy (New York: Dutton, 1983); Joseph Balkoski, Beyond the Beachhead (Harrisburg, Pa: Stackpole, 1989); Joseph Sullivan, "The Botched Air Support of Operation Cobra," Parameters (March 1988): 97–110; Etienne Fouilloux and Dominique Veillon, "Mémoires: Du Débarquement en Normandie," Annales de Normandie 36 (1986): 105–119; Warren Tute, D Day (New York: Collier Books, 1974); Martin Blumenson, Breakout and Pursuit (Washington: USACMH, 1961); Nigel Hamilton, Master of the Battlefield: Monty's War Years, 1942–44 (New York: McGraw-Hill, 1983); Arthur Tedder, With Prejudice (Boston: Little, Brown, 1966); W. F. Craven and J. L. Cate, The Army Air Forces in World War II, vol. 3 (Chicago: University of Chicago Press, 1951); Max Hastings, Overlord: D-Day and the Battle for Normandy (New York: Simon and Schuster, 1984); James A. Huston, "Face of France: Liberation and Recovery, 1944–63" (West Lafayette, Ind.: Purdue University Studies, 1963); and Dwight D. Eisenhower, The Papers of Dwight David Eisenhower, The War Years, vol. 3, ed. Alfred D. Chandler, Jr. (Baltimore: John Hopkins University Press, 1970).

25. *Irish Times*, July 24, 1944. Huston, "Face of France," p. 62.

26. See Ruge, *Rommel in Normandy*; D'Este, *Decision in Normandy*; Balkoski, *Beyond the Beachhead*; Hastings, *Overlord*; *St.-Lô*, and *Army Times*.

27. *St.-Lô*, p. 125.

28. Ruge, *Rommel in Normandy*, pp. 233–234.

29. Carenten and Isigny, to the north; Caumont and Bayeux, the east; Périer and Lessay, the west; and the Coutances highway, the southwest. *St.-Lô*, p. 5.

30. Huston, *Face of France*, pp. 56–59.

31. Huston, *Face of France*, p. 90.

32. Ruge, *Rommel in Normandy*, pp. 233–234. Pamphlet quoted in Ruge, *Rommel in Normandy*, p. 237.

33. Sullivan, "Botched Air Support," pp. 98, 99. *St.-Lô* mentions the air offensive in only the most general of terms and in one sentence alone: "On 25 July the armor, infantry, artillery, and air power assembled for COBRA began the attack that broke through to Marigny" (p. 126). When Tedder was absent from an important meeting, Leigh-Mallory said: "Either I am allowed to direct . . . the whole Air Forces available . . . or I shall resign on that issue" (p. 99).

34. Sullivan, "Botched Air Support," p. 102.

35. Sullivan, "Botched Air Support," p. 103.

36. In the Thirtieth Division, for example, on July 25 alone, 25 were killed and 131 wounded; on the next day, 61 were killed and 374 wounded; there were also 60 missing and 164 in shell shock. According to another official document—covering a broader period of time—these estimates were timid: from July 7 to 22, the Thirtieth suffered 3,934 casualties. See *St.-Lô*, p. 126. After two weeks there was a 75–80 percent turnover of replacements, none of whom had any training regarding the hedgerows.

37. Sullivan, "Botched Air Support," p. 105.

38. Fouilloux and Veillon, "Mémoires du Débarquement en Normandie," pp. 105–119.

39. *St.-Lô*, p. 119.

40. See O'Brien, *Beckett Country*, pp. 316, 320.

41. Huston, *Face of France*, p. 66.

42. Huston, *Face of France*, pp. 53, 60.

43. O'Brien, *Beckett Country*, p. 342.

44. The *Irish Red Cross Bulletin* 1945, vol. 5, as cited in O'Brien, *Beckett Country*, p. 320.

45. Lawrence E. Harvey, *Samuel Beckett: Poet and Critic* (Princeton: Princeton University Press), p. 218.

46. O'Brien, *Beckett Country*, pp. 322, 384.

47. O'Brien, *Beckett Country*, pp. 384, 327.

48. O'Brien, *Beckett Country*, p. 385 (saying that "It is unknown if the broadcast took place") publishes it in full from a typescript that is signed by Beckett. Others report that the broadcast did occur: Brater, *why beckett*, p. 44; Dougald McMillan, "Beckett at Forty: The Capital of the Ruins and 'Saint Lo,'" *As No Other Dare Fail* (New York: Riverrun Press, 1986), p. 71; and John P. Harrington, *The Irish Beckett* (Syracuse, N.Y.: Syracuse University Press, 1991), pp. 144–145.

Index

248